Tae The Lasses

by

Maureen Bell

An Appreciation of
The Women in the Life of Robert Burns

First published by Sleepytown Books
Woodend Leask, Ellon, Aberdeenshire.
Telephone 01779-841-543
Fax 01779-841-849
Email info.sleepytown@virgin.net

Frontispiece silhouettes based on John Miers silhouettes
of Burns in 1787
and Clarinda in 1788.

ISBN 1-904072-00-3
Printed and bound by The Bath Press, Bath

ACKNOWLEDGEMENTS

This book is dedicated to my husband Ronnie Cairns. Without his hard work, organisation, and at times magical intuition, it would never have seen the light of day and would have remained an exercise on paper.

I would also like to dedicate the book to my son Gareth for his sterling work in helping me with the research and index arranging.

Special thanks is given to Catherine Christie Hughes and the late Dr Ian M. Hughes who helped me understand that the warmth of Burns words exist only when the songs are sung in the Scots tongue, as Burns intended.

There's ae wee fau't they whiles lay to me,
I like the lasses – Gude forgi'e me!
For mony a plack they wheedle frae me
At dance or fair;
May be some ither thing they gie me,
They weel can spare.

(Epistle to John Lapraik – April 1st 1785)

Contents

PREFACE

'If others have climbed more successfully the heights of Parnassus, none certainly ever outshone Burns in the charms – the sorcery I would almost call it – of fascinating conversation; the spontaneous eloquence of social argument, or the unstudied poignancy of brilliant repartee...

......such was the irresistible power of attraction that encircled him – though his appearance and manner were always peculiar, he never failed to delight and to excel...

......his voice alone could improve upon the magic of his eye; sonorous, replete with the finest modulations, it alternately captivated the ear with the melody of poetic numbers, the perspicuity of nervous reasoning, or the ardent sallies of enthusiastic patriotism...

......where he paid a compliment it might indeed claim the power of intoxication, as approbation from him was always an honest tribute from the warmth and sincerity of his heart...

......his poetical pieces blend, with alternate happiness of description, the frolic spirit of the joy-inspiring bowl, or melt the heart to the tender or impassioned sentiments in which beauty always taught him to pour fourth his own...

......Proudly She (Scotland) will remember that beneath Her cold sky, a genius was ripened without care or culture, that would have done honour to climes more favourable to the development of those luxuriances of fancy and colouring in which he so eminently excelled'.

Thus wrote 'Candidor' (Maria Riddell) in August 1796, less than a month after the death of Burns. Her 'Memoir Concerning Burns' was first published in the Dumfries Weekly Journal and later in Currie's first edition of his Biography of Burns in 1800. It has been described as 'so admirable in tone, and withal so discerning and impartial in understanding, that it remains the best thing written of him by a contemporary critic'.

To say that the ladies loved Robert Burns would be an understatement, and Robert Burns let it be known that he was fair game for them. He may not have begun to enjoy the delights of the flesh until he was in his early twenties, very shortly after his father's death, but he certainly made up for lost time when he did take his place at the starting line.

Burns did not need physical contact to inspire his poetic heart, though he was not averse to it if the occasion arose. His mind and emotions were so highly tuned that the picture he held in his head poured itself on to his written page and became alive in an instant. 'The Braw Wooer' was written for no one in particular, as was 'Tibbie Dunbar'. 'Beware O' Bonie

Ann' and 'A Rosebud By My Early Walk' were written for two young girls, daughters of two of his friends. And when reading or singing the exquisite 'Jamie, Come Try Me' it is hard to imagine that it was not really entitled 'Robin, Come Try Me'. Yet again it was written for no one in particular.

But this book is not about Robert Burns, though he is part and parcel of every page and sentence of it. This book is dedicated to the memories of some of the many women that Burns celebrated in his poetry and song.

These women inspired him by love, friendship and sometimes, like Lesley Baillie or Wilhelmina Alexander, just by being in the right place at the right time. And he repaid them for that inspiration, in that, for as long as his songs are sung and his poems are spoken, the women will remain immortal and forever young.

In as much as Robert Burns loved these women, as I went further into my research so I grew to love them as well. There wasn't one I didn't like. Every new fact I learned seemed like a gift captured from the past.

I remember sitting in the Mitchell Library in Glasgow and holding in my hands two small books. One was by James Adams and was about Jean Lorimer, 'Chloris'. The other was by John D. Ross and was written about Jean Jaffray, 'The Blue-Eyed Lassie'.

James Adams had met Jean Lorimer when he was a very young lad, and the Ross book was a reprint of a tribute that was written by a Mrs Mary Balmanno in 1858, a friend to Jean Jaffray.

This tenuous contact made the women spring to life for me. The descriptions were so good that I could almost feel their presence and hear them talking down the centuries, and I knew the love that James Adams and Mrs Balmanno held for their respective 'Jean'.

In reading the letters between Agnes McLehose and Burns, it is easy to see why each was so taken with the other. Both were incredible 'Drama Queens'.

Agnes may have spent three quarters of her life in the staid Edinburgh society of the time, but she was still a Glasgow Saltmarket lassie at heart. Her letters have been taken apart, analysed, criticised and in some cases demonised, but what has never been pointed out is the humour in them. Agnes was known for her humour, her west coast humour. Burns must have loved her for her ability to make him laugh, and maybe that laughter got her out of many a tight embrace with him. I like Agnes McLehose.

Jean Armour was a better wife to Burns than he was a husband to her. She was all that Burns could have wished for, and far better than he deserved. What Jean gave him was unconditional love. Though I hope that now and then she also gave him a good swift kick, because he certainly merited it. Fate had destined them for each other, though their road was never intended to be a smooth one.

No one will ever know how much Jean Armour contributed to Burns' songs both composed and collected. Like Burns' own mother, Agnes Broun, Jean had a memory bank of old songs and tunes. She was a first class singer, and she was the one that Burns turned to when he wanted to try out a new composition.

Jean Armour was not stupid or unlettered, as was hinted by earlier biographers of Burns, she had an education as befitted the eldest daughter of a master mason, nearly middle class by the standards of Mauchline of the late seventeen hundreds.

Margaret Campbell, 'Highland Mary', existed for a time in the love of Burns. So much fiction, and so little fact is known about this young woman. She was certainly no ephemeral being as portrayed by the Victorian and Edwardian Burnsians. She was real, and like us all, she had her faults.

What Burns felt for her after she left for Argyll in May 1786 we will never know, as any letters written to her from him are alleged to have been destroyed by her father after her death.

Mystery still surrounds her supposed pregnancy. There was no hint of it either when she was alive in Campbeltown, or just after her death in Greenock. Nor does there appear to be any letters from her to Burns from that time, informing him of any impending birth. Even if she were illiterate, as said by some early Burnsians, she would surely have known of someone who would have written to him for her. It is reported that she did attend school, so illiteracy is out of the question, and, as attested to, she could read her bible.

Was she going to emigrate to the 'Indies' with Burns in 1786? Burns bought only one single journey ticket for the ship, costing £9, which he paid for out of the profits of his 'Kilmarnock Edition'.

Robert Burns wrote to Agnes McLehose in January 1788 admitting that the name of the woman who was registered in his 'heart's core' was Peggy Chalmers. He had apparently asked Peggy to marry him in 1787 (although he was technically married to Jean Armour under Scots Law), but she had turned him down, being secretly engaged to Lewis Hay.

On reading Burns' letters to Peggy, there is a familiarity and honesty that is missing, even in the letters to Agnes McLehose. In one letter to her dated 19th December 1787, while in Edinburgh, he unburdens himself.

'My worst enemy is 'Moimeme'. I lie so miserably open to the inroads and incursions of a mischievious, light-armed, well-mounted banditti, under the banners of imagination, whim, caprice, and passion: and the heavy-armed veteran regulars of wisdom, prudence, and fore-thought move so very, very slow, that I am almost in a state of perpetual warfare, and, alas! frequent defeat'.

Undoubtedly Robert Burns deeply loved Peggy Chalmers, and had she accepted his proposal of marriage, well, who knows what would have happened. But his ultimate tribute to Peggy was to compose his last ever song in her honour. 'Fairest Maid On Devon Banks' was written and posted from Brow on the Solway Firth on 12th July 1796, nine days before he died. As far as we are aware the last poetic song line Burns wrote was

> 'No love but thine my heart shall know'!

If Robert Burns ever had a soul mate it must have been Peggy Chalmers.

It's interesting to consider how Burns' life would have changed depending upon which woman he might have married. Elizabeth Gebbie (Ellison Begbie) who moved to Glasgow, Margaret Campbell from Argyll, Agnes McLehose with her Edinburgh contacts and Peggy Chalmers who died in Berne. With each he would have become a different man, and maybe would have taken a different path. Assuredly he would still have been a literary man, but would he have become Scotland's Bard? Maybe only one marriage could have ensured that, and that marriage could only have been with Jean Armour.

I recently found out that circa 1784 there was an eruption from a volcano in Iceland. Millions of particles of dust and dirt were propelled into the air, and spread throughout the Northern hemisphere. Because of this pollution, the temperature dropped by a couple of degrees. In turn the land grew colder and crops became difficult to grow. This was at the time, just after his father's death, when Burns and his brother had taken on Mossgiel farm, and were experiencing problems with seed growth, resulting in failed harvests, and one of the reasons Burns looked to publishing his poetry for his future. It seems that even climatic changes were conspiring to ensure that Robert Burns, *Poet*, was born.

My favourite description of Burns is by Nellie Martin (later Miller) sweetheart of Robert's brother William. Nellie was also acquainted with Margaret Campbell and Jean Armour. The first part is a telling of how 'The Holy Fair' went on its first reading in Nance Tannock's Inn.

'There were present Robert an' his sweetheart, Jean Armour, William an' I, an' anither lad or twa an' their sweethearts. Robin himsel' was in unco glee. He kneelit ontil a chair in the midds o' the room, wi' his elbows on the bak o't, an' read owre the 'Holy Fair' frae a paper i' his han' – an' sic laughan'! we could hardly steer for laughan'; an' I never saw himsell in sic glee'.

Nellie then went on to describe Robert at that time

'In a licht-blew coat o' his mither's makin' an' dyein'; ay, an' o' his mither's sewin' I'se warrand, in these days; an' his bonie black hair hingin' doon an' curlin' ower the neck o't; a buik in his han' – aye a buik in his han' – an' whiles his bonnet aneath his tither ockster, an' didna ken that he was bareheidit – gaun aboot the dyke sides an' hedges; an idler, ye ken – an idler jiest, that did little but read; an' even on the hair'st-rig it was soup an' soup, an' then the buik! He wasna to ca' a bonie man – dark an' strong; but uncommon invitin' in his speech – uncommon! Ye couldna hae cracket wi' him for ae minite, but ye wad hae studen four or five. He was unco by-ordinar engagin' in his talk'.

Mind you, Burns' literary habits did not seem to please an old woman from Dunscore, who is reported to have noticed him riding slowly through the hills, reading. She is said to have remarked

'That's surely no a guid man, for he has aye a buik in his han'!

Robert Burns died far too young, and this has added to his mystique. It has also left Scotland with a feeling of 'unfinished business'. Maybe that's why there is a kind of madness every January 25th.

There will never be another Burns. There will never be a gathering of such women like these again.

From his first song, 'Handsome Nell', to 'The Fairest Maid On Devon Banks', his last, when the glass is raised and the toast is given, the women who inspired Burns to become the poet and song-master we recognise today must never be forgotten.

Tae The Lasses

Maureen Bell
Woodend, Leask, Ellon, Aberdeenshire, AB41 8JY
Telephone 01779-841-543
Fax 01779-841-849

August 2001

PART ONE

Robert Burns
And
His Family

PART ONE
Chapter One – Robert Burns

For a man who entered the world on a bitterly cold January night in the middle of the 18th century, Robert Burns emerged with his own internal flame already lit, awaiting the time for it to create the fire that has blazed a path down nearly two and a half centuries to the present day.

Robert had hardly set foot in the world when his parent's house was shaken to the core by a terrible storm, causing part of the roof to fall in. Had this occurred in Legend, the Oracle would assuredly have had something to say about it. But this event seemed to herald what Burns was to become. What he said shook foundations, whether they were religious or social, and like fire and storm let loose, impossible to control.

From his birth on 25th January 1759 until 1766, Robert lived in the 'Auld Clay Biggin' in Alloway, built by William Burness with his own hands in 1757, and where four of the seven Burness children were born, Robert, Gilbert (1760), Agnes (1762) and Annabella (1764).

At Whitsun (May) 1766, the family moved to Mount Oliphant on the Doonholm estate near Alloway, but this was not a good move. Due to the poor soil, the family, though they worked all the hours that they could, suffered hardship. Successful cultivation of crops was impossible. The children helped as much as they could and according to Gilbert

> 'My brother at the age of thirteen, assisted in threshing the crop of corn, and at fifteen was the principal labourer on the farm, for we had no hired servants male or female'.

How this affected Robert's health, no one can tell, but affect him it did. Again Gilbert says

> 'I doubt not, but the hard labour and sorrow of this period of his life, was in great measure, the cause of that depression of spirits with which Robert was so often afflicted through his whole life afterwards'.

But it was here that Robert took the first step on the road that fate had laid before him. Though he had the choice of rhyming to anything around him, at the age of fourteen and a half, he chose to write his first poem/song to his helpmate in the harvest, his 'Handsome Nell'. She became the first in a long line of women to receive a love poem aimed directly from the quivering heart of Burns.

Another three children were born at Mount Oliphant, William (1767), John (1769), and Isabella (1771). The family soldiered on with their bad bargain until Whitsun 1777, when they moved to a larger farm two miles outside of Tarbolton, called Lochlea (Lochlie).

For Robert this was a happier more contented time. At Lochlea Burns moulded himself into the man he was to become. He formed the Tarbolton Bachelor's Club, learned flax dressing in Irvine, a trade he received prizes for, and began his First Commonplace Book.

Robert was reaching manhood, and his hormones, buffeted by his internal fire and storm, were ready to explode at the sight or sound of a young woman. He was a good-looking young man, with a powerful build, who gave the impression of being very sure of himself, and he was never short of female companionship. According to Gilbert, Robert's

> 'attachment (to the society of women) became very strong, and he was constantly the victim of some fair enslaver'.

Although Lochlea began well, towards the end of the tenure it left the Burness family in dire straits. William Burness became involved in litigation, and the stress related to this did not help his weakened constitution. He died on 13th February 1784. A month later the Burness family left Lochlea and moved to Mossgiel in the parish of Mauchline.

Mossgiel (Mossgaville) was a joint family concern, and every member received wages for the work done. Robert and Gilbert, the main labourers, receiving £7 p.a. each. Robert was now the head of the family, a title he did try very hard to live up to, but unlike his brother, he had not blossomed into a sober god-fearing young man.

By that Spring of 1784 Burns was standing at the threshold of his destiny.

Whether Burns met Jean Armour in the May of 1784 or 1785 is unknown. But what is clear is that by the late Autumn of 1784, his relationship with Elizabeth Paton, a family servant who had helped look after his dying father, was becoming the talk of Mauchline.

Elizabeth was pregnant to Robert, and the Burness home was in an uproar. Agnes Broun wanted Robert to marry the lassie. Robert was not averse to this. He was desperate to wed anyone who would have him, but his brothers and sisters thought that marriage to Elizabeth was not a good idea. Robert bent to sibling pressure.

In May 1785, Elizabeth Paton Burns, Robert's 'Dear-bought Bess', was born. Robert was proud of his daughter and convinced Elizabeth Paton that, after weaning, the child should be brought to the Burns home at Mossgiel to be looked after by his mother. Elizabeth agreed to this.

One of the main reasons against believing that Burns met Jean Armour in 1784 is that she did <u>not</u> become pregnant until December 1785. As Gilbert was to say of his brother, *'he was no platonic lover'*.

It is more likely that they met in 1785 during Race Week (a village gala). When the couple attested to marriage in September of that year, Jean was definitely not pregnant. As was perfectly legal under Scots Law, Robert had in writing, accepted Jean as his wife. The ensuing pregnancy, though incurring during an 'irregular' marriage, was quite legitimate.

1786 started off on a potentially cheery note with the couple happy, though secretive about Jean's condition. As far as they were concerned they were legally married, irregular or not. But by March matters had taken a sombre and angry turn when James Armour, after he had recovered from a swooning fit on finding out who the father of his first grandchild was, appropriated the attestment paper, which he had also just found out about, and caused it to be mutilated and destroyed.

On April 23rd 1786 Jean was sent to relatives in Paisley for the term of her pregnancy, and James Armour repudiated Robert Burns as his son-in-law. Robert was shell-shocked. Because of this rejection it is said Burns took up with Margaret Campbell.

Confusion runs rife around Margaret Campbell. We are led to believe that the relationship between she and Burns budded, blossomed and flowered in three weeks. Certainly it could have happened this way, but we are also told by Isabella Burns that her brother knew Margaret Campbell long before Jean Armour, and that there had been a relationship between them. Did he go back to Margaret Campbell on the rebound?

Whatever the answer, they met, unknowingly for the last time, circa 14th May 1786, before Margaret left to return home to her family and friends. Burns hinted, in later letters to George Thomson, that he and Margaret were planning to go to Jamaica.

Burns certainly did intend to go, but was Margaret included? The letters written by him at the time to various friends don't point to this, nor does the fact that he bought only one single journey ticket for the ship, leaving on September 1st 1786.

Margaret left Campbeltown long after September 1st to come to Greenock. It is reported that she had arranged employment in Glasgow starting at Martinmas (November). If this is true then there certainly was no intention on her part of moving to warmer climes.

On April 3rd 1786 the proposal for the printing of Burns 'Poems, Chiefly In The Scottish Dialect', was sent to the printer. The proposals were published on 14th April, and in June, copy for the book was sent to John Wilson. On the 31st July 'The Kilmarnock Edition' was published at three shillings a copy.

With the publishing of the Kilmarnock Edition began the decade of Burns, a ten year long adventure begun in July 1786, ending full circle with his death in July 1796.

Burns had now crossed the threshold to his destiny.

On September 3rd 1786 Jean Armour gave birth to twins, Jean and Robert, and probably from the moment Burns saw them, all intention of emigration flew out the window. He had already postponed the voyage on the *1st September, whether it was because of the success of his poems or the fact that Jean was so near to having the children is not known, but when he postponed the voyage for the second time on the 27th September, he knew in himself that he would not be going to Jamaica.

* Burns' excuse for not setting out on the ship 'The Nancy' was that he was given only two days notice to embark, but he had known since the 30th July that the ship would be leaving circa the end of August.

His joy at the success of his poems along with the birth of his children was short lived. Shortly after harvest time, in October/November 1786, according to his youngest sister Isabella, a letter arrived which, we are led to believe, informed him of the death of Margaret Campbell. From this time onwards Margaret 'Highland Mary' Campbell becomes the stuff of legend. There would never be any more plans for emigration by Burns.

On 27th November 1786, Robert Burns took another step down the pathway of his fate when he set out on his horse, Jenny Geddes, for Edinburgh.

Henry MacKenzie, writing for 'The Lounger' magazine gave The Kilmarnock Edition an extremely good review on 9th December, and on the 14th, a proposal was issued for a second edition of his poems. This would become the First Edinburgh Edition.

1787 began and ended with a woman. On the 7th January Burns became acquainted with 'a very pretty girl, a Lothian farmer's daughter, whom I have almost persuaded to accompany me to the west-country'. He never mentions her name, but it is commonly believed that she was Peggy Chalmers.

On the 9th April, Burns began his Second Commonplace Book, his 'Edinburgh Journal'. The 17th of that same month saw the publication of his second Edition of poems ('The First Edinburgh Edition'), and on the 23rd April he sold the copyright to his poems to William Creech for One Hundred Guineas.

1787 was also the year when his feet never seemed to stay in the same place for any length of time. This was the year of 'Tours', journeys through Scotland, with the odd sojourn into England when near the border.

Accompanied by a young friend, Robert Ainslie, he set out on the 5th May on his 'Border Tour'. This lasted until 1st June and they took in places such as Coldstream, Melrose, Berwick, Alnwick, Morpeth, Newcastle, Carlisle, before heading home, via Dumfries.

As seems to always happen with Burns, his upbeat is followed by a very, very precipitous downbeat. On his arrival in Dumfries, where he was awarded an 'Honorary Freedom' of the town, he was floored by a letter, which was waiting for him, from May Cameron, a servant girl working in Edinburgh, with whom Burns had had an amorous relationship. The letter informed him that she was pregnant, and, though she did not claim that he was the father, Burns considered it a possibility that he was.

He contacted Robert Ainslie, who had returned to Edinburgh after the tour, and asked him to go to May and help her out financially. May did eventually take a writ out against Burns naming him as the father of her child, but by August 15th, Burns was freed from this writ, the possibility being that May Cameron might have suffered a miscarriage.

By the 8th June, Burns had returned to Mauchline. He had no intention of becoming involved with the Armour family again, but his daughter Jean, a sickly child, was living with them, and he needed to see her. His son, Robert was being cared for at Mossgiel by Agnes Broun, his mother.

With all good intention Burns came to visit his daughter, but on seeing Jean Armour, their natural attraction to one another took over. By the time Burns left Mauchline in late June, Jean was again pregnant.

Burns set off on his 'West Highland Tour' which is shrouded in mystery.
For a time he travelled alone, and this has led to many questions. Did he visit Margaret Campbell's graveside at Greenock? Did he visit her mother in Campbeltown? Margaret's mother is quoted as having said she met Burns, and that she quite liked him, though he did not seem 'husband quality' for her daughter.

No one is completely sure where Burns stopped, as, unusually for him, he did not keep a journal of the trip. Maybe his conscience was troubling him or maybe he needed a rest, the previous year had been quite hectic for him.

On the second part of the tour Burns was accompanied by Dr George Grierson, a Glasgow friend, and this part of the tour was diarised. Their travels included the towns of Arrochar and Inverary.

Burns was back in Edinburgh by 8th August. By the 15th he was freed of the May Cameron writ, and on the 25th, he was off again, this time not on horseback but in a chaise, accompanied by William Nicol, who was not the best travelling companion to choose for a long trip. Nicol had a very irascible temper and changeable nature, plus he had an addiction to quaffing large amounts of alcohol, encouraging Burns to join with him in these sessions. Ignoring this obvious negative side of the journey, they headed off in the direction of the Highlands and the North East, where Burns' predecessors came from.

This was a long journey, covering nearly 600 miles, which took in Bannockburn, Aberfeldy, Killiecrankie, Inverness, Fochabers, Cullen, Old Deer, Ellon, Aberdeen, Stonehaven, Arbroath, Dunfermline, to name but only a few, before returning to Edinburgh on 16th September.

Maybe Burns was enjoying his last taste of the bachelor life, for hardly had he unpacked his trunk on his return to Edinburgh, before he was off again on the 4th October, accompanied this time by another old friend, Dr James Adair. This was his 'Stirlingshire Tour'. This tour took in Clackmannan, Harvieston (where he again met, and apparently proposed to Peggy Chalmers), Dunfermline Abbey and Ochtertyre.

The travellers returned to Edinburgh on 20th October, and Burns rented rooms with William Cruikshank, at St James Square. At least the news was good on this return, as the 'First London Edition' of his poems had now been published.

In November 1787 Robert met with Patrick Miller at Dalswinton to discuss leasing a farm, and he also became more involved with contributing to, and editing James Johnson's Scots Musical Museum.

As stated earlier, the year started off with a woman, and it ended with one.

On the 4th December 1787, at a soiree in Edinburgh, with a guest list carefully manipulated by a young deserted wife, Robert Burns met Agnes McLehose.

If you believe many of the biographers down the decades, this event seemed to be accompanied with sparks flying, rockets launching, fanfares resounding, and, when *Robert's lustrous dark and dangerously magnetic eyes fell upon Agnes' crystal blue open and honest gaze, a feeling of time standing still.*

After this first meeting at Miss Nimmo's house, in Alison Square, Agnes invited Burns to tea at her house in the Potterrow. Unfortunately he could not keep this invitation, as he had, through no fault of his own, fallen from a coach and dislocated his knee-cap.

But unfortunate though it was for the couple, fortunate it was for literary history that this accident happened. Had Robert and Agnes met, we would not have been left such wonderful letters, with such an insight into two truly individual and remarkable people.

On the 18th February 1788 Burns left Edinburgh for Ayrshire. He went via Glasgow, as he was meeting his brother William, and his old friend Captain Richard Brown, in the city. On the 22nd or 23rd of that month, he returned to Mauchline and Jean Armour.

This is not the nicest side we see of Burns, as you will read in a future chapter, and hopefully it was one he regretted. On the 3rd or 9th March (the date is disputed), Jean gave birth to twin girls, sadly both died.

After visiting Ellisland with John Tenant on the 27th February, Burns signed the lease for the farm on 18th March. The rent was £50 p.a. This was about the time he was beginning an instruction course for the Excise, in Mauchline and Tarbolton.

Burns received his commission on 28th April 1788 and though there is no official date as to when it happened, circa this time, Robert and Jean are reported to have celebrated a civil marriage. Burns settled in alone at Ellisland on 11th June 1788, making it ready for Jean to join him. Life was not easy, but he had a lot to look forward to.

On 5th August, a Kirk Service was performed recognising the marriage of Robert and Jean. Third time lucky for the couple. His friendship with the Riddell family at neighbouring Friar's Carse began at this time.

Then came November 1788, and Burns was informed that Jenny Clow, Agnes McLehose's young servant girl, with whom he had had a brief fling, had given birth to his illegitimate son. In December Jean Armour joined Burns in rented accommodation at 'The Isle', a farm near Ellisland. (Some biographers have thought that the name Ellisland actually is 'Isle's Land' and that the two were once one property).

1789 began with Jenny Clow taking a writ out against Burns naming him as father of her son. In February he visited Edinburgh to settle things with Jenny and to sort out William Creech, who still had not paid him the money he was owed for the copyright to his songs.

Burns now took on the mantle of good husband and father. On the 7th September he began work as an Excise officer at £50 p.a., exactly the same amount as the rental of his farm at Ellisland. Unfortunately in November of that year his weak constitution took its toll and he was laid low with a severe fever.

By January 1790, Burns was back at his Excise work, and riding up to two hundred miles a week, in all weathers, as well as running his farm, and writing his poetry. No one could ever accuse Robert Burns of being work-shy or a shirker. But he was still physically and mentally weak, and complained of incessant headaches and feelings of depression.

In June/July 1790, Burns had been transferred to the Dumfries Third Division of the Excise. This meant that some nights he could not get home to Ellisland and had to stay over in Dumfries. These spells in town led to a short relationship with Anna Park, resulting in another illegitimate daughter, (also called Elizabeth), who eventually came to be cared for by Jean Armour.

January 1791 began with Burns suffering an injury received when he fell

9

'with his horse'.   On the 31st of March Anna Park gave birth to her daughter, and on the 9th April, Jean Armour gave birth to her son, William Nicol.

For work reasons, Burns had made up his mind to leave Ellisland and move into Dumfries.   On 25th August his crops were auctioned at a sale held on the farm.   After the sale the countryside resounded to the sounds of merry-making and celebrations of the severely inebriate kind. Burns formally renounced the lease on Ellisland on 10th October.

On 11th November 1791, the family moved to *Cawart's Vennel in Dumfries. This was a three-roomed apartment above John Syme's office, and must have seemed like a cage in comparison to the space they'd had at Ellisland.   Apparently Jean was not happy at this move though she grew to like living there after all she was originally a town girl herself.

* Cawart's Vennel – 'The Wee Vennel' now 11 Bank Street, Dumfries and later christened the 'Sang-Hoose'.

The family had hardly settled in Dumfries, when Burns received a letter from Agnes McLehose pre 23rd November, informing him of the imminent death of Jenny Clow.   Burns told Agnes that he would come to Edinburgh to see Jenny, and also to see Agnes herself.

He was granted time off from the Excise and travelled to Edinburgh on 29th November, staying in the city until 11th December.

Although he had not seen her in three years, Burns was stunned when Agnes informed him that she was intending to leave Scotland and try for reconciliation with her estranged husband in Jamaica.

Burns and Agnes met and parted for the last time on 6th December at Lamont's Land in Edinburgh.   On the 27th December, Burns sent her a letter containing three songs.   'Behold the Hour, the Boat Arrive!', 'Ance Mair I Hail Thee, Thou Gloomy December!', and the eternal 'Ae Fond Kiss, and Then We Sever'.

The following year saw Burns again in his hard working mode.   In February 1792 he was transferred to the Dumfries Port Division with a rise in his salary of £20 p.a., and he could make £15-£20 extra p.a. in basic essentials.

On February 29th Burns was involved in an Excise assault on a smuggler's ship, 'The Rosamond', at Gretna.   This entailed wading up to his chest through freezing water.   Burns, though strongly built, had a weak constitution, and this ice-cold shock to his system did not do his heart any favours.

An event that threw a cloud over the year is the suggestion of Burns' buying and then trying to send four small cannons, captured from the 'Rosamond', to the Revolutionaries in France.   It brought his politics to the attention of his superiors, and left him, a government employee, on a very shaky footing. To be fair to Burns, Britain was not then at war with France, therefore this was not a treasonous act, though possibly for one in his position, a little foolhardy.

On the 31st December, John Mitchell, Collector of Excise, was ordered by the Board to investigate Burns for his political views *'as a person disaffected to Government'*. Burns was in imminent danger of losing his job, something he could not allow to happen. He had a family to support and Jean had just given birth to another child, a daughter this time, whom he named after Elizabeth Riddell.

On the 5th January 1793, Burns went before Excise Commissioner, Robert Graham of Fintry, to defend himself. He was successful in this defence, but he must have known that he would now have to tread very warily.

On the 19th May the Burns family moved to 'Millbrae Vennel'. This was a much bigger house and was on two floors, with its own front door. The house stands on what today is known as Burns Street.

Two months later, on 27th July, Burns and John Syme set out on their 'First Galloway Tour', lasting until 2nd August. Places visited included Kenmure, Kirkcudbright, Selkirk, and Girvan.

But the year ended on a very sour note. An incident occurred at Friar's Carse, home of Robert Riddell. The incident is described in a future chapter but is often referred to as the 'Rape of the Sabines'. It took place when Burns had drunk more than usual and found himself in a situation in which he considered he had been 'set-up'. This debacle ended the friendship between Burns and Robert and Elizabeth Riddell, and caused a major split between Burns and Maria Riddell, one which lasted for over a year.

1794 began with Burns again in a working frame of mind. He put together a proposal to reorganise the Dumfries Excise Service. Sadly before he could be reconciled with Robert Riddell, his friend died on 21st April at the age of 38. In June, Friar's Carse was put up for sale.

Burns and Syme set out on a Second Galloway Tour on 25th June. This was a short excursion and lasted only until 28th June. Places visited included Castle Douglas, Newton Stewart and Portpatrick. On 25th June, from the Carlinwalk Inn, Castle Douglas, Burns wrote a long letter to Agnes McLehose, nearly two years since he had last written to her.

August 12th saw the birth of his son James Glencairn. Life was beginning to look up for Burns when, on 22nd December 1794, he was promoted to Acting Supervisor of Excise, Dumfries. He was also tentatively resuming correspondence with Maria Riddell, which pleased him greatly. But as usual the good times didn't last.

In January 1795, although he was working harder for the Excise, his income was dropping at an incredible rate. This was due to Britain's war with France which had been ongoing since 1793. As Burns wrote

'These accursed times, by stopping up Importation, have for this year at least lopt off a full third of my income'.

He was still sympathetic to the revolutionaries, which he wrote in a letter to his friend, Mrs Dunlop on the 12th January. Unfortunately Mrs Dunlop had relations on the royalist side and took this letter as a personal insult. He wrote to her on several occasions, but Burns did not read a letter from her in his lifetime again.

To make the point that he was still a patriotic Exciseman, Burns became a founder member of the Dumfries Volunteers, the 18th century version of the 'Home Guard'. Dumfries was becoming a garrison town, and uniforms of all colours were bedecking the streets, thoroughfares, and social gatherings.

Not to be outshone in this extravaganza of vibrant pulsating colours, The Royal Dumfries Volunteers chose their uniform at their second meeting on the 3rd February 1795. It was, according to the description in the small book 'Robert Burns As A Volunteer' by William Will

'a blue coat half lapelled with red cape and cuffs, and gilt buttons with the letters R.D.V. engraved on them; a plain white Cassimere vest, with small gilt buttons; white trousers made of Russia tweeling, tied at the ankle; white stockings; a black velvet stock; hair to be worn short, or turned up behind; a round hat turned up on the left side with a gilt button, a cockade, and a black feather; their shoes to be tied with black ribbon; and the only distinction between the officers and privates, in point of dress, is that the Major Commandant and two Captains are to wear two epaulets, and the other Commissioned Officers one'.

On the 28th March, they made a slight change on the type of trousers to be worn, which were now to be *'white Cassimere breeches, buckled at the knee, and half gaiters'*. Burns must have looked quite the dandy in that uniform.

In losing one friend in Mrs Dunlop, he regained another when he and Maria Riddell were fully reconciled in the February/March of 1795, and were to remain so for the rest of his life.

In April we have, so far as we are aware, the last painting of Burns done from life. Alexander Reid produced a miniature of him, which first Burns liked, and then he didn't. But he was not a very well man during this time.

In September, Burns was again unwell. His whole being was sent crashing when he learned of the death of his and Jean's only surviving daughter, Elizabeth who, with her mother, was on a visit to relatives in Mauchline. Due to this illness Burns could not be present at his daughter's funeral. Burns went into a decline.

From December 1795 through January 1796, Robert suffered *'a most severe Rheumatic fever'*, and could hardly move from his bed. By the 31st of January, he was *'beginning to crawl across my room'*.

Burns was also very worried as he realised that, because of his illness, his salary would be cut. Though what he would have been able to buy was questionable as between January and March of 1796 there was famine in Dumfries. Many families, as well as Burns' own, *'are absolutely without one grain of meal; as money cannot purchase it'*. The embargo of foreign imports into Britain because of the war with France, was hiking up the price of home-grown produce. In fact from the 12th-14th March there were food riots in the town of Dumfries.

Though he was not to know it at the time, Burns was on his last walk down that highway that destiny had laid before him.

By February Burns was back at the Excise and was also supplying George Thomson with new songs. From then until June he was between work and ill-health on quite a few occasions.

The poet's last illnesses can be followed through his pay-checks. On 3rd March 1796 he received a normal wage of £6, his next wage, on the 14th April was £3. On June 2nd he received £6, but on 14th July, a week before his death, he received only £2.

Many of Burns' last letters were about songs and song writing, and addressed to either James Johnson or George Thomson. His body was failing, but his Muse was still with him.

At the beginning of June 1796, Maria Riddell, who had moved to Halleaths near Lochmaben, invited Burns to join her and her friends in celebrating King George III's birthday. Burns declined the invitation, due to illness *'rackt as I am with rheumatism'*.

On 26th June, Burns presented Jessy Lewars with an inscribed copy of the Scots Musical Museum, which he apologetically requested from James Johnson at the beginning of June.

Burns' financial situation was beginning to press on him severely, to the point of his writing to people to whom he had lent money, requesting in the politest manner possible, if they could direct even the smallest repayment his way.

There appeared to be no way that the medical men could cure, or even help

Burns by normal means, so Dr Maxwell, possibly Dr Alexander Brown, and some other medical friends suggested that sea-bathing, fresh country air, and horse-riding would be the best way to tackle the cure. At the beginning of July, Robert Burns left Dumfries, trusting in the advice given to him by his medical friends. He spent nearly three weeks at Brow Well, drinking the waters of the spring near the Raffles Burn.

The most horrifying advice given to him was that he was to wade up to his armpits in the icy cold Solway. He was debilitated, had no strength, was emaciated and had a weak heart. Yet it must have been an inner strength that kept him going.

On the 5th July, Maria Riddell, who had been advised to go to Brow because her own health was failing, invited Burns to dine with her at her lodgings. She sent her carriage to fetch him, and when confronted with how ill he really was, she was shocked and upset at his appearance, *'he seemed already touching the brink of eternity'*. They talked through the evening then he left. They met again the next day, for the last time.

Tradition reports that Burns visited the wife of a Rev John Craig and their daughter at Ruthwell one sunny July afternoon. Where he was seated in their house, the sun shone in his eyes. The daughter Agnes, thinking that this was making him uncomfortable got up to close the curtains. It is reported that Burns stopped her saying

> *'Thank you, my dear, for your kind attention; but, oh, let him shine he will not shine long for me'.*

Did this kind gesture from young Agnes Craig in Ruthwell recall to Burns' mind the other Agnes Craig (McLehose) he left behind in Edinburgh in December 1791?

From Brow, on 12th July, Burns sent a letter to Thomson requesting a loan of £5. In lieu of this loan he enclosed his last song ever written, 'Fairest Maid On Devon Banks', a song meant solely for Peggy Chalmers, she whom he held in his 'heart's core'. Another circle completed. From 'Handsome Nell' to 'The Fairest Maid', his first love to his last, and maybe only, true love.

On Monday 18th July, Robert Burns returned to Dumfries, riding in a gig borrowed from John Clark of Locharwoods.

According to Jean Armour in an interview with John McDiarmid, on his return home Burns' mind began to wander because of the fever. He was aware of this, and requested that when this happened, Jean should touch him to bring him back to himself. Three days before he died he managed to get out of bed. Jean found him sitting in the corner of the room with the bedclothes around him. He allowed himself to be led back to bed. The day before he died he called out, in a hale voice *'Gilbert! Gilbert!'*

Robert Burns died at home in Millbrae Vennel in Dumfries, at five o'clock on the morning of 21st July 1796, aged thirty-seven and a half.

His final days and hours were tortured with thoughts that he, like his father before him, would die in debt, and that his wife and children would be left penniless and possibly even homeless. But Robert Burns, when he joined the Excise, actually did something financially correct, maybe for the first time in his life. He joined a pension plan.

Burns paid six shillings a quarter towards the 'Excise Incorporation', which was a fund for the widows and orphans of Excise Officers. From the start of his employment, until his death in 1796, he had paid in less than £10.

From his death Jean was entitled to £8 per annum until 1821. From 1821 until her death in 1834, the pension was raised to £12 per annum. Thus making a total of £356. It was not a great fortune, but it probably kept the wolf from the door on many occasions.

In the end his fears for his family were unfounded. Burns' children, legitimate and illegitimate, did well for themselves, and with the exception of a few wavers from his eldest son Robert, those that survived into adulthood did not let their father down. Nor could he have ever left behind a more loyal and exceptional envoy for his memory than Jean Armour, who grew in stature, love and respect until her own death.

Unfortunately this allegiance cannot be attributed to some of his supposed male friends who, now that Burns was out of the way, did nothing for his *esteem* with their selective memories and braggardship as to his *'frailties'*, while they thrived on the fame of being a familiar of his true genius.

Robert's 'Lasses' emerge as the most loyal in their recollections. For them he wore his beating and beaten heart on his sleeve, and despite themselves they could not help but love him for this openness and honesty, remaining true to him and his memory till finally their own time to pass came.

Above: A portrait of Burns (Paisley Libraries).
Below Left: Isabella Burns Begg – Burns' Sister (unknown artist).
Below Right: Agnes Brown – Burns' Mother (unknown artist).

PART ONE
Chapter Two - The Burns Family

THE PARENTS

Mother - Agnes Broun - (17ᵗʰ March 1732 - 14ᵗʰ January 1820)

Agnes was ten, and the eldest of six children, when her mother died. Tradition maintains that she was born at Whitestone Cottage, Culzean, and was brought up at Craigenton, her grandparent's farm, in Kirkoswald parish, which was tenanted by her father, Gilbert Broun and her mother Agnes Rennie. Two years after the death of her mother, on Gilbert Broun's remarriage, she was sent to live with her grandmother Mrs Rennie, in Maybole, who could recall back to the time of the Covenanters and who had a vast memory bank of old ballads and songs. Agnes met William Burness shortly after breaking off her seven-year engagement, circa 1756, to ploughman William Nelson, because of Nelson's philandering, and she and William Burness were married on 15ᵗʰ December 1757.

According to her youngest child, Isabella Burns Begg, Agnes Broun

> 'was rather under the average height; inclined to plumpness, but neat, shapely and full of energy; having a beautiful pink and white complexion, a fine square forehead, pale red hair, but dark eye-brows and eyes often ablaze with a temper difficult to control. Her disposition was naturally cheerful; her manner, easy and collected; her address, simple and unpresuming; and her judgement uncommonly sound and good. She possessed a fine musical ear, and sang well'.

After her husband's death in 1784, Agnes lived most of her life with her second son, Gilbert. Robert had settled an annuity on her of £5 per year for her care. She died at Gilbert's home, at Grant's Braes, East Lothian, and is buried in Bolton Kirkyard.

Father - William Burness - (11ᵗʰ November 1721 - 13ᵗʰ February 1784)

William was born at Clochnahill Farm, Dunnottar, Kincardineshire, and was a gardener to trade. He worked in Edinburgh from 1748-50 landscaping 'The Meadows' in the city, then moved on to Ayrshire. He was head gardener at the Doonholm estate of Provost William Ferguson of Ayr. During the Summer/Autumn of 1757, a few months before his marriage, he began to build, with his own hands, the 'but and ben' at Alloway, which he called 'New Gardens'. His intention was to start up a market garden business. His contribution to his son's history is now known as 'Burns Cottage'.

According to Isabella Burns Begg, William Burness

'was a thin, sinewy figure, about five feet eight or nine inches in height, somewhat bent with toil; his 'haffet-locks thin and bare', with a dark swarthy complexion'.

It is from his father that Burns inherited his swarthy complexion, not from his mother, as wrongly stated by 'Honest' Allan Cunningham in his 'Life Of Burns', a complexion which stood out so noticeably in the salons of the Edinburgh gentry.

William Burness is buried in Alloway Kirkyard.

From 'Wood's Songs Of Scotland'

> 'Men who rise to celebrity in the world are generally supposed to inherit their genius from the maternal side. If it shall be said that Burns inherited his love for ballad lore from his mother, we may presume that he derived his strong manly sense from his father; as to his genius
>
> > 'The light that led astray, was light from Heaven'.
>
> It may be traced in many of his poems, and flashes out in his lyrics like sheet-lightning in a summer's eve, when sung to the simple, yet deeply pathetic melodies of his native land'.

BROTHERS AND SISTERS

Brother - Gilbert - (28th September 1760 - 8th November 1827)
Gilbert, like Robert, was born at Alloway. He married Jane Breckenridge on 21st June 1791 and fathered eleven children, five girls and six boys.

When Robert left Mossgiel, Gilbert took on the responsibility for his mother and sisters, as well as for Burns' illegitimate daughter Elizabeth Paton Burns, 'Dear-bought Bess'.

After he left Mossgiel, he farmed at Dinning, Nithsdale for two years, before becoming manager of Captain John Dunlop's farm, Morham, West Mains, East Lothian in 1800. In 1804 he became factor on Lady Katherine Blantyre's East Lothian Estates, living at Grant's Braes, near Haddington, where he died. Gilbert is buried in Bolton Kirkyard.

Sister - Agnes - (30th September 1762 - 17th October 1834)
Agnes married late in life in 1804 a William Galt, who became land-steward on Matthew Fortescue's Irish estate. They had no children. She died in Stephenstown, County Louth, and is buried in St Nicholas' Churchyard, Dundalk.

Sister - Annabella - (14th November 1764 - 2nd March 1832)
Died unmarried at Grant's Braes, and is buried in Bolton Kirkyard.

Brother - William - (30th July 1767 - 24th July 1790)
William was the oldest of the three children born at Mount Oliphant. He became an apprentice saddler in Longtown, near Carlisle, before moving to

Newcastle where he worked for Messrs. Walker & Robson, saddlers. He then became a journeyman saddler in London with William T. Barber, situated at 181, The Strand. He is said by John Murdoch, ex-tutor to the Burns family to have died from 'putrid fever', another name for typhus, while living in London.

Brother - John (10th July 1769 - October 1785)

John died from an unknown illness at sixteen years of age. He was buried in Mauchline Kirkyard on November 1st 1785.

Sister - Isabella (27th July 1771 - 4th December 1858)

Isabella was the youngest of Burns brothers and sisters and the one who lived longest. This enabled her to pass on information to many biographers regarding the life of her brother, although many today question the accuracy of her recollections.

She married John Begg, quarrier, on 9th December 1793 at Mossgiel. After her husband's accidental death in 1813 she lived first at Orminston in East Lothian, then Tranent, finally settling at Bridge House, Alloway. Isabella Burns Begg is buried in Alloway Kirkyard beside her father.

THE CHILDREN

Daughter - Elizabeth Paton Burns - (22nd May 1785 - 8th January 1817)

The illegitimate daughter by Elizabeth Paton an account of whom is given in Part Two – Chapter Two.

Son - Robert - (3rd September 1786 - 14th May 1857)

Robert and his twin sister Jean were born to Jean Armour in Mauchline. He was educated at Dumfries Grammar School, Edinburgh University and Glasgow University. He held a position in the Stamp Office in London, which to all accounts did not really suit him, retiring from there in 1833.

Robert married Ann Sherwood on 24th March 1809 and had one daughter, Eliza, baptised 23rd August 1812. The couple separated some years later. Ann Sherwood died in 1835. When his wife was still alive, he formed a relationship with Emma Bland, with whom he had another four children, Jessie (1827-19th August 1847), Francis William (9th September 1829 -?), Jane Emma (1831- 24th September 1916), and Robert III (1833 - 1879).

According to a letter written by Elizabeth Park Burns in 1844

'Robert was a kind-hearted man, but was addicted to the bottle. He had fathered eleven children of whom only one was alive'.

From the Dumfries Courier of May 1857, is the report of the death of Robert

'We have to announce the demise of Mr Robert Burns, which occurred on the afternoon of the 14th instant at Dumfries. Mr Burns was born at Mauchline in September 1786, so that he had nearly completed his 71st

19

year.   In several respects, in point of intellect, the deceased was no ordinary man, but yet he was chiefly remarkable throughout life as being the eldest son of Robert Burns, the national poet of Scotland.   Burns died in 1796, and his eldest son was nearly ten years of age at the time of that premature decease.   Of the father the son preserved a vivid remembrance, and was wont to describe the walks taken together on the banks of the Nith.   Mr Burns was educated at the Dumfries Academy, where he distinguished himself, especially in the classics.   Even before his father's death he gave promise of ability which filled the parental heart with pleasure, while the poet did not fail to lend a helping hand in the preparation of the school tasks of his son, as was discovered by Rector Gray from the eloquence of the language in which his youthful pupil's translations from the Latin were couched.   After completing the curriculum of the local seminary, Mr Burns prosecuted his studies at Glasgow College and the University of Edinburgh, becoming an excellent classic scholar as well as an advanced mathematician.   His own natural bent was for tuition, but an appointment to a clerkship in the Stamp Office having been offered him by the prime minister, Mr Addington, he proceeded to London in 1804, and entered upon his duties at Somerset House, where it was anticipated that a prosperous career had opened up for him.   For a work of a public office, however, he was not well suited, and, indeed, throughout his life he continued comparatively a child in matters of business.   He remained at London until 1833, a period of nearly thirty years, during which he had eked out a limited income by his favourite occupation of tuition; he retired at that time on a pension and returned to Dumfries, where he has since resided almost constantly. During the past winter it had become evident that his vigorous constitution was giving way, but it was not until the 6th inst. that the disease, or rather decay of nature, which terminated his existence became serious.   Mr Burns as we have already mentioned, was an accomplished scholar.   Endowed with a prodigious memory and great powers of application, he had amassed a vast quantity of knowledge on a great range of subjects.   His enthusiasm in the acquisition of information continued to almost his last days, and for some years he had been almost passionately attached to the study of the language of the Gael.   In music he was a proficient student, possessing both a theoretical and practical knowledge of the art.   A portion of the father's poetic mantle had fallen upon the son, and in his earlier years he composed verses of considerable intrinsic merit.   His remains were laid on Tuesday beside those of his father in the Mausoleum, St Michael's Churchyard, the vault of which has not been opened for upwards of twenty years[1].*

Daughter - Jean - (3rd September 1786 - c. 20th October 1787)

Robert was being raised at Mossgiel by Burns' mother Agnes Broun, while Jean his twin sister, a sickly child, remained at the Armour home with her mother.   She died at little more than one year.   The cause of death is unknown.   Jean Burns is buried in Mauchline Kirkyard.

Twin Daughters - (3rd/9th March 1788 - 10th March 1788)
- (3rd/9th March 1788 - 22nd March 1788)
Born to Jean Armour at Mauchline, two girls unnamed and unbaptised.
They are buried in Mauchline Kirkyard.

Son - Robert Burns Clow - (c.   November 1788 – Date of death unknown)
Very little is known about this illegitimate child born to Janet Clow in
Edinburgh, except that in later years he did very well for himself, becoming
a successful merchant who married into society. He also named his eldest
son Robert Burns Clow II, and it appears that he did not use his famous
father's name to get on in life.

This eldest son, Robert Burns Clow II, was born in 1820 and was educated
at a boarding school in Islington called Gerrit van de Linde's.   Apparently
of an adventurous nature, circa 1840 he travelled to the East Indies and
North Borneo.   He returned to Britain in 1849 to testify to atrocities
committed under the rule of Sir James Brook in Sarawak, and a Royal
Commission was set up in Singapore to investigate the matter.

On the 12th September 1851, pirates captured and boarded Robert's
schooner, 'The Dolphin', and Burns Clow, his partner and five of the crew
were murdered.   As a result of this attack, ships of the Royal Navy and the
East India Company set out on an expedition against the south sea pirates.
The village of Raja Muda was attacked and destroyed in reprisal for the
murders of Burns Clow and his crew.

Daughter - Helen Armstrong (1789 - 1887)
The illegitimate daughter by Helen Hyslop born in Moffat, an account of
whom is given in Part Two – Chapter Two.

Son - Francis Wallace (18th August 1789 - 9th July 1803)
Born to Jean Armour whilst living at Ellisland.   A Mr Shaw had arranged
for his cadetship in the East India Company, but Francis died, possibly
from consumption, before he could leave for that country.   He is buried in
the Burns Mausoleum in St Michael's Churchyard, Dumfries.

From a letter written in 1803 to James Currie by John Murdoch once tutor
to the Burns family

> *'Mr James McClure wrote me from Dumfries, dated July 8th, that poor
> Frank Wallace Burns came home from Edinburgh in April last in a bad
> state of health, and that, after having all the best medical advice that
> could be procured, his life was despaired of.   When I showed this to Mr
> Alderman Shaw he expressed much concern; for (as I suppose you know)
> this was the lad for whom he had procured the promise of an excellent
> appointment in the service of the East India Company.   Next post
> brought me the Dumfries weekly journal of the 12th, in which was this*

paragraph:- 'Died at Dumfries, yesterday, Francis Wallace Burns, second son of the late celebrated Robert Burns, the Scots bard, in the 14th year of his age. He was a very promising youth''.

Daughter - Elizabeth Park Burns - (31st March 1791 - 13th June 1873)
An illegitimate daughter by Anna Park, born possibly at Leith, an account of whom is given in Part Two – Chapter Two.

Son - William Nicol - (9th April 1791 - 21st February 1872)
This son by Jean Armour was born at Ellisland and was named after Burns' friend, William Nicol.   William married Catherine Adelaide Crone from Dublin. They had no children.   Catherine died in India on 29th June 1841.

William's cadetship in the East India Company commenced in 1811 and he joined the 7th Madras Infantry.   He became Lieutenant-Colonel, reaching the position of Colonel in 1855.   On his retirement he moved to England, living in Cheltenham with his brother, James, when they were both widowed.   Though he died in Cheltenham, he is buried in the Burns Mausoleum in St Michael's Churchyard, Dumfries.

Daughter - Elizabeth Riddell - (21st Nov. 1792 - pre 23rd September 1795)
Elizabeth was born in the 'Wee Vennel' in Dumfries.   Circa January 1794 it is alleged that the little girl suffered a serious illness, (the illness is not named) and this is hinted at as one of the causes leading to her early death.

In the summer of 1795 Elizabeth was taken to visit relatives in Mauchline. Maybe Burns and Jean knew that it could possibly be the last time the relations would see her alive.   This proved to be correct.   The child died in Mauchline.   Burns was recovering from a recurring illness during this time, which sapped his strength and it affected him very sorely that he could not be present at her funeral.   She is buried in Mauchline Kirkyard beside her three sisters.

Son - James Glencairn - (12th August 1794 - 18th November 1865)
James, born at Millbrae Vennel, was educated at Dumfries Grammar School and Christ's Hospital, London (The Blue Coat School).   His cadetship began in June 1811, when he left for Calcutta, joining the 15th Bengal Native Infantry. He became a Major in the East India Company.

He married Sarah Robinson in 1818, but she died three years later, in November 1821, after the birth of their daughter, Sarah, born on 2nd of that month.   Another son and daughter died in infancy.   His second wife was Mary Becket whom he married in 1828. They had one daughter Ann.

In 1833 James was appointed Judge and Collector at Cahar in India.   On retiring in 1839, they moved to England and lived in London until Mary died on 13th November 1844. When widowed he shared a house with his brother William who lived in Cheltenham.   He was promoted to Lieutenant-Colonel in 1855.

James died from a fall down a flight of stairs at his Cheltenham home, and is buried in the Burns Mausoleum St Michael's Churchyard, Dumfries.

In a letter to James Currie, written from London in 1803 by John Murdoch, we are informed that circa that time his mother, Jean Armour, was living with the knowledge that James might lose his sight

> *'James has been in the sick ward upwards of three months. He has had from time to time a considerable degree of fever, and twice so violent an inflammation of his eyes that we were under serious apprehensions that he must lose his sight'.*

Son - Maxwell - (25th July 1796 - 25th April 1799)

Born at Millbrae Vennel as his father's corpse was being carried to St Michael's Churchyard, Burns' last child was named after Dr Maxwell by Jean Armour. Burns had intended he be named after his friend Alexander Cunningham. The cause of the boy's premature death is unknown and he also is buried in the Burns Mausoleum in St Michael's Churchyard, Dumfries.

Two further 'children' should be considered. Tradition names Burns as the father to Margaret Campbell's child, but there is no proof that she was ever pregnant. Nor is there any record of a child being born to another acquaintance, May Cameron, who had an unhappy episode with the poet.

Above Left: The grave, in Whitburn Cemetry, of Burns first illegitimate daughter Elizabeth Paton Burns (Dear-bought Bess).

Below: The Buccleuch Arms in Thornhill, where Burns alleged second illegitimate daughter Helen Armstong was in service for thirty years.

Above Right: Elizabeth Park Burns, the third and final illegitimate daughter.

PART TWO

The Lasses

PART TWO
Chapter One

An Introduction to The Lasses

The standard perception of Robert Burns is that he was very much a man's man, but in reality, at his heart's core, he was a woman's man. With a few exceptions he always tried to be on his best behaviour in the company of women, and very few of them had a bad word to say about him.

It was difficult choosing the women to put into the book, but I based my decision on those particular ones that Burns had written for and dedicated songs to. Going further into my researches I found out that some of them led strange but interesting lives, women such as Mary Stewart. Others had contacts in the high echelons of royal society, as did Maria Riddell.

I chose to leave out some important women who had a profound effect on Burns. Women like Mrs Dunlop, Catherine Stewart of Stair, The Duchess of Gordon and others such as Louisa Fontanelle, Eliza Burnett and Jane Ferrier. Though I think that Jean Scott, Kirstie Flint and Jean Glover would add a frisson, if a further book were written.

I have introduced the 'Lasses' as Burns would have met them in his lifetime. As far as I am aware this is chronologically correct. The songs dedicated to the women are also in the accepted chronological order, as Burns would have written them, and the titles are included in each chapter. The songs, with the appropriate music, are included in Part Three of the book, with remarks written by Burns regarding some of them.

The following is a dip into the chapter of each of the 'Lasses' in the book.

1.   Handsome Nell
Was the very first of Burns' charmers to be celebrated in rhyme. This was when he was at the tender age of about fourteen and a half, circa 1774. Unfortunately Burns did not leave the last name of 'Nell' for posterity, so we are left with two claimants to the title of the song.

Nellie Kilpatrick
Nellie was born in February 1759, and lived with her parents at Purclewan, less than two miles from Mount Oliphant, her father being the miller there. After marrying William Bone she lived on the Newark Estate, where she died circa 1820. It was Burns sister Isabella who named her as 'Handsome Nell'.

Nellie Blair
Was born sometime in 1760 and at the time of the harvest would have been

about a year younger than Burns as stated in his biographical letter to John Moore. Her name was give as 'Nell' by a correspondent to the 'Scotsman' newspaper in 1828.

2. Margaret (Peggy) Thomson

Peggy was born circa November 1762 at Main Street in Kirkoswald. Her house was next to Hugh Rodger's school, which Burns attended in the summer of 1775. He first saw Peggy when he ventured out to the back of the school to take the 'sun's altitude', and it was love at first sight.

3. Agnes Fleming

Agnes was known to have a beautiful singing voice, one of the main attractions in a woman for Burns. He wrote one of his loveliest ballads to her. Was she a lover, who knows!

4. Isabella Steven (Tibbie Stein)

Lived at Littlehill Farm, about a mile or so from Lochlea. Burns fell in love with her, unfortunately she did not look on him in the same way. Her family moved to Tarbolton village to a house once situated at the corner of Burns Street and Garden Street. Burns had done with her when, on turning up at her house unannounced, he found she was entertaining another, richer, suitor for her hand.

5. Anne Rankine

Was the daughter of a neighbouring farmer friend of Burns called John Rankine, who lived at Adamhill Farm. Gossip, passed down in tradition, states that she and Burns had a sexual relationship, which Anne, in later interviews, neither denied nor admitted. She later married a John Merry, innkeeper of Cumnock Inn. Anne is buried in Cumnock Old Kirkyard.

6. Ellison Begbie/Elizabeth Gebbie

There is doubt about the actual name of this lass and she goes under either. According to Isabella Burns Begg, Ellison lived at Old Place and worked at Carnell House by the River Cessnock. Burns was very serious about her and had high hopes of marriage to her. According to some letters it is thought that he proposed, but was gently refused.

7. Mary Morison

Is thought to have lived at Brownlea or The Place, both situated in Mauchline. She died from a riding accident at a young age. Although she did meet Burns, she is not now thought to be the Mary Morison of the song composed by him. Mary is buried in Mauchline Kirkyard.

8. Montgomerie's Peggy

Peggy was another woman who refused Burns' proposal of marriage. According to Isabella Burns Begg, 'Peggy' worked at Coilsfield House ('Castle O' Montgomerie') and used to meet Burns at Tarboth Mill. She could easily be confused with Elizabeth Gebbie or Margaret Campbell.

9.   Anne Ronald (Ronalds of the Bennals)

Burns liked Anne Ronald of Bennals Farm near Tarbolton, but considered her to be a bit above him.   The relationship got nowhere.   Anne later married a Matthew Paterson of Aikenbrae Farm and is buried, alongside her husband, in Monkton Kirkyard.

10.   The Mauchline Belles

Were six young women friends in Mauchline, round about the same age. Burns very soon became acquainted with them when he and his family moved into the area.

Jean Markland

Jean married Tarbolton Excise officer James Findlay, a friend of Burns. They moved to Greenock because of his work, where Jean is buried.

Elizabeth (Betty) Miller

She was a daughter of the innkeeper of the Sun Inn, Mauchline.   Burns had a short relationship with her, though not a very serious one.   She married William Templeton in 1794 and died giving birth to her first child.

Helen Miller

Helen was the sister of Betty.   She married Dr John MacKenzie, 'midwife' to Jean Armour, and moved to Irvine when his work took them there.   She is buried in Irvine Parish Kirkyard.

Christina Morton

She was the daughter of Hugh Morton, owner of Morton's Ballroom in Mauchline, where Jean and Robert were said to have first become acquaint. It is said she carried a small torch for Burns herself.   She married Robert Paterson, a Mauchline merchant.

Jean Smith

Married Dr James Candlish, friend of Burns.   She moved to Edinburgh when her husband took up a teaching position at the University.   When he died she also taught to support her family.   Buried in Old Calton Churchyard, Edinburgh, she is thought to be the last of the 'Belles' to die.

Jean Armour

Of whom much is written elsewhere in this book.

11.   Elizabeth Paton

Lived at Largieside, but was servant at Lochlea during the period of William Burness' last illness.   Her sexual relationship with Burns resulted in his first child.   She later married John Andrew in 1788.

Elizabeth Paton Burns

Born in 1785, she is Burns' daughter by Elizabeth Paton.   She was brought up at Mossgiel by Burns' mother, Agnes Broun until her marriage to John Bishop.   They later moved to Rumlinskye near Whitburn.   She died at the age of 31 and is buried in Whitburn Cemetery.

12. Margaret (Peggy) Kennedy

Peggy was a young woman with whom Burns became acquainted in late 1784. She lived at Daljarrock House near Pinwherry. Her story is of a love gone horribly wrong, with fatal consequences.

13. Mary Anne Whitefoord

Was the daughter of Sir John Whitefoord who lived at Ballochmyle House close to Mossgiel, until 1785 when the estate was sold to pay off some of Sir John's debts. Mary Anne later married Henry Kerr-Cranston.

14. Wilhelmina Alexander

Wilhelmina was the sister of Claud Alexander who bought Ballochmyle House near Mauchline in 1785 from the Whitefoord's. Burns came across her when he was seeking inspiration in the evening ambiance. He wrote a poem and sent it to her regarding the incident. She did not acknowledge it. Wilhelmina never married and lived in Glasgow with her sister.

15. Elizabeth (Betty) Miller

One of 'The Belles of Mauchline'.

16. Margaret Campbell - 'Highland Mary'

Margaret was born at Auchamore Farm, Dunoon. When she came to Mauchline she worked first for the Montgomeries at Coilsfield House and later for Gavin Hamilton at Mauchline as nursemaid to his baby son.

In 1786 Burns decided to go to the West Indies. Tradition and Burns alleges that Margaret was to go with him. But first she had to return to her parents home, in Campbeltown, to get herself organised and to say goodbye to them. Burns and Margaret made their parting on the Banks of the Ayr at Failford, within a few months Margaret would die of typhus.

17. Jean Armour

Jean Armour was born in February 1765 in the Cowgate in Mauchline. She was twenty when she met Burns on attending a dance at Morton's Ballroom in the village, during Race Week. Jean and Robert were together for just over a decade. In that time Jean gave birth to nine children, four daughters and five sons.

Jean's loyalty to Burns before their marriage, during the lifetime of their marriage and throughout her long widowhood of nearly thirty-eight years stands unquestioned, and the crowds who came to her funeral after her death on 26th March 1834 equalled those of her illustrious husband in 1796.

18. Margaret (May) Cameron

Margaret Cameron was born in Fortingal in Perthshire. She met Burns in Edinburgh having moved there to find work. In 1787 she informed him by letter that she was in a delicate condition although she did not state outright at the time that he was the father.

19. Euphemia Murray

'Phemie' was born at Lintrose, the only daughter of Mungo Murray. She was known as 'The Flower Of Strathmore'. She met Burns at the house of her uncle, Sir William Murray, at Ochtertyre in Strathearn in October 1787. Euphemia is buried in the Canongate Cemetery, Edinburgh.

20. Margaret (Peggy) Chalmers

Peggy Chalmers was born in Kirkcudbrightshire and lived at Braehead Farm two miles south of Mauchline. Of all of the charmers who entered Burns life, she was probably the nearest thing to a soul-mate. Burns is said to have proposed marriage to Peggy whilst visiting her at the home of her uncle at Harvieston, near Dollar in 1787. She turned him down.

After her marriage to a Lewis Hay she lived abroad. For a while in widowhood, she came back to live at Buccleuch Place in Edinburgh before returning to Switzerland, where she died and is buried.

21. Charlotte Hamilton

Charlotte was cousin to Peggy Chalmers and a half sister to Gavin Hamilton, Burns' lawyer friend. She first met Burns at Harvieston in 1787. She married a travelling companion of Burns, a Dr Adair in 1789, and moved to Harrogate. On her husband's death she returned to Edinburgh where she died in 1806.

22. Agnes Craig McLehose - 'Clarinda'

Down the decades she has become known as Clarinda the charming Edinburgh grass-widow, but she was born, Agnes Craig in the Saltmarket area of Glasgow.

Agnes was sent to boarding school in Edinburgh at age 15, to polish up on her manners. Unfortunately within a short while she met and eventually married James McLehose, and returned to live in Glasgow. When the marriage failed she took refuge in her father's house in the Saltmarket.

After her father's death she moved her family to a small flat in Potterrow in Edinburgh. It was whilst living here that she first read Burns' poetry. She was keen to meet him and finally did so at a party in December 1787.

Agnes died in 1841 and is buried in Canongate Cemetery in Edinburgh.

23. Janet (Jenny) Clow

Very little is known about Jenny who was born in Newburgh in Fife. Whilst employed in the service of Agnes McLehose she had a brief fling with Burns and gave birth to one of his illegitimate children, Robert Burns Clow in November 1788.

24. Jane Cruikshank

Jane was the only child of Burns friend, William Cruikshank, and an excellent harpsichord player and singer. Burns lodged with the Cruikshank family in Edinburgh in October 1787.   In 1804 she married James Henderson, a Jedburgh solicitor, dying there in 1835.

25.   Jean Jaffrey/Jeffrey
Jean was the daughter of Rev Andrew Jaffrey of Lochmaben Church, Dumfriesshire, a good friend of the bard. Burns wrote two songs in her honour.   She married a Liverpool merchant called James Renwick in 1794 and emigrated to New York, settling there at 18 Cortland Street, becoming a member of the New York literati set.   A volume of her writings was published after her death in 1850.

26.   Helen Hyslop and Helen Armstrong
Helen Hyslop was a local beauty born in Langholm who, tradition relates, had a short relationship with the poet, which it is said produced another of Burns' illegitimate children, Helen Armstrong.   The child was born in Moffat in 1788/1789 and lived a long life during which she worked for 30 years as cook at The Buccleuch Arms Inn, Thornhill.

27.   Ann Masterton
Very little is known about Ann Masterton.   She was the daughter of Allan Masterton, musician friend of Burns.   She married a Dr Derbishire and, because of her husband's work, moved to Bath and then on to London. She had one son.

28.   Anna Park
Burns had a short relationship with Anna, a barmaid at the Globe Tavern in Dumfries, resulting in a daughter, Elizabeth Park Burns.   Anna moved to Edinburgh where she met and married John Greenshields.   Where and when she died is unknown, but it was before 1799 when he remarried.

29.   Elizabeth Park Burns
The illegitimate daughter of Burns and Anna Park, Elizabeth was raised by Jean Armour as her own daughter, a promise Jean still kept to after Burns death in 1796.   Elizabeth married Private John Thomson and moved to Glasgow, living at Langside and Pollokshaws.   She is buried in the Vennel Cemetery/Old Burgher Churchyard, Glasgow.

30.   Maria Riddell
Burns met her sometime in late 1791 probably at Friar's Carse, the home of her brother in law, Robert Riddell.   Maria and her husband Walter lived at Woodley Park (Goldilea) about four miles from Dumfries.

Burns and Maria had a falling out at the end of 1793 which stopped them talking for about 18 months.   They last met in July of 1796 when both had been sent to Brow on the Solway to take the sea air for their health.   This meeting took place 5th/6th July, a couple of weeks before Burns' death.

After her first husband, Walter Riddell, died in 1802, she moved to London where she married a Mr Phillips Lloyd Fletcher. She died soon after in Chester, possibly from 'Graves Disease', a disease of the Thyroid, and is buried in the family vault at Overton. In August of 1796 she wrote the first, and considered the best, eulogy to Robert Burns under the name of 'Candidor'.

31. Mary (Polly) Stewart
Mary was a daughter of Burns friend, William Stewart. She lived at Brownhill near Closeburn. After two failed marriages, she returned to stay with her father at Maxwelltown. She then fell in love with a Swiss soldier called Fleitz and moved abroad with him. She died in 1847.

32. Deborah Duff Davies
Was the daughter of Dr Davies of Tenby, and was either a friend or a distant relation of the Riddell's of Friar's Carse. It is though that she probably met Burns at Woodley Park, home of Maria and Walter Riddell. She apparently went to Fontainbleau sometime in 1793 because of bad health and is reported to have died soon after of consumption.

33. Lesley Baillie
Lesley and her family met Burns in August 1792. She lived at Mayville House, Stevenston, with her father and her sister. In 1799 she married a Robert Cumming of Logie. She died in Edinburgh on 12th July 1843, where she is buried. Her father had a memorial column erected in memory of her mother when she died, and Lesley's name was added to it in 1929. It stands on the east side of Glencairn Street, Stevenston.

34. Jean Lorimer – 'Chloris'
Jean was born at Craigieburn, near Moffat in 1775 and moved with her family to Kemys Hall near Ellisland circa 1790. She and her father were often visitors to Burns' house.

Whilst still in her teens, Jean made a serious error when she ran off to Gretna Green to marry a waster called Whelpdale. The marriage lasted only a few weeks.

She contracted tuberculosis and moved to lodgings in Middleton's Entry, Potterrow. Jean died in September 1831, and was one of the first burials in the newly opened Preston Street Cemetery.

35. Jean McMurdo
Jean was the eldest daughter of John McMurdo of Drumlanrig, a friend of the bard's, to whom Burns wrote a song/poem called 'There Was A Lass And She Was Fair'.

36. Philadelphia (Phillis) McMurdo
Phillis was the youngest daughter of John McMurdo of Drumlanrig. She married Mr. Norman Lockhart of Carnwarth. Burns had a great problem

writing a song to her to that 'crinkum-crankum' air 'Robin Adair'.

37.   Jessy Staig

Jessy was the second daughter of Provost David Staig of Dumfries.   Burns sent her the song 'Young Jessy' in the spring of 1793.

She married Major William Miller, brother to Patrick and Janet Miller, and had two sons.   Jessy died while still a young woman, and is buried beside her father in St Michael's Churchyard, Dumfries.

38.   Janet Miller

Janet was the eldest daughter of Patrick Miller of Dalswinton.   Burns dedicated to her his poem/song 'Where Are The Joys'.   She married Thomas Erskine, later the 28th Earl of Mar, in 1795.

39.   Lucy Oswald (Louisa Johnston)

Lucy was the wife of Richard Oswald and lived at Auchincruive, (Oswald Hall - now part of the Scottish Agricultural College).   Burns was very impressed with her, her husband and their family life.   He rededicated the song 'O Wat Ye Wha's In Yon Toon' in her honour, changing the name of the heroine from Jean to Lucy.   She became ill with Pulmonary Tuberculosis and went to Lisbon to recuperate.   She died there circa December 1797/January 1798.

40.   Jessy Lewars

Jessy originally hailed from Ryedale Cottage in the parish of Troqueer. She moved to Dumfries after her father's death and lived with her elder brother across the road from the Burns family in Millbrae Vennel   She helped look after Burns through his last months of illness and cared for Jean Armour and her children in the months following his death.

Burns prophesied that she would marry a young lawyer named James Thomson, which she did.   After her husband's death she lived the rest of her life in Maxwelltown.   She is buried in St Michael's Churchyard, Dumfries, close to the Burns Mausoleum.

Top Left: Lochmaben Kirk where Jean Jaffray's father was minister.

Top Right: Highland Mary's monument in the West Churchyard, Greenock.

Left: Wilhelmina Alexander's Memorial Stone at Mauchline.

Below: Ballochmyle House owned by Maria Woodfoord's family then later by Wilhelmina Alexander's. The latter was 'The Bonnie Lass o' Ballochmyle'.

PART TWO
Chapter Two – The Lasses

1. Nellie Kilpatrick / Nellie Blair - (Handsome Nell)
2. Margaret (Peggy) Thomson
3. Agnes Fleming (My Nanie O)
4. Isabella Steven (Tibbie Stein)
5. Anne Rankine
6. Ellison Begbie/Elizabeth Gebbie
7. Mary Morison
8. Montgomerie's Peggy
9. Ronalds Of The Bennals (Anne Ronald)
10. The Belles Of Mauchline
11. Elizabeth Paton / Elizabeth Paton Burns
12. Margaret (Peggy) Kennedy
13. Mary Anne Whitefoord
14. Wilhelmina Alexander (Lass O' Ballochmyle)
15. Betty Miller
16. Margaret Campbell (Highland Mary)
17. Jean Armour
18. Margaret (May) Cameron
19. Euphemia Murray
20. Margaret (Peggy) Chalmers
21. Charlotte Hamilton
22. Agnes McLehose (Clarinda)
23. Jenny (Janet) Clow
24. Jane Cruikshank (The Rosebud)
25. Jean Jaffray (The Blue-Eyed Lassie)
26. Helen Hyslop / Helen Armstrong
27. Ann Masterton (Bonie Ann)
28. Anna Park (Anna of the Golden Locks)
29. Elizabeth Park Burns
30. Maria Riddell
31. Mary (Polly) Stewart
32. Deborah Duff Davies (The Bonie Wee Thing)
33. Lesley Baillie
34. Jean Lorimer (Chloris)
35. Jean McMurdo
36. Philadelphia (Phillis) McMurdo
37. Jessy Staig
38. Janet Miller
39. Lucy Oswald (Louisa Johnston)
40. Jessy Lewars

1.

NELLIE KILPATRICK
Born Feb 1759 – Died 1820

NELLIE BLAIR
Born 1760 – Died ?

Chronology : Autumn 1774

On his own testimony, 'Handsome Nell' ('Once I Lov'd A Bonie Lass'), was the first song ever composed by Burns and written when he was in the Autumn of his fifteenth year, the Autumn of 1774.   Unfortunately he doesn't name for whom the song was actually transcribed, but he does state that it was dedicated to a young girl who was partnering him in the work of the fields during that harvest time.

The two challengers for the title of ownership of the song are Nellie Kilpatrick and Nellie Blair.

An earlier biographer of Burns, the Rev Hamilton Paul of Ayr, in 1819 stated of 'Handsome Nell' after interviewing her

> 'The nymph was afterwards married to a Carrick farmer, and became the mother of many sons and daughters, and who, when we saw her in 1811 still retained the characteristic of sonsiness, which so fascinated her helpmate in the work of the harvests as to betray him into the sin of rhyme.   She sung delightfully, and he wrote a copy of verses to her favourite air or reel'.

But the Rev Paul did not clear up the mystery either, as he did not mention the last name of the 'Nell' he was interviewing, though at the time, according to some of the earliest biographers of Burns, local tradition held that 'Nell' was Nellie Blair.

It was only after 1851, when Isabella Burns Begg, the youngest sister of Burns, threw in the name Nellie Kilpatrick that the problem of ownership to the title of the song began.   Mrs Begg was being interviewed by Robert Chambers for his biography of Burns and she recalled the last name of the young girl of the harvest as being Kilpatrick.

Nellie Blair was first openly identified as 'Handsome Nell', in a letter written to the Scotsman newspaper in 1828.   According to the writer of the letter, Nellie Blair was a servant in the house of the correspondent's friend.

A house often frequented by Burns.   The lady herself when interviewed remembered Burns when 'a ploughman-lad'.   The newspaper report read

> 'At the kitchen of my friend's father, Burns visits were of such frequency and duration as to call down the animadversions of the lady of the house, the alertness of her damsels in the morning being at times impaired by his unreasonable gallantry.   This was supposed to be occasioned by a penchant he had formed for a certain Nellie Blair, a pretty girl, a servant in the family, and whom he celebrated in more songs and odes than her name appears in – the only one likely to be applied to her now being one he himself transcribes – My friend describes him *(Burns)* as being considered at that time a clever fellow, but a 'wild scamp''.

Like so many of the Burns mysteries, the person who wrote the letter has not been named, neither has the friend to whom he refers.   But if indeed this letter paints a true picture of Burns in his young manhood, then it means that somewhere along the line we have lost many poems and songs written by him when a youth.   It also means that his first venture into the fields of love lasted a little longer than the short time of the harvest.

James Mackay, in his 1992 Biography of Burns, has done some thorough investigation into dates of the many lasses that passed through Burns' life and hands.   He found out that, though there was no trace of Nellie Blair's birth in the Ayrshire parishes of the time, a fact that means she could have been born elsewhere, a Helen Blair married a John Smith at Dreghorn on 13th September 1788, and gave birth five months later to a daughter, also named Helen, at Dailly on 18th February 1789, with several other children following on after.   Mrs. Smith certainly sounds like she could be the 'Carrick farmer's wife' interviewed by the Rev Hamilton Paul in 1811.

Now we are introduced to the testimony of Mrs Begg.   Isabella was born in 1771, and would have only been about three when Burns was dallying in the meadowland.   She would have relied on the information passed down from the senior members of the family regarding Burns' early life.

> 'The first touch of an emotion which afterward gushed upon him was now experienced in his seventeenth autumn on the harvest field, the cause being that 'bonnie, sweet, sonsie lass', a year younger than himself, who had been assigned to him as the partner of his labours, Nelly Kilpatrick by name, and the daughter of the same blacksmith, it appears, who lent him his first book, 'The Life of Wallace''.

Nellie Kilpatrick was the daughter of Allan Kilpatrick, miller of Purclewan in the parish of Dalrymple.   According to parish registers she was baptised on 1st March 1759, which would mean she would have been born a couple of days earlier.   So she was only a month younger than Burns, not a year

40

younger as Burns states of 'Nell' in his autobiographical letter of 1787.

Nellie Kilpatrick married a William Bone, who was coachman to the laird of Newark and lived at Newark Estate. She died in 1820 and is presumably buried in the district Kirkyard.

In his letter to Dr John Moore dated 2nd August 1787 Burns wrote

> 'This kind of life – the chearless gloom of a hermit, with the unceasing moil of a galley-slave – brought me to my sixteenth year; a little before which period I first committed the sin of RHYME. You know our country custom of coupling a man and woman together as Partners in the labours of Harvest. In my fifteenth autumn, my Partner was a bewitching creature who had just counted an autumn less. My scarcity of English denies me the power of doing her justice in that language, but you know the Scotch idiom: She was a bonnie, sweet, sonsie lass. In short, she, altogether unwittingly to herself, initiated me in a delicious Passion which, in spite of acid Disappointment, gin-horse Prudence, and book worm Philosophy, I hold to be the first of human joys, our dearest blessing here below! How she caught the contagion I can't tell; you medical people talk much of infection by breathing the same air, the touch, etc.; but I never expressly told her that I loved her. Indeed I did not well know myself why I liked so much to loiter behind with her, when returning in the evenings from our labours, why the tones of her voice made my heartstrings thrill like an Eolian harp and particularly why my pulse beat such a furious ratan, when I looked and fingered over her hand to pick out the nettle-stings and thistles. Among her other love inspiring qualifications, she sang sweetly; and 'twas her favourite reel to which I attempted giving an embodied vehicle in rhyme. I was not so presumptive as to imagine that I could make verses like printed ones, composed by men who had Greek and Latin; but my girl sung a song which was said to be composed by a small country laird's son, on one of his father's maids with whom he was in love; and I saw no reason why I might not rhyme as well as he; for excepting smearing sheep, and casting peats, his father living in the moors, he had no more Scholarcraft than I had. Thus with me began Love and Poesy; which at times have been my only, and till within this last twelvemonth have been my highest enjoyment'.

But, whichever Nellie partnered Burns at harvest, she unknowingly helped him choose his pathway in life.

In August 1783 Burns, in his First Commonplace Book, describes the poem 'Handsome Nell'

> 'The expression is a little awkward, and the sentiment too serious... The seventh stanza has several minute faults, but I remember I composed it

in a wild enthusiasm of passion, and to this hour I never recollect it but my heart melts, my blood sallies, at the remembrance'.

Burns says he met 'Nell' in his fifteenth autumn, Mrs Begg says it was in his seventeenth year. Maybe she made a mistake at the interview, after all she was eighty at the time, or maybe Burns was boasting a little to Dr Moore as to when he started to take notice of the opposite sex.

The problem here is that if we start to question Mrs Begg's testament too closely, and say that because of her advanced age, she may be mistaken in her recollection, then it throws everything else she says into doubt. She would become an unreliable witness.

In truth, all of the members of the Burns family were unreliable witnesses, a little backwards in coming forwards with the truth about the Bard. This is understandable. The family knew him and knew the truth. Those who wanted to know about him were strangers, and maybe his failings appeared more serious to unsophisticated country dwellers than they really were. Maybe they decided that it was better for the family to shut up, close ranks and say nothing.

With hindsight it would have been fitter if they had come clean and spoken about Burns, warts and all, and not left his 'frailties' to other people's fertile imaginations, especially those with an axe to grind. Even his brother Gilbert's defence of Burns, as to his supposed continuous over indulgence of an alcoholic nature, can be read as very weak and 'wattery'.

As regards ownership of the poem 'Handsome Nell', until anything else comes to light 'Nell' will remain twins for a long time to come.

The story of the composition of 'Handsome Nell' was given in the verse-epistle reply to the 'Gudewife Of Wauchope House'. It was written in March 1787 and sent to Elizabeth Scott of Wauchope House near Jedburgh. This was after she had started a correspondence with Burns on reading his poems in the Kilmarnock Edition. Burns visited her on 10th May 1787 during his Border tour with his friend Robert Ainslie.

The parents of Nellie Kilpatrick, Allan Kilpatrick, born at Milmannoch and his wife, Margaret Good, are buried at Low Coylton Kirkyard, where there is a gravestone erected by Nellie's brother, William, inscribed

'Erected by William Kilpatrick, Drumgabs, In memory of his Father, Allan Kilpatrick, late Miller in Percluan: Born at Millmannoch, 4th November 1725, Died 1st May 1782, Age 57. And Margaret Good, his Mother: Died 12th August 1770, Aged 37. And of said William Kilpatrick, Late in Barnhill: Born September 1765, Died 21st November 1841, Age 77'.

Associated Songs

Song : Handsome Nell
Tune : Untitled in S.M.M.
Period : Autumn 1774

2.

MARGARET (PEGGY) THOMSON
Born Nov 1762 – Died ?

Chronology – Summer 1775

Burns was sent by his father to finish his education in Kirkoswald   This entailed studying Mensuration, Surveying, Dialing… and such, at a school run by a schoolmaster called Hugh Rodgers who was considered to be a first class teacher of mathematics, as well as being employed as a practical land-surveyor.

Burns lived with his maternal uncle, Samuel Broun, farm-labourer, fisherman, dealer in wool (as well as sometime dealer in smuggled goods), and his wife, who resided at the farmhouse of Ballochneil, which was about a mile from the village of Kirkoswald and close to the Corriston Burn. This was during the summer of 1775.

It was in the August of that year Robert met Peggy Thomson, who lived in Main Street right next to Rodgers' school.

In a letter dated 2nd August 1787 he wrote to Dr John Moore

'Another circumstance in my life which made very considerable alterations in my mind and manners was, that I spent my seventeenth summer on a smuggling coast, a good distance from home, at a noted school, to learn Mensuration, Surveying, Dialing, etc., in which I made a pretty good progress; but I made greater progress in the knowledge of mankind.   The contraband trade was at that time very successful, and it sometimes happened for me to fall in with those who carried it on. Scenes of swaggering riot and roaring dissipation were as yet new to me; and I was no enemy to social life.   Here, though I learnt to look unconcernedly on a large tavern-bill, and mix without fear in a drunken squabble, yet I went on with a high hand in my Geometry, till the sun entered Virgo – a month which is always carnival in my bosom – when a charming Fillette, who lived next door to the school, overset my Trigonometry, and sent me off in a tangent from the sphere of my studies.   I struggled on with my Sines and Co-sines for a few days more; but stepping into the garden one charming noon, to take the sun's altitude, there I met my Angel –

'Like Proserpine gathering flowers,
Herself a fairer flower'.

43

It was in vain to think of doing any more good at school. The remaining week I staid, I did nothing but craze the faculties of my soul about her, or steal out to meet with her; and the two last nights of my stay in the country, had sleep been a mortal sin, I was innocent'.

Writing in April 1783 in his Commonplace Book, Burns says of this early experience

'If anything on earth deserves the name of rapture or transport, it is the feeling of green eighteen (*'green eighteen' is a slight exaggeration as in August of 1775 he was sixteen and a half*) in company of the mistress of his heart, when she repays him with an equal return of affection'.

His 'Proserpine gathering flowers' may not have been as romantic as Burns would like to make out.

Behind every house in the row where the school was situated, there was a small kail-yard where vegetables for the family were grown. As Burns took his 'sun's altitude' he was more likely to see his 'Proserpine' cutting a large cabbage for the evening meal, rather than a bunch of flowers for the family's visual delight. But Burns always had an eye for a good poetry setting, as well as a highly charged imagination.

The friendship with Peggy petered out for a while, but apparently picked up at a later date and evolved into a romantic and possibly physical relationship.

Thomas Orr, a pupil at Rodgers' school, became a friend of Burns and took messages between Burns and Peggy in the summers of 1782 and 1783. He worked as a harvest hand at Lochlea in 1780 and 1781. Orr is reported to have gone to sea in 1785, and is said to have drowned on his first voyage.

Unfortunately none of the Burns/Thomson letters have survived. Peggy most likely destroyed them before she got married, just to be on the safe side, and maybe to keep her reputation intact, if nothing else.

But three letters written to Orr by Burns have survived. One concerns the forthcoming marriage of Peggy Thomson and is dated 11th November 1784

'I am much obliged to you for your last letter tho' I assure you the contents of it gave me no matter of concern --I am at present so cursedly taken in with an affair of gallantry that I am very glad Peggy is off my hands as I am at present embarrassed enough without her. – I do'n't chuse to enter into particulars in writing but never was a poor rakish rascal in a more pitiful taking…'

It is thought that the above quote refers to the situation that he had found himself in, due to his fathering Elizabeth Paton's as of yet unborn child, and the ensuing family dilemma that was being caused by it.

Burns' mother wanted him to marry Elizabeth as she was a good country lassie and she liked her very much, but his siblings were totally against this liaison and thought that he would be making a big mistake if he went through with a marriage to Elizabeth.

Burns always remained fond of Peggy Thomson and presented her with a copy of the Kilmarnock Edition of his poems with the inscription on the flyleaf

Lines to an old Sweetheart

Once fondly lov'd, and still remembered dear,
Sweet early object of my youthful vows,
Accept this mark of friendship, warm, sincere-
Friendship! 'tis all cold duty now allows;-
And when you read the simple, artless rhymes,
One friendly sigh for him – he asks no more –
Who distant burns in flaming torrid climes,
Or haply lies beneath th' Atlantic roar.

This was written in 1786 when Burns was intent on emigration to the West Indies and the book was meant as a parting gift to her. The evening he left her house, Peggy's husband accompanied Burns on the first three miles of his journey, before they took their farewells of each other.

The above lines are included in the 'Glenriddell Manuscript' with the notation below written by Burns in his own hand

'Poor Peggy! Her husband is an old acquaintance and a most worthy fellow. When I was taking leave of my Carrick relations, intending to go to the West Indies, when I took farewell of her, neither she nor I could speak a syllable. Her husband escorted me three miles on my road, and we both parted with tears'.

Peggy's husband was William Neilson of Minnybae Farm, Kirkoswald whom she married on 23rd November 1784. After William's death she lived for many years in the village of Kirkoswald, where she was the proprietor of a little shop. She finally moved to Ayr, where she died at an apparently respectable old age.

Associated Songs

Song	: Now Westlin Winds		Song	: I Dream'd I Lay
Tune	: Port Gordon		Tune	: I Dream'd I Lay
Period	: August 1775		Period	: circa 1776

3.

AGNES FLEMING
Born 1765 – Died ?

Chronology – 1776/1777

According to 'Honest' Allan Cunningham, Agnes Fleming was the daughter of John Fleming of either Calcothill (Coldcothill) Farm or of the nearby Doura (Dowery) Farm, which was situated about half a mile from Lochlea.   She was a serving maid in the house of Burns' friend Gavin Hamilton in Mauchline.

Burns wrote in his Commonplace Book for 1784

'As I have been all along a miserable dupe in Love, and have been led into a thousand weaknesses and follies by it, for that reason I put the more confidence in my critical skill in distinguishing foppery and conceit from real passion and nature.   Whether the following song will stand the test, I will not pretend to say, because it is my own; only, I can say, it was, at the time, real'.

The song that followed was 'My Nanie O'.

Rev Hamilton Paul (contemporary and biographer of Burns) when writing to Dr Chambers in 1819 said of Nanie (who he named as Agnes Sherriff)

'In Kilmarnock, Burns first saw Nanie, the subject of one of his most popular ballads.   She captivated him as well by the charms of her person, as by the melody of her voice.   As he devoted much of his spare time to her society, and listened to her singing with the most religious attention, her sister observed to him that he paid more attention to Nanie's singing than he would do to a preaching, and he retorted, with an oath: 'Madam, there's no comparison''.

Gilbert Burns seemed to have a different viewpoint on Agnes, whom he named as 'a farmer's daughter in Tarbolton parish with the surname of Fleming, as one to whom the poet paid some of that roving attention which he was 'continually devoting to someone'.   When interviewed Gilbert reportedly said

'Her charms were indeed mediocre, but what she had were sexual, which was the characteristic of the greater part of the poet's mistresses, for he was no platonic lover, however he might otherwise pretend to suppose of himself'.

46

Isabella Burns Begg, Burns' youngest sister, apparently held the same opinion of Agnes Fleming as that of her brother Gilbert. When Captain Charles Gray, in an interview with her, mentioned Agnes as the heroine of 'My Nanie O'

'She could scarcely repress her resentment; assuring us that Agnes Fleming, whom she knew, had no pretensions, either morally or physically, to be considered the heroine of that fine song. Who was the heroine? Peggy Thomson was the reply'.

The problem we have is that if this song was written for Agnes Fleming round about 1777 Agnes would have been a very young child of about twelve. Maybe Gilbert and his sister were getting their Agnes' mixed up!

Down the years other names were put forward to claim ownership of the song. As we have heard, Isabella Burns Begg said it was Peggy Thomson. The poet's aunt Mrs Broun of Kirkoswald said it was Agnes McIlwraith of Pinvalley, Barr, who he met at *Kirkdamdie Fair. Local tradition in Girvan states it was Nanie Brown, whom he also saw home from Kirkdamdie Fair. She was the daughter of the proprietor of the 'Ship Inn' in Girvan (and remember Burns had put forward his choice of the River Girvan as a substitute for the River Stinchar in his letter to Thomson). While Hamilton Paul added Agnes Sherriff of Kilmarnock to the ever lengthening role.

*The Kirkdamdie Fair, held annually on the last Saturday in May, was the largest feeing fair of South Ayrshire. It was centuries old, and was held on the grounds of the ruined Kirkdominie Church which was situated on the River Stinchar, and as well as work prospects, it was also considered the perfect place and time to meet future marriage partners.

The song first appeared in the Edinburgh Edition in 1787, and in Thomson's 'Scottish Airs' in 1793. Thomson, in his typical wisdom, wanted to change the tune for another one. Burns stuck to his guns as regard to the old tune 'My Nanie O' and won out. The song also appears in the Scots Musical Museum of 1803 to a different tune, an air by a Durham musician, Thomas Ebdon.

The river mentioned in the original version of the song, 'The Stinchar', was changed to 'The Lugar', so that the 'charming, sweet and young creature, might be connected with a sweeter sound.

To George Thomson on 26th October 1792 Burns wrote of the river's name

'The name of the River is horribly prosaic – I will alter it.' He went on to say that 'Girvan is the river that suits the idea of the stanza best'.

Thomson chose the harsh sounding Lugar, which is not surprising, as Thomson's lack of taste and judgement with some of Burns' songs is astounding.

As regards the 'Airs', Burns had also used another when he entered the song in his First Commonplace Book. This was the tune 'As I Came In By London Town O'. But the old melody has always been the one that worked best.

Apparently 'My Nanie O' was one of the few poems that William Burness, Robert's father knew, and he, surprisingly, approved of the sentiments in it, so maybe Gilbert and Isabella were wrong in miscalling Agnes Fleming. William Burness was a very religious man and would certainly have been very vocal in his condemnation if Robert were writing poems to someone of such a questionable character.

Much of what Allan Cunningham has written has been proved to be of his own fabrication, so maybe he was wrong in his choosing Agnes Fleming as the holder of the title, or maybe he did not take down the correct name from the woman he interviewed. But whomsoever he spoke to claimed the song was written for her alone.

According to Cunningham, Agnes Fleming died unmarried and at an advanced age, and maybe the old woman should be left with the last word

'Aye, atweel he made a great wark (fuss) about me'.

Associated Song:

Song   : My Nanie O
Tune   : My Nanie O
Period   : 1776 / 1777

4.

ISABELLA STEVEN (TIBBIE STEIN)

Chronology : c 1777

According to Isabella Burns Begg, 'Tibbie Stein' was the daughter of a farmer at 'Little Hill' the neighbouring farm adjoining 'Lochlea'. He owned three acres of Peat Moss and was entitled to the name of landowner.

Tibbie was regarded as a very beautiful young woman, and Burns was in love with her. Their courtship seemed to be proceeding well, until she came into an inheritance of £75. At that time this was a very large amount of money. Burns and his brother only earned £7 each per annum for their farm wages, so Tibbie had now become ten times richer than Burns.

This windfall obviously changed matters for her. Tibbie began to consider herself as having moved quite a bit further up the social ladder and therefore had to look for a more suitable, and obviously richer, suitor who had potentially more prospects than Burns appeared to have.

According to Tarbolton tradition, at some time (the date is unknown) her family moved from 'Little Hill' into the village of Tarbolton and took up residence in a house which used to stand on the west side of Burns Street at the corner of Garden Street, opposite Manson's Inn (demolished decades ago). The house stood there for years before it too was knocked down and was always referred to 'Tibbie Stein's House'.

Again, according to local oral tradition, it is said that the relationship came to an end when Burns called on Tibbie at her home one evening, whether at 'Little Hill' or Tarbolton village is unknown, and was told by an unnamed relative who answered the door, that Isabella was unavailable to see him as she was entertaining another visitor/suitor.

Cut to the bone and very severely humiliated Robert turned on his heels and strode off into the night. He never went back to see Tibbie again.

She is reported to have married the other suitor, said to be a man called Mr Allan, soon after, but not before Burns composed a caustic song about her and her love of 'siller', of which this is one verse

<blockquote>
I doubt na, lass, but ye may think,
Because ye hae the name o' clink,
That ye can please me at a wink,
Whene'er ye like to try.
</blockquote>

What Tibbie thought of this song at the time can only be guessed at. It's unlikely that she'd be pleased having her business spread about the village, and her with her foot poised on the first rung of that social ladder. There's no doubt Burns would have made sure that the poem was read by as many as was possible in order to assuage his hurt pride and deflated dignity.

But there was a sort of happy ending to the event. Though there might have been a big stramash at the time when Burns wrote his poem about her, it is reported that when Tibbie was an old woman, she was proud to say that she was once held deeply in the poet's affections, to the point of having him court her with a view to them being married. And she apparently was even prouder of the fact that Burns had conferred on her an immortality to be eternally the 'Tibbie' of his song.

Associated Song

Song   : O Tibbie I Hae Seen the Day
Tune   : Invercauld's Reel
Period : circa 1777

5.

ANNE RANKINE
Born 1759 – Died 20th August 1843

Chronology : c 1781 but possibly earlier.

Anne Rankine was the youngest daughter of John Rankine, farmer at Adamhill near Tarbolton. She is described as being a tall and masculine looking woman.

Tradition has it that John Rankine, being very fond of Burns, would have liked his daughter and the poet to be married to each other. With this end in mind it is said that he would regularly leave them alone in the house hoping that Nature and hormones would take it's course.

Apparently Nature did take it's course, but not in the comfort of her father's house. Their trysting place was among the rigs o' barley, which local tradition informs us Anne chose, having respect for the parental home. Happy as the experience was for both of them, she and Burns did not marry. Anne's father was deeply disappointed.

Burns liked Anne a lot. After he had become well known, he made her a present of a lock of his hair and one of his miniature likenesses. She is reported to have treasured these gifts, along with her song, all her long life.

Anne married a John Merry in December 1782. He was an innkeeper in Cumnock, and when he died in 1802, she ran the Inn on her own until her death. Burns, when in the vicinity of Cumnock, used to stay at the Inn and there are letters written by him from there on at least two occasions. One letter is to Thomas Campbell dated the 19th August 1786, just after the Kilmarnock Edition was published, and another letter is to Agnes McLehose, dated the 3rd March 1788, written less than a month after parting from her in Edinburgh.

Living until 1843, Anne was interviewed by many people about Burns, and delicately asked as to what her relationship with him really was.

One of these interviewers was Dr Robert Chambers, who enquired of her if she remembered when and why the song was written. 'Yes', was the reply 'when I was a fair young lassie amang the rigs o' barley'.

To another interviewer, Anne reported on a meeting with Burns after the publication of the 'Kilmarnock Edition' of his poems in 1786. 'Corn Rigs' was one of only two songs included in the volume and she remarked to Burns that she was surprised to see it there as she little expected to be celebrated in print. To which Burns is said to have replied

'Oh ay, I was just wanting to give you a cast among the lave'!

In 1817 in one of the earliest interviews Anne gave, conducted by James Grierson of Dalgoner, a collector of anecdotes of Burns, she was asked if she could remember nights with Burns among the rigs o' barley. According to Grierson, Anne said

'No', with considerable naevity, but then added with a twinkle in her eye, 'I mind o' mony a happy nicht wi' him tho'.

One story Anne like to tell, related to Burns' first visit to the Rankine house at Adamhill. According to Anne, when Burns entered into the parlour, he made a circuit, to avoid a small carpet in the centre, this she assumed was either because he had at that time had no acquaintance with carpets, or too great a veneration for them to tread upon them with his ploughman's shoes, or then again, 'maybe it was just 'sly burlesque''.

In the song 'Rigs O' Barley' ('Corn Rigs Are Bonie') Burns considered the last stanza the best he had ever written. It summed up his attitude to life and living. As Burns hinted in his autobiographical letter to Dr Moore, August (Lammas) was a month that made his heart go tapsalteerie

'When the sun enter Virgo, a month that is always carnival in my bosom'.

Her family reported that until she died Anne would often sing her very own song, and always spoke with affection of memories of the poet.

John Rankine, Anne's father, died on 2nd February 1810 and is buried in Galston Kirkyard. Anne Rankine Merry is buried in Cumnock Old Churchyard.

In 'Wood's Songs of Scotland' there is a letter from a Miss Janet Logan of Cumnock, daughter of Hugh Logan, Esq., which had been sent by the Rev James Murray to the Editor of the aforesaid book, Mr George Farquhar Graham, circa 1849. It contained recollections from her regarding Burns and Anne Rankine Merry. The letter reads that Miss Logan

'Remembers having met with Robert Burns the poet, about sixty years ago, in the house of Mrs Merry, Old Cumnock. He had not then visited Edinburgh, but was a farmer of Mossgiel, in the neighbourhood of Mauchline. Mrs Merry was the youngest daughter of John Rankine of Adamhill, whom Burns, in one of his productions, describes as 'Rough, rude, and ready-witted'. Mrs Merry was well known to be the heroine of 'The Lea-Rig'. Some say it was another person, but it was not so'. (She then goes on to relate the carpet story). She remembered that Burns 'wore his hair tied – was good-looking – thick set – not very tall. Has heard that he played the violin, but never was present when he played on that instrument. Never heard him sing'. The letter was signed, Janet Logan.

Both mother, (at the time the unmarried Miss Farquhar who later became Mrs Colonel Graham) and grandfather (George Farquhar) of the Editor of the aforementioned 'Wood's Songs', knew Robert Burns from Edinburgh, where he often frequented the grandfather's (George Farquhar) house. Mr Farquhar Graham's mother often talked of Burns' remarkable conversational powers, but added that

'No one of the portraits of Burns that she has seen – not even the one by Skirving – gives an idea of the extraordinary fire and expression of Burns' eyes'.

According to George Farquhar Graham, his mother, when a young woman, played the tune, 'Lochaber No More', for Burns on the harpsichord one evening when he was visiting her and her father at their home.   She said that he listened to it attentively, and then exclaimed with tears in his eyes, 'Oh that's a fine tune for a broken heart'!

Associated Songs

Song	: The Rigs O' Barley
Tune	: Corn Rigs Are Bonie
Period	: circa 1782 (pre his 23rd year)

Song	: The Lea-Rig
Tune	: My Ain Kind Dearie O
Period	: 26th October 1792

6.

ELLISON BEGBIE/ELIZABETH GEBBIE
Born 22nd July 1762 - Died pre-1823

Chronology : November 1780

Ellison (Alison) Begbie was one of Burns' early serious loves. He met her shortly after the 11th November 1780 when he formed the Bachelor's Club in Tarbolton and was paying earnest attention to her in 1781. This was when he was about 22 and at an age when he was, according to his brother Gilbert, desperate to be married.

Ellison came from the Galston, area, reputedly from a farm called 'Old Place', and was the daughter of the farmer who worked the land there. She was employed as a servant at Carnell House (Cairnhill House) near the Cessnock River, and it is surmised that Burns wrote five letters to her. Well five letters have been found.

Unfortunately her name is not actually mentioned in any of the correspondences, just the first initial. But at the time of writing Ellison fits the jigsaw.

In one of the letters that first initial is 'A' and not 'E'. But that has been explained away as – 'A' stands for Alison, 'E' stands for Ellison and as Ellison was the Ayrshire pronunciation of Alison, then probably the five letters are a unit. A wee bit of ham-fisted logic there! The fourth letter is a very formal proposal of marriage. The recipient of the proposal turned Burns down, which is acknowledged in the fifth letter.

Writing to a friend called Willie Niven, on 12th June 1781 Burns states

> 'I know you will hardly believe me when I tell you, that by a strange conjuncture of circumstances, I am intirely got rid of all connections with the tender sex, I mean in the way of courtship: it is, however absolutely certain that I am so; though how long I shall continue so, Heaven only knows; but be that as it may, I shall never be involved as I was again'.

According to the earlier part of this letter the rejection happened sometime between February and June of that year.

When interviewed in 1847 by Chambers, the poet's sister, Isabella Burns Begg, says

> 'About two miles eastward from Lochlea, a shining stream, called

Cessnock Water, flows past in a northerly course through Galston Parish into the River Irvine. A young woman, named Ellison Begbie, the daughter of a small farmer near Galston, was then in service with a family whose house was on Cessnock Bank at the distance mentioned from the farm of William Burness. The youthful poet had got acquainted with Ellison, and was so much charmed with her superior manners and agreeable person, that he courted her with all his ardour during several months, with a serious view to future marriage. It was on her that composed the very poetic 'Song of Similes', called 'The Lass of Cessnock Banks'.

In another interview, this time with Captain Charles Gray (Wood's Songs of Scotland), round about the same time as the previous interview, Captain Gray states 'upon the testimony of Mrs Begg, from whom this information is drawn, the old lady said

'That Miss B was no ordinary person; on the contrary, that she was possessed of great natural abilities: that all the members of William Burness' family looked upon her as a very superior person, accomplished in manner, and of great personal attractions, more so than anyone with whom they were then acquainted. In fact, Miss Begbie was a gentlewoman of nature's own making –

'Not bred in courts – though formed in courts to shine;
A diamond polished, ere it leave the mine''.

Isabella Burns Begg seems inclined to think, that Ellison Begbie was the first sweetheart to whom Burns was sincerely and ardently attached. According to Captain Gray's interview, after her marriage Ellison Begbie visited the poet, occasionally with her husband, and for a time some correspondence was kept up between them, though to date no letters have ever been found to support this. But he also claims that the 'Verses to an old sweetheart after her marriage' were meant for Ellison, whereas today we know that they were written for Peggy Thomson.

Family tradition, again via Isabella to Captain Gray, claims that Burns, on returning from Edinburgh after the publication of his second edition of his poems, 'in a crack by the chimla cheek, in the family circle at Mossgiel', in speaking of his former sweethearts, declared, that of all the women he had ever courted, he had met with none that he could have made such a companion of for life as Ellison Begbie.

In a letter to Dr Moore in August of 1787 Burns says of the time

'In my twenty third year a belle-fille whom I adored and who had pledged her soul to meet me in the field of matrimony, jilted me with particular circumstances of mortification'.

Jilted is not really the term to be used when someone has just refused your proposal of marriage. She didn't leave him standing at the altar in front of a packed congregation. But Burns obviously still felt more than a little hurt by the rejection. Rejection being something which he never could take gracefully.

Gilbert Burns, in 1820, stated when asked about 'Mary Morison', the song written round about 1784/85, that if his brother had anyone in mind, 'Mary Morison' was not the lady's real name, but he believed that she was the same lady who was subject of 'And I'll Kiss Thee Yet, Peggy Alison', and this was the lady named at the head of this chapter.

James Mackay in researching his biography of Burns combed through the parish registers of Galston of the time to see if in fact there was an Alison/Ellison Begbie around. He found no trace of a family named Begbie anywhere, but did find several families with the name Gebbie, who were all related to one another. John was a farmer at Millhill. Alexander was a miller at Cessnock Mill. Thomas was a farmer at Pearsland.

Alexander had a daughter who was born on 21st November 1761, and Thomas had a daughter who was born on 22nd July 1762. Both children were called Elizabeth.

On the 30th April 1788 Alexander's daughter Elizabeth married a carpenter or wright, called Hugh Guthrie, at Riccarton, which is south of Kilmarnock, and she and her husband settled in Woodhead, where she later gave birth to two sons.

Thomas' daughter Elizabeth is considered to be the recipient of the marriage proposal, which was turned down 'In the politest language of refusal'. Maybe this was because she had more than one string to her beaux, and needed time to make up her mind between Burns and another suitor.

On receiving her letter of rejection Burns wrote in his fifth letter to her from Lochlea in June 1781 that he

'Expects in a few days to move farther off, and you I suppose will perhaps soon leave this place. I wish to see you or hear from you soon'.

It is reported that Ellison/Elizabeth was not regarded as a beauty but from this letter in June, it is clear that she had more going for her than good looks. Burns had high hopes regarding the lady, and he obviously esteemed her greatly, her sense, her goodness, her disposition -

'All these charming qualities, heightened by an education much beyond any thing I have ever met in any woman I ever dared to approach, have made an impression on my heart that I do not think the world can ever efface'.

Although he did have misogynistic tendencies towards some women, Burns did appreciate a woman who was intelligent and talented, and it is quite clear that the 'E' of the letters was a good opponent in his intellectual duels. Probably more so than any of his male friends who would have had the same outlook as himself, and were probably, on the whole, a wee bit less bright than he was.

Elizabeth Gebbie did leave Galston and married a Hugh Brown at Newmilns, in Louden parish, on 21st November 1781. He was seven years older than her and a stocking maker to trade. They had three daughters and one son.

Robert Hartley Cromek in his 'Reliques of Robert Burns' (published 1808) traced Elizabeth Gebbie Brown to Glasgow and interviewed her there. Cromek was also the first editor to publish the song 'The Lass of Cessnock Banks'. As he states in his book

> 'This song was an early production. It was recovered by the Editor from the oral communication of a lady residing in Glasgow, whom the Bard in life affectionately admired'.

When James Mackay checked the burial registers in the Glasgow parishes for the first three decades of the nineteenth century, he found no trace of a date of death for Elizabeth. 'Even a search through the tombstones of Glasgow has so far proved fruitless.' No doubt he'll be successful one day. But Elizabeth was definitely dead by 1823 when her husband, Hugh Brown, widower, had a will made up in favour of his children.

The business that Hugh started up when he and Elizabeth moved to Glasgow expanded from King Street to 100-104 Virginia Street when his son took over in 1829. Hugh Brown, Stocking Manufacturer, then became Hugh Brown and Company.

It is interesting to contemplate what would have happened if Burns had actually married Elizabeth Gebbie. Would she have taken him down another pathway in his life? Maybe moved him from Ayrshire to Elsewhere? Or would he have encouraged her to remain in her environs? Either way, would he have been a different type of poet or even a poet at all? Maybe if he had moved to the big city he would have become a playwright. This was something he had tucked away in his mind to try in the future.

And the big question is would Burns have died at such a young age had he succeeded in getting Elizabeth to accept his proposal of marriage?

Maybe doctors in a bigger city would have recognised that Burns had a weak heart and was not suffering from what Dr Maxwell and other local medicals diagnosed as 'flying gout', and maybe their cure would have been less draconian and tragic than having him sit immersed up to his armpits in the ice cold sea waters of the Solway Firth. Who knows!

Regarding the song 'From Thee Eliza', in his letter to Dr Moore, Burns says that the song was written before 1782, which makes it impossible to apply to either Elizabeth Miller or Elizabeth Barbour, two women earlier biographers claim it was written for. 'From Thee Eliza' was included in the 1793 volume of the 'Scots Musical Museum'.

This was the second rebuff of marriage that Burns had to contend with. The first one was from Tibbie Stein. He could not have been well pleased at all.

Associated Songs

Song	: Farewell To Eliza/From Thee Eliza (See Betty Miller)
Tune	: Gilderoy
Period	: 1782 – Pre his 23rd Year
Song	: Lass Of Cessnock Banks
Tune	: The Butcher Boy
Period	: Pre 1782
Song	: Mary Morison
Tune	: Duncan Davidson
Period	: Pre 1784/85
Song	: And I'll Kiss Thee Yet, Bonie Peggy Alison
Tune	: The Braes O' Balquidder
Period	: circa 1788?

7.

MARY MORISON
Born 1771 – Died 29th June 1791

Chronology : Pre 1784

Mary Morison was the daughter of Adjutant Morison of the 104th Regiment and is buried in Mauchline Kirkyard. It is suggested that she lived in two places in Mauchline. The first, was a house called 'Brownlea', at the junction of Castle St. (Back Causeway) and The Knowe. The second was in a tenement building called 'The Place', which was east side of 'The Cross'. However this Mary Morison is considered unlikely to be the 'Mary' of Burns' song.

The song was one he wrote when he was young, maybe in his early 20's. He said himself that it was one of his 'juvenile works', pre 1784/85, which would make this Mary about twelve or thirteen when the song was composed. It is unlikely Burns, quite definitely a young man, would be writing a love song to a child of that age. This is the same age problem that we have with 'Agnes Fleming'.

The 'Mary Morison' buried in Mauchline Kirkyard died after a horse riding accident, not consumption as some others report, in which her foot had to be amputated. Probably blood poisoning set in.

Another point against this being the Mary Morison of the song is that when Burns wrote to George Thomson in 1793, including the song in his letter, although he said that it was written at an earlier time, no mention was made of Mary Morison having died. Burns in general liked to supply information on his songs, so it would have been unusual for him to avoid commenting upon the unfortunate death of the young woman especially in such an unusual accident.

But according to tradition Burns did meet the above Mary Morison of Mauchline and her family, though only once. The meeting took place at tea in a friend's house.

The Rev Dr Edgar, minister at Mauchline Parish Church, from his book 'Old Church Life in Scotland' wrote

'I am informed, on authority, that a member of the adjutant's family, who lived to be a grandmother, used to speak of Burns (with aversion, I may add), as one whom she knew personally, when he lived at Mauchline, and that, she believed her sister Mary was the 'Lovely Mary

Morison' whom the poet admired. She often spoke of this long lost Mary, who died in early youth, from the amputation of a foot that had been accidentally injured, as 'one of the fairest creatures the sun ever shone upon'.

In a letter to George Thomson on 20th March 1793 Burns wrote

'My dear sir, - The song prefixed ('Mary Morison') is one of my juvenile works. I leave it in your hands, I do not think it very remarkable, either for its merits or demerits'.

Considering how popular the song has become over the past two centuries, maybe it shows that Burns could make mistakes in his critiques of his own compositions.

In 1825, A. N. Carmichael, the nephew of Mary Morison erected a tombstone in Mauchline Kirkyard in memory of his young dead aunt, the poet's 'Bonnie Mary Morison'. Thus history is misled.

Associated Song :

Mary Morison – For nearly two hundred years, the song 'Mary Morison' has, by most biographers, been associated with E. Begbie/Gebbie, spoken of in the previous chapter. This is due to a comment made by Gilbert Burns.

8.

MONTGOMERIE'S PEGGY

Chronology   : pre 1785 (possibly 1782)

Isabella Burns Begg, regarding Burns and 'Montgomerie's Peggy' stated

'They sat in the same church and contracted an intimacy together, but she was engaged to another before they ever met'.

Gilbert Burns also attested to the fact that Burns and 'Peggy' often met at Tarboth Mill, also known as Tarbolton Mill or Willie's Mill (Willie being Willie Muir, who Jean Armour went to live with when her father is alleged to have put her out of the house in December 1787, after finding out that she was again pregnant to Burns).

Very little is known about this heroine of Burns except that she was the housekeeper at 'Coilsfield House', the Castle O' Montgomerie, which was the residence of Colonel Hugh Montgomerie, 12th Earl of Eglinton.

Burns Commonplace Book of September 1785 states

'My Montgomerie's Peggy was my deity for six or eight months. She had been bred in a style of life rather elegant. But, as Vanburgh says in one of his comedies, 'my damn'd star found me out', there too; for, though I began the affair merely in a 'gaiete de coeur', or, to tell the truth, what would scarcely be believed, a vanity of showing my parts in courtship, particularly my abilities at a 'billet-doux' (which I always piqued myself upon), made me lay siege to her; and when, as I always do in my foolish gallantries, I had battered myself into a very warm affection for her, she told me one day in a flag of truce, that her fortress had been for some time before the rightful property of another, but with the greatest friendship and politeness, she offered me every alliance except actual possession. I found out afterwards that what she told me of a pre-engagement was really true; but it cost me some heart Achs to get rid of the affair'.

This quote from Burns appears to express his attitude to the art of wooing, which with the young women of his class is far different to the way he tackled his upper class dalliances. It is, in today's world, quite an insulting non-equal attitude, that of conqueror and that of conquered. It seems to show that although Burns may have liked women's company, even professing to like the intelligence of women, he can display a complete lack of respect for them, even the ones he leads us to believe he loves.

When compared with the upper class women, to whom he wrote many quite sycophantic letters, he cared very little for any responsibility towards the women of what he would consider his class, especially once he had bedded them. Though, to be fair to him, he did make sure his 'bastard weans' were looked after.

Even Jean Armour his future wife who clearly adored the man, Burns being quite aware of that fact, was written of in a very insulting and unnecessarily demeaning manner in a letter sent to Agnes McLehose in March 1788, and even more so in another distasteful letter that he sent to Robert Ainslie round about the same period.

For most of this time Burns appears to be a man out of control of his emotions where women and sex are concerned, capable of working himself up into a complete lather for no reason at all. Every rejection, a personal insult every glance in his direction, an invitation.

Though no one knows who the mysterious Montgomerie's Peggy was, a possibility that has been considered is that she could have been Margaret (Highland Mary) Campbell, who had worked on at least two occasions at the House of Montgomerie, maybe as early (or even earlier) than 1784.

This being true it would mean that Burns could have met 'Margaret 'Mary'/Peggy' before 1785 and not the Spring of 1786 as is generally believed to have been the case, and that there had been an ongoing relationship with her long before Jean Armour came on the scene.

Burns met Margaret Campbell at church as he did Montgomerie's Peggy. He also kept trysts with Margaret at Tarboth Mill as he did with the other woman. But Margaret Campbell had not been 'bred in a style of life rather elegant'. On the other hand someone who was bred in that style is mentioned in another chapter. Elizabeth Gebbie! She was also a housekeeper at a large house and had been his deity for several months, and was betrothed to another and turned Burns' marriage proposal down. The song could easily have been entitled 'Montgomerie's Gebbie'? This woman is really the most confusing out of all of Burns' relationships.

But, supposing 'Montgomerie's Peggy' was Margaret Campbell and she did come to work at Coilsfield as early as 1784, what was Burns playing at? Was he courting her at the same time as he was bedding Elizabeth Paton, the mother of his first child, 'Dear-bought Bess'?

Montgomerie's Peggy was claimed to be a Mrs Derbishire by Gilfillan, an earlier Burns biographer in 1872, but this was not borne out.

Associated Song:
Song   : Montgomerie's Peggy
Tune   : Galla Water
Period : circa 1782-1784

9.
THE RONALDS OF THE BENNALS

Chronology : c 1784

William Ronald was a wealthy farmer who owned a two hundred acre farm in the Tarbolton area. He had four daughters and one son.

Isabella, born in 1756, married an Alexander Bruce of Shaw
Jean, born in 1759, married a John Reid of Langlands
Anne, born 1767, married a Matthew Paterson
Mary, born in 1769, married a Robert Steven
Hugh – no information

Burns was a little in love with Anne Ronald.

Anne and her sister Jean, whom Robert's brother, Gilbert Burns, had a hankering after, were considered to be the catch of the area. Needless to say, due to their higher position in Mauchline society, Robert was not successful in his courtship of Anne Ronald who eventually married Matthew Paterson, a friend of his, and a fellow member of the Bachelors Club in Tarbolton.

In the 1988 Burns Chronicle there is an article written by Heather B. Ronald regarding the 'Ronald' family of Tarbolton. She is married to one of the descendants.

She quotes an article, which was printed in the Kilmarnock Standard of 14th January 1905, in which there was an item written concerning an earlier interview with an unnamed old woman who knew Anne Ronald. The old lady went on to say

'Oh, Aye, I kenn'd Jean, tae, an' a' the Ronalds o' the Bennals fine... They were coonted big folk lang syne, Mr Ronald was laird o' his ain fairm'.

According to the newspaper article, Anne died in 1828 at the age of 61, and then went on to report that the old lady, who had been a 'servant lassie' at the Bennals, had been quoted as saying that 'old Mrs Ronald didn't like Burns', and whenever she saw him coming (to see her daughters) she asked the servant to 'hunt him off the premises'.

Whether that was because she knew of his reputation, or that he was unsuitable because he was just a poor farmers son, who knows? But, one way or the other, she was probably correct in her assessment of Burns and in protecting her daughter, and her daughter's reputation, from him.

There is a nice little story regarding Burns and the two Ronald sisters, related in the book 'Interesting and Characteristic Anecdotes of Burns' edited by John Ingram in 1893

'At a preaching at Tarbolton, Burns happened to be a hearer. Two young ladies of good position, and at the time slightly acquainted with the poet, were seated on the opposite side of the congregation in the open air. A heavy shower passed over the audience, when there was no available shed to screen the 'countra gentry'. Burns, who happened to have an umbrella, rare enough in those days, walked deliberately round to shelter the ladies, who had none: this he did by standing respectfully behind their chair, and holding the umbrella over their heads. When the rain ceased, and the gaping crowd expected to see him take advantage of the situation by remaining in their neighbourhood, he quietly closed the umbrella, and walked deliberately round again to his original position, where he remained a devout and attentive listener till the conclusion of the service. The ladies in question were two of the Miss Ronalds of the Bennals – one of them remarkable for her piety, and a subsequent correspondent of Burns himself, on topics concerned with religion'.

Anne and Matthew Paterson went on to farm Aikenbrae farm. They are both buried in Monkton Kirkyard.

There was a letter from Burns to his brother William dated 10th November 1789 telling him that a William Ronald had been made bankrupt. Many earlier biographers accepted that the letter referred to William Ronald of Bennals farm, but this is incorrect. The letter refers to a William Ronald, Merchant and Tobacconist who traded in Mauchline at the same time.

As for Jean Ronald, who turned down Gilbert's proposal of marriage. She went on to become the wife of John Reid of Langlands farm near Tarbolton, and it only took two generations before Jean's grandson, Sir George Reid, became the Prime Minister of Australia in 1904.

Associated Verses:

Poem : The Ronalds Of The Bennals
Period : circa 1784

10.
THE BELLES OF MAUCHLINE

Chronology : 1784

The Belles of Mauchline were.

Helen Miller (Sept 1762 - 2nd March 1827)
She was 'Nell' in Burns poem 'A Mauchline Wedding', and was the eldest daughter of John Miller of the Sun Inn in Mauchline. She was a very attractive young woman although she was afflicted with blindness in one eye. But she covered up this disability well, by draping her hair over her blind eye, making the eye less noticeable.

Helen married a Dr MacKenzie, midwife to Jean Armour, on 29th August 1791. The couple eventually moved to Irvine on the invitation of Lord Eglinton where Dr MacKenzie became the family physician, as well as a local magistrate. Later with David Sillar, he formed the Irvine Burns Club. Helen's son was the antiquarian, John Whitefoord MacKenzie, who died in Edinburgh in 1884 at the age of ninety.

Helen died at Seagate House, Irvine, on 2nd March 1827. She is buried in Irvine Parish Kirkyard. Her husband retired shortly after her death and moved back to Edinburgh, where he died at 4 Shandwick Place on 3rd January 1837. He is buried in New Calton Burying Ground, in a railed graveside, beside the Skene Monument.

Jean Markland (1765 - 30th September 1851)
She was a neat woman with a good figure and a pleasing manner. Jean and her parents were brought before the Kirk Session in 1779 and charged with accusing another woman of witchcraft. The charge was dropped.

She married James Findlay in September 1788, an Excise officer in Tarbolton who had been introduced to her by Burns. They moved to Greenock in 1792 when her husband was promoted in the Excise. She died there in 1851 at age 86. 'Tae A Louse' is reputedly to have been written about an incident involving her at a kirk service.

Jean Smith (1768 - 20th January 1854)
She was small, dark-eyed, lively, witty, clever, a very managing person, 'free as the wind to act as she pleased'. She was the sister of one of Burns' oldest and closest friends, James Smith. Jean married James McCandlish, another close boyhood friend of Burns, around about 1788. He went on to become a medical lecturer in Edinburgh.

When her husband died Jean became a teacher in order to support her four children, thus helping her son, Dr Robert S. Candlish along the road to becoming the well-known and respected Free Church Theologian.

Jean died aged 86 on 20th January 1854, and is buried in Old Calton Churchyard in Edinburgh. The family tomb overlooks Waverly Station.

Betty Miller (Feb 1768 - 1795)
She was the sister of Helen Miller and held the post of Postmistress at Mauchline. She had once suffered from smallpox, which left her face quite badly scarred. For a time Betty was the 'Tenant of Burns' heart', a short time before Jean Armour's return to his affections in 1786. Burns is reputed to have proposed to her but she refused his proposal. She, like her sister Helen, is also mentioned in 'A Mauchline Wedding'.

Betty married a William Templeton, a draper from Auchinleck and died at the birth of her first child. There is more about Betty in Chapter 15.

Christina Morton (Aug 1768 - ?)
Was the daughter of Hugh Morton, who owned Morton's Ballroom. in Mauchline. She was said to be the most attractive of all the 'Belles'. She was certainly the wealthiest of them, having a personal fortune of £500. She was considered a young woman of great propriety of demeanour and sweetness of manners.

It is said that she carried a torch for Burns but seeing that his attentions were directed elsewhere, she became a go-between to Jean Armour and Burns. Traditionally it is reported that she accompanied Jean on her first meeting with Burns. Christina left Mauchline soon after to assist in harvest operations in New Cumnock as she is reported to have said

> 'There were so many clashes going on about Robert Burns and her, she wished to be out of the way'.

It was alleged that she was 'much affected when his preference for Jean Armour became evident'. Christina married a Mauchline merchant Robert Paterson on 27th December 1788 and had two daughters and four sons.

Jean Armour (1765 - 1834)
Married Robert Burns.

Associated Songs:

Song	: The Belles Of Mauchline	Song	: O Leave Novels
Tune	: Bonie Dundee	Tune	: Ye Mauchline Belles
Period	: circa 1784/1785	Period	: circa 1784/1785

11.

ELIZABETH PATON
Born 1760 – Died pre 8th March 1799

ELIZABETH PATON BURNS
Born 22 May 1785 – Died 8 Jan 1817

Chronology : 1783

Elizabeth Paton

Elizabeth Paton came from Largieside near Lochlea, and was employed as a servant girl to the Burns family from 1783, during the period when their father, William, was dying. After his father's death, on 13th February 1784, Burns found 'solace' in and with Elizabeth Paton to the extent that she gave birth to his first child, Elizabeth Paton Burns his 'Dear-bought Bess'. The child was born on the 22nd May 1785, and was baptised two days later on the 24th May 1785.

Burns' mother, Agnes Broun, was fond of Elizabeth Paton. She considered her an honest country girl, and wanted Burns to marry her, but his brothers and sisters were set against this.

From a letter written by Burns' niece, Isabella Burns Begg jnr., to Robert Chambers when he was collecting information for his 1852 biography of Burns, comes a description of Elizabeth Paton passed down from her mother, Isabella (snr.)

'She was an exceedingly handsome figure, but very plain looking; so active, honest and independent a creature, that she had become a great favourite with her mistress *(Agnes Broun)*, who, when her situation became known, was most anxious that Burns should have married her, but both my aunts *(Agnes and Annabella Burns)* and uncle Gilbert opposed it. The girl herself acknowledged he had broken no promise to her. They thought the faults of her character would soon have disgusted him. She was rude and uncultivated to a great degree, a strong masculine understanding, with a thorough (tho' unwomanly) contempt for every sort of refinement...My mother *(Isabella Burns Begg, snr.)* says she does not believe that ever any woman loved man with a more heartfelt devotion, than that poor creature did him. She married, some time after, a farm-servant lad named Andrew, and made a most excellent wife. In fact, except in that one instance, her behaviour was exemplary'.

The niece also went on to say that Burns' affection for Elizabeth Paton was very different to her affection for him but 'he never treated her badly'.

Unfortunately, though he never treated her badly, Burns repaid her love by writing his braggard's 'Epistle to J. R.' (John Rankine, a man twice Burns' age and father of Anne 'Rigs o' Barley' Rankine), comparing his seduction of Elizabeth Paton in a hunting metaphor, which was boorish, uncouth and mean spirited of Burns to say the least (though not quite as nasty as the 'horse-litter' diatribe written regarding Jean Armour). But again it shows Burns attitude to women of conqueror and conquered.

Then again to be fair to Burns, he was willing to marry Elizabeth, at first anyway. Maybe this was because many of his former marriage proposals had been rejected, and he thought that this would be his best chance of becoming a husband. He knew that Elizabeth Paton would have married him without a moment's hesitation.

Elizabeth, being of the country, would also have been a very able and knowledgeable worker round the farm, and she was not averse to hard work. According to Gilbert Burns, from his late teens, early twenties, Robert was desperate to be married, though it is unlikely, even at that early age that the idea of being faithful ever entered into the equation.

It must have been a very confusing and upsetting time for Burns. In just a few short years he had been rebuffed in marriage by Isabella Steven, Elizabeth Gebbie, Montgomerie's Peggy, Anne Ronald, Elizabeth Miller. And that's just the ones we know about. His self-esteem must really have taken a nose-dive.

Now here he was with Elizabeth Paton, his chance to enter into in the matrimonial stakes, and his family, who he presumably thought would be delighted with his new found air of responsibility shining through, were dead set against it, even though he was proud to admit that he was the father of Elizabeth's child, and trumpeted it far and wide. This really was not fair.

When the kirk found out about Elizabeth's delicate situation, Burns took his first trip to the * 'creepie chair'. It cost him a guinea fine, which he paid to the Tarbolton Kirk Session. It was also something that he boasted about to his friends and acquaintances and swore that when Elizabeth had given birth to her child he would return to her to get his money's worth paid in kind. Not a very nice attitude.

*A 'creepie chair', 'cutty stool' or 'stool of repentance' was described by R. H. Cromek in his book 'Remains of Nithsdale and Galloway Song' in 1810

'The stool of terror was fashioned like an arm-chair, and was raised on a pedestal, nearly two foot higher than the other seats, directly fronting the pulpit. (Arrayed 'in the black sack-cloth gown of fornication'), the culprit stood three Sundays successively, his face uncovered, and the awful scourge of unpardoning divinity hung over him. The women stood here in the same accoutrements, and were denied the privilege of a veil'.

On the 1st December 1786 Elizabeth Paton, who had eventually made a claim on Burns over the paternity of her child, accepted a settlement of £20, which was paid out of the profits of the 'Kilmarnock Edition'. It is conjecture as to whether the child was referred to as Dear-bought because of this payment to her mother.

On 9th February 1788 Elizabeth Paton married a widower, John Andrew, who was employed as a farm labourer, and had another four children with him. John Andrew married Jean Lees, his third wife on 8th March 1799, and therefore it is assumed that Elizabeth Paton had died before that date.

Associated Songs:

Song   : My Girl She's Airy
Tune   : Black Joke
Period : 1784

Song   : The Fornicator
Tune   : Clout The Caudron
Period : Summer 1785

Song   : The Rantin Dog (may also have been written for Jean Armour)
Tune   : Whare Wad Bonie Annie Ly
Period : 1785

Elizabeth (Bess) Paton Burns
When Bess Paton Burns was born, Burns dedicated a poem to her, entitled 'A Poet's Welcome To His Love-Begotten Daughter', or as he was to put it in some of his several versions, 'A Poet's Welcome To His Bastard Wean'. Nevertheless he was proud of this achievement of parenthood, as it was the first instance that entitled him to the 'venerable appelation of Father'.

Bess, after she was weaned, did not live with her mother. Burns had convinced Elizabeth Paton that the child would be better being looked after by his mother at Mossgiel. Maybe he also managed to convince Elizabeth that her own future marriage prospects would be improved without having a child in tow.

According to his niece Isabella Burns Begg jnr., when Burns was getting married to Jean Armour in 1788, he and Jean offered to take the little girl into their home at Ellisland, but she remained at her grandmother's house.

'When Burns went to Ellisland, the child Elizabeth *(Bess)* Paton Burns came to Mossgiel to my grandmother *(Agnes Broun)*, and attended school at Mauchline till the poet's death. Elizabeth Paton *(Elizabeth*

Paton Andrew, her mother) then took her home, where she lived till she *(Bess)* was married to John Bishop, who acted as land-steward to Baillie of Polkemmet. She *(Bess)* was a good spright creature, and when she died, the minister of the parish wrote a beautiful character of her to my grandfather *(this has to be her paternal grandfather)'*.

John Bishop was brought up at 'Roadheid' near Shotts, and after their marriage he and Bess moved to a place called 'Rumlinskye' near Whitburn on the road to Pedenstone.

'Dear-bought Bess' had seven children and died at the young age of 31 on 8th January in 1817. Tradition infers that she may have died in childbirth. She is buried in Whitburn Churchyard. Made of cast iron, hers is the only metal tombstone in the cemetery. Shortly after her death, one of her children, Mary Lyon, died on 26th April 1817 at the age of 23 months.

On the back of Bess' gravestone there is an inscription saying 'Here lies the Daughter of Robert Burns the National Bard'.

After the death of Bess, John Bishop remarried and he died on 20th June 1857 aged seventy-five. Many of his children from that marriage are buried in the Whitburn area.

In a twist of fate, like poetical justice, one of Bess' daughters married a James Weir, and one of the descendants from that marriage became Lord Weir of Cathcart. Viscount Weir had his estate near Mauchline. How Bess Paton Burns must be tickled pink, wherever she is watching from. As they say, what goes round comes round.

'Dear-bought Bess' was never mentioned in the biographical letter to Dr Moore, which Burns wrote in August of 1787 nor was she ever mentioned by Gilbert Burns, her uncle, though he had accepted responsibility and financial support for her. Burns had given over his half share of Mossgiel to Gilbert, as well as monies received from the sale of the 'Kilmarnock Edition' in order that Gilbert would look after Bess, which also contributed towards the support of Agnes Broun, their mother.

All of this happened when Burns was thinking of making his escape to the West Indies to avoid the threat of reprisals that James Armour had in store for him for being the instigator of his daughter, Jean's unfortunate condition.

12.

MARGARET (PEGGY) KENNEDY
Born 1766 – Died Feb. 1795

Chronology : Autumn 1784

Peggy Kennedy was one of the daughters of Robert Kennedy of Daljarrock, the factor to the Earl of Cassilis situated in the parish of Colmonell. Her older sister was Helen Kennedy, the wife of Burns' friend Gavin Hamilton.

Burns first met Peggy in the Autumn of 1784 when she was engaged to a Captain Andrew McDoual of Logan, Wigtownshire whom she met a year earlier when she was just 17.

On the completion of his song 'Young Peggy' Burns wrote to her

'MADAM - Permit me to present you with the inclosed SONG as a small, though grateful tribute, for the honor of your acquaintance. I have, in these verses, attempted some faint sketches of your Portrait in the unembellished simple manner of descriptive Truth. – Flattery, I leave to your Lovers, whose exaggerating Fancies may make them imagine you still nearer Perfection than you really are'.

He finishes the letter with

'That the Arrows of Misfortune, however they should, as incident to Humanity, glance a slight wound, may never reach your Heart – that the snare of Villainy may never beset you in the road of Life – that Innocence may hand you, by the path of Honor, to the dwelling of Peace, is the sincere wish of him who has the honor to be, Madam, your most obedient and very humble servant'.

Peggy contracted a secret marriage with McDoual and in 1794 they had a daughter. He denied paternity and also that there had ever been such a marriage. He dropped Peggy, married the daughter of a Dumfriesshire laird, and took over his father's estate in Logan. Peggy raised an action in Court of 'declarator of marriage' and for damages of seduction, but before the case was ended Peggy died, of a broken heart it is said.

In 1798 the Consistorial Court of the Church declared the irregular marriage legal according to Scots Law, and legitimised the child. McDoual however, with his numerous contacts, managed to get this overturned by the Court of Session and the poor child was made illegitimate again, though the Court awarded damages of £3000 to the dead woman and alimentary provision for the child.

McDoual was an MP who represented Wigtownshire in Parliament, but he was considered a blackguard, corrupt, untrustworthy, and anyone's for the buying of. In the political poems that Burns wrote, wherever he is mentioned it is in a derogatory manner. His name is synonymous with skulduggery, dishonesty and sleaze.

An unpleasant man, even Chambers called him a 'noted Lothario'. McDoual was one of the many admirers of Maria Riddell. Unfortunately though we do not have her impression of him.

Whatever Burns wished for Peggy, the last paragraph in his letter was a prophetic one for this unfortunate woman. He also commented, 'Peggy Kennedy loved not wisely, but too well'.

The song 'Young Peggy' was published in the Musical Museum in 1787.

There is an interesting little insight into Burns' attitude to Peggy Kennedy, which was written by Burns niece Isabella Burns Begg jnr. in October 1850

'Burns met Miss Kennedy at Mr Hamilton's, where she lived sometime. My mother *(Isabella Burns Begg snr.)* remembers a conversation between Robert and Gilbert, on the har'st rig, respecting the young lady and the song, which had been written upon her. Gilbert said he did not think quite so much of her. Robert said she had a great deal of wit. One Sarah Weir, who was often about Mr. Hamilton's, working, and knew them all well, was shearing on the same ridge with my mother. At the poet's remark about the wit of Miss Kennedy, Sarah stopped and asked him if it was not of a shallow kind. The bard only replied with a look of contempt, which greatly amused my mother at the time, and which still remains imprinted on her memory'.

In Edinburgh's Buccleuch Cemetery, Jane one of Peggy Kennedy's sisters is buried. Her inscription on the north wall reads

'Sacred to the memory of Mrs Jane Kennedy of Daljarrock, who died on 8th July 1797, aged 29 years, who lies buried 18 feet from West Dike, and 105 feet from back of Chapel. As a testimony of regard this stone is erected by her Affectionate Husband, Robert Thomson, Esq., late of the Island of Jamaica'.

Jane's actual grave is placed near the grave of Miss Sophia Johnson, within the west wall of new Church Hall.

Associated Songs:

Song	: Young Peggy	Song	: The Banks O' Doon
Tune	: Loch Eroch Side	Tune	: Caledonian Hunt's Delight
Period	: Autumn 1785	Period	: March 1791

Song	: Ye Flowery Banks O' Bonie Doon
Tune	: Cambdelmore
Period	: March 1791

13.

MARY ANNE WHITEFOORD

Chronology : pre 1784/1785

Mary Anne was the eldest of Baronet, Sir John Whitefoord's four daughters. He occupied the Ballochmyle Estate, near Mauchline, which was owned by the Whitefoord family. It was in their possession until the 1785 when John Whitefoord was eventually forced to sell because of the losses made by collapse of the Ayr Bank (Douglas, Heron and Co.), a few years previously, in which he was a partner. The Whitefoord's then moved to Edinburgh, where they took up residence in *Whitefoord House.

On the song 'The Braes O' Ballochmyle', Burns remarks

'I composed the verses on the amiable and excellent family of Whitefoord leaving Ballochmyle'.

The following poem was found among the manuscripts of Burns after his death, and is thought by some earlier biographers to have been written about Mary Ann (although unsubstantiated), who was considered to be a local beauty, and to whom he was immediately attracted when one day he saw her walking along the Mauchline streets.

> Her flowing locks – the raven's wing –
> Adown her neck and bosom hing;
> How sweet unto that breast to cling,
> And round that neck entwine her!
> Her lips are roses wet wi' dew!
> O what a feast her bonie mou'!
> Her cheeks a mair celestial hue,
> A crimson still diviner!

Mary Anne married the grandson of the fifth Lord Cranston, Henry Kerr-Cranston. Her husband's sister became the second wife to Professor Dugald Stewart, proprietor of the Catrine woods and lea, mentioned in the song, and which adjoined Ballochmyle. The estate was about two miles outside of Mauchline. Professor Stewart later became a friend of Burns.

The tune written and also named after the song, 'The Braes O' Ballochmyle', was composed by Allan Masterton a very good friend of Burns, and one of the participants in his poem 'Willie Brewed A Peck O' Maut'. Masterton was a man whom he had known for many years, and shared a few libations with when the occasion and need arose.

Following the departure of the Whitefoord's from Ballochmyle, the estate was ought by the Alexander family, to the daughter of which, Wilhelmina Alexander, Burns wrote the song 'The Bonnie Lass O' Ballochmyle.' Burns did not like the Alexander family at all.

*Whitefoord House was not the first residence lived in by the family in Edinburgh. According to Williamson's Directory they resided at number 25 St Andrew's Square, after its completion in 1778, and then moved to a house 'at the head of Leith Walk' circa 1783, which Sir John advertised at the yearly rental of £4. Sir John died at Whitefoord House on the 8th April 1803.

Associated Song:

Song   : The Braes O' Ballochmyle
Tune   : The Braes O' Ballochmyle
Period : Autumn 1785

14.

WILHELMINA ALEXANDER
Born April 1756 – Died 5th June 1843)

Chronology : 1785/86

Wilhelmina was born in Paisley and was the sister of Claud Alexander, who bought the Ballochmyle Estate from the Whitefoord Family when he retired from the East India Company in 1785, becoming the Laird of Ballochmyle. Claud was the son of a landed proprietor in the west of Scotland and had gathered a vast fortune from his job as paymaster-general of the East India Company's troops in Bengal.

In 1786 while out walking on the Banks of the Ayr, Burns saw Wilhelmina walking through the verdure. He thought that she may not have seen him. On his return home to Mossgiel he composed the song 'The Lass O' Ballochmyle'.

But apparently Wilhelmina had seen him and reported on returning that

'The grounds being forbidden to unauthorised strangers – the evening being far advanced, and the encounter being very sudden – she was startled, but instantly recovered herself, and passed on'.

Burns wrote to her asking her permission to include his song to her in the 'second edition of my poems', though it was not necessary for her to have given her permission for him to do this. But Burns was always on the lookout for patronage, and maybe he thought that this would get his foot in the door with the Alexander Family. She never replied to his letter.

Burns' recollection of the incident

'I had roved out as chance directed, in the favourite haunts of my muse, on the banks of the Ayr, to view nature in all the gaiety of the vernal year. The evening sun was flaming over the distant western hills, not a breath stirred the crimson opening blossoms or the verdant spreading leaf. It was a golden moment for a poetic heart. Such was the scene, and such the hour, when, in a corner of my prospect, I spied one of the fairest pieces of nature's workmanship that ever crowned a poetic landscape, or met a poet's eye; those visionary bards excepted who hold commune with aerial beings'!

Maybe Wilhelmina could be forgiven a little for not replying to Burns' letter. According to a relative

75

'On receiving the letter and poem, Miss Alexander was taken aback. She was suspicious of him. Was he making improper advances? She was an unmarried virgin in her early thirties – not a 'bonnie lass'. She made enquiries about him and opinions offered to his character were unfavourable. 'Feeling it necessary to decline yielding to his request, she thought that her decision would be intimated most delicately to him, by allowing his letter to remain unanswered'.

As the years went by, Wilhelmina mellowed a little, and wherever she went, the original manuscript of the song went too. Belatedly appreciating the immortality conferred on her by the poet.

Burns smarted sorely from the insult of being ignored by his ill-mannered 'betters'. He copied his letter to Wilhelmina in the Glenriddell Manuscript, and added that Miss Alexander was 'too fine a lady to notice so plain a compliment'. Of her brother Claud, and 'great men' of his ilk he wrote

'When Fate swore that their purses should be full, Nature was equally positive that their heads should be empty. Men of their fashion are surely incapable of being impolite!! Ye canna mak' a silk-purse o' a sow's lug'.

Another reason for Burns anger towards the Alexander family, was that *Saunders Tait, an older Mauchline rhymer who thoroughly detested Burns and his family and had written many scurrilous verses about them, had composed a poem on Wilhelmina called 'Lady Ballochmyle's Chariot'. Not only had she read and acknowledged the poem, but she also requested that Saunders Tait come to Ballochmyle to perform the poem in person. From then on he became a regular visitor at the estate.

*Saunders (Alexander) Tait was a tailor to trade, but he owned several houses in Mauchline, thus making him a landlord. He was a bachelor and lived in a very small attic. At the annual 'June fair' he turned his attic home into a 'poet's corner' whereupon he sold drink to the locals and to the visitors to the fair, becoming, for a short while, a publican.

Tait published a book of poetry in Paisley in 1790 containing 304 pages. It is said to be of much quantity but very little quality. There was no comparison between Tait and Burns, nor was his poetry ever near the standard of Burns. In fact if it hadn't been for Robert Burns and the unpleasant poems Tait wrote about Burns and his family, the name of Saunders Tait would never have been remembered at all.

Wilhelmina Alexander never married and died at eighty-seven, in Glasgow. Her house was situated on the East Side of the then recently built 'George Square', and was later demolished to make way for today's Municipal Buildings. Apparently in her later years, her home became like a shrine to the poem, which she had framed and put in a prominent place for all of her visitors to see.

No one is sure where Wilhelmina is buried, but one of the places suggested is an old disused cemetery, which is within the bounds of Glasgow Airport, although the traditional burial spot of the Alexander's is Mauchline Kirkyard.

Years later a nephew of Wilhelmina erected a summerhouse, called the 'Fog House' to commemorate the place where Burns saw her walking. In this small folly type building there was a facsimile of two verses of the manuscript of 'The Bonnie Lass O' Ballochmyle'. Unfortunately vandals set fire to the 'Fog House' in 1944, and it was completely destroyed.

There is an interesting article in the Burns Chronicles of 1974 relating to Wilhelmina, written by one of her modern day relatives, Boyd Alexander. He gives us a little insight into 'The Lass O' Ballochmyle'.

She is first heard of in a letter from her uncle, William Cuninghame of Craigends, who wrote to her father, Claud Alexander of Newton, in April 1756, commiserating with him on the birth of a fourth daughter. To get rid of her meant he had to find a fourth dowry. 'Tho' these girls are troublesome, we must submit and be thankful', states her uncle.

Like her sisters, Wilhelmina was a very attractive looking young woman. In fact a Robert Barclay, the family lawyer, wrote to her elder brother Claud in May of 1782, saying

> 'I find you are rather surprised that none of the young ladies are settled, and indeed it is to be regretted as they are handsome and in their prime'.

But Wilhelmina chose to remain unmarried. She had many suitors and was in great demand in the Glasgow Society of the day, though there was becoming a shortage of young men of her station, as they were enlisting in the regiments because of the popularity of the American War. She was a very independent young lady. As an old woman she is reported as saying 'I'm a true Alexander and cannot put up with it'.

Wilhelmina writes of Glasgow and its business in her diaries

> 'Some individuals in Glasgow have made great fortunes by it *(the war)*, but in the main it has been most distressing to it. Will Clark has been most successful what with tobacca, insurances, prizes, and some say gaming. He has made a great sum and keeps such a grand house he has bought an estate upon Loch Lomond a beautiful laying place with the finest garden in the country'.

As a young woman, in her letters she appears to be forthright and spirited, with a lively and attractive personality as well as appearance, but as she grew older her letters show her as having deep religious feelings, loyalty to the throne and to be a strong supporter of Conservatism.

She and her unmarried sister, Peggy, lived together at number 12 George

Square, until Peggy's death in 1834.   Wilhelmina attended the funeral service for her, which was held in St George's Presbyterian Church where

> 'our own minister gave us most excellent prayers: poor me quite stupid – sometimes could not walk – often thought or feared I had entirely lost my mind; yet the almighty supported me and enabled me to do my duty in all things'.

Because of the custom of the time, and prevented by her age, she had to watch from the window in George Square as the hearse containing her 'Angel sister's' remains left for Paisley, followed by the mourning coach which held her brothers and an empty carriage, representing Wilhelmina as the chief mourner.

Years later, when informed by her niece, Mary, of a new biography on Burns, written by Motherwell & Hogg, and how much James Hogg would have travelled far to see her she wrote to an acquaintance

> 'She (*Mary*) also asks me if I have seen the new Life of Burns, edited by the Ettrick Shepherd – where she thinks he maybe mentions the 'Lass' – is uncommonly good.   Do ask my good friend Mr Lockhart, if he thinks so much of it.   A gentleman told me he had heard the Shepherd say that so much was he delighted with what Burns said of her that he would go one hundred miles to see her; how lucky he never did – he would have been much disappointed!   Don't mention me in this at all, I know you will not'.

Hogg had written

> 'Burns took it heinously amiss that Miss Alexander never made any reply to the flaming letter which he sent her along with the song.   I think it would have been very unnatural if she had; for how could she think with patience of a great black curly ploughman, with brawny limbs and broad shoulders, straining her nightly to his bosom.   It was really too much of a good thing this'!

Maybe, for the 'Lass's' sake, we should repeat the last ten words again!

> 'It was really too much of a good thing this'!

Associated Song:

Song   : The Lass O' Ballochmyle
Tune   : Ettrick Banks
Period : September 1786

15.

BETTY MILLER
Born February 1768 – Died 1795)

Chronology : 1784/85

One of the Mauchline Belles, Betty was said to be romantically involved with Burns during 1785.   She was a daughter of John Miller, owner of the Sun Inn in Mauchline.

According to a Matthew Leerie, who knew the Miller family, when interviewed for the small book 'Mauchline Memories of Robert Burns'

> 'She might perhaps have been what Burns styles her, 'braw', if her face had not suffered severely from the ravages of small-pox'.

Apparently Mrs Miller, Betty's mother was one of the few parents who actually liked Burns.   When Matthew Leerie's father, a mason to trade, came knocking at the door of the Sun Inn early one morning to begin work on one of the rooms, Mrs Miller told him that he could not start at that time as 'ye wad disturb oor twa lasses, who were awa last night at Mossgiel seeing that nice young lad Robin Burns'.

That the song 'From Thee Eliza' was written for Betty is to be questioned. According to Burns he composed it three years before he met her, round about 1781/82.   It is thought more likely to be meant for Ellison Begbie/Elizabeth Gebbie after she turned down his proposal of marriage and left the district on marrying someone else, to live in Glasgow.

But the words of the song are of the man leaving the woman, not the other way around as happened when Begbie/Gebbie left Burns.   Burns had been considering emigration to Jamaica long before 1786, but he'd also been considering being a soldier too.   So who has ownership to the song is still up in the air.

What cast her out as the 'tenant of Burns' heart'?

Tradition tells that William Miller, a brother of Betty and Helen, married an heiress.   Gossip said supposedly for the sake of the £500 inheritance left to her by her brother.   The Miller family considered themselves to have gone up in the world by this matrimonial connection, and thus a poor farmer like Robert Burns was not quite a suitable partner through life, even although Mrs Miller still thought of him kindly.

Burns wrote of the occurrence in a letter to Mrs Dunlop on 21st August 1788

'You would know an Ayrshire lad, Sandy Bell, who made a Jamaica fortune & died some time ago – A William Miller, formerly a mason, now a merchant in this place, married a sister german of Bell's for the sake of 500£ her brother had left her – A Sister of Miller's who was then Tenant of my heart for the time being, huffed my Bardship in the pride of her new Connection; & I, in the heat of my resentment resolved to burlesque the whole business, & began as follows'.

He enclosed the poem 'A Mauchline Wedding' describing the events of the marriage of William Miller and Agnes Bell, which took place in July 1785.

There is a slightly different variation to the story as reported in the small book 'Mauchline Memories of Robert Burns'. There it is stated that the one who went away was an Alexander Miller *(another brother to the two women)*. He is said to have gone out to India, made his fortune and returned home, his health broken and totally blind. Apparently he also brought back to Mauchline a young Asian boy who seemingly was given to Sir John Whitefoord as a present.

The boy was sent to the local school and was given a 'good Christian education'. At the age of 17 the local kirk was packed to the gunnels when he was baptised into the church where he took the name of John Cartwright. The first name, John from Sir John Whitefoord, and surname Cartwright from Lady Whitefoord's maiden name. (The only problem here is that Sir John Whitefoord may have at that time actually sold his residence at Ballochmyle, and moved to Edinburgh).

It appears that Betty had returned for a short duration to Burns' affections sometime in the autumn of 1786 post 'Highland Mary' and pre Jean Armour with the birth of her twins. In a letter to John Richmond dater 27th September 1786 Burns writes

'I received yours of Connel's last return, and I have just a moment at present to tell you that I am in the land of the living, and in the place of hope – I am going perhaps to try a second edition of my book – If I do, it will detain me a little longer in the country; if not, I shall be gone as soon as harvest is over - Bettsey Miller waits me'.

According to Robert Chambers regarding Betty Miller

'She appears to have been an amiable girl, and it is not improbable that she had sympathised with Burns during his various distresses. Gratitude may have inspired a kind of affection, which, as usual, he expressed in the language of adoring love'.

Betty married a William Templeton from Auchinleck on the 8th September 1794. Templeton became the draper in Mauchline when James Smith, brother to another 'Mauchline Belle', Jean Smith, moved away.

Her sister Helen, another of the Mauchline Belles, married a Dr John MacKenzie who lodged at the Sun Inn. Helen and her husband then moved to Irvine. She is buried in Irvine Parish Kirkyard.

After Helen left to go to Irvine with her husband, Betty was employed as the post-mistress to the village. Sadly she died at the birth of her first child, within a year of being married. It is unknown if the child survived.

Gilfillan, a biographer of Burns, states that 'Farewell to Eliza' was written for Elizabeth Black, who married an innkeeper of Alloa, but this unsubstantiated.

Burns was certainly busy during the year 1785/86. Montgomerie's Peggy, Elizabeth Paton, Betty Miller, Jean Armour, Margaret Campbell, and no doubt others who will remain unidentified. Burns must have felt that he was on the crest of an ever-rising wave.

Associated Song:

Farewell To Eliza – but more likely to have been written for Ellison Begbie/Elizabeth Gebbie

16.

MARGARET CAMPBELL
(HIGHLAND MARY)
Born circa 18th March 1766 – Died circa 20th October 1786

Chronology : Pre-Spring 1786 but possibly during 1784/85.

Margaret (Highland Mary) Campbell was born in Auchamore, which forms the southeast and southwest parts of Kirn and Dunoon, and was baptised in Dunoon on 18th March 1766.

We have James Mackay to thank for discovering in his investigations that her name was Margaret, not Mary, and that she was the eldest of four children.

Agnes Campbell of Auchamore was her mother, and Archibald Campbell of Dailing was her father. Because of his work, he was a hand on board a revenue cutter, she also resided at Ardrossan, Lochranza, Campbeltown, and finally Greenock. It is also reported that Archibald was self-employed, owned an old sloop and that he carried coal to the neighbouring islands.

According to family tradition, passed down through Julia McNeill, daughter of Elizabeth Campbell McNeill, a cousin to Archibald Campbell, Margaret was greatly loved by all who knew her.

When the family moved to Campbeltown from Dunoon they lived in a house where Gayfield Place is today. Margaret attended a small school in Watson's Row near her home, and was known for her pleasant manners, her good temper, and her willingness to help anyone in need.

She is reported as tall with a fair complexion, light yellow hair, blue eyes and carried herself in a graceful manner. Above all she was sincere and honest. Even as a young girl she was considered a good singer, as were her mother and her sister. Her first language was Gaelic not English.

Tradition relates that in 1778 at the age of twelve, Margaret began in domestic service. She worked for a family named Kirk who lived in Campbeltown. At the end of 1778 she is thought to have moved to Lochranza where she became housemaid to the Rev David Campbell, said to be a maternal relative. Round about 1780 she is reported to have left Lochranza and moved to the mainland to work where she was allegedly employed in Irvine in 1782 (Burns was living in Irvine in late 1781).

Though none of this can be proved.

In 1784, Margaret may have been employed as a dairymaid at Coilsfield, the house belonging to Colonel Hugh Montgomerie, to which Burns whimsically gave the name 'Castle o' Montgomerie'.

*Coilsfield was styled Quyllisfield in the charter of John de Graham conveying it, with other lands, to the monks of Melrose in 1342. It came into the hands of the Montgomerie family through a Colonel James, fourth son of Alexander, sixth Earl of Eglintoun c 1640.

In 1785 Margaret worked for Burns' friend Gavin Hamilton who employed people on a half yearly basis. An old woman by the name of Nellie Martin (nee Miller) gave an interview recorded in the small book 'Mauchline Memories of Robert Burns'. Nellie was born in July 1766, the same year as Margaret, and knew her very well as both worked at Hamilton's. Mrs Martin had a high opinion of Margaret and said of her in the interview

'She was an unco bonnie bit lass, wi' twa fine black een, but gae an' Heelan' spoken'.

Delving into past memories, Mrs Martin recalled that Margaret Campbell had yet not come to Mauchline in January 1785. The Kirk Session was interviewing potential servants of Gavin Hamilton's in this month, and Margaret was not one of them, but by the Autumn both Nellie and Margaret had left his employ.

At a later date Gavin Hamilton employed Margaret in the post of nursemaid to his children in Mauchline. This was from Candlemas (February 1785) to Lammas (August 1785), although others say May to November 1785. His son was born on 13th July of that year. However, as already stated by Nellie Martin, before the end of the year, she had left Hamilton's and is reported to have returned to Coilsfield. Others say she may have gone to Stairaird Farm.

Nellie Martin died in the winter of 1858 shortly after giving the interview.

When interviewed years later, Gavin Hamilton's second daughter Williamina, recalls Margaret as being 'Very pleasant and winning though not a beauty'. (It is reported that Margaret had traces of smallpox scars on her face). Williamina married Rev. J. Todd in 1806, and died in 1858 at the age of 79.

With other members of the Coilsfield household Margaret worshipped at Tarbolton Parish Church, (memories of Montgomerie's Peggy), and with her noticeable highland accent she was soon christened 'Highland Mary'. It is reported that Margaret was very devout, and it was often commented on how wrapped up she appeared to be in her Bible during the services.

According to local tradition it is said she became acquainted with Burns in Tarbolton, probably meeting him when he occasionally attended the church there. It was not his usual or local place of worship, but he liked to try out new preachers and new sermons in the area.

Burns insinuates that he met Margaret in the spring of 1786 when he was extremely low, and on the rebound from Jean Armour. Jean was pregnant to him, and although he was more than willing to marry her, (and indeed, under Scots Law, <u>had</u> married her) at the end of March, her father sent Jean to Paisley to stay with relatives until the birth was passed.

Old Armour was out to get Burns by any means, fair or foul. He went as far as to have the contract which Robert and Jean had drawn up stating they were husband and wife, perfectly legal under Scot's Law, destroyed. That is after he had recovered from his fainting fit on hearing that Jean was first of all pregnant, and worst of all pregnant to Robert Burns of all people, the man whom he detested most in the world. Why?

Could it be that if Margaret had been around since the beginning of 1785 James Armour was aware that there was something going on between Burns and her. Mauchline was a small place and few secrets or liaisons could be kept quiet for very long before they became common knowledge.

If James Armour was suspicious something was going on between Burns and Margaret Campbell, then Jean Armour would have known for definite.

As far as Robert was concerned insult was being added to injury when Jean went to Paisley. He had been deserted. Now he was ready to give it all up and emigrate to the West Indies, leaving Jean, her betrayal and her loathsome family to their own devices.

Burns was feeling quite sorry for himself, and was ready for some emotional healing, when, according to him sometime in April 1786, Margaret Campbell appeared on the scene, a young woman whose

'bosom is fraught with truth, honour, constancy, and love'.

Tradition leads us to believe that after a whirlwind romance Margaret had agreed to go to the West Indies with Burns. We are informed that she left her place of employment at Mauchline in May 1786 to return to Campbeltown, where she was to prepare for the move abroad. She was to say her farewells to her family and friends and then join Burns at Greenock for their voyage into their future.

Fact or fiction has it that they met on the second Sunday in May 1786, stood on opposite banks of a small stream, called 'The Faile', just before it falls into the River Ayr, and plighted their troth in the ancient tradition of Scotland. According to Cromek (in his 'Reliques') the couple washed their hands in the water, to show purity, clasping them over the running stream, and held Margaret's Bible between them, the significance being that 'as long as the stream continued to run, and as long as the book held true, for that length of time they would be true to one another'.   The couple then exchanged Bibles and made their last (though they were not to know this) farewells to each other.

This intense relationship was allegedly crammed into a four-week period (unless of course Margaret was indeed 'Montgomerie's Peggy', which meant that the association was of a much longer duration).

When Margaret Campbell put one foot outside of Mauchline, to set off on the road to Campbeltown, to some early biographers she all but took on the mantle of martyrdom.

On 9th June 1786, three weeks after Margaret departed for Campbeltown, Jean Armour returned from Paisley.   The question is - Why?

Maybe Jean had heard about Burns' intention of leaving for The Indies? Maybe she had been worried about the relationship with Margaret?   Either way there was a possibility that Jean was going to lose the man she loved. If she remained in Paisley there was no way that she would be able to influence the outcome.   So she came home.

Jean must really have loved Burns with all of her heart, to come home at this time and suffer her father's wrath.

Margaret remained in Campbeltown from May until the beginning of October 1786 then she returned to the mainland where her boat docked at Greenock.   This was supposed to be the first leg of the journey prior to leaving Scotland for The Indies.   Margaret was travelling with her brother and they were met on the quay by a ship-owner called Andrew Munro.

It is reported that when Margaret disembarked from the ship, Andrew Munro thought that she did not appear too well and took her to a house at 31 Upper Charles Street in Greenock, where she stayed with some maternal relatives called McPherson.

Some biographers have said that where Margaret lived on arrival in Greenock was Minch Collop Close, a very run down and unhealthy part of the town at the time, but according to Margaret's nephew, Archibald Campbell, the McPherson's moved to Minch Collop Close after the death of Margaret.   Archibald also stated that Margaret's mother, his grandmother, had often taken him to show him the house where his aunt had died, so he knew that to be true.

Margaret's brother had been travelling to Greenock after being chosen for an apprenticeship, possibly in Messrs Scott. Shipyard.   He was to go through an initiation called a 'brothering feast' in order that he could enter the craft of carpenter.   At the celebration after the initiation, Margaret, who had recovered her health, helped to serve the company.

The next day her brother could not go to work.   Margaret apparently commented on his alcohol intake the previous evening.   Her uncle, Peter McPherson is jokingly said to have commented 'Oh then, it's as well, in case of the worst, that I have agreed to purchase that lair in the kirkyard.'

Unfortunately what her brother was suffering from was no hangover. He had contracted typhus. There was a very severe outbreak in Greenock in the Autumn of 1786. His illness worsened. Margaret tended to him and, luckily, as he was young and strong, within a few days he began to recover.

But, sad to say, due to the close contact with her brother when caring for him, Margaret caught the fever herself and died in Greenock, sometime between the 12th and the 20th October 1786. She was buried in McPherson's recently purchased plot in West Church burial ground.

Although the actual date of Margaret's death is not known, we do know that the lair was purchased, by Peter McPherson, on the 12th October 1786, having previously been assigned, on 14th January 1760, to Duncan Robinson, a carpenter to trade. Margaret was the first member of the extended McPherson family to be interred in it.

McPherson's daughter gave the above information regarding Margaret's time in Greenock to Robert Chambers in the mid 19th century.

Whether Margaret was pregnant to Burns no one knows, but she may have survived the typhus epidemic if she were not. Medical opinion of the time thought that pregnancy strengthened the disease and death was considered the inevitable outcome. But if Margaret had reached Greenock in a weakened state, pregnant or not, (Captain Munro had noticed that she was looking pale) if her resistance to infection was low, then the disease could have taken a firm grip on her system with again the same inevitable result.

According to Isabella Burns Begg jnr., her mother, Burns' youngest sister, said that Burns had received a letter late in 1786, at the end of the harvest, which after having read, he then left the room in an agitated state. She did not know what was in the letter.

Biographers over the decades have surmised that this letter could have been from a member of the Campbell family informing him of Margaret's death, and, if Margaret had been pregnant, it would also have meant the death of their child.

The following paragraph is included in Cromek's 'Reliques', as one of the missing interleaved notes of the Scots Musical Museum. It was a note to the song 'My Highland Lassie, O', which was included in the second volume. Burns writes of Margaret, and of the last time he saw her.

'This was a composition of mine in very early life, before I was known at all in the world. My Highland Lassie was a warm hearted, charming young creature as ever blessed a man with generous love. After a pretty long tract of the most ardent reciprocal attachment, we met by appointment, on the second Sunday of May, in a sequestered spot by the Banks of Ayr, where we spent the day in taking farewell, before she should embark for the West Highlands to arrange matters amongst her friends for our projected change of life. At the close of the Autumn following she crossed the sea to meet me at Greenock, where she had scarce landed when she was seized with a malignant fever, which hurried my dear girl to the grave in a few days, before I could even hear of her illness'.

Burns makes no mention of Margaret again until three years later when he composes his song 'Thou Ling'ring Star', which was copied into a letter to Mrs Dunlop dated 8th November 1789 as 'a Song I made the other day'.

Even in the autobiographical letter to Dr Moore carrying his life up to 1787, Burns never recognises Margaret's existence. Why? A 'pretty long tract' covers much more ground than does four or five weeks, the time between Jean Armour going to Paisley and Margaret Campbell leaving Mauchline.

Also the question that must be asked is, that if he had intended to take Margaret with him to the West Indies, why did he purchase only a single one way ticket, costing him £9, which he paid for from the sales of his 'Kilmarnock Edition'? Apparently he did not tell any of his friends that he was intending to take Margaret with him on his journey.

In letters that were written by him during the time of May-October 1786, the time when Margaret and he were supposed to be engaged and leaving the country for a new life abroad, there is no mention of her name anywhere, though Jean Armour is mentioned on numerous occasions.

Was it the fact that although the agreement between Burns and Jean Armour was irregular, and the paper it was written on, destroyed, it was still legal under Scots Law, and therefore any marriage that he entered into after that date would have been bigamous? There had been witnesses to the signing of the marriage document between him and Jean Armour, Burns would not have had a leg to stand on.

What is known is that Burns had decided against going to The Indies by the beginning of September, especially after Jean's twins were born. This was before Margaret had left Campbeltown for Greenock.

Did Burns tell Margaret about his change of plan? He did write to her when they were apart, (her father is alleged to have destroyed these letters after her death) so why didn't he mention the fact that he had decided against leaving Scotland. We don't know the date of their last correspondence, and apparently there is no trace of any letter from Margaret Campbell to Burns.

Burns is quite clear in his afore mentioned quote that Margaret was coming to Greenock to meet him on the first stage of their new life together. Did her wasted journey cost her life? Burns certainly was not there to meet her when the boat docked. Margaret had been in Greenock for a while before her death, yet apparently he did not try to contact her. Why?

If all these things are true, then Burns was correct to feel guilt for the death of Margaret Campbell. He did not bring the typhus to Greenock, but he did bring Margaret Campbell there on a fool's errand, where she caught the disease and died.

A statue of Margaret was erected on the Castle Hill, Dunoon, where she is faced looking over to Ayrshire, for eternity still awaiting her Bard. She was buried in the West Highland Churchyard at Greenock.

In 1920 the Churchyard land was needed because of the expansion of the shipyard. On the 5th November of that year Margaret's grave was opened and the contents of the exhumed. Fourteen people oversaw the event.

Among the remains was found the base of a baby's coffin interred in the grave, and, at the time, this was considered conclusive evidence of Margaret's death in childbirth. But no examination of the child's bones seems to have taken place to find out if the remains were of a stillbirth, or of a child maybe a few weeks old.

It does seem strange that there is information about Margaret's burial, scant though it is, even down to the alleged act of her father cursing the name of Burns at the graveside, but no child or pregnancy is hinted at by anyone at the time, and in October, Margaret would have been at least five months pregnant.

Surely if she or her brother were aware of any pregnancy then there is no way that either of them would have wished for her or her unborn child to be put in such a dangerous situation of nursing a typhus victim, family loyalty or not?

It was also noted at the exhumation, that there were at least two other bodies in the grave with Margaret, so unless the remains of the child were checked with the remains of Margaret and Burns through DNA, then the truth will never be known.

If Margaret had given birth to a full term child, whether the child had survived or not, and we accept the fact that Burns was the father, it means that he definitely knew Margaret earlier than April 1786, the earliest being January of that year. It may even be as early as 1784, when she worked at Coilsfield House as a dairymaid, or the Summer of 1785 when she was employed at Gavin Hamilton's home as nursemaid to his son.

Earlier knowledge of Margaret Campbell is more believable than later knowledge of her. Hamilton was his friend. Montgomerie was his friend. Burns was up to the minute on all the available young females of the surrounding districts.   It is highly unlikely that a woman, a foreigner to those parts, who would stand out like a sore thumb, would slip past Burns' attention so easily.   He was never one to let an occasion pass never mind a period nearing a full year, to become acquainted.

In 1789, around about the third anniversary of Margaret's death, Jean Armour remarked in an interview with John McDiarmid, that she became aware of Burns sinking in to a depressed state.   He went out walking along the banks of the Nith at Ellisland, and stood staring at the brightest light in the sky.   He sat in the shelter of a corn stack for several hours contemplating this light in the winter sky whereupon on his return home he sat down at his desk and immediately started writing his poem/song 'Thou Ling'ring Star'.   Approaching the sixth anniversary of Margaret death he composed the song 'Highland Mary'. To Thomson he wrote

'The foregoing song 'Highland Mary' pleases myself; I think it is in my happiest manner: you will see at first glance that it suits the air.   The subject of the song is one of the most interesting passages of my youthful days; and I own that I should be much flattered to see the verses set to an air, which would insure celebrity.   Perhaps, after all, 'tis the still glowing prejudice of my heart that throws a borrowed lustre over the merits of the composition'.

Thomson's reply was

'Your verses upon 'Highland Mary' are just come to hand; they breathe the genuine spirit of poetry, and, like the music, will last for ever…I have heard the sad story of your Mary: You always seem inspired when you write of her'.

Burns wrote to Thomson on 26th October 1792 regarding the song 'Will Ye Go The Indies'

'In my very early years, when I was thinking of going to the West Indies, I took the following farewell of a dear girl. – It is quite trifling, & has nothing of the merit of 'Ewe-bughts'; but it will fill up this page'.

It is important to point out that not everyone who knew Margaret thought that she was pure, virginal and respectable.   John Richmond, a contemporary and friend who shared a room and bed with Burns during his first sojourn in Edinburgh, is quoted in the Train Manuscript stating

'Mary's character was loose in the extreme, she was kept for some time by a brother of Lord Eglinton's, even while a servant with Gavin Hamilton, and during the period of Burns' attachment, it was well known that her meetings with Montgomerie were open and frequent. The friends of Burns represented to him the impropriety of his devotedness to her, but without producing any change in his sentiments'.

Richmond's story relates that Margaret and Montgomerie were at a tavern in Mauchline called 'the Elbow'. Burns' friends were aware that the couple were there, and to prove to Burns that there was something going on, they took Burns along to the pub. Nothing happened for a while, but just as Burns was accusing his companions of fabrication, Margaret appeared from one of the rooms, blushed and went in again. After another lengthy period, Montgomerie came out of the same room.

'Burns coloured deeply – compressed his lips – and muttered 'damn it'.

Burns' friends thought that that would be it with Margaret but in a few days he returned to her 'Like the dog to it's vomit'.

But there is also another name to disturb and colour the murky waters of this story. In Mauchline, during this time, another highland lassie was living. She was also called Margaret, Margaret McCrae. She had been before the Kirk Session on quite a few occasions for the sin of fornication. It is reported that this Margaret was having an affair with Thomas Montgomerie, another brother to the laird. Are these two stories getting mixed up with the passing of the years? Who knows!

Another name creeps into this convoluted story. According to the Burns Chronicle of 1892 it is reported that there was a 'Mary' Campbell living at Dundonald in 1783 but she had moved to Mauchline by April 1784. This 'Mary' was of a dubious character and had been called before the Kirk session in Dundonald on 25th April 1784 confessing that she had brought forth a child in the parish of Mauchline, stating that John Hay of Paulstone was the father. By 26th February 1786 she was living in the parish of Stair, still looking for John Hay to accept responsibility and pay maintenance for his child. This he eventually did on 17th December 1787.

Now for number four tale in the 'Highland Mary' series, this time from an Archibald Munro who heard it from Margaret Campbell's nephew, Archibald Campbell.

A man called John Blair, a friend of Margaret's uncle, Peter McPherson, met Margaret 'a braw buxom lass, a weel faured dame wi' cheeks like roses', in August 1786 on the road between Kilmacolm and Greenock. Apparently Margaret had come by gig, which had been driven by her lover, from Kilmarnock to Kilmacolm.. As a parting gift he had given her a copy of the Kilmarnock Poems, which was just hot off the press. She was going to the McPherson house and then on to Campbeltown.

According to John Blair, he met with McPherson later that evening and McPherson had the book of poems with him. McPherson went on

'It was Mary (?) Campbell, Jean's (his wife) cousin, wha brought the

90

book wi' her frae Ayr. It's jist new oot ye see. She's awa tae Argyll tae see her freens, an she's comin back in a week or twa tae be merit. An wha dae ye think till? Well it's jist tae the chiel wha made that book'.

He also threw in a wee bit of gossip about Burns who apparently had been fighting in the Kirk, and that he thought 'the lassie might help tae haud him straucht'. (The Glasgow Herald, 30th January 1877)

Yet another story is that a Mr Andrews of Tarbolton is said to have cared for Margaret, but had lost out to Burns. He, it is said, took her and her belongings back to Argyll, when she left Coilsfield. His description of her was that 'she was plain in appearance, but virtuous and amiable'.

Archibald Munro reports that when she was at Campbeltown, Margaret did not busy herself in preparation for her marriage, pregnancy or impending emigration, although she had received letters from Burns, which may or may not have mentioned all three.   (According to *Annie Campbell, Margaret's younger sister, these letters contained poems and songs which were lost when Margaret's father destroyed them).

Instead it is said that Margaret had arranged to take a position with a Colonel McIvor in Glasgow, which she was due to begin at Martinmas (November). She left Campbeltown for Greenock in late September. Due to problems with her father's boat, it was October before she arrived in Greenock. Just in time for the typhus epidemic.

*Miss May Anderson (Mrs Kilgour) resident of Ayr, Ontario and later Chicago told Robert Chambers that her grandmother, (Margaret's sister Annie) had become the confidant of her elder sister as neither of her parents wanted to hear anything about Robert Burns. Annie also learned the songs which Burns sent to Margaret in his letters and when older used to sing them to her own children and grandchildren. According to Mrs Kilgour

'These songs were never in print, although William Anderson (her father, Annie's son, a Canadian emigrant and possessor of the Burns Bibles) had given some of the songs he had heard his mother sing to a William Motherwell who was collecting all he could in regard to Burns' poems, for a work he was busy with then. But he died before it was ready to be published, so the songs were never printed'. (Taken from 'Concerning Highland Mary' by Rev. William Wye Smith).

In June 1787, Burns went on his West Highland Tour, apparently alone. Unusual for him, he did not keep a journal. Whether he took the time to visit Margaret Campbell's grave, no one knows.   But according to Margaret's mother, he did find time to visit her. The old lady had a grand nephew, J.C. Douglas who lived in Greenock, and he asked his grand aunt if Burns and Margaret would ever have gotten married.   She said she couldn't know what would have happened had Margaret not died, but that

'She didn't think her sweet lassie could have ever been happy with so wild and profane a genius as Burns'.

But she went on to say that he was a 'real warm-hearted chiel', for that was the impression he had given when he had visited her.

Agnes Begg, daughter of Isabella, Burns' youngest sister, sent a letter to Robert Chambers on 21st January 1850 from Bridgehouse in Ayr regarding Burns and Margaret Campbell.

'Mr Douglas *(William Scott Douglas)* is perfectly right with regard to Burns and his 'Highland Mary's' short love passage. It was in 1786, just as he supposes; at least so my mother has all along thought, from a revulsion of feeling attendant on the heartless desertion of him by Jean Armour. He just then became acquainted with Mary Campbell, who was acting as nursery-maid in the family of Gavin Hamilton. He must have known her previously to that time, though his love-fit had only begun then. My mother has no doubt that he meant to marry her'.

As James Mackay points out in his biography of Burns, although her name was Margaret, everyone, including all of her family members, seemed to fall under the spell of referring to her as Mary, allowing the legend of 'Highland Mary' to flourish. The fact that she was hardly ever spoken about by the Burns family, her workmates, James Currie in his biography, or even her own family, allowed the legend to take on the mystery and mystique which it still holds today, over two hundred years later.

Mary's father is buried in Kilkerran Cemetery, Campbeltown. Her mother, who died on 27th September 1827 in Greenock is reputed to be buried beside Margaret. (It is also alleged that they may both be buried in the same grave as Margaret). Chambers reports that old Mrs Campbell, her sons Archibald who died in 1817 and Robert who died in 1821 are buried in the Duncan Street Burying-ground. Annie, Margaret's younger sister married a James Anderson, stonemason in Greenock on 6th August 1792. He died at Renton on 23rd March 1828 and Annie died on 23rd January 1824. Margaret has two nieces buried at Renton.

As a footnote, the song 'Flow Gently Sweet Afton' was claimed to have been written for a young woman called Mary Murdoch of 'Ashmark' New Cumnock, a niece of Burns' friend John Logan of Laight. Burns often stayed over with John Logan, who was included in the poem 'The Kirk's Alarm', named as 'Afton's Laird'. Burns is said to have been very fond of Mary, who was a great favourite of his.

Associated Songs:

Song   : The Highland Lassie O
Tune   : McLauchlin's Scots Measure
Period : 1786

Song   : Afton Water
Tune   : Afton Water
Period : pre 5th February 1789

Song   : Thou Ling'ring Star
Tune   : Captain Cook's Death
Period : circa October/November 1789

Song   : Will Ye Go To The Indies
Tune   : Ewe-Bughts Marion
Period : 27th October 1792

Song   : Highland Mary
Tune   : Lady Catherine Ogie
Period : 14th November 1792

17.

JEAN ARMOUR
Born 25th February 1765 – Died 26thMarch 1834

Chronology : Either circa May 1784 or circa May 1785

Jean Armour was born on 25th February 1765 in Mauchline, the daughter of master mason James Armour and his wife Mary Smith. She was the second child and eldest daughter of eleven children born to the Armours, who lived in the Cowgate in the centre of Mauchline. She remained with her family until she was nearly twenty-three years of age, when, allegedly, her parents turned her out of their house after learning of her second pregnancy to Robert Burns.

Jean was her father's favourite, and for her part seems to have had a great deal of respect for the man, which may have contributed to her having received a much better education than did most of the other girls of the village at that time. Jean was a good reader and letter writer, and in no way could considered illiterate, a slur which has been cast on her by some of the early biographers of Burns who chose to portray Jean as unlettered, naïve and very unsophisticated.

Jean used to help Burns by reading through his poems, giving her opinion on them as any critic would. She would also sing through his songs to him, until he transcribed them to his satisfaction. Burns appreciated and trusted her advice, and this he mentioned in quite a few of his letters.

Burns knew of Jean's love of the 'Scotch Tongue', and was aware that her memory for the old tunes and the old words were second to none. He never underestimated her, she was his own personal researcher, and she would be the first one he turned to if he needed words for an air, or an air to fit his words. Their home must have been a very musical one.

Jean, with her amazing memory bank of traditional songs, would sing to Burns, with her 'wood-note wild'. Vocally it is said she had an easy Top B, which means that she probably had a couple of notes higher to play with if she needed them. She was definitely in the country of the first soprano. This could be why so many of Burns' songs are in the high setting. From her singing of the old 'sangs', Burns would take down the words and the music in order to preserve them for future generations.

We probably owe a lot to Jean Armour for many of the songs around today as without her recall they may well have been lost in the mists of time.

Although Burns had many 'flings' in his short lifespan, the women that he was really serious about, Peggy Chalmers, Agnes MacLehose, Jean Lorimer, Maria Riddell, Jean Armour and Margaret Campbell, all had verse and song coursing through their veins. Even people like Agnes Fleming and Anna Park attracted him more because they had beautiful voices.

I suppose, at the end of the day, Jean Armour must have considered herself lucky that he became a poet and not a choirmaster. He could have fathered a small village from the soprano section alone.

Peter J Westwood, in his book 'Jean Armour, Mrs Robert Burns' says of her

'From the description handed down by those who knew her at the early and later part of her life, we gather that she was a remarkably sweet and attractive brunette of a bright affectionate nature, gifted with an attractive smiling face, lightened by a pair of very bewitching dark eyes. Her person was well formed and firmly knit and her movements were at all times graceful and easy. In manner she was frank and unaffected, kindly and winning in her disposition'.

Nellie Martin (nee Miller) said of Jean in the booklet 'Mauchline Memories of Robert Burns', that she was

'a common looking lass, with nothing remarkable about her but her black eyes, and that she was always either singing or dancing'.

A man called John Brodie gave his opinion of her in the book 'Dumfries and Galloway Lore'

'She was weel-faured an kind, only a wee bit thouless; a better natured woman I never saw. She needed, for Rob was nae saunct'.

Though sibling rivalry from her sister Janet, sixteen years younger than Jean, states

'Oor Jean wisna bonnie, I was a far bra'er lass masel'.

Other descriptions of the young Jean said that she was above middle height, dark complexioned, had irregular features, a neat figure, jet black eyes, a pleasing address, a gentle disposition and was a fine singer and a graceful dancer. Or as Burns puts it in one of the verses in his 'Address to the Deil' (before his falling out with the Armours)

'Lang syne, in Eden's happy scene
When strappin' Adam's days were green'
And Eve was like my bonie Jean-

My dearest part'
A dancin', sweet, young, handsome queen,
O' guileless heart'.

On her death in 1834, John McDiarmid, editor of the Dundee Courier and friend of Jean for the last fifteen years of her life, wrote

'When young she must have been a handsome, comely woman, if not indeed a beauty, when the poet saw her for the first time on a bleach-green at Mauchline. Her limbs were cast in the finest mould; and up to middle life, her jet-black eyes were clear and sparkling, her carriage easy, and her step light. The writer of this sketch never saw Mrs Burns dance nor heard her sing; but he has learnt from others that she moved with great grace on the floor, and chaunted her 'woodnotes wild' in a style but rarely equalled by unprofessional singers. Her voice was a brilliant treble, and in singing 'Cooleen', and 'I Gaed a Waefu' Gate Yestreen' *(written by Burns for Jean Jaffrey)* and other songs, she rose without effort as high as a B natural'.

Burns obviously saw something that he liked, because although he had his choice of the young women of the area, he considered Jean Armour 'the jewel for me o' them a''.

The traditional story that has passed down of the first meeting of Jean and Burns is that…there was a building in Mauchline called Morton's ballroom, which held weekly dances. Hugh Morton, father to Christina, one of the 'Mauchline Belles' owned this ballroom. At the end of race week circa end of April/beginning of May 1784 or 1785, (depending on the biographer, but today considered to be more likely 1785), Burns and Jean were in attendance at the dance there, but not in each other's company. Both were dancing with other partners, when Burns' dog came on the floor and followed him around while he was still dancing. Burns is supposed to have remarked that 'He wished he could get any of the lassies to like him as his dog did'.

A few days after the dance, Burns was walking through the green in Mauchline where Jean was spreading out the clean clothes on the grass to bleach in the sunshine. His dog ran onto her washing with its muddy paws. She shouted at Burns to get the dog under control, this he did apologising. During their conversation Jean is reputed to have asked him

'Have you found any lassie yet to love you as well as your dog'?

The relationship grew from there.

Jean disagreed with this account, maybe not wanting to appear forward, and when interviewed by John McDiarmid in 1827 she gave her version

'The first time I ever saw Burns was in Mauchline. His family then lived in Mossgiel, about a mile from the village. I was spreading clothes in a bleach-green along with some girls, when the poet passed on his way to call on Mr Hamilton. He had a little dog, which ran on the clothes, and I scolded, and threw something at the animal. Burns said 'Lassie, if ye thought ought o' me, ye widna hurt my dog'. – I thought to myself – 'I wadna think much o' you at ony rate'! I saw him afterwards at a dancing-room, and we fell acquainted'.

This meeting took place round about April 1785 and by the Autumn of that year they were considered a courting couple, though not with the approval of Jean's father, who was kept in the dark. Before the year was out, love and nature had taken its course and Jean was pregnant.

There is another story of the first meeting of Robert and Jean, which is recounted in Peter Westwood's book 'Jean Armour' and this reads thus.

Jean Armour came from a musical household. Her mother loved music and wanted her children to be as proficient as they could in it, and apparently the house was always full of singing and dancing. Jean, who had an excellent voice, was sent to singing lessons. *John Blane, a friend of Burns, was also a pupil at the same singing school.

*In 'Wood's Songs of Scotland' there is information regarding some of the people who were acquainted with Burns. This information was collected by Captain Charles Gray, and apparently when Burns' sister, Mrs Isabella Begg, heard of the death of John Blane, whom she did not seem to like, she is reported to have said to one of her daughters

'There that impudent bodie, John Blane, has slippit awa' before I could get to Kilmarnock to scold him for the great lees he told about my brother'.

One night at a Fasten's E'en (Shrovetide) *'rocking' at Mossgiel, Blane was discussing with Burns a male singer called Ralph Sillar who obviously had a high vocal opinion of himself. Blane commented 'I would not give Jean Armour for a score of him'.

*Gilbert Burns explained the term 'rocking as

'derived from those primitive times when the country-women employed their spare hours in spinning on a rock or distaff. This simple instrument is a very portable one, and well fitted into the social inclination of meeting in a neighbour's house; hence the phrase of going a-rocking or with the rock. As the connection the phrase had with the implement was forgotten when the rock gave place to the spinning-wheel, the phrase came to be used by both sexes on social occasions, and men talk of going with their rocks as well as women'.

Burns is supposed to have commented that Blane was always talking about Jean Armour and maybe Blane had a thing going for her. He said that he wanted to see this Jean Armour for himself.

The story carries on that the next night Burns and Blane waited outside the music school for the singing class to finish. Jean was approached by Blane, who was acting as the poet's 'black-foot' (go-between) and asked if she would like to meet with Burns. She agreed, but only if she were allowed to bring a companion, (obviously hearing of Burns' reputation, maybe that is where the attraction lay). She took Christina Morton (who it is claimed also had a penchant for Burns), and the relationship began from that time.

Whatever story is the correct one, Jean still ended up pregnant. Gilbert Burns told Currie, the first Biographer of Burns, that when Robert found out about the pregnancy, the couple worked out a plan

'It was agreed therefore between them (Jean and Robert) that they should make a legal acknowledgement of an irregular and private marriage; that he should go to Jamaica to push his fortune, and that she should remain with her father till it might please Providence to put the means of supporting a family in his power'.

When Jean's father found out about the pregnancy, and especially who the father was, he was humiliated, scandalised and shocked to such a degree that he fainted away and had to be brought to with the administration of a cordial by his, also very upset, but less overly-ostentatious wife.

William Patrick, who knew old Armour, was interviewed by William Jolly in 1859 and was asked why old Armour objected to Burns courting his daughter?

'The thing was, he hated him, an would raither hae seen the De'il himsel comin tae the hoose tae coort his dochter than him! He cu'dna bear the sicht o'm' and that was the way he did it'.

In this interview, recorded in Mauchline, William Jolly gave this description of James Armour from Mr Patrick's testimony

'Old Mr Armour was a kind of contractor or master builder employing other masons, he and his sons being 'as guid workmen as ever lifted mell' (a maul or a wooden hammer used by masons to drive the iron chisel). He owned his own house and several others near it in the Cowgate, had a good business, thought himself of the well-to-do class, and held no small opinion of his own consequence. He was of the stricter or 'Auld Licht' sort and therefore, by instinct and profession, disliked all freer ways, especially when combined with cleverness and sarcastic power. He would seem, however, not to have been perfectly correct in his own habits, though hard on others. It is certain he had little liking for the poet when he came courting his daughter'.

'What kind of man was old Armour'? Asked Mr Jolly. 'Surely a person of consequence in Mauchline, judging from his treatment of Burns'? 'Ow he was only a bit mason body, who used to snuff a good deal, and gay af'en tak a bit dram'.

The *legal acknowledgement that Burns and Jean had drawn up was intended to show to everyone that they considered themselves to be husband and wife. Under Scot's Law of the day it would have been considered lawful

Jean's father thought that it was, as he took it to the lawyer Robert Aiken and demanded that he mutilate and deface the document making it null and void.   To calm James Armour down, Robert Aiken, although a lawyer and a friend of Burns at the time, cut the names of the parties concerned out of the offending paper.

The question is would Aiken have done this if the contract were in any way binding, as he would have been in serious trouble with the Legal Establishment had they ever found out?   Then again the document had been witnessed and that adds to its legitimacy.   Another question could also be asked, that if there were witnesses to this verbal arrangement between Burns and Jean Armour, was a piece of paper necessary anyway?

*The doctrine laid down by Erskine on this subject is

> 'Marriage may be without doubt perfected by the consent of parties declared by writing, provided the writing be so conceived as necessarily to impart their present consent.   The proof of marriage is not confined to the testimonies of the clergyman and witnesses present at the ceremony.   The subsequent acknowledgement of it by the parties is sufficient to support the marriage, if it appears to have been made not in a jocular manner, and with deliberation'.

But maybe on balance mollifying an angry and threatening James Armour, builder to trade, who had friends with large muscles, might have seemed the more prudent thing to do at the time, if only to stop him from turning blue and having a heart seizure in his office.

Where the document went from there, from that day to this no one knows, as it has never seen the light of day since.

According to 'Honest' Allan Cunningham there is another tale to the document story

> 'The father of Jean Armour, heard with much anguish, of his favourite daughter's condition, and when on her knees before him she implored forgiveness, and showed the marriage lines, his anguish grew into anger which overflowed all bounds, and heeded neither his daughter's honour nor her husband's fame.   He snatched the marriage certificate from her, threw it into the fire, and commanded her to think herself no longer the wife of the poet.   It must be accepted proof of paternal power that Jean trembled and obeyed; she forgot that Burns was still her husband in the sight of Heaven, and according to the laws of man. She refused to see him or even hearken to aught he could say; and in short was ruled in everything by the blind hatred of her father'.

Cunningham, as usual, is a bit melodramatic, and his versions of the Burns story must all be taken with a large packet of salt.   He was more like a tabloid reporter than a serious biographer.   Jean Armour was very unhappy with what Cunningham was saying about Burns after his death.

Somewhere between these two stories may lie the mystery of the disappearance of the mutilated document, one that may never be solved.

Whichever story is correct as to what happened to the marriage contract, Burns took the destruction of the document very badly, and in a letter to Gavin Hamilton, which supports the first version of events, and Robert Aiken's part in it, on 15th April 1786 he writes

'Apropos, old Mr Armour prevailed with him to mutilate that unlucky paper yesterday - Would you believe it? Tho' I had not a hope, nor even a wish, to make her mine after her (damnable) conduct, yet when he told me, the names were all cut out of the paper, my heart died within me, and he cut my very veins with the news - Perdition seize her falsehood, and perjurious perfidy! But God bless her and forgive my poor, once dear, misguided girl - She is ill-advised - Do not despise me, Sir, I am indeed a fool, but a knave is an infinitely worse character than any body, I hope, will dare to give the unfortunate Robt Burns'.

In late March Jean's parents sent her to relatives in Paisley, to an uncle called Andrew Purdie, who was a carpenter. There she could have her child away from the snooping of the Kirk Session officers. Her parents probably also intended to keep her away from Burns until she had come to her senses as regards him. For about nine weeks Jean lived with her mother's sister and her husband at Sneddon.

Entry in the minutes of the Mauchline Kirk Session on 2nd April 1786 -

'The Session being informed that Jean Armour, an unmarried woman, is said to be with child, and that she has gone off from the place of late, to reside elsewhere, the Session think it is their duty to enquire...But appoint James Lamie and William Fisher (*Holy Willie*) to speak to the parents'.

Entry for April 9th 1786 –

'James Lamie reports that he spoke to Mary Smith, mother to Jean Armour, who told him that she did not suspect her daughter to be with child, that she was gone to Paisley to see her friends, and would return soon'.

Apparently at the last visit, when Jean's mother answered the door, James Armour hid behind the door in another room, as he was too embarrassed to meet the kirk's men. At least he didn't faint this time...

James Armour hoped that Jean would soon forget all about Burns in her stay in Paisley, and maybe take up with someone else, someone a bit more suitable, a man more fitted to old Armour's taste.

Into the picture stepped a Mauchline man who was living in Paisley at this time. He was Robert Wilson, a prosperous weaver. Wilson was about eighteen years older than Jean, and had moved to the Paisley area to set up a factory there. Wilson was obviously aware of Jean in Mauchline, and may have carried a torch for her. He must have realised about the pregnancy. But this did not seem to matter to him.

He showed interest in her by calling on her on a number of occasions. But Jean was not interested in Robert Wilson, even when he told her that if she were not to become the wife of Robert Burns, he would engage himself to no other girl, while she remained single. This man was serious.

Though Wilson was a good catch, seemed to care for Jean a lot and obviously would have been much more in line with what her father wanted for a son in law, Jean refused his marriage proposal and turned him down gently. There was no hope for Wilson or anyone else for that matter, not when there was a Robert Burns still available for the taking.

But what would worry Jean were the stories that were coming from Mauchline regarding Burns and Margaret Campbell. She would hear about Robert through letters from friends, and from the visitors that came to her uncle and aunt's house. Of course, when she was visited by any of her family, Burns would not have been left with a name to call himself.

That was Paisley, but what was happening in Ayrshire?

With Wilson coming from Mauchline, Robert would have known him and probably realised that he was a serious contender for Jean's affection. Wilson may have been a lot older, but he could supply, at the time, the stability and security that Burns could not. He would also be aware that old Armour's preference was for this man, and that the old man would be trying with all his might to get Wilson and Jean together.

When false rumour reached him that Jean and Wilson were to be married, no doubt helped along by Jean's parents, he was furious and more than a little jealous. The idea of another man bringing up his child did not sit very well on his shoulders either and worried him a great deal.

Years later Burns got his revenge on Jean for this episode, when he wrote the song 'The Gallant Weaver' which was about Robert Wilson's attempted courtship of Jean Armour. It must have appealed to Burns' sense of humour to have Jean sing this song for him, the song written about his rival in love, over and over again until he got it down to his satisfaction.

Poor Jean no matter how much she may have argued that it was not her idea to go to Paisley, and that she had been parentally evicted from Mauchline, she was on a hiding to none. The song must always have ended in gales of laughter.

To return to 1786. Burns was a proud man and his pride had been hurt. He had been ready and willing to marry Jean, but she had deserted him (totally ignoring the fact that it had been her parents who had sent her away). Jean had let him down badly when she gave the marriage document to her father, which ended in it being destroyed (again ignoring the fact that old Armour was of a stern, unbending Calvinistic nature used to being obeyed, especially in his own house by his own children).

The fact that James Armour was also attempting to have Burns jailed, thus making the poet flee the village and go into hiding till the dust settled, didn't help matters, even if this action was all just a little exciting to someone with a brilliant imagination, especially to a poet with words pulsing through his veins instead of blood.

Burns decided that he had had enough of Jean and her father. He asked for and eventually received a certificate from the Kirk Session to show that he was, in the eyes of the Kirk, a single man again. He received this certification of bachelorhood after his third sitting at the 'creepie-chair' in August and his third admittance of his part in the affair with Jean.

Jean had admitted her guilt by letter, and apologised to the session on her return to Mauchline on 9th June 1786. She, sensible woman, did not appear in person and her letter said

'I am heartily sorry that I have given and must give your Session trouble on my account. I acknowledge that I am with child, and Robert Burns in Mossgiel is the father. I am, with great respect, your most humble servant, Jean Armour'.

From the minutes of the August Kirk session

'August 6th 1786 – Robert Burns, John Smith, Mary Lindsay, Jean Armour and Agnes Auld appeared before the Congregation professing their repentance for the sin of fornication, and they having each appeared two several Sabbaths formerly, were this day rebuked and absolved from the scandal'.

The rebuke went as follows

'You appear there to be rebuked, and at the same time making profession of repentance for ye sin of fornication.

The frequency of this sin is just matter of lamentation among Christians, and affords just ground of deep humiliation to the guilty persons themselves.

We call you to reflect seriously in contrition of heart in all the instances of your sin and guilt, in their numbers, high aggravation, and unhappy consequences, and say, having done foolishly, will do so no more.

Beware of returning again to your sin, as some of you have done, like the dog to his vomit, or the sow that is washed to her wallowing in the mire'.

Why Jean came back from Paisley nearly three months before her babies were due no one knows. She obviously respected her parents and their wishes when she left for Paisley, so she knew that they would be very angry with her for returning. Her parents had also lied to the Kirk Session regarding Jean's pregnancy. But it also showed that Jean was made of stern stuff.

Maybe she had heard of Burns intention to go abroad? Maybe she had heard of his carryings on in her absence, and felt he was getting out of control? Burns himself admitted to 'mischief and other such things' in a letter to a friend. Maybe she had heard about Margaret Campbell being on the scene? Maybe she just missed the man? She had always been in love with Burns, heart and soul, totally and completely.

Jean was not stupid. She had been given a good education as befitted the child of a self employed master tradesman, and in Mauchline terms this meant being one of the middle-class. She must have realised that unless she was in Mauchline, there was no way she would be able to have any influence on anything that happened. If Burns' intention was to emigrate, so be it. If his intention was to marry 'Highland Mary', so be it.

The way she felt about this man, she could not watch from the sidelines. Being a bystander was not an option. Even if she lost the main role, at least she could still have an impact on the play. If both the aforementioned things were to happen, Burns emigrating, Burns marrying Margaret Campbell, by being on the scene she would have satisfied herself that she had done all she could to hold on to the only man she could ever love.

Jean must have considered that what she was doing was correct, and it certainly showed an element of spirit. Returning to Mauchline would prove to her family how much she really did love Burns.

Through the grapevine she may have become aware that Robert was becoming less enthusiastic about going abroad, and little or nothing was being heard regarding Margaret Campbell, who was by now at home in Campbeltown many, many miles away.

With no one else in the picture Jean must have thought that it was only time before she and Burns would be officially husband and wife, especially as she would soon have the goods in her arms, their child.

Jean probably thought the timescale for their official marriage would be greatly shortened when on Sunday 3rd September 1786 she gave birth to twins, a girl and boy.

Burns visited Jean and was delighted by his children. He brought presents for them and their mother, and even gifts for Jean's parents. As the twins were illegitimate (but were they?) the tradition in those days, was that they were named after their parents as opposed to their grandparents.

The strange anomaly about Burns is that although he was not a particularly natural and faithful husband, he did appear to be a natural born father as regards his children. He always had time and patience for them, and, on Jean Armour's testimony, their noise did not seem to bother him, even when he was working.

To Robert Muir in Kilmarnock he wrote.

'You will have heard that poor Armour has repaid my amorous mortgages double. A very fine boy and girl have awakened a thousand feelings that thrill, some with tender pleasure and some with foreboding anguish, thro' my soul'. At the end of the letter he finished with 'I believe that all hopes of staying at home will be abortive'.

Robert had been changing his mind about Jamaica, especially since the publishing of the 'Kilmarnock Edition' of his poems and the success it had achieved. Jamaica didn't seem like such a great prospect now, although he was still swithering back and forwards.

To Robert Aiken he wrote that everything seemed to point to him going, but the birth of his children made that different now

'All these reasons urge me to go abroad, and to all these reasons I have only one answer – the feelings of a father. This, in the present mood I am in, overbalances everything that can be laid in the scale against it'.

He also had Jean on his mind when he wrote to Gavin Hamilton in the first week of 1787

'To tell the truth among friends, I feel a miserable blank in my heart, with want of her, and I don't think I shall ever meet with so delicious an armful again. She has her faults; and so have you and I; and so has everybody'.

The twins were brought up in separate households. The boy, Robert, was with Burns' mother at Mossgiel while the girl, Jean, who was a sickly child, remained at the Armour house with her mother. Burns seems to have kept out the way for a time in 1787, though it must have been hard on him being separated from one of his children.

From May to June of that year he went on his Border tour with Robert Ainslie. On his return from the tour he visited his daughter at the Armour's house.

On this summer visit the Armour's treated Burns in a much pleasanter manner, it was in fact so pleasant that he felt sickened at their behaviour. At some point or another, Burns and Jean were left alone.

The parents must have been very naïve if they thought that the couple, who obviously still had the 'hots' for each other, would, when alone, find only the weather to discuss. On the first chance they had some quality time together since the twins had been born, they did what came naturally to them. Ending with the exact same consequences as before.

Burns left soon after this visit to go on his West Highland tour, half of which, it is thought, he made on his own. The other part of the tour was made with George Grierson, a friend from Glasgow.

This solo tour is allegedly when he called on Mrs Campbell, Margaret's mother, but neither she nor he mentioned if he had visited Margaret's grave in Greenock.

On his return to Mauchline, he very quickly set off again on another Highland tour, this time with William Nicol, and when this one was over he returned home again only for a short time, before he set off on his Stirlingshire tour with Dr Adair. He spent the rest of 1787 and the first two months of 1788 in Edinburgh. So he may not have seen Jean again for at least six months.

Jean's parents were furious and disappointed with her when they found out about her second pregnancy to Burns, even although Robert was gaining celebrity status. A second edition of his poems was being considered for publication, and he may have become a respectable son in law for them to acquire if only they would relent a little bit. They allegedly refused to allow her to stay under their roof, and in the winter of 1787 Jean had to find other accommodation.

Burns was in Edinburgh dallying, by letter, with Agnes McLehose in the winter of 1787. For most of December 1787 and January 1788 he was laid up with an injured knee, which he received in a fall from a carriage caused by an inebriate coachman. A letter arrived from his brother Gilbert, telling him about the unfortunate situation Jean was in, having been 'cast out' of her parent's home (as per Gilbert's account).

According to Burns, he sent a letter to a Willie Muir, owner of 'Tarbolton (Willie's) Mill, asking him to give Jean shelter until he could return to Mauchline. Jean testifies that she was the one who went to the 'Muir's' herself, long before Burns wrote his letter, asking for lodgings in order to get away from her seriously angry and disappointed father.

Jean had no reason whatsoever to lie about this. She had always been her father's favourite child, a fact she was very aware of, and he felt let down by her behaviour.

Burns did return, on the 22nd February 1788, where he arranged for a room in the town for Jean and a Dr MacKenzie, who later married Helen Miller one of the Mauchline Belles, to look after her.

What went on in Burns head on his return to Mauchline is a mystery. He wrote letters at this time to Agnes McLehose and Robert Ainslie regarding Jean, none of which are complimentary. He seems to be looking for a big pat on the back a judgement of how good he is to this poor creature, ignoring the fact that he is at least half to blame for her condition.

In Agnes' letter dated 23rd February he writes

'I, this morning, as I came home, called for a certain woman *(Jean Armour).* I am disgusted with her – I cannot endure her! I, while my heart smote me for the profanity, tried to compare her with my Clarinda; 'twas setting the expiring glimmer of a farthing taper beside the cloudless glory of the meridian sun'.

This is how he wrote of the woman who must have been so grateful and happy to see this man again who owned her completely.

Another distasteful letter written to Robert Ainslie on 3rd March 1788 *(sometimes referred to as the 'Horse litter' letter)* describes his return to Mauchline and his meeting again with Jean, where a very angry and aggressive bout of lovemaking took place. This was after, on his own admittance, he used his power to scare the vulnerable young woman.

Burns hadn't seen Jean for the eight months of her pregnancy. She had been allegedly kicked out of her family home and was alone, living with strangers, at a time when she should have been being cared for at home by a loving partner or at least loving parents, and during that eight months one of her children had died. Jean, the little girl passes away, circa 20th October 1787, according to Burns by 'careless, murdering mischance'.

And where was Burns? He certainly was not there for her when she needed him. It really took a big man to frighten and bully a lonely young woman in the final month of her pregnancy. The letter to Ainslie reads

'I have been through sore tribulation and under much buffeting of the Wicked One since I came to this country. Jean I found banished, like a martyr – forlorn, destitute and friendless: All for the good old cause. I have reconciled her to her fate, and I have reconciled her to her mother. I have taken her a room. I have taken her to my arms. I have given her a mahogany bed. I have given her a guinea, and I have f----d till she rejoiced with joy unspeakable and full of glory. But, as I always am on every occasion, I have been prudent and cautious to an astonishing degree. I swore her privately and solemnly never to attempt any claim on me as a husband, even though anybody should persuade her she had such a claim (which she had not), neither during my life nor after my death. She did all this like a good girl, and I took the opportunity of some dry horse litter, and gave her such a thundering scalade that electrified the very marrow of her bones. Oh, what a peacemaker is a guid wee-willy pintle! It is the mediator, the guarantee, the umpire, the bond of union, the solemn league and covenant, the plenipotentiary, the Aaron's rod, the Jacob's staff, the prophet Elisha's pot of oil, the Ahasuerus' Sceptre, the sword of mercy, the philosopher's stone, the Horn of Plenty, and Tree of Life between Man and Woman'.

It is interesting to note that most of the Victorian Burnsians refuse to print this letter in full, and in many of the old biographies there is just a line of dots after the words 'I have reconciled her to her mother...' Quite clearly this letter showed the nasty, shallow, distasteful side of Burns, which these people were intent on hiding. What we must also remember is that there is no excuse that this letter was written with a bottle of port by his side. It was from the heart, and written completely sober.

Jean gave birth to another set of twins, girls this time, in the first week of March (the family bible states - March 3rd 1788, were born to them twins again, two daughters, who died within a few days of their birth), one died on March 10th the other March 22nd.

The date of the birth of these children has been disputed, and some biographers consider that they were born on the 9th March, which would fall in line with the dates given by the parish burial register. Neither child was baptised and the Mauchline burial register has two entries 'Jean Armour's child, unbaptised' on both the aforementioned dates.

In none of his correspondences during or after this time does Burns ever make any comment on these children. It is as though they never existed.

Did Burns link his bullying temper, aggressive lovemaking and unnecessarily violent attitude to Jean on his return to their deaths? Who knows! It is possible that at a time when child mortality was high, they would have died anyway.

Jean was under a great deal of stress at this time. She had not seen Burns for practically the whole of her pregnancy. When her furious parents had found out about her condition she was allegedly cast out into the wintry elements by her furious parents. Added to this was her grief over the death of her first daughter. All of these things could have combined to weaken her strength and the children in her womb, though they were both carried to full term. But we can certainly be sure that Burns' inexcusable behaviour did not help to reduce Jean's anxiety in any way.

Jean's account of this time, taken from a 'Memoranda by Mr McDiarmid from Mrs Burns' Dictation' is

'The father *(James Armour)* was no doubt angry that his daughter

107

continued to correspond with the Bard – after he had written to her – but he had no opportunity of turning her out of doors.   Her mother had warned her that her father was angry, and that she had better remain from home a little.   She was then on a visit to William Muir, miller, Tarbolton Mill'.

So does this testimony mean that Jean chose to leave home, rather than face her father's anger?   And does this mean that her father has been vilified for two centuries for throwing her out in the middle of winter with nowhere to stay, when all he needed was time to calm down?

The house in Mauchline rented for Jean by Burns, was opposite Nance Tannock's Inn, and had two rooms, one of which was a kitchen.   It is said that this is the room that Burns rented and in that room Jean gave birth to their twins, not Willie's Mill, as some have thought.

Burns eventually married Jean in a civil service, though he kept it secret for a while.   Why all this cloak and dagger carry on, no one knows, especially as marriage was one of the suggestions put to him, which would help his entry into the Excise.   Jean, as usual, complied in this secret.

Burns was very keen to become an Exciseman and now as a married man with a family to support, he was looked on as being more dependable and responsible, though his relationship with Jean was one that everyone knew about anyway.

The marriage is said to have taken place in the writing office of Gavin Hamilton in Mauchline, and was performed by John Farquhar-Gray J.P of Gilmilnscroft, Sorn.   Ronald's Inn and Morton's Ballroom have also been put forward as alternative places where the marriage took place.

He wrote to his friend, James Smith who was now living in Linlithgow on the 28th April 1788

'There is, you must know, a certain clean-limbed, handsome bewitching young Hussy of your acquaintance, to whom I have lately and privately given a matrimonial title to my Corpus.   I hate to presage ill-luck; and as my girl in some late random trials has been doubly kinder to me than even the best of women usually are to their Partners of our Sex, in similar circumstances; I reckon on twelve times a brace of children against I celebrate my twelfth wedding-day'.

This is the first letter in which Jean is openly referred to as Mrs Burns by Robert and it is thought that the marriage took place late March early April 1788, but no document to show the actual date has come to light.   Yet!

Above: Jean Armour in later years.

Below: Willie's Mill (Photo circa 1900). Jean left her parents' home to live here for a while during her second pregancy to Burns. The birth was at Mauchline and produced twin girls both of whom died within a few days.

There was a Rev Dr Niven, minister of Dunkeld, who knew Burns in his younger days, and according to his son, John Dick Niven, his father told him that a Professor Walker and himself were present when Burns first acknowledged Jean Armour as his wife. This information was related to George Farquhar Graham, Editor of 'Wood's Songs of Scotland'. There is another little tale regarding the friendship between Dr Niven and Burns.

Dr Niven, when he was attending College in Edinburgh, fell into a severe illness. Burns visited him every evening bringing along with him humorous verses he had composed to be used as epitaphs on Niven's imaginary tombstone. No doubt all the laughter helped cure him in double quick time.

Others heard of the marriage second hand. Agnes McLehose heard of it from Robert Ainslie, and Mrs Dunlop heard it from her son Andrew. In August 1788 the private marriage was recognised by the Kirk Session, and Burns made his peace with them, for the time being anyway.

'1788, August 5th – Compeared Robert Burns, with Jean Armour, his alleged Spouse. They both acknowledge their irregular marriage, and their sorrow for that irregularity, and desiring that the Session will take such steps as may seem to them proper, in order to Solemn Confirmation of the said marriage

The Session, taking this affair under their consideration, agree that they both be rebuked for this acknowledged irregularity, and that they be taken solemnly engaged to adhere faithfully to one another as husband and wife all the days of their life.

In regard the Session have a title in Law to some fine for behoof of the Poor, they agree to refer Mr. Burns his own generosity.

The above Sentence was accordingly executed, and the Session absolved the said parties from any scandal on this account.

William Auld, Moderator
    Robt. Burns
    Jean Armour
(Mr. Burns gave a guinea-note for behoof of the poor).

After years of proposing and being rejected, Burns was eventually a married man, and marriage seemed to be to Burns' liking. In a letter to Mrs. Dunlop date stamped 17th July 1788

'In short, I can easily fancy a more agreeable companion for my journey of Life, but, upon my honor, I have never seen in individual instance! – You are right that a Bachelor state would have assured me more friends; but from a cause you will easily guess, conscious Peace in the enjoyment of my own mind, and unmistrusting Confidence in approaching my God, would seldom have been of the number'.

Jean and Burns had nine children together. Jean was an exceptionally caring and incredibly understanding woman. She took in not one but two of Burns' illegitimate children to her household, Elizabeth Paton Burns, until her return to Mossgiel, and Elizabeth Park Burns, bringing them up as her own, though her statement (if she ever really did say that) 'our Robbie should have had twa wives' is a bit out of place today.

Jean Armour was Burns' rock, his constant, his touchstone. Jean's very fine singing voice, her 'woodnote wild', was one of the first things that attracted Burns to her. Maybe that spurred his interest in collecting Scots song, as up until the time they met, most of what he had written was verse. It must have been a great help to him to know what his songs would sound like when he had finished painting his musical canvas. Jean would sing them through until they sounded the way he wanted. She also read though all of his poetry and was a keen critic.

When Burns was on duty for the Excise, which often kept him away from home, Jean oversaw the farm and the workers, making sure it ran like clockwork. Not bad for a lassie who was not country bred, and who has on occasions been summarily dismissed as being illiterate and bland.

On writing to Margaret Chalmers Burns says of Jean

'If I have not got polite tattle, modish manners, and fashionable dress, I am not sickened and disgusted with the multiform curse of boarding-school affectation; and I have got the handsomest figure, the sweetest temper, the soundest constitution, and the kindest heart in the country'.

Robert Ainslie in a letter to Agnes McLehose said of Jean, whom he apparently did not take to when he met her in the winter of 1790 at a kirn-night at Ellisland, when the harvest-home was celebrated.

'With regard to the helpmate. She seems Vulgar and Common-place in a considerable degree – and pretty round & fat – She is however a kind Body in her Own way, and the husband Tolerably Attentive to her – As to the house, it is ill-contrived – and pretty Dirty, and Hugry Mugry – Tho' last, not least our Friend himself is as ingenious as ever, and Seem'd very happy with the Situation I have described. His mind, however, seems to me to be a great mixture of the poet and the Exciseman…From his conversation he Seems to be frequently among the great – but No Attention is paid by people of any rank to his wife…Having found that his farm does not answer, he is about to give it up, and depend wholly on the Excise'.

First of all, Jean was again pregnant, so that would take care of the 'round & fat' statement, secondly Ainslie sounds a little jealous, though whether of Robert or Jean, who knows?

Mrs Dunlop thought more of Jean when she met her in 1791.

'Mrs Burns I found in all the rosy bloom of health and beauty. I was

111

delighted with the cheerful openness of her countenance, the intelligence of her eyes, and her easy, modest, unaffected manners'.

Burns knew he had a standing to keep up, especially when he moved to Dumfries, and this was reflected in his household. Robert, his eldest son remembered the house in Millbrae Vennel as

'being one of a good order, such as were used in those days by the better class of citizens, and the life of his father and mother as being comparatively 'genteel'. They always had a maid-servant, and sat in their parlour. That room and the two principal bedrooms were carpeted and otherwise well furnished. The poet possessed a mahogany dining-table, and good company often put their legs under it...The poet received many presents of game and country produce from his country friends, besides occasional barrels of oysters from Hill, Cunningham, Alexander and other friends in town. It is just possible that he was as much envied by some of his neighbours as he has since been pitied by the world'.

According to Jessy Lewars Burns

'Was always anxious that his wife should be well and neatly dressed, and did his utmost to counteract any tendency to carelessness – which she sometimes excused by alleging the duties of a nurse and mother – not only by gentle remonstrance, but by buying for her the best clothes he could afford. He rarely omitted to get for her any little novelty in female dress. She was, for instance, one of the first persons in Dumfries to wear a dress of gingham – stuff which was at its first introduction rather costly, and used almost exclusively by the well-to-do'.

If Burns had lived another two centuries, he might, by now, just be on the brink of becoming a 'new man'.

As Burns coffin was carried to his resting place on 25th July 1796, and the bells tolled for the passing of the poet, Jean gave birth to her last son. She was aged just 31, newly widowed and bringing her ninth child into the world, to the funereal sounds of her husband leaving it.

Within a few days of Burns' death 70 guineas was raised towards support for Jean and her children. With some of this she paid off Burns' debts as well as the cost of the funeral, which came to under £16. Burns was also owed £180 from Gilbert his brother, his library had a value of £90, and he had money drafts of £15 in the house.

Burns did not die a pauper. But his last days were filled with the dread that he had become one. As Burns was slipping in and out of consciousness, his own father's situation when he himself was dying seemed to be pressing on Burns' fevered mind.

Appeals for money for Jean and her family went throughout Scotland, and even as far south to cities such as Liverpool and London. By the Spring/Summer of 1797 a very respectable amount had been amassed, which would look after Jean comfortably for the rest of her life and make sure her children, and two of the children that Burns had fathered illegitimately, were financially taken care of.

There is some contention as regards the donations collected for Jean. It is said that they slowed down when articles began to appear in the papers, some written by Burns' supposed friends, that he was a philanderer and a drunkard, and that the last few months of his life was spent in debauchery.

It was even said that his last illness was caused when he fell asleep in the street, on a snowy January night, after crawling out from the Globe Inn in Dumfries in a state of drunkenness. This was another melodramatic accusation by 'Honest' Allan Cunningham, who would even put a hardened tabloid reporter to shame, with his fabricated stories.

Jean remained in the same house, which she had shared with Burns, for the next thirty-eight years of her life and was hostess to hundreds of visitors, from all walks of life, who wanted to know about the poet.

Alfred Lord Tennyson called on her, and recited the poem 'Thou Ling'ring Star'. He might have picked a more suitable poem to recite than one which was written for one of Burns' lovers, one that Burns was seeing when he and Jean were still an item, even though Jean was pregnant in Paisley and she, for whom it was written, was now dead.

Jean was interviewed on many occasions tolerating all of the questions, good or bad, put to her, answering with manners and graciousness. A generous woman, she would also sometimes give away minders of Burns, to those who had the cheek to ask for something. This included some of his precious books. This does not show so much the naivety of Jean as much as it does the ignorance and cupidity of the visitors.

There is a likeness of Jean, a portrait of her when she was old, painted by Samuel McKenzie round about 1826, sitting alongside her grand-daughter, Sarah Eliza, whom she brought up after the child's mother died. *There are no paintings of Jean as a young woman, though she did have a silhouette made circa 1811, and very few descriptions of her as she grew older, but a Mrs Grant met Jean when she was fifty-five and found her

'a very comely woman, with plain sound sense and very good manners'.

It is said the Alexander Reid painted a minature of Jean, at the time he painted the one of Burns, but if this painting were done, it has now become lost.

Round about 1822 a Hew Ainslie, later to become a poet in America, visited

Jean in Dumfries, and according to his biographer Thomas C. Latto, the house at the time was overrun with visitors. When the visitors had left, Hew held on a little and he and Jean supped tea together. He would have been a young man of about 28 then, and they had some 'twa-handed crack'.

After a short while Hew asked if he could take a walk along the paths that Burns had walked, Jean agreed and accompanied him on this stroll. They walked to Lincluden Abbey, stopping at a sheltered spot. Jean must have been taken back many years. Maybe she had not visited this particular place in a while, and she is reported as saying

'It was just here that my man often paused, an', I believe, made up mony a poem an' sang ere he cam' in to write it down. He was never fractious – aye gude-natured, an' kind baith to the bairns an' me'.

George Thomson asked Jean on quite a few occasions to come and visit Edinburgh, and meet with the many friends that her late husband had made there. She eventually accepted in 1828 and stayed at his house in High Street adjoining Exchange Square. There were musical parties held for her and she consented to display her singing voice for all to hear.

Though it was not the same as when she was a young lassie, her voice seemed to cast a more beautiful spell because of the retrospective history surrounding it.

Jean enchanted the company when she sang the songs that Burns had written to her, and also those inspired by some of his other charmers, and she danced the night away when one of the young men ventured shyly to ask her up on the floor. She told the lad that had been waiting to be asked to dance all evening. When asked about Burns and his language she said

'He never spoke English, but spoke very correct Scotch'.

Agnes McLehose visited Jean when she was in Edinburgh during this time. No one knows what the conversation was like, but in a short while of meeting they were certainly getting on well and seemed to like each other.

Thirty-two years had passed since Burns' death, and Jean would have known that nothing happened between Agnes and her husband, and she would have recognised that this was because of Agnes, not Burns.

Jean apparently said, maybe tongue in cheek, maybe not, that she was fortunate in possessing charms that in the end triumphed over those of her talented and pretty rival

'How happy Robin was with either when t'other was away'.

Another person Jean met on her visit to Edinburgh was Sir Walter Scott, though not at the house of George Thomson. No report of this meeting was ever made.

She also had time to call on Jean Smith, a 'Mauchline Belle' who was then residing in Nicolson Street, before she later moved to South Charlotte Street to live in the house of her son, Principal Candlish, the theologian.

A long article was written by A. Munro for the 'Scotsman' newspaper of 1894 regarding the time spent in Edinburgh by Jean Armour, and is reprinted in Peter Westwood's book, 'Jean Armour.' Apparently this Mr Munro met Jean Smith in 1846 and was impressed with her wit and vitality, although she was heading well into old age. It was to the same Mr Munro that we owe the report of Jean Armour's visit from Agnes McLehose.

As she got older, Jean developed high blood pressure and suffered a series of strokes, which left her partially paralysed. Jean's granddaughter Sarah helped to look after her.

Jean died at home in Millbrae Vennel, on Wednesday 26th March 1834, after becoming totally paralysed on the previous Sunday.

According to the medical reports, the sad fact was that her mind was still active, but she could not move nor speak...just look. Late Tuesday night or early Wednesday morning, she fell into unconsciousness and within twenty-four hours, was dead. She was interred in the Burns Mausoleum on the 1st April of that year.

Sarah, her grand-daughter, gave an account of Jean's passing

'I used to read a chapter out of the family Bible, and I can vividly remember seeing her, after her last seizure, lying speechless with her eyes closed. After our minister Dr Wallace prayed, she opened her eyes and looked around the room to me, and as I went up beside her the tears coursed down her cheeks, and I think she pressed my hand, but she never spoke again'.

Jean's body was carried out of her house and her coffin was placed on spokes and carried along to St Michael's Kirkyard. No sooner had one person touched a spoke than another took their place.

Though only a short distance to the cemetery, hundreds had a hand in bringing this well loved woman to her last resting place beside her husband the poet, and two of her sons that had died in childhood.

Inscribed on her coffin, 'Jean Armour, widow of Robert Burns, aged 69'.

All in all, Burns didn't deserve a woman like Jean Armour. Her tolerance helped make him the poet he became, and gave him freedom. He could wander knowing that with her looking after his children, whom he did love unconditionally, and his home, he had no worries.

The question is did he love her? Burns loved all women. He was able to compartmentalise his love. So yes somewhere in his brain he had a compartment where he loved Jean Armour, with the deep love that we save only for those we take for granted.

Being cynical, she was always there to go running back to when things got a little too hot in the love stakes, then his marriage became like a sanctuary or more-so a bolt-hole.   As she commented herself, showing her own natural sense of humour, it was 'Nae joke bein' a poet's wife'!

We have a good idea what was going on in Burns' mind because of his writings, but there is nothing left behind from Jean on paper, of her thoughts during the years she knew Burns.

She had seen him through little more than a decade, but what a decade it was.   If we don't know how much of an influence she had on Burns' writings, how would she ever be expected to know.

It was a different age, with different expectations for women.   It took Jean Armour three times in all to get her Robin, one irregular marriage, one civil marriage and eventually one kirk recognised marriage but she got him in the end.   Maybe having Burns, with all of the problems that went with him was all she ever wanted in life.   If so then she truly was a happy woman.

Jean and Robert's five sons are buried in the Mausoleum in Dumfries. Their four daughters are buried in Mauchline Kirkyard, as is Robert Wilson, 'The Gallant Weaver' who once set his cap and hopes on Jean Armour, but lost out to a 'Ploughman Poet'.

The Following is a report on the 'Death and Character of Mrs. Burns' as printed in the Dumfries Courier, April 1834 ('The Illustrated Family Burns')

> 'At a late hour on the night of Wednesday, 26th March 1834, the world and its concerns closed forever on Mrs. Jean Armour – the venerable relict of the Poet Burns.   On the Saturday preceding she was seized with paralysis, for the fourth time during the last few years; and although perfectly conscious of her situation, and the presence of friends, became deprived, before she could be removed to bed, of the faculty of speech, and a day or two thereafter of the sense of hearing.   Still she lay wonderfully calm and composed, and, in the opinion of her medical attendant, suffered from weakness rather than from pain.   Frequently she gazed, with the greatest earnestness, on her granddaughter Sarah; and it was easy to read what was passing within, from the tears that filled her aged eyes and trickled down her cheeks.   To another individual she directed looks so eager and full of meaning, as to impress him with the idea that she had some dying request to make, and deeply regretted that it was too late; for even if her salvation had depended on the exertion, she was fortunately incapacitated from uttering a syllable, guiding a pen, or even making an intelligible sign.   The mind, in her case, survived the body; and this, perhaps, was the only painful circumstance attending her deathbed – considering how admirable her conduct had always been, her general health so sound, her span protracted

beyond the common lot, her character for prudence and piety, and her situation in life in every way so comfortable. On the night of Tuesday, or the morning of Wednesday, a fifth shock, unperceived by the attendants, deprived Mrs Burns of mental consciousness; and from that time, till the hour of her death, her situation was exactly that of a breathing corpse. And thus passed away all that was left of 'Bonnie Jean' – the relict of a man whose fame is as wide as the world itself, and the venerated heroine of many a lay, which bid fair to live in the memories of the people of Scotland, and of thousands far removed from its shores, as long as the language in which they are written is spoken or understood.

The deceased was born at Mauchline, in February 1765, and had thus entered the seventieth year of her age. Her father was an industrious master mason, in good employment, who enjoyed the esteem of the gentry and others within the district, and reared the numerous family of eleven sons and daughters, four of whom still survive – viz. Robert, a respectable merchant in London; James, who resides in the town of Paisley; Mrs Lees and Mrs Brown. The alleged circumstances attending Mrs Burns union with the bard are well known, and may be dismissed with the remark, that we have good authority for saying, that they have been incorrectly narrated by nearly every writer who has touched upon the subject. To the poet, Jean Armour bore a family of five sons and four daughters. The whole of the latter died in early life, and were interred in the cemetery of their maternal grandfather in Mauchline Churchyard. Of the sons, two died very young viz. Francis Wallace and Maxwell Burns, the last of whom was a posthumous child, born the very day his father was buried. Of the said family of nine, three sons alone survive – Robert, the eldest, a retired officer of the Accountant-General's Department, Stamp-Office, London, now in Dumfries; William, ultimately a colonel, and James Glencairn Burns, a lieutenant-colonel in the Hon. the East India Company's Service.

Burns certainly left his family poor (and how could it be otherwise?), but it was not true, as Collector Findlater has most successfully shown, that they were in immediate want, or lacked any necessary comfort. The relief fund annuity of an Exciseman's widow is known to be small (now, we believe, about £12 per annum); but Providence, shortly after the husband and father's decease, raised to the family many valuable friends. Passing exigencies were supplied from this honourable source; and no lengthened period elapsed until the active and disinterested benevolence of Dr. Currie, in conjunction with his excellent talents, placed at the feet of the family, to the great delight of the people of Scotland, very nearly £2000 sterling, in name of profits arising from the Liverpool Edition of the poet's works. The poet died in 1796, and up to 1818 his widow's income exceeded not, if

it equalled, sixty pounds per annum. But on this sum, small as it
may appear, she contrived to maintain a decent appearance, was
never known to be in debt, or wanting in charity – so unaspiring
were her ambition and views, and undeviating her prudence,
economy and frugality. At the period just mentioned, Captain
James Glencairn Burns wrote in breathless haste, from India, to
say, that having obtained promotion through the kindness of the
Marquis of Hastings, he had been able to set apart £150 yearly for
the use of his mother, and, as an earnest of affection, transmitted a
draft of £75. And it is due to this gentleman to say, that from first
to last, including some assistance from his brother, and
allowances for his infant daughter Sarah, he remitted his mother
in all the handsome sum of £2400 sterling. Leave of absence, and
some other circumstances, at length impaired the means and
changed the fortunes of the individual alluded to; but Captain
William Burns, in later life, very cheerfully took his brother's
place, and discharged, with equal promptitude, generosity, and
affection, duties dear to the best and kindliest feelings of our
nature. In this way, for sixteen years at least, Mrs Burns enjoyed
an income of £200 per annum – a change of fortune which enabled
her to add many comforts to her decent domicile, watch over the
education of a favourite grandchild, and exercise on a broader
scale the Christian duty of charity, which she did the more
efficiently by acting in most cases as her own almoner.

The term of Mrs Burns' widowhood extended to thirty-eight years,
in itself rather an unusual circumstance – and in July 1796, when
the bereavement occurred, she was but little beyond the age at
which the majority of females marry. But she had too much
respect for the memory of her husband, and regard for his
children, to think of changing her name, although she might have
done so more than once with advantage; and was even careful to
secure on lease, and repair and embellish, as soon as she could
afford it, the decent though modest mansion in which he died.
And here, for more than thirty years, she was visited by thousands
on thousands of strangers, from the peer down to itinerant
sonneteers – a class of person to whom she never refused an
audience, or dismissed unrewarded. Occasionally, during the
summer months, she was a good deal annoyed; but she bore all in
patience, and although naturally fond of quiet, seemed to consider
her house as open to visitors, and its mistress, in some degree, the
property of the public. But the attention of strangers neither
turned her head, nor were ever alluded to in the spirit of boasting;
and had it not been for a female friend who accompanied her on
one occasion to the Kings Arms Inn, to meet by invitation the
Marchioness of Hastings, no one would have known that the
excellent lady directed the present Marquis, who was then a boy,
to present Mrs Burns with a glass of wine, and at the same time

remarked, that 'he should consider himself very highly honoured, and cherish the recollection of having met the poet's widow, as long as he lived'. Her's, in short, was one of those well-balanced minds that cling instinctively to propriety and a medium in all things; and such as knew the deceased, earliest and latest, were unconscious of any change in her demeanour and habits, excepting perhaps, greater attention to dress, and more refinement of manner, insensibly acquired with frequent intercourse with families of the first respectability. In her tastes she was frugal, simple, and pure, and delighted in music, pictures, and flowers. In spring and summer it was impossible to pass her windows without being struck with the beauty of the floral treasures they contained; and if extravagant in anything, it was in the article of roots and plants of the finest sorts. Fond of the society of young people, she mingled, as long as able, in their innocent pleasures, and cheerfully filled for them the cup 'which cheers but not inebriates'. Although neither a sentimentalist nor a 'blue-stocking', she was a clever woman, possessed great shrewdness, discriminated character admirably, and frequently made very pithy remarks; and were this the proper place for such a detail, proofs of what is stated might easily be adduced.

When young, she must have been a handsome comely woman, if not indeed a beauty, when the poet saw her for the first time on a bleach-green at Mauchline, engaged like Peggy and Jenny at Habbie's Howe. Her limbs were cast in the finest mould; and up to middle life her jet black eyes were clear and sparkling, her carriage easy, and her step light. The writer of the present sketch never saw Mrs Burns dance, nor heard her sing, but he has learned from others that she moved with great grace on the floor, and chanted her 'wood-notes wild' in a style but rarely equalled by unprofessional singers. Her voice was a brilliant treble, and in singing 'Cooleen', 'I Gaed A Waefu' Gate Yestreen', and other songs, she rose without effort as high as a B natural. In ballad poetry her taste was good, and range of reading rather extensive. Her memory, too, was strong, and she could quote when she chose at considerable length and with great aptitude. Of these powers the bard was so aware, that he read to her almost every piece he composed, and was not ashamed to own that he had profited by her judgement. In fact, none save relations, neighbours, and friends could form a proper estimate of her character. In the presence of strangers she was shy and silent, and required to be drawn out, or, as some would say, shown off to advantage, by persons who possessed her confidence and knew her intimately.

But we have perhaps said enough, and although our heart has been thrown into our words, the portrait given is so strictly true to nature, that we conclude by saying, in the spirit of friendship not of yesterday – peace to the manes, and honour to the memory, of

119

'Bonnie Jean'.

The remains of Mrs Burns were interred in the family vault on Tuesday, the 1ˢᵗ April, with marks of public respect, in presence of an immense crowd of spectators. Independently of the Bard's Mausoleum, St. Michael's Churchyard is perhaps the most remarkable cemetery in Britain; amidst innumerable tombs thousands on thousands sleep below; and on the day alluded to public interest or curiosity waxed so intensely, that it became, if such an expression may be used, instinct with life as well as death. By many a strong wish was expressed that the funeral should be made public. The Magistrates and Commissioners of Police politely offered to mark their respect for Mrs Burns' memory by attending her funeral in their public capacity – an offer so honourable that it was at once acknowledged and acceded to by the trustees'.

Associated Songs:

Song   : The Mauchline Lady
Tune   : I Had A Horse And I Had Nae Mair
Period : circa 1785

Song   : The Lament
Tune   : Scots Queen
Period : Spring 1786

Song   : Tho' Cruel Fate
Tune   : She Rose And Let Me In
Period : Autumn 1786

Song   : Again Rejoicing Nature Sees
Tune   : Jockey's Grey Breeks
Period : circa Autumn/Winter 1786

Song   : To The Weavers Gin Ye Go
Tune   : To The Weavers Gin Ye Go
Period : circ Spring 1788

Song   : Of A' The Airts The Wind Can Blaw
Tune   : Miss Admiral Gordon's Strathspey
Period : May/June 1788

Song   : O Were I On Parnassus Hill
Tune   : My Love Is Lost To Me
Period : August 1788

Song   : Louis, What Reck I By Thee
Tune   : Louis, What Reck I
Period : circa December 1788

Song   : Out Over The Forth
Tune   : Charles Graham's Welcome Hame
Period : 11th March 1791

Song   : The Bonie Lad That's Far Awa
Tune   : The Bonie Lad That's Far Awa
Period : 1792

Song   : It Isna Jean, Thy Bonie Face
Tune   : The Maid's Complaint
Period : 1792

Song   : I Hae A Wife O' My Ain
Tune   : I Hae A Wife O' My Ain
Period : 1792 (originally dated to 1788)

Song   : The Gallant Weaver
Tune   : The Gallant Weaver (The Weaver's March)
Period : 1792

Song   : She Is A Winsome Wee Thing
Tune   : My Wife's A Wanton Wee Thing
Period : 8th November 1792

Song   : Their Groves O' Sweet Myrtle (also for Jean Lorimer)
Tune   : Humours Of Glen
Period : April 1795

Song   : Altho' My Back Be At the Wa' (Here's To His Health In Water)
Tune   : The Job Of Journey Work
Period : unknown

18.

MARGARET (MAY) CAMERON
Born 19th August 1766 - Died?

Chronology : circa early 1787

Margaret (May) Cameron was born in Fortingal, Perthshire, to Hugh Cameron and Catherine Kennedy in 1766. When she moved to Edinburgh to work, she resided in the Tollbooth area of the city.

From the 28th November 1786, until 5th May 1787, Burns shared a room with his friend, John Richmond in Baxter's Close in Edinburgh. The owner of the house was a Mrs Carfrae. Traditionally it is thought that May Cameron was a maid in Mrs Carfrae's home, and that is how she and Burns came to know one another.

On the 1st June 1787, Burns arrived in Dumfries, at the end of his Border tour. He had been accompanied on this tour by Robert Ainslie, who had by the beginning of June, returned to Edinburgh. On the 4th June Burns was delighted to be awarded the freedom of the borough of Dumfries.

Unfortunately on his arrival in Dumfries, he was also met with a letter, informing him that May Cameron was pregnant and that there was the possibility the child was his.

The letter delivered to Burns was dated 26th May 1787, and is believed to have been written by a friend on behalf of May. It is reported that May could neither read nor write. She apologised for sending him the note

> 'But out of quarters, without friends, my situation is really deplorable. I beg, for God sake, you will write and let me know how I am to do. You can write to any person you can trust to get me a place to stay till such times as you come to town yourself'.

Wallace, a Victorian biographer of Burns, saw the letter and reported

> 'The poor girl, who had to get a friend to write for her, did not reproach Burns, nor did she say directly that he was the cause of her 'trouble'. She described herself as his 'sincere well-wisher', and apologised for writing'.

An undated letter from Burns, thought to be of 1st June 1787, was sent to Robert Ainslie in Edinburgh saying

'My first welcome to this place was the inclosed letter. – I am very sorry for it, but what is done is done. Please call at the James Hog *(who was a shoemaker at Buchanan's Land, which was at the head of the Canongate)* mentioned and send for the wench and give her ten or twelve shillings, but don't for Heaven's sake meddle with her as a Piece. – I insist on this. On your honour; advise her out to some country friends...Call for God's sake, lest the poor soul be starving. Ask her for a letter I wrote to her now, by way of token. It is unsigned. – Write me after the meeting'.

This request Ainslie complied with.

Burns accepted that the child was his, though at the back of his mind there was a lingering doubt, which he wrote of, again to Robert Ainslie, on 25th June 1787 from Arrochar

'The Devil's Day-book, only April 14th or fifteenth so cannot yet have increased her growth much. I begin, from that, and some other circumstances to suspect foul play; and to tell the truth I w...'

In other words Burns and May Cameron had had sexual relations circa 14th April 1787. As her letter to him, which he received in Dumfries, was sent approximately five weeks into the pregnancy it was unlikely that May's predicament would be obvious.

A few weeks later, on the 29th July 1787 Burns again wrote to Robert Ainslie, and after mentioning Jean Armour added

'And Peggy *(Cameron?)* will bring me a gallant half-Highlander – and I shall get a farm, and keep them all about my hand'.

May Cameron issued a writ against Burns in 'meditatione fugae' for monetary support, naming him as the father of her unborn child, but it was cancelled on the 15th August 1787. (Burns carried this document around with him, on the back of it he had written two verses of an old song).

The reason for this cancellation is not known. But the possibility is that May had suffered a miscarriage. There was no trace in the registers of Edinburgh of her having given birth to a live child at this time.

After this unhappy episode with Burns, May married a cattle-drover called Mungo Forbes of New Grayfriars Parish on 5th September 1788. He was her first cousin, born on 18th January 1766, his parents being Neil Forbes and Christian Kennedy who came from the neighbouring parish of Dull.

May and Mungo went on to have three children. Their eldest child was Katherine Campbell Forbes, born on 4th April 1790 in Edinburgh. A son named David was born on 9th May 1795 and a second daughter named Catherine was born on 20th June 1804.

19.
EUPHEMIA MURRAY
Born 1769 – Died 29th April 1845

Chronology : October 1787

Burns recalled

'I composed these verses while I stayed at Ochtertyre with Sir William Murray. The lady, who was also at Ochtertyre at the same time, was a well-known toast, Miss Euphemia Murray of Lintrose'.

'The Flower of Strathmore', Euphemia Amelia Murray, was born at Lintrose, the only daughter of Mungo Murray. In 1794 she married David Smythe Of Methven Castle, one of the Senators of the College of Justice, who became a judge at the Court of Session. They had several children.

Burns met Euphemia at the house of her uncle, Sir William Murray and his wife *Lady Augusta MacKenzie, in Ochtertyre (Auchtertyre) in Strathearn, where Burns had been invited to visit, during his Clackmannanshire tour with Dr Adair. Euphemia was 18 at the time, and it is said she lacked appreciation of the honour done to her by Burns dedicating his poem 'Blythe, Blythe And Merry Was She' to her.

Maybe some of her reluctance was because the poem was set to an old drinking song 'Andro And His Cutty Gun'. It was a well-known fact at the time, that the 'cutty gun' was a metaphor for the phallus. Not quite the right sentiment for a pretty, well brought up young woman, a regular attendant at the St. Cecilia concerts, not forgetting her membership of the upper class circles.

Burns knew the alternative meaning of the title of the music. Was he playing games? Did he have a problem with young 'Phemie'? Probably!

Burns also wrote the poem 'On Scaring Some Water-Fowl On Loch Turit' on the same occasion. From a relative comes this quote

'Mrs Smythe always manifested a disinclination to speak on the subject of her meeting with Burns. But once she told me she remembered his reciting the poem 'On Scaring The Wild Fowl', one evening after supper, and that he gave the concluding lines with the greatest possible vigour'.

It looks as if there was a possibility that they did not get on very well. Maybe Burns thought that she was upper-class and spoiled, or maybe their personalities did not hit it off.

I suppose it's unlikely that Euphemia ever carried the words and music of her song around with her, unlike another well brought up young matron called Wilhelmina Alexander. After all for a judge's wife to be associated with a 'cutty gun' and all of it's graphic descriptions, hidden or otherwise, would be considered just a tad down market.

Lucky for Euphemia she chose a husband whose Christian name was David and not Andrew.

Euphemia Murray is buried in the eastern section of the Canongate cemetery, in the tomb of her husband, David Smythe, Lord Methven.

Over the grave, the monument bears an inscription in Latin recording the death of Lord Methven and also that

> 'Alongside are deposited the mortal remains of Euphemia Amelia Murray, daughter of Mungo Murray of Lintrose, the truly inestimable wife of David Smythe. She died 29th April 1845, aged 77'.

*The Traditional story is that Lady Augusta's father was the Third Earl of Cromarty, a Jacobite, who was imprisoned in the Tower of London in 1746, awaiting execution with Kilmarnock and Balmerino. Her mother, who was heavily pregnant at the time, had gone down to London to plead for her husband's life.

During this time Augusta chose to enter the world, apparently born in the Tower, and it is said she bore what all her friends believed to be the image of an axe upon her neck. Her father survived, but his two companions were executed.

Unfortunately the truth is that Augusta was born in July 1747. In November of that year, her father published a poem in The Gentleman's Magazine entitled 'Occasioned by a reflection lately published on the new-born daughter of Mr MacKenzie, late Earl of Cromartie'.

> 'Ill flows the verse that brands an infant's name,
> And loads a babe yet innocent with shame;
> Heir to misfortune let its fate suffice.
> Nor for the father's crimes the child despise;
> The generous heart laments the guiltless moan,
> The future sighs, for follies not its own;
> E'en there perhaps we err – succeeding days
> May see this child our warmest wishes raise'
> Retrieve the honours that her father lost,
> And match some Briton, Britain's future boast,
> Who, fired, celestial Liberty, by thee,
> From hell-born faction shall his country flee'.

Associated Song:

Song   : Blythe, Blythe And Merry Was She
Tune   : Andro And His Cutty Gun
Period   : October 1787

20.
MARGARET (PEGGY) CHALMERS
Born 1763 – Died 3rd March 1843

Chronology : circa 1786 or early 1787

'Some folk hae a hantle (many) o' fauts, an' I'm but a ne'er-do-weel!
(letter to Peggy Chalmers 21st November 1787)

Peggy Chalmers was born at Fingland, Kirkudbrightshire, but later moved to Braehead Farm near Mauchline when her father, James Chalmers, was forced to sell his estate because of financial difficulties. Her mother was Euphemia Murdoch of Cumloden in Galloway whose two sisters were Barbara, who became stepmother to Gavin Hamilton a friend of Burns, and Charlotte Tait, who was deceased.

When or where Burns met Peggy is unknown. But it was either in Mauchline or Edinburgh. An earlier biographer of Burns, Ferguson, names a letter, dated to January 1787 as written to her

> 'My Dear Countrywoman, I know you will laugh at it, when I tell you that your pianoforte and you together have play'd the deuce with my heart. I was once a zealous Devotee to your sex, but you know the black story at home. My breast has been widowed these many months, and I thought myself proof against the fascinating witchcraft; but I am afraid you will 'feelingly convince me what I am'. I say, I am afraid, because I am not quite sure what is the matter with me, I have one miserable bad symptom, which I doubt threatens ill: when you whisper, or look kindly to another, it gives me a draught of damnation'.

Whoever the letter was written for, it was clear that Burns was once again head over heels in love.

Peggy told the poet Thomas Campbell that Burns had proposed to her in October 1787 when he visited Harvieston, home of her uncle, John Tait, widower of Peggy's aunt Charlotte, but she was already engaged to Mr Lewis Hay, son of Captain John Hay, an Edinburgh banker.

Peggy Chalmers refused Burns proposal of marriage but so gently that he never took umbrage or reverted to his natural inclination, which was to write something unpleasant about the one who had let him down or offended him in some way. Instead he remained in love with Peggy for the rest of his life.

Peggy and Lewis were married on the 9th December 1788 and set up home in Parliament Square, in Edinburgh, in a property owned by Lewis' employer, Forbes Bank.

Despite her marriage Burns remained in love with Peggy for the rest of his life. His admiration and esteem for her never wavered or waned. He enjoyed her conversation and intellectual abilities, something that Burns was not used to in a woman, especially at that time in his life. You will recall in the earlier chapter on Elizabeth Gebbie, that Burns was also enamoured of her intelligence.

He wrote to Peggy on many occasions. She was one of the first to be told that he had at last married Jean Armour, and any mention of Jean in his correspondences to her are always of a positive nature. She was also one of the first to be told that he had taken on the farm at Ellisland in a letter dated 14th March 1788, sent from Edinburgh

'I know, my ever dear friend, that you will be pleased with the news, when I tell you that I have at last taken a lease of a farm. Yesternight I completed a bargain with Mr. Miller, of Dalswinton, for the farm of *Ellisland, on the banks of the Nith, between five and six miles above Dumfries. I begin at Whitsunday to build a house...'

*Burns had been given the choice of 'Foregirth', rich farming land, 'Bankhead', just a little less rich and 'Ellisland'. Ellisland was the not the best choice, but the views were superb and according to the factor, Alexander Cunningham, Burns made 'a poet's, not a farmer's choice'.

Burns referred to Peggy as 'one of the most accomplished of women', and the following quote from a letter dated 16th September 1788 which he wrote to her from Ellisland, seems to be tinged with regret for lost opportunity and possibilities. There were no class barriers to stop them marrying, just bad timing.

'When I think of you – hearts the best, minds the noblest, of human kind, when I think I have met with you, and have lived more of real life with you in eight days, than I can do with almost anybody I meet in eight years – when I think on the improbability of meeting you in this world again – I could sit down and cry like a child'.

Later on in the same letter he comments upon Jean Armour and says of his marriage that it

'Was not in consequence of the attachment of romance perhaps; but I had a long and much loved fellow creature's happiness or misery in my determination, and I durst not trifle with so important a deposit. Nor have I any cause to repent it. If I have not got polite tattle, modish manners, and fashionable dress, I am not sickened and disgusted with the multiform curse of boarding-school affectation; and I have got the handsomest figure, the sweetest temper, the soundest constitution, and the kindest heart in the country'.

In 1787 he sent Peggy copies of the songs he had written to her. She didn't want one of them, 'My Peggy's Face', to be published and sent a letter telling Burns of this. He in turn was not happy with her less than ecstatic attitude. His words were meant as a compliment to her not something to compromise her.

It is interesting to read how Burns writes in this letter dated November/December 1787. There is no foppery in it, no cajoling, no cloying words. It is a letter sent to someone that Burns felt comfortable with, comfortable enough to speak frankly to, though you can imagine him beating her over the head with his first edition just to make the point.

For me it is one of the best letters ever written by Burns and in my opinion one of the funniest. Honest, direct, like an arrow from the tongue. No messing! Even his compliments are delivered with all the gentleness of a cudgel. Peggy Chalmers was well and truly put in her place.

'My Dear Madam,

I just now have read yours. The poetic compliment I pay cannot be misunderstood. They are neither of them so particular as to point you out to the world at large; and the circle of your acquaintances will allow all I have said. Besides I have complimented you chiefly, almost solely, on your mental charms. Shall I be plain with you? I will; so look to it. Personal attractions, madam, you have much above par, wit, understanding, and worth, you possess in the first class. This is a cursed flat way of telling you these truths, but let me hear no more of your sheepish timidity...'

In Peggy's defence, she was secretly engaged to Lewis Hay at this time. It is no wonder that she did not want anything published for the whole region to see, she felt she would be compromised, and in rhyme too.

Everyone knew about Burns and his affectionate nature towards the ladies. But Peggy was aware of his talent and she must have been secretly delighted about the honour he had bestowed on her. She was one of his top five heroines, if not his soul mate, immortalised in poem and prose forever.

'When Braving Angry Winter's Storms' appeared in the second volume of the Scots Musical Museum, but 'My Peggy's Face' didn't appear in print in Burns' lifetime. Burns honoured her wishes, which showed how much he cared for her.

None of Peggy's letters to Burns have ever come to light though it was apparent that Burns took a great delight in his letters to her. It is stated by Cromek, in his 'Reliques', that Charlotte Hamilton, Peggy's cousin through her aunt Barbara, for some unknown reason threw Peggy's letters to Burns into the fire after his death, and those that were salvaged were too badly damaged to be of use to anyone, but this has not been proved. Maybe Charlotte was just looking after her cousin's 'honour'.

Peggy Chalmers was a relative of Dr Blacklock from Pear Tree House in Edinburgh. He was a poet who had been blinded by smallpox as a child, and was the one who had first invited Burns to come to Edinburgh in 1786, after hearing Burns' poems read.

Peggy used to play the keyboard for Dr Blacklock. It is reported that she possessed a very good voice, and she would sing to Dr Blacklock many of the songs of the day, which would inevitably include songs composed by Robert Burns.

On 10th January 1788 Burns revealed in a letter written to Agnes McLehose that 'The name I register in my heart core is Peggy Chalmers'.

Burns also let Agnes McLehose read Peggy's letters. Agnes replied after reading them

'Why did not such a woman secure your heart? O the caprice of human nature, to fix on impossibilities'.

When interviewed years later a relative said of Peggy

'Her heart was warm, her temper even, and her conversation lively. I have often been told that her gentleness and vivacity had a favourable influence on the manner of Burns'.

Another relative describing her to Robert Chambers

'In early life, when her hazel eyes were large and bright and her teeth white and regular, her face possessed a charm not always the result of the accompaniment of fine features. She was short, but her figure was faultless. Her conversation was cheerful, but intelligent. She talked rarely of books yet greatly liked reading. She spoke readily and well, but preferred listening to others'.

Peggy and Lewis moved abroad with their three daughters and three sons. After Lewis' death on 28th February 1800 she returned to Scotland. Up until about 1820 she lived at Buccleuch Place in Edinburgh, then she again went abroad to live. She died at Pau in Berne on the 3rd March 1843. Her obituary was printed in the Inverness Courier and the Scotsman (1st April 1843) and read as follows

We observe the following announcement in the Edinburgh papers of last week:-

'Died at Pau in Bearn, on the third inst. Mrs. Lewis Hay, daughter of James

Chalmers, Esq. Of Fingland, and widow of Lewis Hay Esq., one of the partners of the banking house of Sir William Forbes, J. Hunter and Co., Edinburgh'.

It may interest the lovers of Scottish poetry to know that Mrs Hay was one of the special favourites of Burns during his Edinburgh sojourn, and to her are addressed some of the most excellent of his letters in his printed correspondence. This accomplished lady was then unmarried, and is addressed by the poet as 'Miss Margaret Chalmers'. Next to Mrs Dunlop, Miss Chalmers seems to have stood highest in Burns' estimation, and the unreserved disclosures which he made to her of his feelings and sentiments and private views are the best evidence of the entire confidence which he reposed in her admirable good sense, taste and judgement. Mrs Hay was also celebrated by Burns in his song –

> *My Peggy's face, my Peggy's form,*
> *The frost of hermit age might warm.*

Burns, it will be recollected, was fond of displaying the little knowledge of French which he had picked up by a fortnight's tuition by his old preceptor Murdoch; and on this head Mrs Hay used to relate an amusing anecdote which we give in the words of Mr Campbell, the poet.

One of his friends (Mrs Hay, then Miss Chalmers) carried him into the company of a French lady, and remarked with surprise that he attempted to converse with her in her own tongue. Their French, however, was mutually unintelligible. As far as Burns could make himself understood, he unfortunately offended the foreign lady. He meant to tell her that she was a charming person and delightful in conversation; but expressed himself so as to appear to her to mean that she was fond of speaking; to which the Gallic dame indignantly replied that it was quite as common for poets to be impertinent as for women to be loquacious'.

In September 1787 Burns finished a letter to Peggy with the words

'as for friendship, you and Charlotte have given me pleasure, permanent pleasure, 'which the world cannot give, nor take away', I hope; and which will outlast the heavens and the earth'.

Maybe he himself made this possible, as the last song ever written by him, nine days before his death on 12th July 1796, was written in memory of the time he, Peggy and Charlotte Hamilton spent the day on the River Devon.

The song 'Fairest Maid On Devon Banks', was thought by some earlier biographers to be written for Charlotte Hamilton, but knowing how much he loved Peggy there is no doubt that during his few remaining days on earth many of the last thoughts of Burns' life led him down that pathway to she who was 'registered in his heart's core', Peggy Chalmers.

There are traditional anecdotes regarding both sides of Peggy Chalmers' family

1. The Murdoch's of Cumloden received lands for help given to Bruce in a time of danger.

2. Peggy was related to Grizel Cochrane of Ochiltree who had saved her father's life. John Cochrane had been condemned to die in Edinburgh for his share in Argyll's rebellion during the times of James VII.   Grizel is said to have disguised herself in male attire, attacked the post-messenger as he crossed the border, and robbed him of the warrant of execution with her father's name on it.   Grizel later became Mrs Kerr of Morriston in Berwickshire, and apparently at her home in Morriston there was a picture painted of her as a girl of seventeen, leaning on a table on which is placed the pistols and the disguise that she wore.

Associated Songs:

Song   : My Peggy's Face
Tune   : My Peggy's Face
Period : October 1787

Song   : Where Braving Angry Winter's Storms
Tune   : Niel Gow's Lamentation For Abercairney
Period : October 1787

Song   : Fairest Maid On Devon Banks
Tune   : Rothiemurche's Rant (Rothiemuchus)
Period : 12th July 1796 (Last Song Ever Composed)

21.

CHARLOTTE HAMILTON
Born 1763 – Died 1806

Chronology : August 1787

Charlotte was the elder daughter of John Hamilton of Kype, a lawyer at Mauchline and his second wife Barbara Murdoch. She was also the half-sister to Gavin Hamilton a lawyer friend of Burns. Burns first met her on 27th August 1787 at Harvieston, near Dollar, and was taken with her immediately. He wrote to Gavin Hamilton the next day after the meeting

> 'Of Charlotte I cannot speak in common terms of admiration. She is, not only beautiful but lovely. Her form is elegant, her features not regular, but they have the smile of sweetness, and the settled complacency of good nature in the highest degree. Her eyes are fascinating, at once of good sense, tenderness and a noble mind'.

Together with Peggy Chalmers, Burns and Charlotte rode to see the 'Falls of Devon'.

Of the song written for her, 'The Banks Of The Devon', which appeared in the second volume of the Musical Museum, Burns wrote to Peggy Chalmers in 1788

> 'Talking of Charlotte, I must tell her that I have, to the best of my power, paid her a poetic compliment, now completed. The air is admiral - true old highland. It was the tune of a gaelic song which an Inverness lady sang to me when I was there. I was so charmed with it, that I begged her to write me a set of it from her singing, for it had never been set before. I am fixed that it shall go in Johnson's next number, so Charlotte and you need not spend your precious time in contradicting me'.

As usual, Burns had a penchant for Charlotte Hamilton, even though Peggy Chalmers, her cousin, was 'registered in my heart's core'. But Burns had a penchant for just about every woman who crossed his path.

Charlotte did not return his affection, and she stands accused, by one of the earliest of Burns' biographers, Cromek, of throwing Peggy Chalmers letters to Burns into the fire after his death, though how she would have got a hold of the letters to Burns is a mystery. If she did throw letters in the fire then surely it would be more likely to be Burns' letters to Peggy Chalmers.

The only explanation for this act is that after Burns' death, many of the letters he received during his lifetime were returned to those who had sent them to him, people such as Robert Ainslie, Agnes McLehose, Maria Riddell etc.

Peggy's letters may have been returned to Charlotte because Peggy herself was not living in Scotland at the time, and if Charlotte had read over these youthful correspondences, she may have believed that Peggy might have found herself compromised. She could have thought that the best action to take would be to destroy the letters. But that is only supposition.

'Fairest Maid On Devon Banks' was penned on 12th July 1796, just nine days before he died and was the last song written by Burns. Although reported by earlier biographers to be written for Charlotte the song is actually meant for her cousin Peggy Chalmers.

The song was sent to George Thomson in Edinburgh along with a letter imploring Thomson to lend him £5 to stop a haberdasher, who, on hearing of Burns' illness and possible impending death, had taken out a lawsuit against him for monies owed. Burns was afraid that the tailor would have him removed from his sick bed and incarcerated in jail.

Charlotte married a Dr James Adair, a travelling companion of Burns, on 16th November 1789 at Harvieston *(Scots Magazine)*.

Dr Adair set up a medical practice in Pleasance in Edinburgh before moving to Harrogate. Charlotte was referred to as 'Mrs Adair of Scarborough'. They had five children.

James Adair died on 24th April 1802 in England, aged only 37. Charlotte returned to Edinburgh soon after his demise. She outlived him by only four years, dying in Edinburgh, where she is buried.

Associated Song:

Song   : The Banks Of The Devon
Tune   : Bhannerach Dhon Na Chri
Period   : October 1787

22.

AGNES CRAIG MCLEHOSE
(Clarinda)
Born 26th April 1758 – Died 22nd October 1841

Chronology : 4th December 1787

'The heart's aye, the part aye, that maks us richt or wrang'

Burns wrote the following words to an old friend, Captain Richard Brown, on 30th December 1787.

'Almighty love still reigns and revels in my bosom, and I am at this moment ready to hang myself for a young Edinburgh widow, who has wit and wisdom more murderously fascinating than the stiletto of the Sicilian Banditti, or the poisoned arrow of the savage African'.

Agnes was born in Glasgow's Saltmarket area on 26th April 1758, near the Merchant's Hospital situated at the southwest corner of the Trongate. She was baptised on 8th May 1758, the third of four daughters born to a well-known Glasgow surgeon, Mr. Andrew Craig. According to her grandson, W. C. McLehose, there was also a son born to the family, but he apparently died young and there is no information regarding him.

Dr Craig worked at the Town Hospital and the Merchant's Hospital, and was thus permitted to rent a tenement flat, near to Glasgow Cross, which belonged to the hospital.

Agnes was a sickly child but had an inner built sense of survival. She gradually gained her health, and became quite robust. Unfortunately the same cannot be said for the others in her family. There is sadness in her childhood. By the age of eleven, she had lost two sisters, a brother and her mother, Christian McLaurin who died in 1767.

Agnes' remaining sister, Margaret, six years her senior, married Captain James Kennedy of Kailzie on 30th April 1771, but she died sometime in 1772 in childbirth. Her child was stillborn.

The dates of birth of the Craig sisters were

| Margaret | 27th June 1752 | Lilias | 25th July 1754 |
| Agnes | 26th April 1758 | Mary | 11th May 1764 |

At the age of fifteen in the spring of 1774, motherless and with no surviving siblings, Agnes was sent to boarding school in Edinburgh. Her father's intention was for her to have a finishing school education, which would give her a touch of culture, brush up on the basics and make her ready to enter the society where he intended she would spend the rest of her life.

There may also have been another reason for her father sending her to Edinburgh, as 'the pretty Miss Nancy' had become one of the beauties of Glasgow, and was voted top of the 'Toast List of 1773' at the famous 'Glasgow Hodge-Podge Club', established in 1752 for professional men.

As this was when Agnes was at the tender age of hormonal advance with a mind of her own, it probably sent alarm bells ringing in Mr Craig's ears. Coincidentally, one of the founders of the Hodge-Podge Club was Dr John Moore, to whom Burns sent his biographical letter in August 1787.

Agnes although sad at leaving the last remaining member of her immediate family, seemed to be quite happy going off to Edinburgh to enjoy excitement, adventure and explore her pastures new, but other events and other people came on the scene.

As mentioned before, Agnes Craig was a very good-looking girl with a wicked charm and devastating sense of humour, and did not want for male company. But in matters of love she was very inexperienced.

She had several suitors, but one young man in particular was more insistent that any of the others. He was a law agent named James McLehose. Born in 1752 he was six years older than Agnes, and from their first meeting circa 1773/74, he had done everything but kidnap and brainwash her to ensure she became his.

Agnes' father was less enamoured of McLehose than his daughter. Nor were any of her other relatives pleased with Agnes' choice of a life partner. Mr Craig did not approve of McLehose. McLehose was a mistake. McLehose was a bad type, blessed with the gift of a silver tongue. McLehose was also a jealous, violent drunk.

It is unlikely that Agnes was aware of this side to his nature, as he would be on his best behaviour towards her during the courting period. Agnes was eighteen, hormones were at an all time high, and she was head over heels in love. On July 1st 1776 she married James McLehose.

The marriage may have taken place in St Andrew's Church where her uncle was a minister, and is recorded in the Glasgow parish register as

'1776, July – James McLehose, writer in Glasgow, and Agnes Craig, residing there, regularly married the 1st inst.'.

Agnes had four sons in four years with McLehose.   They were

William	born 23rd May 1777 (died in infancy)
Andrew	born 1st July 1778 (died 21st April 1839)
William no. 2	born April 1780 (died August 1790)
James	born 21st April 1781 (died pre November 1784)

Agnes soon realised that marriage to McLehose was a mistake and later she referred to it as ' the result of disinterested affection on both sides'.   There were many arguments, and McLehose was not averse to using his fists on her, either in or out of drink.

But Agnes had been brought up playing in the streets of Glasgow with a mix of children working class as well as middle class, (maybe this is where she got her strong sense of justice) so she could give as good as she got.

The old Scottish quotation 'To rule a wife and have a wife is a difficulty of old experience with the lords of the creation' probably suited the McLehose marriage well.

James McLehose was a bully, and Agnes, who was a strong character and used to a great amount of freedom, was not used to being ruled, either by an iron fist or by a velvet glove.   Her husband could not accept this, and could not understand why he could not break this woman.   He was master and she was his possession.   According to her

'Only a short time had elapsed ere I perceived, with inexpressible regret, that our dispositions, tempers, and sentiments, were so totally different, as to banish all hopes of happiness.   Our disagreement rose to such a height, and my husband's treatment was so harsh, that it was thought advisable by my friends that a separation should take place, which accordingly followed in December 1780'.

In the last quote Agnes appears to be ambivalent about leaving McLehose. The decision reads as though it has to be made with the support and agreement of others.   This may have had something to do with her religious beliefs.   She had taken a vow in God's church, possibly in front of her uncle, to marry for life.

Her pride was also to be taken into consideration.   Her family may have warned her that marriage to McLehose could only end in disaster. Walking out on him would prove them correct.

Agnes was a very complex woman, but she should never be despised for this complexity.   Too many earlier Burns biographers went down this road with her.   She had underlying courage, free spirit and a strong sense of justice beating in the same heart, and her religion and beliefs in justice were her touchstone to reality.

Agnes moved out of the matrimonial home, in December 1780, before her last son was born and went back to live with her father in the Saltmarket.

Being a lawyer, with all of his contacts, her estranged husband managed to get custody of the elder two boys. To rub salt into the wound, cruelly, McLehose removed the baby from Agnes as soon as he was weaned.

This behaviour was bad enough from this drunken, brutal bully, but then she was struck by another blow. Eighteen months after the separation, on 13th May 1782, her father died. Mr Craig had suffered a long illness. Agnes nursed him throughout. Regrettably as his condition made him unable to work, his savings were used up. This meant that there would be no inheritance for Agnes.

But her father did try to do his best for Agnes. Realising that his health was worsening and that there was no chance of recovery, Mr Craig, before he died, managed to ensure that Agnes would be left with two annuities from societies he had contributed to during his working life. These two annuities amounted to £18.

Mr Craig also had some property, which he left to be invested on Agnes' behalf, first of all making sure that James McLehose could not gain ownership to this property as her husband. Though the interest amounted to just £7 per year, Agnes gained a small sense of financial independence. There was no contribution from McLehose. These monies gave her an income of under ten shillings a week to live on.

With support of friends, Agnes had moved to Edinburgh shortly after the death of her father in May 1782, where she had rented a small first floor flat at the back of General's Entry in the Potterrow. She was uncomfortable and afraid, living in Glasgow beside her estranged husband and his relations, never knowing what he would do next. She felt alienated in her own birth city, hounded by the lies that McLehose was spreading.

In August 1782 Agnes eventually retrieved her children from the hands of their father and returned to the Potterrow with them. As Agnes said

'The income being left me by my father being barely sufficient to board myself, I was now distressed how to support my three infants. With my spirits sunk in deep dejection, I went to Glasgow to see them. I found arrears due for their board. This I paid, and the goodness of some worthy gentlemen in Glasgow procuring me a small annuity from the Writers (£10), and one from the Surgeons (£8), I again set out for Edinburgh with them in August 1782; and by the strictest economy made my little income go as far as possible. The deficiency was always supplied by some worthy benevolent friends, whose kindness no time can erase from my heart'.

Above: Clarinda's House in Potterow in Edinburgh by an unknown artist.

The only apparent reason for James McLehose to have taken the children from Agnes seems to be because he could. He wanted to hurt her and get revenge on her for leaving him. During the separation he abandoned his children, leaving them with his mother and various other relatives, paying nothing for their upkeep. He then disappeared off to England.

After he left Scotland for England in 1782, McLehose's family did not contribute in any way towards the upkeep of their grandchildren, although they were reasonably well-off and they knew of Agnes' financial position.

James McLehose lived in London for a while, and managed to get himself incarcerated in the Fleet prison for non-payment of debts. His family paid off what he owed, thus obtaining his release from gaol. This was on the understanding that he went abroad as soon as possible.

McLehose was encouraged to go Jamaica, which he did in November 1784, but before leaving he sent a letter to Agnes saying

'For my part, I am willing to forget what is past, neither do I require an apology from you: for I am heartily sorry for those instances of my behaviour to you, which caused our separation. Were it possible to recall them, they would never be repeated'.

If that was to be the start of a hopeful reconciliation, Agnes was not too pleased with it and never answered his letter. She had nearly four years separation from him to think about what she had suffered in their doomed marriage, and did not consider that she had anything to apologise for.

It was McLehose not her, who was the drunkard and bully. It was he who had forcibly removed her children and denied her the right to see them. It was he who then abandoned them, running off to England for his own pleasures. Agnes had not left him destitute without a roof over his head.

1784 was a very trying and upsetting time for her, as her youngest son, James died, and another son, William, was unwell, with ulcerated legs.

So with a shrug of his shoulders and not one look backwards, James McLehose took off to Jamaica, to a new and successful life, and eventually a new 'wife' and new family.

Many old friends had made Agnes welcome in Edinburgh and helped her settle in. Others were encouraged to come along and make her acquaintance. Her cousin *William, later Lord Craig, introduced her to the literary society of the city, and she bloomed.

*Born in 1745, Lord Craig died in 1813. His obituary in the 'Scot's Magazine' says of him

'As a judge he was highly honourable and upright – endowed with persevering talents and a complete knowledge of his profession...In private life he was gentle, affable and unassuming, and in an eminent degree, hospitable and benevolent. He possessed the warm esteem of a circle of select friends, to whom he was extremely attached'.

With her charming personality, quick wit, repartee and banter Agnes became very popular. But I wonder how often she had to bite her tongue when it was said to her 'I told you so' as regards her failed marriage.

Settling very quickly into Edinburgh society, Agnes began to widen her circle of friends. Educationally she realised that she was not up to scratch due to her early marriage to James McLehose and she soon became aware how much had slipped away from her. Ever the optimist, she moved on.

She began to look at how she could expand and improve herself both personally and professionally. Agnes became a voracious reader, soaking in facts like a gigantic sponge. She was also considered an excellent letter writer, which in turn helped her towards becoming a wonderful conversationalist. At length she acquired what then was known as 'a correct style' and composed in prose and verse with power and elegance.

But she was still aware of her precarious financial state.

Stories were returning to Scotland relating to James McLehose who evidently was making a fortune in Jamaica. He had become an attorney-at-law there and was earning a hefty one thousand pounds per annum.

Suddenly the annuities, which had been arranged by Mr Craig, stopped.

The Trustees believed that as McLehose was now very successful in Jamaica, it was time for him to shoulder his responsibilities. He was still her husband as neither Agnes nor he had sued for divorce. He should be paying for the upkeep of his family no matter whether together or apart.

Though financially McLehose had gained tremendously, his cruelty had not changed in his years abroad. He still refused to contribute anything towards supporting Agnes or his children, though Agnes wrote to him on many occasions informing him of the 'straits' his *children were suffering.

Even William Craig, her cousin on her father's side, wrote to McLehose reminding him of his responsibility, to his children at least. To no avail!

Circa early 1787 her son William became very ill, and the expense for his care ate into her funds. William died in August 1790, long after her meeting with Burns. She informed McLehose of the boy's death immediately. It took him a year to reply to her letter.

McLehose never did reimburse his parents and family who had paid off his debts and fines in London in order to get him freed from gaol. They had also purchased his ticket for Jamaica.

When he was appealed to for money for his aged mother, by Agnes as well as his family members, whose income was too small to support her, he never acknowledged the request.

William Craig made up the deficit in her finances. He was genuinely fond of Agnes, (possibly even living in hope that one day, if she did decide to divorce McLehose, he might be lucky enough to make Agnes his wife), and gave paternal support to her sons.

Though there are few paintings of her, the Meirs silhouette being the best known but not the only one, there are quite a few descriptions of Agnes round about 1787, the time when she met Robert Burns, from various people who knew her. Here are a couple

> 'Short in stature, her form graceful, her hands and feet small and delicate. Her features were regular and pleasing, her eyes lustrous, her complexion fair, her cheeks ruddy, and a well-formed mouth displayed teeth beautifully white'.

> 'She was of a somewhat voluptuous style of beauty, of lively and easy manners, of a poetical cast of mind, with some wit, and not too high a degree of refinement or delicacy'.

Agnes as part of her self-improvement had become a rhymer and had absorbed Burns' poetry. Learning that he was in Edinburgh in the winter of 1787, she was desperate to meet him. She was sure that they would have much in common.

But her cousin William Craig disliked Burns, 'that ploughman with pretensions to poetry', and refused to invite him to any of his soirees, no matter how much Agnes pleaded.

But fate intended that they meet.

Burns had intended leaving Edinburgh on the 4th December, which he stated in a letter to Isabella Mabane dated 1st December 1787, but he was invited along to a party at the last minute, and decided to take up the invitation. Agnes, who had been nagging her friends for weeks about

140

meeting him, orchestrated Burns' invitation to the party.

The eventual meeting of Burns and Agnes took place at the party on 4th December 1787, held in a house owned by Miss Erskine Nimmo in Allison Square, in an Edinburgh where Burns had gained celebrity status.

From that first meeting their platonic friendship blossomed into a full-blown non-physical bodice ripping love affair, lasting only about ten weeks at the most, but which has passed down the centuries as one of the most celebrated love stories in history.

The day after the party Agnes sent a note to Burns asking him to come to tea with her later in the week. She gave him two dates. He could not manage the first one on the 6th, but was sure he could come on Saturday 8th December, 'and embrace the opportunity with the greatest pleasure'.

Sadly for Agnes, Burns, though having every intention of seeing her, especially in her own lair, did not manage the visit on the 8th, due to the fact that he had fallen from a coach on the evening of the 7th when he was returning from another Edinburgh soiree. The fall, he said, was due to the antics of a drunken coachman, which had dislocated his kneecap.

It is highly unlikely that Burns would have been intoxicated. Burns was very aware of his precarious standing in Edinburgh and would not want to jeopardise any helpful relationship that may have passed his way. The drunken coachman story is probably correct.

Neither could Burns' constitution tolerate a lot of alcohol and he was always very aware of not letting himself down when in the presence of the upperclass. He had a name to make for himself. He wanted that name to be 'poet' not 'drunk'. That he left to his hosts.

'Lang Sandy Wood', his Edinburgh doctor, made Burns rest at his lodgings in the Cruikshank residence in 2 St James Square, his leg stretched out on a pillow until the swelling had gone down and the kneecap healed again.

Apart from the pain and discomfort Burns was in, remaining indoors and virtually static must have seemed like purgatory for a man used to the freedom of tramping the fields or riding through the countryside.

Though he remained behind in Edinburgh on the 4th, he had been making plans to leave on the 13th December after various bits and pieces of business had been dealt with. He was trying to get the money he was due from William Creech an Edinburgh printer, to whom he had sold the copyright of his poems, but the injury to his knee had put paid to that idea.

But for compensation there was the young 'widow' he had met at the Nimmo party, who was obviously taken with him. Now was as good a time as any to sharpen up his correspondence technique with someone whose contacts may be of use to him in the future.

Whether Burns expected this 'letter game' to create the momentum it did, or to become as serious as it did, is unknown. But his flirtation touched a heart that for so long had been void and dark, no matter what her outward appearance said. Burns threw a switch and Agnes seemed to flood with brilliant light.

And so the letters begin.

On 8th December, after informing Agnes of his accident, Burns' charm offensive commenced

'I cannot bear the idea of leaving Edinburgh without seeing you - I know not how to account for it – I am strangely taken with some people, nor am I often mistaken. You are a stranger to me; but I am an odd being: some yet unnamed feelings; things not principles, but better than whims, carry me farther than boasted reason ever did a Philosopher'.

She replied immediately, writing a long letter to him on the same evening after receiving his letter. She enclosed one of her poems for him to read, and to criticise as he liked, saying

'I have often composed rhyme (if not reason), but never one line of poetry. The distinction is obvious to everyone of the least discernment. Your lines were truly poetical: give me all you can spare'.

Burns was virtually confined to his room for the next six weeks during which time numerous letters and poems passed between them, at a later date under the contrived names of Sylvander and Clarinda.

At Agnes' insistence these names were to be used in case any of their letters fell into the wrong hands. If that happened Agnes would have been the one to suffer, not Burns. Respectability was so fragile, but necessary for one in her situation. The loss of it would be devastating, and could have led to her being ostracised from 'decent' society.

In her letter of the 8th, Agnes tells Burns she had always wanted to meet him, and admitted that she had nagged Miss Nimmo on quite a few occasions to have him invited to her house when she was there. Then she commented upon the 'unnamed feelings', he had mentioned in his letter, which she said she completely understood. She goes on

'Pardon any little freedoms I take with you...If I was your sister, I would call and see you, but 'tis a censorious world this, and in this sense 'you and I are not of this world'. Adieu. Keep up your heart, you will soon get well and we shall meet. Farewell. God bless you'.

On 12th December 1787 Burns replied to her letter of the 8th, with a critique of her poem

'Your lines, I maintain it, are poetry, and good poetry; mine were, indeed, partly fiction, and partly a friendship which, had I been so blest as to have met with you in time, might have led me – God of love only knows where. Time is too short for ceremonies. I swear solemnly, (in all the tenor of my former oath), to remember you in all the pride and warmth of friendship until – I cease to be'!

Agnes was unhappy with the use of the word 'love' and replied on 16th

'When I meet you, I must chide you for writing in your romantic style. Do you remember that she whom you address is a married woman? or, Jacob-like, would you wait seven years, and even then, perhaps be disappointed, as he was'.

But it was not a serious chastisement, as can be seen when the letter is read in it's entirety. This has been the problem with Agnes' letters. They have all been taken as serious pieces. No one has ever wanted to see the humour in them.

Agnes Craig was born and brought up in the centre of Glasgow, playing with all classes of children, and had a very sharp Glaswegian humour, which could not help but come out in her writing and her conversation.

This inborn humour seems to have been lost in the minds of most of the biographers of Robert Burns, especially the earlier ones. Mind you what chance did Agnes ever have, when even her honesty, confusion and level headedness as to her survival, is used against her by many of these writers.

Agnes could not bed Burns because she had too much to lose, and she recognised she was still married, even if her wayward husband had decided he was not. But that did not mean that she could not go in for a spot of 'heavy breathing', or even a lot of it. Agnes was in her prime and Burns was, according to him, unattached, and anyone's for the taking.

In another letter written round about the 20th December, Burns says that his heart may 'have gone astray a little, but I can declare upon the honor of a poet that the vagrant has wandered unknown to me'.

He then goes on to play some very serious emotional games with her, which probably caused her a great deal of confusion and gave her a bout of the vapours. How many phials of smelling salts did she have to carry about her person when reading his letters, I wonder?

From a letter dated 20th December 1787 it can be seen that the idea of using aliases was Agnes' idea

'I have proposed to myself a more pastoral name for you, although it be not much in keeping with the shrillness of the Ettrick Pipe. What say you to Sylvander? I feel somewhat less restraint than when I subscribe myself CLARINDA'.

Robert replied on 28th December,

'You cannot imagine, Clarinda, (I like the idea of Arcadian names in a commerce of this kind)…I do love you if possible still better for having so fine a taste and turn for Poesy. – I have again gone wrong in my usual unguarded way, but you may erase the word, and put esteem, respect or any other tame Dutch expression you please in its place'.

This really got to her now. There he was using that word love again, and after her having been separated from her husband, vile though he was, for seven years, with all that that entails. She probably had another bout of the vapours. Trying to brush it aside in the next letter she ended with

'I entreat you not to mention our corresponding to one on earth. Though I've conscience innocence, my situation is a delicate one'.

Agnes, realising that they could be getting in a little too deep, offered to introduce him to her friend, Mary Peacock, whom she told Burns

'Would have been a much better Clarinda. She is comely, without being beautiful, - and has a large share of sense, taste and sensibility, added to all, a violent penchant for poetry. If I ever have an opportunity, I shall make you and her acquainted'.

I wonder what *Mary Peacock would have thought of that description 'comely, without being beautiful', her self-esteem would have probably sunk to the level of a cobblestone. But Agnes was bright enough to know that Mary Peacock would be no contender for the poet's soul, because that was going to belong to her alone.

*Mary Peacock was the second wife of James Gray, master in the High School, Edinburgh and Principal of Belfast Academy in 1822. He entered Holy Orders and was sent overseas to a Chaplaincy in India, where he died at Bhuj in 1830. Mary is also said to have died there.

Eventually 'Lang Sandy' allowed Burns to get out the house. In January 1788 he visited Agnes about six times, mostly getting about in a sedan chair. Agnes was worried about him being seen too often at her flat.

Agnes' small abode, situated over the alley called General's Entry in the Potterrow, was surrounded by the homes of many people who knew both she and Burns. More than that, they knew of Burns' reputation with the ladies, and a small amount of tittle-tattle as regards any imagined goings on with him, could ruin any woman's reputation.

The first visit Burns made to Agnes was on the 4th January. This was a whole month, several gallons of ink and at least two small trees since they last met. These visits must have put a strain on both of them.

After a rendezvous with Burns, on the 12th January, Agnes wrote in a long letter dated Sunday evening, 13th January, and written over three days

'I will not deny it, Sylvander, last night was one of the most exquisite I ever experienced. Few such fall to the lot of mortals! Few, extremely few, are formed to relish such refined enjoyment. That it should be so vindicates the wisdom of Heaven. But though our enjoyment did not lead beyond the limits of virtue, yet today's reflections have not been altogether unmixed with regret. The idea of the pain it would have given, were it known, to a *friend to whom I am bound by the sacred tie of gratitude, (no more)'.

*The friend is probably William Craig, her cousin.

In the letter Agnes tells Burns of a meeting she had had earlier that day at the house of a woman friend 'with whom I sat between sermons'. She had met another woman at the friend's house, and neither she nor the second woman liked each other from the start.

'She eyed me with minute, supercilious attention, never looking at me, when I spoke, but even half interrupted me, before I had done addressing the lady of the house...I was disgusted at the fawning deference the lady showed her; and when she told me at the door that it was my Lord Napier's sister, I replied, 'Is it indeed? By her ill-breeding I should have taken her for the daughter of some upstart tradesman!

Sylvander, my sentiments as to birth and fortune, are truly unfashionable; I despise the persons who pique themselves on either, - the former especially...A person of a vulgar, uncultivated mind I would not take to my bosom, in any station; but one possessed of natural genius, improved by education and diligence, such an one I would take for my friend, be her extraction ever so mean'.

The letter was topped up on Tuesday 15th when Agnes added to the end another long paragraph

'Just returned from the Dean, where I dined and supped with fourteen of both sexes: all stupid. My Mary (*Peacock*) and I alone understood each other. However, we were joyous and I sang in spite of my cold; but no wit. 'T'would have been pearls before swine literalized'.

In other words, 'I sang to them, because I know I am a good singer, but by heaven's I made sure they knew I wasn't enjoying it'. Agnes on her high horse must have been an exquisite, and very humorous sight.

Burns sent Agnes a reminder in his letter of the 15th January that he would have to be returning home soon. He began

'O, Clarinda! Why would you wound my soul, by hinting last night must have lessened my opinion of you. True, I was behind the scenes with you; but what did I see? A bosom glowing with honor and benevolence; a mind ennobled by genius, informed and refined by education, and reflection...'

Burns finished his letter with

145

'Oh, my angel! How soon must we part! – and when can we meet again? I look forward on the horrid interval with tearful eyes! What have not I lost by not knowing you sooner! I fear, I fear, my acquaintance with you is too short to make that lasting impression on your heart I could wish'.

Burns' leg was healing fast. In her letter of 16th, after mentioning that 'you are the first letter-writer I ever knew. I only wonder how you can be fashed with my scrawls', she says

'I am happy to hear of your being able to '*walk*' – even to the next street. You are a consummate flatterer; really my cheeks glow while I read your flights of fancy. I fancy you see I like it when you peep into the Repository…If I grow *affected* or *conceited* you are alone to blame. Ah, my friend! These are disgusting qualities! But I am not afraid. I know any merit I have perfectly – but I know many sad counterbalances'.

The subject of Lord Napier's sister came up again, and Agnes writes

'You carry your warmth too far as to Miss Napier (not Nairn); yet I am pleased at it. She is sensible, lively, and well-liked, they say. She was not to know Clarinda was 'divine,' *(a nice little dig at herself)* and therefore kept her distance. She is comely, but a thick bad figure, waddles in her pace, and has rosy cheeks.

> Wha is that clumsy damsel there?
> 'Whisht! It's the daughter of a peer,
> Right honorably great!'
>
> The daughter of a peer, I cried,
> It doth not yet appear
> What we shall be (in t'other world),
> God keep us frae this here!
> That she has *Blude*, I's no dispute,
> I see it in her face;
> Her honor's in her *name*, I fear,
> And in nae other place.

I hate myself for being satirical – hate me for it too'.

They met on the 18th January. On Wednesday 23rd the temperature must have risen quite high between them, with Agnes teetering on the brink of temptation. Writing to Burns the next day she says

'To drop my metaphor, I am neither well nor happy today; my heart reproaches me for last night. If you wish Clarinda to regain her peace, determine against everything but what the strictest delicacy warrants. I do not blame you, but myself. I must not see you on Saturday, unless I find I can depend on myself acting otherwise'.

In another note written on 24th, Agnes remarks how things will calm down after he returns to Ayrshire

'You and I are capable of that ardency of love, for which the wide creation cannot afford an adequate object. Let us seek to repose it in the bosom of our God'.

The letter was delivered by her maidservant, Jenny Clow, on Friday morning, 25th January, his twenty-ninth birthday. Poor Jenny Clow who was used by Burns to alleviate his frustration on, then forgotten about until he found out she was unfortunately pregnant.

Jenny was sent back to Agnes with a letter from Burns informing her that he would be visiting her on Saturday 26th

'I had proposed bringing my bosom friend, Mr. Ainslie, to-morrow evening, at his strong request, to see you; as he has only time to stay with us about ten minutes, for an engagement. But I shall hear from you this afternoon for mercy's sake! – for, till I hear from you, I am wretched. O Clarinda, the tie that binds me to thee is intwisted, incorporated with my dearest threads of life'.

If, as is suspected, he had bedded Jenny Clow that afternoon, his words were totally hypocritical.

Burns wrote to Agnes again on Saturday 26th informing her that he and his friend, Robert Ainslie, would visit. Also at that meeting was Mary Peacock.

'We only propose staying half an hour- 'for ought we ken' – I could suffer the lash of Misery eleven months in the year, were the twelfth to be composed of hours like yesternight- You are the soul of my enjoyment all else is of the stuff of stocks & stones'.

They met on the 28th January where they apparently had had a falling out, and another on Tuesday 29th. In a letter dated Wednesday 30th January, Agnes talks about someone who had become very fond of her. She did not mention his name, (though it was probably her cousin, William Craig, who looked after her and her family so well, and who never married).

'He was, for near four years, the one I confided in. When I had hardly a friend to care for me in Edinburgh, he befriended me. I saw, too soon, 'twas with him a warmer feeling: perhaps a little infection was the natural effect. I told you the circumstances, which helped to eradicate the tender impression in me; but I perceive (though he never tells me so) – I see it in every instance – his prepossession still remains. I esteem him as a faithful friend; but I can never feel more for him. He sees no man half so often with me as himself; and thinks I surely am at least partial to no other. I cannot bear to deceive one in so tender a point,

147

and I am hurt at his harbouring an attachment I never can return. I have thoughts of owning my intimacy with Sylvander, but a thousand things forbid it'.

This, to me, shows that Agnes McLehose was an honourable woman. It would have been easy for her, with her looks and charm, to find a husband who would keep her in a style befitting to her, but she did not sell herself down that road. She could only marry for love. Even the marriage to McLehose was for love, though love there was definitely blinded by hormones and bad choice.

They were together again on Friday 1st February. On the 2nd Agnes opened her heart to Burns

'I am wishing for, Sylvander, the power of looking into your heart. It would be but fair – for you have the key of mine. Last night must have shown you Clarinda not 'divine' – but as she really is. I can't recollect some things I said without a degree of pain...For many years, have I sought for a male friend, endowed with sentiments like you, one who could love me with tenderness, yet unmixed with selfishness; who could be my friend, companion, protector, and who would die sooner than injure me...Last night can leave you at no loss to guess the man:

Then, dear Sylvander, use it weel,
An' row it in your bosom's biel;
Ye'll find it aye baith kind an' leal,
An' fou o' glee;
It wad na wrang the vera deil, -
Ah, far less thee!

How do you like this parody on a passage of my favourite poet? – It is extempore – from the heart; and let it be to the heart'.

This is the cry of a lost soul, alone in the world. Parents dead, three sisters and a brother dead, half of her children dead, and the man she loved, trusted and married, a brutal bully, who took her children from her, just because he could. She was left in dire straits while he went abroad and made his fortune, which neither she nor her remaining children were to share in. Agnes couldn't have said anymore of herself in this paragraph if she had taken time to write a tome of pages. She finished the letter with a quote from Oliver Goldsmith, obviously intended for Burns

'In Nature's simplest habit clad,
No wealth or power had he;
Genius and worth were all he had,
But these were all to me'.

Agnes, in the years she had lived in Edinburgh, had built a shielding wall around herself and her emotions. She had lost just about everything and everyone she had ever cared for and loved. But every day she put on the motley to face the world.

No wonder Agnes kept Burns at arms length and use religion as her defence. If things looked like getting out of hand at least she could bring God into the conversation. She was aware that she was the one with everything to lose. Burns would be leaving soon. She was sure that she could hold out against his fascinating sorcery, for a few more days, at least.

Agnes sent him a letter on Thursday 7th February giving him news of Mary Peacock. Mrs Alison Cockburn, the poet, had read a poem of Mary's called 'Henry' and apparently had 'admired it greatly', so Mary was on top of the world. Apparently Agnes, Mary and Burns had met the previous night, the 6th. It was a good night, but Mary's attitude worried Agnes

> 'What a cordial evening we had last night! I only tremble at the ardent manner Mary talks of Sylvander! She knows where his affections lie, and is quite unconscious of the eagerness of her expressions. All night I could get no sleep for her admiration. I like her for it, and am proud of it; but I know how much violent admiration is akin to love'.

From the meeting of Agnes, Burns, Mary Peacock and Robert Ainslie, on 26th January, it was well and truly 'almost nearly quite' out in the open in Edinburgh society, that there was 'possibly a whiff of a suggestion' that there might be something going on between the two of them.

This 'whiff' reached the ears of Agnes' cousin, William Craig and her minister The Rev John Kemp, who apparently was not sinless himself in his dalliances with the ladies. With the amount of stones cast in his direction, he could have built his own small church.

Kemp wrote to Agnes telling her that she was wrong to carry on this affair and must cease the liaison immediately. Burns name was not mentioned. She sent the letter round to Burns on Wednesday 13th February with a note saying that he must cease to love her. He refused saying 'I must love, pine, mourn and adore in secret; this you must not deny me'.

He followed this declaration by

> 'Thou Redeemer of Mankind! Ye look down with approving eyes on a passion inspired by the purest flame, and guarded by truth, delicacy, and honor; but the half-inch soul of an unfeeling cold-blooded, pitiful Presbyterian bigot cannot forgive anything above his dungeon-bosom and foggy head'.

The next day he sent another letter

> 'How shall I comfort you who am the cause of the injury? Can I wish

that I had never seen you?   That we had never met?   No; I never will'.

(Is this the forerunner to Ae Fond Kiss?)

Robert advised Agnes that she was not answerable to either Craig or Kemp, and told her to keep her own council

> 'I do not think they are entitled to any information.   As to their jealousy and spying, I despise them'.

By the middle of February 1788 the affair was coming to an end.

Many people question the fact that it was an affair.   Agnes certainly thought that it was.   She may not have given herself physically to Burns, but in the heart and soul department, she had already admitted she was his, and she remained his for the rest of her days.   For some people the giving of the soul is a thousand times more binding than the giving of the body.   I think Agnes was one of those people.

They met on Saturday 16th February.   Burns left Edinburgh and headed for Glasgow on Monday 18th February 1788.   He wrote to her from 'The Black Bull', in Argyll Street, where he was spending a little time, in the company of his brother, William, and his friend Captain Richard Brown.

> 'Every milestone that marked my progress from Clarinda, awakened a keener pang of attachment to her.   How do you feel, my love?   Is your heart ill at ease? I fear it'.

Agnes missed him when he left Edinburgh, in a letter sent to him at Mossgiel in Mauchline on 19th/20th February she mentions that she had been visited by Kemp, and goes on to say

> 'Yesterday I thought of you and went over to Miss Nimmo, to have the luxury of talking of you.   She was most kind, and praised you more than ever, as a man of worth, honor, genius.   Oh, how I could have listened to her for ever!...I wish you were here tonight to comfort me, I feel hurt and depressed.......Mary was at my bedside by eight this morning.   She tells me her defence of you was so warm, in a large company where you were blamed for some trivial affair, that she left them impressed with the idea of her being in love.   She laughs, and says, "tis pity to have the skaith, and nothing for her pains'...I think the streets look deserted-like since Monday; and there's a certain insipidity in the good kind of folks I once enjoyed not a little...Miss Wardrobe supped here on Monday.   She once named you, which kept me from falling asleep.   I drank your health in a glass of ale – as the lasses do at Hallowe'en, - 'in to mysel''.

Burns wrote to Agnes from Kilmarnock, on 22nd February, on his way to Mauchline to take his responsibility for Jean Armour.   He arrived there on

22nd/23rd February 1788.

He put pen to paper to Agnes again on 23rd February, making very unpleasant and insulting remarks about Jean, saying she was like a farthing taper compared to Agnes' sun, and that he was still hoping to go to the Indies. Then he went on to say that he will write to her from Dumfries, 'if these horrid postages don't frighten me'.

He didn't manage to write again until 2nd March from Cumnock as he had gone to Dumfriesshire to view Mr Miller's farms on the banks of the Nith.

I wonder when Agnes began to question his sincerity. Did she ever falter in her belief of him on her earlier pronouncement to Miss Nimmo in reply to her asking Agnes what she thought of Burns, 'He is ane o' god's ain; but his time's no come yet'.

If he could insult Jean, someone whom he had professed to love at one time, someone who obviously was deeply in love with him and who was the mother to their children, what could he be saying about her, maybe to people that they both knew? She even picked up on his quibble on postage costs in her letter of March 5th.

> 'How could you ever mention 'postages'. I counted on a crown at least; and have only spent one poor shilling. If I had but a shilling in the world you could have sixpence; nay eightpence, if I could contrive to live on a groat. I am avaricious only in your letters…'

Burns left Mauchline and set out to return to Edinburgh on the 10th of March in order to deal with business with Creech and others, which had not been resolved earlier. He saw Agnes on many occasions, the last being Saturday 22nd March 1788 sending her a pair of small drinking glasses, along with the verses beginning 'Fair Empress of the poet's soul'.

Burns' sister, Mrs Begg, said that on his return from Edinburgh he wore a breast-pin with a miniature of Agnes in it, which was later exchanged for a miniature of Jean Armour, Jean Armour being sent to Glasgow with her brother-in-law, William to have the miniature painted.

Burns could be hard headed and business like when he chose. He had made up his mind that he wanted to return to farming again and probably realised, after his last meeting with Agnes, that if he were to go back to the country life, then she would be a totally unsuitable helpmate for him.

If he was successful in being accepted into the Excise, he intended to use Ellisland as a dairy farm to supplement his income. While he would be out on his Excise rounds, he needed someone he could depend on and trust to look after his investment I don't think he could imagine Agnes McLehose up to her ankles in farm effluence, churning butter till her blond hair was like rats tails, or having to dispose of a chicken for dinner.

With all these evaluations, and more, to take into consideration it probably spurred him on to finally accept Jean as his wife. Which she was anyway under Scots Law. His relationship with Jean had never been a secret, except to her father in the early days, but then Burns was not in the position of becoming a government official, and it had been inferred that he would stand a better chance of entering the Excise if he legitimised his relationship with Jean, thus becoming a dependable married man.

Burns married Jean in April 1788. He did not tell Agnes about this 'second' marriage, leaving that to Robert Ainslie. Agnes was upset and once again felt that fate had dealt her another blow. Maybe during the separation she had warmed towards the idea of marrying Burns. Then, in the summer, came the second body blow. Jenny Clow was pregnant, and the father of her child was Robert Burns.

Agnes had no contact with Burns for a year. Then she broke her silence in a letter telling him, circa March 1789, what she thought of his actions. She was still hurting, still felt used and betrayed. He had spent all that time with her in Edinburgh with not a hint of his intention to marry Jean.

Burns replied to this letter on 9th March 1789 telling Agnes that when he left her he had no intention of marrying Jean, but circumstances beyond his control laid this path in front of him.

Burns in his letter carries on to show what a good fellow he was in not taking advantage of Agnes

'When you call over the scenes that have passed between us, you will survey the conduct of an honest man, struggling successfully with temptations the most powerful that ever beset humanity, and preserving untainted honour in situations where the austere Virtue would have forgiven a fall. Situations that I will dare to say, not a single individual of all his kind, even with half his sensibility and passion, could have encountered without ruin; and I leave you to guess, Madam, how such a man is likely to digest an accusation of perfidious treachery'.

Not such a good fellow as regards Jenny Clow though! Agnes certainly was not amused when she found out about Jenny, her young maidservant having given birth to Burns' illegitimate son. Though in a later letter Burns said that he had offered to take 'my boy from her long ago, but she would never consent'.

Agnes wrote to Burns in November 1791, informing him of the imminent death of Jenny Clow. Jenny had contracted tuberculosis. Burns took leave of his Excise work to come to Edinburgh, and possibly try to convince Jenny that their son would be better off living with him and Jean. It also gave him a chance to meet Agnes again, after a period of nearly four years.

Agnes and Burns met for the last time on 6th December 1791 in Lamont's Land in Edinburgh, exchanged locks of each other's hair and kissed for the last time. They were never to meet again.

On 27th December 1791, Burns, now living in the 'sang-hoose' in the Wee Vennel in Dumfries, sent her the songs 'Ae Fond Kiss', 'Aince Mair I Hail Thee, Thou Gloomy December' and 'Behold The Hour, The Boat Arrive'.

Agnes had also reached a turning point in her life and had decided to go to Jamaica to have one last chance at reconciling with her husband.

The decision to go to Jamaica was sparked when Agnes received a draft for £50 from her husband, and an invitation to come over in order that they could be reconciled. William having died in August 1790, she settled her surviving son Andrew into boarding school and prepared for the voyage.

Burns sent her a large amount of letters during this period before she left. One dated the 15th December said he was going to have the lock of her hair made into a ring.

She wrote to Robert on his thirty-third birthday in January 1792

> 'And now, my dearest Sir, I have a few things to say to you, as the last advice of her who could have lived or died with you! I am happy to know of you applying so steadily to the business you have engaged in; but oh remember, this life is a short, passing scene! Seek God's favour - keep His commandments – be solicitous to prepare for the happy eternity! There, I trust, we will meet, in perfect and never-ending bliss'.

Not exactly the cheerful birthday letter Burns would have hoped to receive. But somehow or another Agnes always seemed to be happiest talking about sin, repentance and death. Still it is nice to have something to look forward to.

Agnes sailed from Leith for Jamaica on the 'Roselle' on 29th January 1792. As fate would have it, this was the same ship that Burns would have sailed in had he actually gone to the West Indies in the late winter of 1786.

When she reached Jamaica she found out her estranged husband had taken a Jamaican mistress, Ann Chalon Riviere, and had had a child with her, Ann Lavinia McLehose.

McLehose didn't meet her when the ship anchored, and Agnes was left on the dockside until he decided he was ready to turn up to collect her. He arrived drunk and aggressive as usual, leading to more arguments.

In Jamaica, Agnes lived in the large house owned by McLehose in an area today known as Kingston Gardens. She could stand in the tropical heat, a change from the winds of Edinburgh, and view the Blue Mountains about 20 miles away. What thoughts must have passed through her mind as she

Song Tune, Rory Dall's port

Ae fond kiss, & then we sever;
Ae fareweel, & then for ever!
Deep in heart-wrung tears I'll pledge thee
Warring sighs & groans I'll wage thee.——

Who shall say that Fortune grieves him,
While the star of hope she leaves him:
Me, nae chearful twinkle lights me,
Dark despair around benights me.——

I'll ne'er blame my partial fancy,
Naething could resist my Nancy:
But to see her, was to love her;
Love but her, & love for ever——

Had we never lov'd sae kindly,
Had we never lov'd sae blindly:
Never met——or never parted
We had ne'er been broken-hearted——

Fare-thee-weel, thou first & fairest!
Fare-thee-weel, thou best & dearest!
Thine be ilka joy & treasure,
Peace, Enjoyment, Love & Pleasure!

Ae fond kiss, & then we sever!
Ae fareweel, alas, for ever!
Deep in heart wrung tears I'll pledge thee,
Warring sighs & groans I'll wage thee——

Facsimile from the original M.S. sent to Mrs. McLehose in the collection of the late W. F. Watson Esq. Edinburgh

The note beneath reads – 'Facsimile from the original M.S. sent to Mrs. McLehose in the collection of the late W.F. Watson, Esq. Edinburgh.

realised the mistake she had made in coming out at her husband's request.

James McLehose was still the same dishonest cheat in Jamaica as he was in Scotland, and still the same bully. Almost always drunk, he was also in the habit of beating his servants. It is reported that Agnes tried to stop him from doing this on quite a few occasions, but was threatened with violence for these courageous acts.

Becoming more sick and depressed as the days passed, she eventually came under the care of a Dr Fife who confirmed that she was on the edge of nervous collapse, and he feared that she would suffer a complete nervous breakdown. There was no other place for her to go, and nothing else to do but return home.

Three months later she came back to Scotland, arriving in Leith in August 1792, again on the 'Roselle' on it's return voyage home. McLehose still refused to pay maintenance for her and his son, although he was a very wealthy man. Agnes returned home with £21 in her pocket. She did not inform Burns that she was back in Scotland. Her own description of the period is as follows

'...As my constitution never agreed with heat, I felt its bad effects as soon as we had crossed the Line; but the very cold reception I received from Mr McLehose on landing, gave me a shock, which, joined to the climate, deranged my mind to such a degree as made me not answerable for what I either said or did. My husband's after-kindness could not remove the complication of nervous disorders, which seized me. They increased to such a height that Dr Fife, the professional gentleman who attended me, and whose soothing manner I can never forget, was of opinion that my going home was absolutely necessary – otherwise my reason if not my life, would fall a sacrifice. Accordingly in June I took leave of Mr McLehose. Our parting was most affectionate. On my part, it was with sincere regret that my health obliged me to leave him. Upon his, it was to all appearances equally so. However, we parted with mutual promises of constancy, and of keeping up a regular correspondence. After getting into the cool air, I gradually recovered my health'.

Again Agnes seems to need to share the responsibility for her return to Scotland, saying that it was Dr Fife's opinion that her going home was necessary as either her sanity or life would be at stake. Like the breakdown of her marriage, in 1780, she seems to be taking a bystanders view, not being totally involved in the decision.

Apparently during this time, Burns had written letters to Agnes via Mary Peacock. Agnes did not want any letters sent out to Jamaica for her husband to find, and use against her. Mary informed Burns that she did not receive any letters from him for Agnes.   Maybe they were lost in the post.   On the 6th December 1792 Burns again wrote to Agnes via Mary

> 'I have written so often to you and have got no answer, that I had resolved never to lift up a pen to you again, but this eventful day, the sixth of December, recalls to my memory such a scene!   Heaven and earth!   When I remember a far distant person'!

Mary did respond very quickly to this letter, telling him that Agnes was back in Scotland, but had returned suffering from nervous collapse due to her experience at the hands of her husband in Jamaica.   This letter also got mislaid, this time at his house in the 'Wee Vennel' in Dumfries.   It was found some months later behind a chest of drawers.

When he did eventually find the misplaced communication Burns replied to it, in a letter dated to circa March 1793, with all the excitement he could muster asking why Agnes had not informed him that she had returned home.   He stipulated that the response he wanted back from her had to be honest, passionate to a degree and not 'baptised in the font of sanctimonious Prudence'.   He also included the fourth volume of the Scots Musical Museum as a gift to her.

Burns wrote again on 25th June 1794 from the Carlinwalk Inn, Newton Stewart.   This was the first communication in 15 months.   He told her how he had tried to write to her before 'in friendship' but it was impossible.

> 'When I take up the pen, Recollection ruins me.   Ah!   My ever-dearest Clarinda! – Clarinda! What a host of memories tenderest offspring crowd on my fancy at that sound! – But I must not indulge that subject - you have forbid it…You would laugh were you to see me where I am just now.   Would to Heaven you were here to laugh with me, though I am afraid that crying would be our first employment!   Here am I set, a solitary hermit, in the solitary room of a solitary inn, with a solitary bottle of wine by me, as grave and as stupid as an owl, but like that owl, still faithful to my old song; in confirmation of which, my dear Mrs. Mac, here is your good health…You must know, my dearest Madam, that these now many years, where ever I am, in whatever company, when a married lady is called as a toast, I constantly give you, but as your name has never passed my lips, even to my most intimate friend, I give you by the name of Mrs. Mac'.

The letter Burns sent to Agnes enclosed the verses on the 'Monody On A Lady Famed For Her Caprice', the poem he had addressed to Maria Riddell, as well as the Epigram meant for her 'If you rattle along like your mistresses tongue, etc.'.   Walter Riddell was not forgotten either, as Burns included the Epitaph he had composed on him.

> 'The subject of the foregoing is a woman of fashion in this country, with

whom, at one period, I was well acquainted.   By some scandalous conduct to me, and two or three other gentlemen here as well as me, she steered so far to the north of my good opinion, that I have made her the theme of several ill natured things.   The epigram struck me the other day, as I passed her carriage'.

None of the poems in the letter were very nice, and Agnes did not reply. On this bitter note ended one of the most famous unconsummated love stories of all time.

When Burns died, his friends, realising his contribution to the literature of Scotland, and also his importance to future generations, set about gathering as much information, relics and correspondence there was relating to him. Letters received from him or ones sent by him.

Many people were very unhelpful.   Agnes up to a point was one of them. She was very protective of the letters that she sent to him.   She didn't want her reputation sullied in any way.   Various people, including his first biographer James Currie, who really had no right to do such a thing, destroyed many letters from and to Burns.   At least Agnes kept all of hers.

Agnes lived until she was over eighty-three, dying on the 22nd October 1841.   She is buried in the Canongate Cemetry in Edinburgh.

Agnes never forgot Burns.   An entry in her diary dated 6th December 1831, the fortieth anniversary of their parting

'This day I can never forget.   Parted with Burns in 1791, never more to meet in this world.   May we meet in Heaven'.

When Agnes' life is scanned, to a psychologist at least, her actions are understandable

By the time she was fifteen she had lost a mother, brother and three sisters. She was then sent away from Glasgow to a boarding school in Edinburgh, and took up with someone who was totally unsuitable, a drunkard and a wife beater who charmed her with his flattering tongue.   She had four children in four years to him, the oldest child dying in infancy.   She then separated from her husband because of his drunkenness and cruelty.

When she returned to her father's house, her husband made sure he got custody of the children, and when her youngest was weaned he also took him away from her.   McLehose didn't look after the boys but farmed them out to various relatives, nor did he support them financially.

Shortly after moving back to her father's home, he died leaving her virtually penniless except for a couple of annuities from his medical career and some monies from a property investment.

Gathering her children together, McLehose was in England at the time, she moved to Edinburgh. She had approximately ten shillings a week to live on to support her family and even that was taken away from her. Her children were not the healthiest and sadly she was left with only one son.

In 1791 James McLehose offered reconciliation to her. She followed him out to Jamaica, but because of his aggressive behaviour there was no happy ever after for Agnes. She returned to Scotland. Agnes never again saw the man she loved, Robert Burns, and that was that!

The only true sparkle, light and energy seemed to come when Burns entered her life. She came alive with feelings she had probably suppressed for years. But she couldn't help the fact that she had to be very sensible and sensitive to her situation. Deep down inside she probably knew nothing would ever come of the relationship, and if anything physical happened then she would certainly have been left holding the baby, and a ruined reputation.

She was certainly more honest in her feelings for Burns that he was in his feelings towards her. For him it seems more like a paper exercise to while away his hours when he had 'nothing else to do'. Did Agnes love Burns? Oh Yes, Agnes did love Burns. But trust him?

Even if they had got together it was a relationship unlikely to survive. Burns could not or would not help himself. Agnes would have become another conquest, which he could coldly turn away from. Burns' emotions were Burns led and had to do with what he wanted and what he was feeling at the time, others were only co-stars. But that doesn't make him a bad poet, and it certainly does not make Agnes McLehose a tease.

A paragraph in a letter sent to Agnes dated 8th January 1788 reads

'These are my tenets, my lovely friend; and which, I think, cannot be well disputed My creed is pretty nearly expressed in the last clause of Jamie Dean's grace, an honest weaver in Ayrshire:- 'Lord, grant that we may lead a gude life! For a gude life mak's a gude end: at least it helps weel!' Good night, my dearest Clarinda'! 'SYLVANDER'

Above Left : Agnes Craig McLehose (Clarinda) by an unknown artist.
Above Right : Clarinda's Grave at Canongate Cemetry in Edinburgh.

Epilogue

Many people met Agnes McLehose in her middle and old age.   Most had good things to say of her though others had not.   One who liked her was a Dr James Adams who wrote of Agnes whom he met at a party in 1835

> 'There was present a chirpy old lady, who, from subsequent information, I know must have been about seventy-five years of age, but it was a considerable time afterwards I learned that in her an angel had entertained me unawares; and that the 'Mrs McLehose', with whom I shook hands and interchanged ordinary civilities during the evening, was the far-famed 'Clarinda'...a next door neighbour of my host'.

During the evening the company sang Scottish Songs and Adams sang 'She Says She Lo'es Me Best Of A' and he

> 'often regretted I did not take note of Clarinda's face as she listened to almost the only song of Burns that was sung that evening'.

Adams went on to say that Agnes sang and danced with as much gusto as she must have done in her youth and laughed broadly at the humour.   But he did not like her habit of snuff taking (also a habit that Burns had), which

159

he said she seemed addicted to.

A Captain Charles Gray met Agnes McLehose in her old age

'Her features are now somewhat harsh and haggard, very different from the rather attractive silhouette hanging in her little parlour. I cannot promise that you would discern in her now any traces of her once remarkable grace and beauty, but her interesting talk would be ample compensation for the loss of personal charm'.

Chambers description of her is someone

'of a somewhat voluptuous style of beauty, of lively and easy manners, of a poetic fabric of mind with some wit, and not too high a degree of refinement or delicacy'.

Her grandson's description is as follows

'My personal recollection of her does not extend beyond her middle life. She was short in stature; her hands and feet small and delicate; her skin fair, with a ruddy colour in her cheeks, which she retained till the end of her life; her eyes were lively, and evinced great vivacity; her teeth well formed and beautifully white; her voice was soft and pleasing'.

Sir Walter Scott wrote of her

'Clarinda was a Mrs Meiklehose (sic) wife of a person in the West Indies, from whom she lived separate but without any blemish, I believe, on her reputation. I don't wonder that the Bard changed her 'thrice unhappy name' for the Classical sound of Clarinda. She was a relative of my friend the late Lord Craig, at whose house I have seen her, old, charmless and devote. There was no scandal to her philandering with the Bard, though the Lady ran risques, for Burns was anything but platonic in his amours'.

She remained an active woman into her old age and would be seen walking round Calton Hill on the arm of Margaret, her servant. Agnes moved there sometime in 1810, (according to the earliest Post Office Directory for Edinburgh, first to number 3 and then in 1811 to the first floor flat of number 14), where she remained for the rest of her life.

In 1825 Captain James Glencairn Burns visited her at her house in Calton Hill, but she saw no trace of his father in his features.

Jean Armour met with Agnes McLehose in 1828 when Jean paid a visit to Edinburgh, lodging at George Thomson's house in the High Street, and apparently the two women got on very well.

Mrs Moodie, widow of the Commissary-General of Van Dieman's Land, and who became a neighbour to Agnes, kept a journal, which included mention of Agnes in the months leading up to her death.

'10th March 1841 – An accidental circumstance has brought me acquainted with one who was the friend and correspondent of the poet. This is the Celebrated 'Clarinda'...I have had many opportunities of conversing with her. Her memory is greatly impaired and being also a little deaf, and seldom now quitting her house, common occurrences have ceased to interest her...But it is satisfactory to observe how much remains in that mind to cheer the hours of solitude and to give consolation to the close of a life prolonged beyond the common lot...'

'30th March 1841 – Owing to sickness in my family, I did not see Mrs McLehose for a short time. When I called, I found this interesting old lady much altered in appearance, though not in spirits. She lives in great simplicity, and is very sensible of the great blessing of health'.

'June 1841 - ...She is perfectly conscious that her intellectual powers are much abridged. She remarked upon the loss of her memory, -'it was the strongest organ I possessed: therefore, having been so much exercised, it is no wonder it has taken leave the first...' *(Agnes still showing signs of a sense of humour).*

Mrs Moodie goes on to say that although Agnes was forgetful of daily occurrences, her memory for past events was extra-ordinary. She could converse on any subject and relate anecdotes to anytime in her past. 'Indeed, her mind is still the receptacle of fine thoughts'.

She recalled that if there were many people in the room, Agnes seemed confused and didn't take part in the conversation, but Mrs Moodie put that down to her deafness, not her lack of understanding.

Mrs Moodie received a letter from Agnes ten days before she died, maybe the last she wrote. The letter was written in a firm, distinct hand.

'My dear Mrs Moodie, I am wearying to see you. Do give me a call. I am very poorly. I shall never forget your great kindness to me, and your being a stranger. I can give you no return, but my earliest wish that God may bless you and your little ones. May they be spared to you for a blessing, and at last may they be heirs of glory, is the wish and prayers of your earnest friend, A.M. 12th October, 1841'.

On the advance of old age Agnes spoke of the 'loss each year sustains' by quoting 'He gives, and when He takes away, He takes but what He gave'.

On the 22nd October 1841 the entry in Mrs Moodie's journal records

'Our old friend, Mrs McLehose, died this morning. She is gone, and I fully believe to her rest, for she was humble and relied for the acceptance upon the atonement. It has been a source of satisfaction to us to witness the composure of the last days of 'Clarinda.' To some who saw this old lady latterly, the apathy of age, and the loss of memory, gave the idea of greater feebleness of mind than was really the case. There were intervals in which she was still capable of a degree of mental exercise; and corresponding sentiments often served to elicit something of that mental activity for which she had been remarkable. We have frequently found her very collected and clear upon subjects, which interested her. I had the blessing of prayer with her frequently; and on the day of her death I prayed by her bedside, but she could not join; she only pressed my hand and said, 'I am much obliged to you'. She went off peacefully. Amongst her last words were, 'I go to Jesus'. When her faithful servant said to her 'Do you fear death'? she answered 'Not so much now'......After a short time she felt very cold, and pressing her servant's hands, exclaimed Margaret! Margaret! and expired'.

From her grandson

'...As her feelings were naturally strong, so were her attachments. She always considered ingratitude as one of the basest of sins. She would have been a devoted wife, had it not been her misfortune to be united to a man utterly incapable of appreciating her, or of affording her happiness...As a mother, she was fond and indulgent; and the only son who was spared to her, was the object of her warmest affections and most tender solicitude'.

Was it Agnes' curse to outlive her entire family? Agnes' daughter in law Mary, died on 21st April 1838, and her son Andrew, exactly a year later on 21st April 1839.

There is a sheer silken thread of black humour running through the Clarinda/Sylvander saga.

On their third meeting, instead of a passionate evening they both have headaches. Agnes hides behind religion and Burns hypochondria. They argue over which one sent the most letters down to the minutest detail.

Agnes, who cannot visit him, for decency's sake, when he is suffering from his dislocated knee-cap, tells him she will walk past his window and he can look out for her, she will see him and acknowledge this. She doesn't look high enough, leaving Burns bouncing around on his sore knee trying to catch her attention, no doubt using all the swear words of the 18th century.

When he does come to visit her at her house on the 4th January she wants him to walk because taking a sedan would only bring him to the attention of her neighbours. This when he was still recovering from his dislocated kneecap and it was in Edinburgh in a freezing January with the wind probably blowing a discrete hurricane, and nor was where he was living at the time just a hop skip and a jump away.

She wanted him to go and hear her favourite minister preach at the Tollbooth Kirk and told him 'you'll easily get a seat'. It must have been a joy to be a fly on the wall and watch their behaviour.

After her death, in amongst some of Agnes' papers was found the following poem. It was obviously written for Burns, but when is unknown. The poem is called 'Sympathy'. It feels like it was written when she was old, as there is a tiredness in it that is not there in some of her other poetry written when she was younger.

> 'Assist me, all ye gentle powers
> That sweeten friendship's happy hours
> Whilst I attempt to sing of thee
> Heaven born emotion, Sympathy.
>
> When first I saw my rural swain
> The pride of all the tuneful train
> That hour we loved, - what could it be
> But thy sweet magic Sympathy.
>
> Nor sordid wealth, nor giddy power
> Could e'er confer one happy hour. –
> One hour like those I've spent with thee
> In loves endearing Sympathy
>
> All hail, the heavens-inspired mind
> That glows with love of humankind.
> 'Tis thine to feel the ecstasy
> Soul linked to soul by Sympathy'.

James McLehose died on Monday 16th March 1812 in Kingston, at the age of 60 and is interred in Kingston Parish Churchyard. He was appointed Assistant Judge of the Court of Common Pleas for the Parish of Port Royal in 1795, was Deputy Clerk of the Court of Common Pleas for Kingston from 1790-1809, becoming Clerk of the same Court in 1810.

His personality didn't change. According to his grandson W.C. McLehose

'…A report reached this country, as being a matter of notoriety in Kingston, that some of his particular friends had, on the approach of his death, sent all his domestics out of the house; and, as soon as the breath quitted his body, carried off whatever cash and documents there were. If so, the friends proved befitting the man. Notice, however, was given to Mrs McLehose that a balance of several hundred pounds, belonging to her husband, was in the hands of Messrs Coutts in London, Which she soon afterwards obtained'.

There is apparently no remaining letters from James McLehose to Agnes, but again, according to her grandson who had read some of them

'His written correspondence with his wife partakes of the same character: The same letter contained alternate passages of the most endearing expressions and most insulting language'.

In the year before 1937 an event happened that would have tickled Miss Agnes Craig the brightest shade of pink.

The Clarinda Burns Club in Edinburgh wished to erect a plaque to Agnes on the site of her house in the Potterrow. This got the Edinburgh Society folks in a 'stour'. Was Agnes McLehose of 'good enough character' to have a public memorial set up in her honour?

The Edinburgh Corporation Education Committee got their various pieces of underwear in a twist and decided that 'it was beneath the dignity of our city to sanction such a tablet in view of Clarinda's character'. Parts of her letters were read out to show her supposed 'immoral leanings', and permission was refused.

Poor Clarinda, her whole life all she could ever think about was saving her 'character and name', and there she was nearly a century and a half later, having done nothing with Burns but getting a bad name for it anyway.

But the Clarinda Club refused to take no for an answer, and Mr Walter Elliott, M.P. raised the question of the plaque with the Secretary of State for Scotland in the House of Commons.

It was referred back to Edinburgh, where finally the plaque was erected on the wall of Bristo Street Technical Institute and unveiled on 22nd January 1937. Mind you it would have been nicer if they had waited until 25th January. It could have been a gift from Burns to Agnes.

Still for Agnes to find herself mentioned in Parliament would have pleased her no end, and would have been just what she felt she deserved.

Associated Songs:
Song   : Your Friendship Much Can Make Me Blest
                      (Talk Not Of Love, Revision)
Tune   : Banks Of Spey
Period : 4th January 1788

Song   : Go On Sweet Bird (Revision)
Tune   : Scots Queen
Period : 21st January 1788

Song   : Clarinda, Mistress Of My Soul (Farewell To Clarinda)
Tune   : Clarinda
Period : January 1788

Song   : Thine Am I (revised for Jean Lorimer, Sept 1794)
Tune   : The Quaker's Wife
Period : circa February 1790

Song   : On Sensibility
Tune   : Cornwallis' Lament For Colonel Moorhouse
Period : 9th July 1790 (to Mrs Dunlop)

Song   : Thou Gloomy December
Tune   : Thro' The Lang Muir
Period : 27th December 1791

Song   : Ae Fond Kiss
Tune   : Rory Dall's Port
Period : 27th December 1791

Song   : Behold The Hour
Tune   : Oran Gaoil
Period : 27th December 1791   (September 1793 – 2nd Version to Thomson)

Song   : Sae Far Awa
Tune   : Dalkeith Maiden Bridge
Period : December 1791

Song   : Wandering Willie
Tune   : Here Awa, There Awa
Period : c1792 in a letter to John McMurdo,
          (but thought to have been written c1791)

Song   : My Nanie's Awa
Tune   : There Are Few Good Fellows When Jamie's Awa
Period : 9th December 1794

Song   : O May Thy Morn
Tune   : The Rashes
Period : December 1794

23.

JANET (JENNY) CLOW
Born 1766 – Died January 1792

Chronology : 1788

Burns' twenty-ninth birthday, on Friday 25th January 1788, was a day that changed the life of Jenny Clow forever, and was certainly another nail in the coffin of the relationship of Burns and Agnes McLehose.

Jenny was born in Newburgh in Fife, daughter of Alexander Clow and Margaret Inglis, and was the youngest of eight children. On that eventful day she had delivered a letter from Agnes McLehose, her mistress, to Burns

'My servant (who is a good soul) will deliver to you this. She is going down to Leith, and will return about two or three o'clock. I have ordered her to call then, in case you have ought to say to Clarinda today'.

The relationship between Burns and Agnes was now reaching the brow of the hill and was nearing the point of its inevitable end. Their meetings during January were passionate but unconsummated.

There was a lot of emotional torment and anger in Burns who was not used to taking 'no' for an answer, as his brother, Gilbert, said of him, whatever he pretended to be 'he was no platonic lover'.

Even in a letter to his youngest brother William, Burns advised the young lad to try for intimacy as soon as possible after meeting with a woman.

Jenny Clow delivered Agnes' letter after another night of unfulfilled unbridled passion for Robert and Agnes. Burns had begged, he had pleaded, he had crawled. He probably used the fact that his birthday was on the Friday, and what a nice present Agnes would give him if she'd just relent a little (well quite a lot really), still to no avail.

After reading her letter, dated Thursday 24th January 1788, which Jenny delivered, he was in no way pleased. The letter began

'Sylvander, the moment I waked this morning, I received a summons from conscience to appear at the bar of Reason. While I trembled before this sacred throne, I beheld a succession of figures pass before me in awful brightness'.

These figures were Religion, Truth, Reputation, Modesty, Consideration, Love and Friendship.

Something did, or didn't, happen on Wednesday 23rd January 1788, that changed things for both Agnes and Burns forever.

It probably was not on Burns' mind when Jenny dropped the letter off from her mistress to seduce the young girl, but by the time he had read and reread the sentiments 'which wounded my soul' he had certainly an inclination to do so when the maid returned to pick up the reply.

If the mistress would not come across with the goods, then with a little encouragement, the maid would.   After all Jenny was of his class and therefore fair game.

Burns at his worst - selfish, uncaring, controlling, angry and probably devoid of any kind emotion during the act.   Burns could turn predator whenever he felt like it, and there is no excusing his actions on that day.

After the coupling, he sent Jenny back with a letter to Agnes saying that he and a friend (Robert Ainslie) would call on her the next night, Saturday 26th, though they could not stay long.

> 'Be reconciled, My Angel, to your God, yourself, and me; and I pledge you *Sylvander's honor* – an oath, I dare say, you will trust without reserve, that you shall never more have reason to complain of his conduct'.

This was such a hypocritical piece of nonsense after he had just seduced her young servant girl.

Another letter followed on Saturday morning 26th, saying that he and Ainslie would visit Agnes and Mary Peacock at seven o' clock.   Burns ends

> 'I could suffer the lash of Misery eleven months in the year, were the twelfth to be composed of hours like yesternight- You are the soul of my enjoyment: all else is of the stuff of stocks & stones'.

In June 1788, shortly after Burns' civil marriage to Jean Armour, Robert Ainslie wrote to tell him that Jenny Clow was pregnant.   Burns replied on 30th June from Ellisland

> 'I am vexed at that affair of the girl, but dare not enlarge on the subject until you send me your direction, as I suppose that will be altered on your late Master and Friend's death'. (Samuel Mitchelson, to whom Ainslie was apprenticed).

'I am vexed at that affair of the girl'.   Nine words were all he could spare in a very long letter to Ainslie.   Mind you he was becoming used to begetting with women of the working class.

He accepted the fact that he could have been the father of Margaret Cameron's child. His daughter with Bess Paton, the family maid at Lochlea, was about three years old, Margaret Campbell may or may not have been pregnant to him and Jean Armour had already given birth to two sets of twins to him.

With the exception of Jean Armour, they were all disposable sexual fodder. Jean Armour may have remained because she would be useful to him in running his farm, and because she would turn a blind eye to his extra-curricular activities, which, to be fair to him, did seem to slow down following his marriage to her.

By the time Burns received the letter from Ainslie, Agnes McLehose would certainly be aware of Jenny's pregnancy. Ainslie would have made sure of that. Later in the year Jenny took out a 'meditatione fugae' against Burns, naming him as the father of her child.

At the beginning of November 1788 Jenny gave birth to a son, who according to the custom of the time, as the child was illegitimate, automatically took his father's name.

On 6th January 1789 Burns wrote to Ainslie

> 'I shall be in town about four or five weeks, & I must again trouble you to find & secure for me a direction where to find Jenny Clow, for a main part of my business in Edinburgh is to settle that matter with her, & free her hand of the process'.

Burns wanted to take their son from her and bring him up at Ellisland, presumably with the consent of Jean Armour. But the boy did not go to Ellisland. Jenny Clow kept him with her.

Jenny's story had no happy ever after ending. In November 1791 Agnes wrote to Burns in Dumfries

> 'Sir, I take the liberty of addressing a few lines in behalf of your old acquaintance, Jenny Clow, who, to all appearances is at this moment dying. Obliged, from all symptoms of a rapid decay, to quit her service, she is gone to a room almost without common necessities, untended and unmourned. In circumstances so distressing, to whom can she so naturally look for aid as to the father of her child, the man for whose sake she suffered many a sad and anxious night, shut from the world, with no other companions than guilt and solitude? You have now an opportunity to evince you indeed possess these fine feelings you have delineated, so as to claim that just admiration of your country. I am convinced I need add nothing further to persuade you to act as every consideration of humanity, as well as gratitude, must dictate.
>
> I am, Sir, your sincere well-wisher'.

Burns replied to Agnes' letter on the 23rd November 1791, writing in the flirtatious style they once used to each other. He really could not help himself playing his literary mind games. He then turned to what Agnes' letter was all about, the dying Jenny Clow. This letter though written to Agnes, addresses her in the third person.

'I am sure she must have told you of a girl, a Jenny Clow, who had the misfortune to make me a father, with contrition I own it, contrary to the laws of our most excellent constitution, in our holy Presbyterian hierarchy.

Mrs M(-) tells me a tale of the poor girl's distress that makes my very heart weep blood. I will trust that your goodness will apologise to your delicacy for me, when I beg you, for Heaven's sake, to send a porter to the poor woman – Mrs M(-), it seems, knows where she is to be found – with five shillings in my name, and, as I shall be in Edinburgh on Tuesday first, for certain, make the poor wench leave a line for me, before Tuesday, at Mr Mackay's White Hart Inn, Grassmarket, where I shall put up, and before I am two hours in town, I shall see the poor girl, and try what is to be done for her relief. I would have taken my boy from her long ago, but she would never consent.

I shall do myself the very great pleasure to call for you when I come to town, and repay you the sum your goodness shall have advanced...
      (Several lines have been cut from the letter).

Burns asked for and received a week's leave from the Excise to go to Edinburgh to attend to the business with Jenny Clow. He left on 29th November and went to see Jenny, where he gave her an amount of money from that he had received from the roup at Ellisland.

Whether the custody of his son was spoken about again, no one knows, but Burns never tried then or after Jenny's death to obtain this, even although he was more than willing to take the boy into his home at an earlier time, and was probably still of the same frame of mind.

Why did Jenny not want Burns to have their son? Maybe she had arranged for someone else to bring the child up, friend or family. Jenny knew she was dying so there must have been a reason why she did not want Burns to have the boy. Maybe she, like Jean Armour before her, saw the unpleasant side to Burns' nature and did not want her son to have anything to do with that. But that is purely speculation.

It was during this week in Edinburgh that Burns had his final meeting with Agnes McLehose, on 6th December 1791, shortly before she travelled to Jamaica to try for reconciliation with her estranged husband.

Jenny Clow died of Tuberculosis in January 1792. Burns never mentioned her or his son in any of his correspondences ever again.

Jenny's son survived and did well for himself. Robert Burns Clow became a wealthy merchant and married into a good family. Though at the start he cared nothing for his father, he eventually named his eldest son born in 1820, Robert Burns Clow II, telling him who his grandfather was.

Robert Burns Clow II eventually settled in Borneo where he married the chief of the Kayan's daughter. Through him descendants of Burns live there today!

Associated Songs:

None

24.

JANE CRUIKSHANK
Born 1775 - Died 25th April 1835

Chronology : Autumn 1787

Burns returned to Edinburgh on 20th October 1787. This was about six weeks before his first meeting with Agnes McLehose, and just after the first anniversary of the death of Margaret Campbell. He found lodgings with *William Cruikshank, a Classics master at the High School in Edinburgh, who was then living in the New Town at 2 *(later 30)* St James Square.

Burns occupied the top two attic rooms of the then relatively new Cruikshank house, his bedroom facing St Andrew's Square and his front room St James Square.

William was a friend of a friend whom Robert had met earlier on in the year, and they had gotten on very well together. As Cruikshank was one of the members of the foremost masonic lodges in Edinburgh, Canongate Kilwinning, he was a very good contact indeed. He was also a member of the Crochallan Fencibles, one of the prominent drinking clubs in Edinburgh.

Jane was the daughter and only child of William Cruikshank, and although only twelve years of age was regarded a good musician and talented pianist. Burns spent many hours listening to her playing and singing his favourite airs. It was here that he adopted and adapted many of his verses to old tunes. Burns lived with her family from Autumn 1787 - February 1788 (during the Clarinda-Sylvander period). It was here that he convalesced with his injured knee-cap.

Professor Josiah Walker, the 26 year-old son of the minister at Dundonald in Ayrshire who was the tutor to the Marquis of Tullibardine, came to visit Burns while he was living with the Cruikshank family and reported

> 'About the end of October I called for him at the house of a friend, whose daughter, though not more than twelve, was a considerable proficient in music. I found him seated by the harpsichord of this young lady, listening with the keenest interest to his own verses, which she sang and accompanied, adjusting them to the music by repeated trials of the effect. In this occupation he was so totally absorbed that it was difficult to draw his attention from it for a moment'.

Regarding the song 'A Rosebud By My Early Walk', according to Burns

171

'The air of the song is by David Sillar, quondam merchant and now schoolmaster in Irvine'.

The melody for 'Beauteous Rosebud', another poem/song written to Jane was also composed by Sillar, according to Burns, but remains untraced.

In 1804 Jane married a Mr James Henderson a solicitor in Jedburgh, and they raised a large family together. Before she died, in Jedburgh in 1835, according to one of her sons she used to love to reminisce about her young and happy childhood in Edinburgh and the special place she had occupied in the life, heart and works of Robert Burns. Her husband survived her by four years, dying in 1839.

*William Cruikshank had been trained under his uncle, also named William, the famous schoolmaster of Duns, and then went on to study at the University of Edinburgh. He was appointed the Rector of the High School of the Canongate in 1770, receiving a classical mastership two years later in the High School of Edinburgh. He was considered a 'very able and successful teacher, as well as a worthy man' by Lord Brougham. He died on the 8th March 1795, and is buried in Old Calton Cemetery. His grave is unmarked.

Associated Song:

Song   : A Rosebud By My Early Walk
Tune   : A Rosebud
Period : circa Winter 1788

25.

JEAN JAFFRAY/JEFFRY
Born 1773 – Died Oct 1850

Chronology : c1788

Jean Jaffray was the daughter of the Rev. Andrew Jaffray, minister of Lochmaben Church, Dumfriesshire. Her mother was Agnes Armstrong in whose honour 'Roslin Castle' was written. Agnes herself was reputedly related to the 'Johnie Armstrong', of whom the border ballad was penned. So Jean had a lot of old Scottish history behind her.

Jean was described as being of medium height with a fine, clear and fresh complexion and the owner of cheeks that dimpled up when she laughed, which, if reports are correct, she did a lot. She had one sister and three brothers, William, Robert and John, and she presided at the table during Burns' first visit to her father's manse.

Due to the miles he had to cover in his Excise work, Burns could not get home some evenings. On many of these occasions he stayed at the nearest friend's house, one of these being the Jaffrey's. Burns often made himself comfortable, singing and talking, and enjoying the family ambience.

In later years, in her reminiscences of Burns, Jean Jaffray would relate

'Many times have I seen Burns enter my father's dwelling on a cold rainy night, after a long ride over the dreary moors. On such occasions one of the family would help to disencumber him of his dreadnought and boots, while others brought him a pair of slippers and made him a warm dish of tea. It was during these visits that he felt himself perfectly happy, and opened his whole soul to us, repeated and even sang many of his admirable songs to us and enchanted all who had the good fortune to be present with his manly, luminous observations, and artless manners. I never could fancy that Burns had ever followed the rustic occupation of the plough, because everything he said or did had a gracefulness and charm that was in an extraordinary degree engaging'.

Of receiving her song 'The Blue-Eyed Lassie', Jean's story is that her father and she had been dining at the house of Willie Nicol in Moffat. As they were leaving the party Jean relates

'I was only fifteen and sic a wee bit lassie that Burns danced out with me in his arms and put me into the carriage to my father, singing 'Green

Grow The Rashes'. It was after dining with the poet at the house of Mr Nicol that Burns sent me the two songs 'Willie Brewed A Peck O' Maut' and 'The Blue-Eyed Lassie''.

The 'Blue-Eyed Lassie' was included in the Scots Musical Museum of 1790 and was set to an air composed by Robert Riddell of Friar's Carse. The music spanned two octaves and one note, and according to James Dick in his 1906 collection of Burns music and song, was 'unsingable'. This criticism is wrong.

In 1794 Jean Jaffray married a Liverpool merchant, an American citizen, named James Renwick. Soon after she emigrated to New York with James.

It must have been quite a culture shock, moving from sleepy Lochmaben to bustling New York, but Jean fitted in very quickly. She began to enjoy the friendship of the literati in that city, but unfortunately she was widowed early in life and left with several children to bring up on her own. She never remarried after her husband's death.

Jean was quite a literary minded woman, and was reported to be a very proficient writer of poetry. A collected volume of her works was published after her death, but remains untraced to date.

Round about 1822 George Thomson's son visited Jean when he was in New York. He had been invited to meet her by one of her sons who was a professor at Columbia College. This account was sent back to his father.

'She is a widow – has still the remains of Burns delightful portrait of her; her twa sweet een that gave him his death are yet clear and full of expression. She has great suavity of manners and much good sense...She told me that she often looks back with a melancholy satisfaction on the many evenings she spent in the company of the great bard, in the social circle of her father's fireside, listening to the brilliant sallies of his imagination and to his delightful conversation'.

Mrs Mary Balmanno, a friend of Jean's, in 1858 wrote a small book entitled 'Memory to Jean Jaffray'.

Mrs Balmanno had high regard of Jean, who was held in great esteem in the echelons of New York society. Included among those whose admiration she won was Washington Irving, the American poet and novelist. She is mentioned in his biography.

Mary Balmanno reports that Jean was very fond of flowers and they bloomed in her house, at 18 Cortland Street, all year round, 'following the colours of all the seasons'. Mrs Balmanno also reports that Jean Jaffray had a relic of Mary Queen Of Scots, 'a pair of silk and silver fringed gloves.' The gloves had been given to Jean by a relative in Aberdeen.

Another story included in the book of recollections of Mrs Balmanno is of how in Scotland, Jean used to attend a dancing class and at least two of the young men who attended the class were rivals for her affection. One, a Mr Cameron, had himself emigrated to America. Mrs Balmanno writes

'Mr Cameron was deeply enamoured of Jennie Jeffrey and had a great jealousy of 'ane Wullie Broon' This 'Wullie Broon' later rose to the peerage as Sir William Brown. Although Mr Cameron and Jean Jaffray were in America, and possibly even New York, at the same time, it appears they never met'.

It was to Mrs Balmanno that Jean showed the other poem written for her by Burns, 'When First I Saw Fair Jeannie's Face'.

The poem was published, for the first time, in the New York Mirror in 1846. Some biographers questioned whether the verses were written by Burns or even whether they were about Jean Jaffray. The 'New York Mirror' categorically stated that the song was copied from paper, which was in Burns' handwriting, and was brought to America by Jean. It is included in most, but not all, of the editions of his poetry to date.

In 'The Burns Calendar' of 1874, a dedication to Jean Jaffray reads

'Miss Jaffray married a gentleman of the name of Renwick and moved to Liverpool, but ultimately settled in New York, where she died in October 1850, at the venerable age of seventy-seven years, much regretted by a large circle of friends. A brief memoir of her life was written in America by Mrs Balmanno, and is included in a collected volume of her writings entitled 'Pen and Pencil', New York, 1858. Mrs Renwick was tenderly sensitive in her regard for the memory of Burns, and corrects the errors of one of his biographers, in a letter to her sister, dated New York, November 13th 1838, she writes –

'An article in the 'Mirror' induced me to procure and read 'Cunningham's Life of Burns', and I think it is, as I predicted, very inferior to that of my departed friend, Dr Currie, wanting sadly his delicacy and refinement. My dear father was never spoken of but with love and reverence, and he is mentioned as 'that veteran in religion and good fellowship'. Cunningham says he received much information from his son Hugh. I never had a brother named Hugh, my own three brothers were William, at the time in the house of Sir Robert of Herries, in London, the second, Robert, was at the same period surgeon of an East Indiaman, on board of which vessel he died some time after, and the third, John, prosperous and happy beyond the common lot of man, so that at the period of spoken of, fortune was using none of them 'hard and sharp' as stated by the biographer. He is wrong also in stating that the poet's visit was a solitary one at the manse, a statement altogether incorrect. It was after dining in the company of the Poet, at the house of Mr Nicol, who was living at Moffat for the benefit of his child's health, that Burns sent to me two songs 'Willie brew'd a

peck o' maut' and 'The Blue-eyed lassie'. I was then only fifteen and sic a bit lassie, that Burns danced out with me in his arms, and put me into the carriage with my father singing 'Green grow the rashes O'. No event of my early happy days that I look back upon with such pride as having sat at the feet of such a man. He was, at the time I speak of, acting the part of an affectionate husband and father, and even envy never spoke evil of him at my father's fireside, and it was not until many years after, when I had long mixed with a hard-hearted world, that I ever imagined he could do, or had done, wrong. Cunningham says the name of Willie Wastle's wife is lost; I could tell him who she was, but there is no use in opening old sores. It is such a great pity that much more of what he has published had not been lost, also, much that poor Burns never intended to see the light'.

Up to the advanced age of seventy-seven, Mrs Renwick adorned a high social position, with all those qualities of heart and mind – all those sweet, captivating amenities of manner – which had, in her youth, when joined to great personal attractions, rendered her one of the most fascinating maidens of Annandale. She is referred to in 'The Life and Writing of Washington Irving', often a guest at her house. All through her life, she cherished a strong, deep love for Scotland. Writing to her niece from New York, 4th April 1848, she says:-

'If there are any persons near you that recollect Jeanie Jaffrey, say to them that my love for the very stones around the old kirk and manse will only be extinguished by the last scene of all. I hear that you are living at Lochmaben, dear Lochmaben! I remember where the very stones and stumps stood when I left it, and am often, in spirit, by the grave of my beloved parents and yours. I have forgotten none of those I loved in my youthful days'.

Her son, Professor of natural Philosophy and Chemistry in Columbia college, New York, thus writes of 'the last scene of all', in a letter dated 21st February, 1851:-

'It is sufficient to say that she left us full of years and honours, respected beyond the usual lot of mortals, and beloved by a wide circle of friends and descendants'.

Associated Songs:

Song   : The Blue-Ey'd Lassie
Tune   : The Blue Ey'd Lassie
Period : circa 1788

Song   : When First I Saw Fair Jeanie's Face
Tune   : Maggie Lauder
Period : circa 1788 (though questionable)

26.

HELEN HYSLOP
Born March 1766 – Died ?

HELEN ARMSTRONG
Born circa 1788 - Died 1887

Chronology : 1788

Helen Hyslop was the daughter of John Hyslop and Janet Howatson. She was born in Langholm and was considered a 'noted local beauty'. Not a lot more is known about Helen Hyslop, but tradition records that she had a relationship with Burns, which produced a daughter (also named Helen) circa 1788.

James Mackay checked all of the local registers of birth in the district, but it transpires that illegitimate births, at that time, often went unrecorded, so no proof of the child's birth exists. But Helen's daughter did exist, living to a great age of ninety-eight.

From a newspaper report of the death of the old woman

'It will surprise many and may interest a few of your readers to learn that there died at Moffat, on the 13th of last month, a veritable, though illegitimate, daughter of the poet Burns. The old lady in question, Helen Armstrong by name, who was ninety-seven or ninety-eight years of age, resided for many years in Moffat, in the same little back street, in which she was born somewhere about the year 1788. The fact of her relationship to Burns was well known in Moffat and the neighbourhood. Her mother, Nelly Hyslop, was a beauty in her day, and Burns was for some time a devoted admirer of her. Helen (the daughter) is said to have borne a strong resemblance to Burns in her earlier days, and indeed the likeness to the portraits of Burns was traceable to the last, in the contour of the face and in the dark, bright eyes. Nor was the likeness confined to physical points. In her mental powers Helen showed a strain of the poetic blood. A few years ago her conversational powers and her quickness of repartee were most amusing and attractive Even a few months since, when well enough to talk, her conversation was highly interesting'. (Pall Mall Gazette 1887)

On Helen's own testament, she went into service at the age of seven, spending thirty years as cook at the Buccleuch Arms Inn at Thornhill, in service to a family called Glendinning. She lived at the Inn until all the family had died out.

Helen met Sir Walter Scott at the Buccleuch Arms Inn when he was on his way to visit the Duke of Drumlanrig. It is reported that he came into her kitchen and took one of the potatoes that were cooking, from the pot. He remarked how clean and burnished her kitchen was saying

'Eh, *Lucky (a nick name she was called), ye hae a' bricht an' shinin' like the siller'.

To which 'Lucky' replied

'Ay, Sir Walter: but it's no a' gould that glitters'.

Sir Walter related the story later that evening among the 'gentry' of the dinner- table at the Duke's residence.

Helen considered herself lucky that she had never had to ask charity from anyone. She, like Jenny Clow's son, did not receive any money from that which was collected for the support of Jean Armour and the children of Burns, which also included his other two illegitimate daughters.

She worked hard all of her long life, and had lived entirely alone since her husband's death which had occurred many years since. They had no children, but Helen was well loved by the many friends she had gathered in the town, and they knew her as a very well respected worthy of Moffat.

According to Helen she 'had had a long life and had seen muckle'.

*Luckie or Lucky was a designation given to an elderly woman who was the mistress of an alehouse. (Literary Landmarks of Edinburgh, Laurence Hutton, 1891)

Associated Song:

None

27.

ANN MASTERTON
Born ? - Died August 1834

Chronology : 1787/88

Very little is known about Ann Masterton, apart from the fact that she was the daughter of Burns' friend, Allan Masterton.

Allan was the joint writing master at the High School in Edinburgh in 1795, along with Dugald Masterton and Dugald Masterton Jnr., and was the composer of the airs 'The Braes O' Ballochmyle, 'Strathallan's Lament', 'Willie Brewed A Peck O' Maut' (about a drinking spree with Willie Nicol, Burns and Masterton which took place in Moffat) and 'Thickest Night Surround My Dwelling'. Allan Masterton died in 1799.

Burns must have liked this young girl a lot having written a teasing little song about her, to her father's musical composition. Maybe she'd had a few of the young lads from the High School fawning after her? Ann married a medical man called Dr Derbishire who practiced first in Bath and then in London, and they had one son.

Associated Song:

Song   : Beware O' Bonie Ann
Tune   : Bonie Ann
Period : circa 1790

28.

ANNA PARK
Born circa 1770 – Died circa 1799

Chronology : 1789/90

Anna Park was second cousin to William Hyslop owner of The Globe public house in Dumfries, and was employed in the tavern as a barmaid. Her father was Joseph Park an Edinburgh coach-maker.

Anna met Burns when she was about nineteen. This was after he had been transferred to the Dumfries Third Division of the Excise in July 1790, though he was probably aware of her before then. It is thought that one of the first things that brought her to his notice was the fact that she had a very good singing voice.

Anna formed such a close relationship with Burns in such a very short time, that on 31st March 1791 in Leith, she gave birth to their daughter. The child was the second of Burns girls to be called Elizabeth, as Anna had called the baby after her own mother, Elizabeth Dick.

Anna Park was given a bad press by Burnsians of the Victorian period. They disliked the fact that this liaison with her proved beyond any doubt that Burns had been unfaithful during his married life to Jean Armour. In fact he'd been married just over two years when deciding to bed this woman more than a decade younger than himself.

'Honest' Allan Cunningham destroyed her reputation when he wrote

> 'She was accounted beautiful by the customers at the inn, when wine made them tolerant in matters of taste; and, as may be surmised from the song, had other pretty ways to render herself agreeable to them than the serving of wine'.

The Victorian Burns supporters who did everything but deify Burns, knew the only way they could excuse his behaviour was to paint Anna as a 'lightskirts', which was another term for a prostitute. Poor Anna didn't have anyone to defend her and refute this accusation.

One of the excuses used by the Victorian Burnsians to shield Burns for this lapse in faithfulness was that Jean Armour had the audacity to prise herself from both the kitchen sink and marital bed and, with her children, visit relatives in Mauchline, leaving Burns to his own devices. Even his sister Isabella Burns Begg used this as a reason to excuse his behaviour.

But no matter how they tried to twist the blame, there was no excuse for Burns' infidelity. Burns was doing what he wanted, with no thought or consideration to his wife or children, and with utter disregard to his responsibilities as a thirty one year old married family man.

For nigh on two hundred years no trace was found of Anna Park after the birth of her daughter. It was assumed that she had died either in childbirth or soon after giving birth. But James Mackay in his researches found that Anna did not die at the time of her daughter's birth, and he traced her and her daughter as follows.

Before Jean Armour had taken Anna's daughter into her house, it appears that the child had been looked after by one of Anna Park's sisters. Anna was then free to get employment as a domestic servant in Edinburgh. She eventually met and married a carpenter named John Greenshields on 11th November 1794. Anna does not appear to have had any other children with Greenshields. Greenshields married again, on 27th September 1799, this time to a woman called Jane Boyd.

From her marriage in 1794 the trail goes cold and there is no trace of what happened to Anna Park from then. It is assumed that somewhere between November 1794 and September 1799, as there is no proof of a divorce, Anna had died, enabling John Greenshields to re-marry. No death certificate has been found to date therefore when she actually died or the reason for her death is unknown.

Tradition states that Anna Park died in childbirth. That certainly didn't happen when she gave birth to Elizabeth Park Burns, but maybe it did with a child she was having to John Greenshields. Until any form of certification comes to light, we will remain in the dark as to whatever became of her.

In a letter to George Thomson, dated September 1793, Burns stated, with regard to his song 'Yestreen I Had A Pint O'Wine' (The Gowden Locks O' Anna)

'The best love-song I ever composed in my life, though not quite a lady's song'.

Associated Song:

Song   : Yestreen I Had A Pint O' Wine
Tune   : Banks of Banna
Period : Summer 1790

29.

ELIZABETH PARK BURNS
Born 31st March 1791 – Died 13th June 1873

Chronology : 1791

Elizabeth Park Burns, Burns' daughter by Anna Park, was cared for, for a short while, by her aunt who lived in Leith, while Anna returned to work in Edinburgh. Burns, possibly with a little help from Maria Riddell, persuaded the aunt to allow his daughter to come and live with him in Dumfries. This may have been with the approval of Anna Park, but there is nothing, either verbal or in writing, to corroborate this supposition.

In one of Burns' letters to Maria, dated February 1792, after she had made a visit to Edinburgh, he includes the lines

> 'As to your very excellent epistle from a certain Capital of a certain Empire, I shall answer it in its own way sometime next week; as also settle all matters as to little Miss. Your goodness there is just like your kindness in everything else'.

It isn't definite that 'little Miss' refers to Elizabeth Park, but many biographers believe that it does.

With Jean Armour's agreement Elizabeth Park Burns came to live with her father, though it is said she was housed for a time with Agnes Broun, at Mossgiel, before settling in at Bank Street in Dumfries in 1792. This was before Burns' legitimate daughter, also named Elizabeth, was born on 21st November of that year.

This meant that Burns had fathered three girls who were named Elizabeth.

A further oral tradition reports that Elizabeth Park came to live with Burns at a much earlier age. There was only just over a week between Elizabeth's Park's birth and the birth of Jean Armour's third son, William Nicol, which took place on 9th April 1791.

According to the second traditional story Jean's father 'old Armour' was visiting the Burns family at Ellisland and as he looked into the cradle. Expecting to see one baby, he saw two. He commented that he did not realise that Jean had again given birth to twins. Jean replied that the other child was one she was looking after for a neighbour.

In this story, it may or may not have been Elizabeth Park in the cradle, indeed it may very well have been a neighbour's child that Jean was looking after.   But if the letter to Maria Riddell is accepted as referring to Anna Park's child, then she would have been around a year old when she came to live with the Burns family.

Although there is no verification, it is reported that Burns had agreed not to acknowledge the child as his, but to refer to her as a 'neebor's bairn'. This may have been in order to assuage Jean's anger and hurt pride, and also his embarrassment.   But the 'neebor's bairn' grew every day to look more like Burns than any of his legitimate children.   No one was fooled.

According to tradition 'Oor Rob should hae hid twa wives' is all that Jean is supposed to have said on hearing of yet another illegitimate child.

Elizabeth barely knew her father, being just over five when he died, and he did not mention her in any of his letters.   Some time after his death, Burns' paternity of Elizabeth was acknowledged by Jean Armour and the child was given the name of Burns.   She stayed in the family home with her half brothers for the next twelve years until her marriage, when she left Dumfries behind.

Elizabeth Park Burns married a soldier, Private John Thomson of the Stirlingshire Militia on 2nd June 1808 in Dumfries, eventually moving to Pollokshaws in Glasgow to live with his parents.   In 1812 when she was 21, she received £200 from the Burns fund, and this enabled her to rent and furnish a home of her own.

One of Elizabeth's Park Burns' sons, James Glencairn Thomson, stated of his mother prior to Burns' death

'though she was but six when he died, my mother minded Burns well. She minded him taking her on his knee and teaching her to sing 'Ye Banks And Braes O' Bonnie Doon'.   She had a beautiful voice, had my mother, and she and Jean would sing together...Then my mother minded him coming home from the Brow in the last days when he was dying.   She never forgot the sight of him sitting huddled up in the cart, his face buried in his hands.   The next she minded was his funeral.   She was at the graveside with the rest'.

It was also through Elizabeth, that we learn of her unfortunate circumstances of her birth, through a story that could only have been passed to her by Jean Armour.

Elizabeth related of when, in the summer of 1790, Jean and her sons had been bought new clothes by Burns.   Jean was longing to show them off to her family and friends in Mauchline, whom she hadn't seen for a long time and probably missed.   So she packed the children and her new glad rags and waving to Burns, said she would be back in a couple of weeks.

Was Jean being naïve, or did she truly trust Burns?   After all they had been married for two years, and Burns may very well have been a faithful hard working husband and father during that time. A fact no one can ever dispute is that he was a very hard working man.

But unfortunately for Jean, given enough rope, Burns formed his own noose and reverted to type. The first sign of a female glance in his direction and his morals flew out the window and straight to the nearest bedroom. And so was made Elizabeth Park Burns.

But was Elizabeth totally accepted into the Burns household? On the whole yes. Though whenever Jean was asked about Burns' children, she only ever referred to her own sons, even while Elizabeth was living with her at the time and had been acknowledged as his child by being given the family surname, Burns.

Elizabeth had cause for complaint in 1844.

During the Burns Festival in Ayr the three brothers, Robert, William and James, their aunt Isabella Burns Begg and her children and James Burness, another relative, were invited as noted and chief guests to the celebration. At the top table also sat Jessy Lewars. No invitation was extended to Elizabeth or her family, and this hurt her deeply.

Although they had not organised the Festival, it seems mean spirited on the brother's part that they did not insist on Elizabeth being seated alongside them, to honour their father. I'd like to think that Jean Armour would have made sure that Elizabeth, and her children would have been sitting alongside her at the top table. But then, Jean Armour was an honourable woman.

Elizabeth felt so angry at this slight that she wrote to all the members of the family who took part on the day to let them know how she felt. Little good it did her. Though the letters she received in reply from her half-brothers were less offensive, the one sent by Robert Burns Begg, son of Isabella (only a nephew) certainly reminded her of where she had come from and where her place in the family was. And it certainly was not with the legitimate family.

Poor Betty Burns always a reminder of her father's errant and wayward ways. Paying for his mistakes in many subtle ways.

After her marriage and subsequent removal to Glasgow, she saw Jean infrequently, though whenever she could afford it, Jean would send money and presents for Elizabeth's children. Jean always referred to her as 'Dear Betty' and her letters closed with 'I am still your affectionate mother, Jean Burns.' Her half brothers always referred to her as 'Dear Sister' closing their letters with 'Your Affectionate Brother'.

Despite everything Elizabeth Park Burns did love Jean Armour. In a letter sent to Isabella Burns Begg in 1846 she wrote

'The names of the last two children (*Sarah Burns and James Burns), were all that Mrs Burns extracted from me as an acknowledgement of her unwearied kindness to me. God was kind to her, my dear aunt, in giving her plenty but she did not hide it under a hedge: she willingly shared it with the poor and needy. The last letter I had from her was July 1833, with £2 in it to buy a frock for my youngest child, then about a month old. The more I contemplate that excellent woman's character, the more I admire it. There was something good and charitable about her, surpassing all women I ever yet met with. She was indeed a true friend, and the best of mother's to me, and I was often ready to think that all friendships for me in the family had gone with her, but I am glad to find it otherwise'.

Yours respectfully,

E Thomson.

*Sarah Burns Thomson was born in Pollokshaws in Glasgow circa 1824. She became the second wife of Andrew Campbell of Campbell Street, Castlemaine, near Ballarat. She died 15th December 1885 and is buried in Campbell's Creek Cemetery, Castlemaine, north of Melbourne, Australia.

Poor Betty Burns, in the last sentence can be seen all of the insecurity she still felt fifty years after her father's death and twelve years after the death of her step-mother. It appears from the above letter, that the debacle of the 1844 gathering had been sellotaped over even if not totally forgotten, and her half-brothers did send occasional financial help after Jean's passing.

But what doesn't feel right is that though Jean died on Wednesday 26th March a letter informing Elizabeth of this was not sent until Saturday 29th March by Robert, the eldest son. With the burial being on 1st April it did not give Betty much time to make arrangements to get to Dumfries by Tuesday the 1st April. She may not even have received the letter until after the burial.

Like Helen Armstrong, Betty Burns resembled her father better than any of his legitimate children. There is no description as to the appearance of Burns' other two illegitimate children, but maybe they bore the Burns stamp just as strongly.

According to Hugh McDonald when visiting Betty in 1851

'We have had the pleasure of meeting with two of the Poet's sons, on both of whom the paternal stamp was obvious; but we were more forcibly reminded of the family lineaments, as represented in the best portraits, on being introduced to Mrs Thomson than we were on that occasion'.

McDonald also reports

'Her son, Robert Burns Thomson, born in 1818, became a poet and songwriter. Apparently he also bore a strong resemblance to Burns, though a little 'slender in person and a shade more fair in complexion' (Burns had a swarthy complexion from his work in the fields, as had his father before him). But he was intelligent, humourful, independant and had 'a taste for poetry and music, in both of which arts he is indeed no mean proficient'.

Another of Elizabeth's sons, James Glencairn Thomson gave a newspaper interview towards the end of the 19th century regarding his mother. He never married and looked after his mother until her death. The interview is in the Burns Chronicles 1992/93.

'My mother, like Jean Armour, became a very religious woman, and to us eight children she was a model of what a mother should be. She had my grandfather's poetic spirit in her, but she could not express it, save in singing his songs. She had a terrible struggle to make both ends meet, both in Langside where I was born, and at Pollokshaws where we lived after.

My mother taught me to love and be proud of my grandfather. Jean Armour had taught her the same. Ye ken, he was a very loveable man, and if he did wrong, the lassies were partly to blame. Never an unkind word did Jean Armour speak to my mother'.

Elizabeth Park Burns Thomson died in 1873 and is buried in the Vennel Cemetery/Old Burgher Churchyard in Glasgow.

Associated Songs:

None

30.

MARIA RIDDELL
Born 4th November 1772 – Died 15th December 1808)

Chronology : Late 1791

Maria Banks Woodley was born in either London or Dorset, the sixth of a family of seven children, and the youngest daughter. Her father was William Woodley, governor and commander in chief of St Kitts and the Leeward Isles. Her mother was Frances Payne, described in her obituary notice in 'The Gentleman's Magazine' (1813) as 'a very lusty lady'.

Maria became the second wife of Walter Riddell, brother of Robert Riddell of Friar's Carse.

Walter Riddell was a widower, eight years older than Maria, who had inherited a fortune from his first wife, Ann Doig, the only child and heiress to William Henry Doig owner of a sugar plantation in Antigua. Ann and Walter married in St Marleybone Parish Church in London on 1st June 1786. She died less than a year later on 5th May 1787 at Hampstead in London.

On the 11th April 1788, Maria and her family boarded the ship 'Britannia', heading out to the West Indies to visit their estate named 'Profit'. Walter met Maria sometime during this visit. She would have been about fifteen.

What appears to be a kind of arranged marriage took place on 16th September 1790, in Nicholas Town, St Kitts. Thereafter the couple lived on Doig's Estate near Rendevouz Bay until their return to England. Walter bequeathed the estate of 'Barters' in Antigua, which he had inherited on his first wife's death, on Maria and any children born to their marriage. For her dowry, Maria's father agreed to pay £6,000 plus 5% interest p.a. to Walter within six years.

Maria and Walter had two daughters. Anna Maria born on 31st August 1791 in South Audley Street, London, and Sophia, born on 23rd November 1792. Unfortunately, Sophia died of whooping cough on 1st March 1797. She is buried in the Church of St Martin In The Fields in London.

Maria and Walter moved to Scotland late in 1791. They spent three months living at Friar's Carse, the home of her in-laws, while her future residence at *Woodley Park was being renovated. The couple began living at Woodley, a mansion house about four miles south of Dumfries, in March 1792. It is believed that during this three-month stay at Friar's Carse, Maria and Burns became good friends.

*The mansion house was formerly called 'The Holm Of Dalscairth' then renamed 'Goldilea' when purchased by a man called Goldie, who added the second half after his wife's maiden name, which was 'Leigh'. Not to be outdone Walter then renamed the mansion 'Woodley', Maria's maiden name.

Maria was a writer and poet. After meeting Burns, and letting him read some of her work, he gave her a written introduction to the publisher William Smellie. Smellie eventually published a book that she had written on her sojourn abroad, called *'Leeward Caribee Islands'.

*In the Scots Magazine of November 1792 it was announced as published under the following title – Voyage to the Madeira and Leeward Caribbee Islands; with sketches of the Natural History of these Islands. By Maria R******, Cadell, London; Hill, Edinburgh. Maria thought that fifty or one hundred copies would be enough, intending to give them as presents to her friends. Smellie disagreed and thought that this amount was far too modest, and suggested a run of five hundred copies. Maria agreed to this number, and the book sold well.

Burns' letter of introduction to William Smellie, 22nd January 1792 read

'I sit down, my dear Sir, to introduce a young lady to you & a lady in the first ranks of fashion. What a task! You, who care no more for the herd of animals called 'Young Ladies' than for the herd of animals called 'Young Gentlemen'…Mrs Riddell who takes this letter to town with her, is a Character that even in your own way, as a Naturalist & a Philosopher, would be an acquisition to your acquaintance. – The Lady too, is a votary of the Muses; and as I think I am somewhat of a judge in my own trade, I assure you that her verses, always correct, & often elegant, are very much beyond the common run of the Lady Poetesses of the day…lest you should think of a lively West-Indian girl of eighteen, as girls of eighteen are too often observed to be thought of I should take care to remove that prejudice - To be impartial, however, the Lady has one unlucky failing; a failing which you will easily discover, as she seems rather pleased with indulging it; & a failing which you will easily pardon, as it is a sin that very much besets yourself: - where she dislikes, or despises, she is apt to make no more a secret of it – than when she esteems & respects'.

The manuscript of Maria's book was sent to Smellie round about the 7th March 1792 with an accompanying letter from her which mentions Burns

'Robie Burns dined with me the other day. He is in good health and spirits; but I fear his muse will not be so frequent in her inspirations, now that he has forsaken his rural occupations in the line of agriculture'.

Smellie was very taken with this young woman and on 27th March 1792 replied to her letter

> 'When I consider your youth, and still more your sex, the perusal of your ingenious and judicious work, if I had not previously had the pleasure of your conversation, the devil himself could not have frightened me into the belief that a female human creature could, in the bloom of youth, beauty and, consequently, of giddiness, have produced a performance of much out of the line of your ladies' works.   Smart little poems, flippant romances, are not uncommon.   But science, minute observation, accurate description and excellent composition are qualities seldom to be met with in the female world'.

In September 1792, *Smellie came to Dumfries and spent some time with both Burns and Maria, who had arranged for a 'good, easy, snug postchaise' to bring him to the town.   It was a very happy time for the trio.

*William Smellie (1740 – 1795) was the son of a prosperous mason. He had been apprenticed to a printer, but during his apprenticeship had also studied at Edinburgh University and at home.   As well as earning a reputation as a scholar and a successful printer of learned books, he became Editor of the first edition of the Encyclopaedia Britannica.

Burns was one of the friends that received a copy of Maria's book in 1792. He thanked her in a letter in November of that year

> 'Madam,
> I return you my most sincere thanks for the honor you have done me in presenting me a copy of your Book.   Be assured I shall ever keep it sacred, as a boasted testimony how much I have the honor to be, Madam
> > Your highly obliged humble servt., Robt. Burns'

In April 1793 Maria went to London, spending quite some time there.

> 'During the season I did so many things that I ought not to have done, and left undone so many things that I ought to have done, that at the expiration of that time there was no health left in me'.

Walter was called from London during this sojourn to tend to business in the West Indies, and Maria came back alone to Woodley Park.   After her return to Scotland in November 1793 in a long letter to Smellie she writes

> 'I am as chaste and domestic, but perhaps not quite so industrious, as Penelope in the absence of her hero.   I resemble rather the lilies of the field: 'I toil not, neither do I spin'; but I read, I write, I sing and contrive to while away the time as pleasantly as any social being like myself can do in a state of solitude, and in some measure of mortification.   I shall write you more fully in my next as to the nature of my present pursuits, and how I found Burns and the other friends here you left behind, for they were not few, I assure you'.

189

In the letter she talks of Walter, who was still in the West Indies

> 'Were I to give you a narrative of all that volatile genius has undertaken, and in some measure compassed, in spite of all the bars and obstacles his evil genius had vainly raised against his plans, you would think I had launched into the regions of romance and Knight-errantry; so I leave them for him to entertain you with sometime over a bottle of claret, whose exhilarating influence may inspire you with some taste and toleration for such exploits'.

In 1793 the war in Europe had turned Dumfries into a kind of garrison town with two regiments of fencible infantry and cavalry. This piqued Burns very much when he found out that some of the soldiers were vying for Maria's attention at the theatre one night.

> 'I meant to have called on you yesternight, but as I edged up to your box-door, the first object which greeted my view was one of these lobster-coated PUPPIES, sitting, like another dragon, guarding the Hesperian fruit...'

Maria's reply must have been to Burns' satisfaction, and he wrote back

> 'On the conditions and capitulations you so obligingly make, I shall certainly make my plain, weather-beaten, rustic phiz a part of your box furniture on Tuesday'.

An incident at Friar's Carse in December 1793, damaged their friendship, and Maria and Burns stopped talking for a long period.

Burns had been invited to attend a dinner party at Friar's Carse (in Burns' time this was a two storied building, since demolished) by his friend Robert Riddell. According to local gossip of the time, after dinner the ladies of the company retired to the drawing room, leaving the men sitting round the table drinking somewhat heavily and conversing. The discussion came round to the Roman tale 'The Rape of the Sabine Women'. There were some army officers in the company and they thought it a good idea for the sorry tale to be re-enacted.

Each 'roman soldier' at the table was given a Sabine woman to home in on and Burns, who had been encouraged to drink more than he normally would by Robert Riddell, was given *Maria. Burns apparently led the charge into the room and flung himself upon his target, suddenly realising that he was the only one doing so, as the others had held back at the door.

Too late he understood that this had been a set up by the 'Officers' to put this 'ploughman poet' in his place and take him down a peg or two.

The ladies were surprised and shocked, though two of them a 'Miss L.' and a Mrs G.' saw through the set up and tried to take Burns' part. But the upper classes held together and Burns was cast out of the house in humiliation and disgrace.

*It has been reported that it was Robert Riddell's wife Elizabeth the hostess of the party, not Maria Riddell, that was the recipient of the assault, but it is not quite clear either way, though highly unlikely it was Elizabeth Riddell. Whether Elizabeth or Maria was the target, did not matter, Burns had blotted his copybook, and both women were extremely angry and wished him out of their presence.

In a lengthy letter, written in a very sober and sorry state to Elizabeth Riddell the morning after the debacle, he tried to give his apology to his furious hostess, while he was suffering with a raging hangover.

'Madam, I daresay this is the first Epistle you ever received from the nether world. I write to you from the regions of Hell, amid the horrors of the damned...
To the men of the company I will make no apology. – Your husband, who insisted on my drinking more than I chose, has no right to blame me; and the other gentlemen were partakers of my guilt. But to you, Madam, I have much to apologise. Your good opinion I valued as one of the greatest acquisitions I had made on earth, and I was truly a beast to forfeit it...
Regret! Remorse! Shame! Ye three hell-hounds that ever dog my steps and bay at my heels, spare me! Spare me!
Forgive the offences, and pity the perdition of, Madam,
Your humble slave!'

*Elizabeth Riddell did not forgive him, nor did her husband have the chance to. Robert Riddell died four months later on the 21st April 1794, at the early age of thirty-eight. A year later the estate was sold.

*Elizabeth Riddell was the daughter of a wealthy textile manufacturer, William Kennedy who was born in Kirkcudbrightshire and moved to Manchester marrying in June 1753 Ann Walter. Elizabeth outlived Robert Riddell by seven years, dying on 21st December 1801, in Bath. She decided to live there because of her failing health. She was nursed by her unmarried sister, Rachel , and was buried in St James Churchyard in Bath, on Christmas Eve 1801.

In the first couple of weeks in January 1794, Burns wrote Maria three letters, which she never replied to, the last, on the 12th January basically admitting defeat in the saving of the friendship.

'Madam, I have returned your Common Place Book. – I have perused it with much pleasure, & would have continued my criticism, But as it seems the Critic has forfeited your esteem, his strictures must lose their value...With the profound respect for your exalted abilities; the most sincere esteem & ardent regard for your gentle heart & amiable manners; the most fervent wish and prayer for your welfare, peace & bliss'.

Walter Riddell was slowly running out of money for the upkeep of

'Woodley Park'.   He returned from the West Indies circa Spring 1794, still short of funds, and on 17th April of that year 'Woodley Park' was put up for sale.   Maria busied herself with her children's education.

There was still the fall-out from the event at Friar's Carse, which Burns took very badly, writing some unpleasant poems about Maria.   His 'Monody On A Lady Famed For Her Caprice', written on Maria, was full of malice and bile.

> How cold is that bosom which folly once fired!
> How pale is that cheek where the rouge lately glisten'd!
> How silent that tongue which the echoes oft tired!
> How dull is that ear which to flatt'ry so listen'd!
>
> If sorrow and anguish their exit await,
> From friendship and dearest affection remov'd,
> How doubly severer, Maria, thy fate!
> Thou diedst unwept, as thou livedst unlov'd.
>
> Loves, Graces, and Virtues, I call not on you:
> So shy, grave, and distant, ye shed not a tear.
> Bur come, all ye offspring of Folly so true,
> And flowers let us cull for Maria's cold bier!
>
> We'll search through the garden for each silly flower,
> We'll roam thro' the forest for each idle weed.
> But chiefly the nettle, so typical, shower,
> For none e'er approach'd her but rued the rash deed.
>
> We'll sculpture the marble, we'll measure the lay:
> Here Vanity strums on her idiot lyre!
> There keen Indignation shall dart on his prey,
> Which spurning Contempt shall redeem from his ire!
>
> EPITAPH
> Here lies, now a prey to insulting neglect,
> What once was a butterfly, gay in life's beam:
> Want only of wisdom denied her respect,
> Want only of goodness denied her esteem.

Further to this, he pinned a nasty poem to her carriage, and sent copies of what he had written of her to her acquaintances.   He copied the 'Monody' and the carriage poem to Agnes McLehose in a letter of 25th June 1794

'The subject of the foregoing is a woman of fashion in this country, with whom, at one period, I was well acquainted – By some scandalous conduct to me, & two or three other gentlemen as well as me, she steered so far to the north of my good opinion, that I have made her the theme of several illustrated things.   The following Epigram struck me the other day, as I passed her carriage'.

> If you rattle along like your mistresses tongue,
> Your speed will out-rival the dart;
> But, a fly for your load, you'll break down on the road,
> If your stuff be as rotten's her heart.

192

Burns managed to twist things around to make it look like Maria was the one in the wrong. Agnes did not reply to this letter. On this note ended the correspondence of Burns and McLehose - Sylvander and Clarinda.

By the end of 1794 Burns and Maria at least seemed to be on writing terms, if not actually meeting in person. *Apparently Maria had never seen any of the poems that Burns had written about her as she and her husband, after putting 'Woodley' on the market, had returned to England on the first leg of heading to Europe, where they had intended to live for two years, in order to economise. But they found it difficult due to the war with France.

*It is reported that the first time Maria became aware of the lines was in 1800 when she saw the 'Monody on a Lady famed for her Caprice' in Currie's biography of Burns. She thought

'The Monody that follows this little poem (sonnet on the late Robert Riddell) is very well written in its way. I had never seen it before. The two concluding lines are strongly pointed, and indeed constitute the chief, almost the whole merit. The idea was a favourite one of Burns. Before, it was appropriated to the personage he calls Eliza, he had affixed it to two or three satirical squibs and epigrams, on as many successive persons who had offended him, or by whom he fancied himself slighted. This is a curious anecdote, but too scurvy a trait of the poor Bard's to be delivered over to the knowledge of his enemies. Poor Burns! Poor Human Nature'!

It seems that even after reading the lines, she still did not appear to recognise that it was written on her, but maybe she was just being diplomatic and a truly professional critic.

By the beginning of 1795 Maria returned north. This time taking a short lease on 'Tinwald House', three miles east of Dumfries, 'a crazy, rambling, worm-eaten, cob-web hunting chateau of the duke of Queensberry', which Maria hoped to quit by May 1795. Walter remained in London.

In the spring of 1795 Burns and Maria were on better terms, Maria having sent him a book, 'Anacharsis Travels', circa January that year. Enclosed with the book she had included one of her poems 'To Thee, Loved Nith'. Burns promised to do a critique on it as soon as his Excise work permitted.

From herein the wound in their friendship began to heal. They exchanged letters and poetic lines, with Burns telling her in a letter of March 1795 of a miniature he was having painted by Alexander Reid. If she wanted to see it for herself before it became public, she would be very welcome

'I think he has hit by far the best likeness of me ever was taken. – When you are at anytime so idle, in town, as to call at Reid's painting-room, & mention to him that I spoke of such a thing to you, he will shew it to you, else, he will not, for both the Miniature's existence & it's destiny, are an inviolable secret, & therefore very properly trusted in part to you'.

A short while later he met a Mrs Scot, a friend of Maria's, in the street and, having the miniature on him, gave it to her to give to Maria along with a note. He had changed his mind about the resemblance by then 'The painter, in my opinion, has spoilt the likeness'. Burns was not a very well man at this time and finished the note 'I am so ill as to be scarce able to hold this miserable pen to this miserable paper'.

May 1795 saw the end of the lease at 'Tinwald' and she and her daughters moved to a new home at 'Halleaths', which was near Lockerbie. Not so handy for trips into Dumfries. In June 1795, both Maria and Burns lost a good friend in William Smellie, who died on the 24th of that month. The correspondence with Burns continued throughout the rest of 1795, but it is unlikely that the pair met during this year.

Early in 1796 Maria was informed of the death of her favourite brother, Captain John Woodley, who perished on 11th December 1795 when the frigate 'The Leda', went down off Madeira, the result of a freak squall, which came over the ship at midnight. Accounts say the squall lasted only about three minutes, long enough to sink a ship. John was twenty-nine.

Burns' last letter to Maria is dated 1st June 1796. She was arranging a ball to celebrate George III's birthday on the 4th, and invited Burns to attend. Burns was very ill and could not attend, even if he had really wanted to

'I may perhaps see you on Saturday, but I will not be at the ball. – Why should I? - 'Man delights not me, nor woman either'! Can you supply me with the Song 'Let us all be unhappy together''?

Le pauvre miserable, RB'

In June/July 1796 Maria's health was poor and she went to Brow on the Solway for sea bathing. She heard that Burns was there for the same reason. On the 5th July she invited him to dine with her at her residence and sent a carriage to collect him. Writing later to a friend she recalled

'I was struck with his appearance on entering the room. The stamp of death was imprinted on his features. He seemed already touching the brink of eternity. His first salutation was, 'Well, madam, have you any commands for the other world'?

He asked after Maria's health noticing that she looked unwell

'He looked at my face with an air of great kindness, and expressed his concern at seeing me so ill, with his accustomed sensibility'.

Burns ate very little at the dinner table and the conversation centred around his family and how proud he was of his children.

'His anxiety for his family seemed to hang heavy upon him, and the more perhaps from the reflection that he had not done them all the justice he was so well qualified to do...He spoke of his death without any of the ostentation of philosophy, but with firmness as well as feeling, as an event likely to happen very soon, and which gave him

194

concern chiefly from leaving his four children so young and unprotected, and his wife in so interesting a situation – in hourly expectation of lying-in of a fifth'.

Burns knew that with his impending death his poetry and papers would go out into the world with no control over them, and he regretted that he had not sorted this out. It was now too late, as he had neither the strength nor the will left to do this for himself.

'He said he was well aware that his death would well occasion some noise, and that every scrap of his writing would be revived against him to the injury of his future reputation; that letters and verses written with unguarded and improper freedom, and which he had earnestly wished to have buried in oblivion, would be handed about by idle vanity or malevolence when no dread of his resentment would restrain them or prevent the censures of shrill-tongued malice, or the insidious sarcasms of envy from pouring forth all their venom to blast his fame'.

But even with these serious thoughts and conversations, Burns still tried to err on the cheery side

'The conversation was kept up with great evenness and animation on his side. I had seldom seen his mind greater or more collected. There was frequently a considerable degree of vivacity in his sallies, and they would probably have had a greater share, had not the concern and dejection I could not disguise dampened the spirit of pleasantry he seemed not unwilling to indulge...We parted about sunset on the evening of that day *(5th July 1796)*. The next day *(6th July)* I saw him again, and we parted to meet no more'.

Tradition informs us that Maria, accompanied by William Smellie's son Alexander, a few evenings after the burial of the poet, went to his grave in St Michael's Churchyard and planted or spread laurel leaves around it. It does sound like something that Maria would need to do.

At the beginning of August Maria wrote a long eulogy to the genius of Burns for the Dumfries Journal, as a friend and as a poet. When requested, by John Syme, to write this tribute, she only agreed to do so as long as she could remain anonymous, signing herself 'Candidor', thus cementing the reconciliation with Burns for eternity.

Maria was given only twenty-four hours to compose this accolade. She was not totally happy with what she considered was just a first draft, and corrected it on at least four occasions in later years.

Maria contributed to the funds being collected for the family of Burns, and was most insistent that a collection of his works and his life be published. She did her fair share in this project.

She became acquainted with James Currie, Burns' first biographer, through John Syme, pre February 1797, when she was living in Scotland, and visited and corresponded with him until his death in 1805, though she was not always happy with his requests.

In one of Currie's first letters to her he had obviously asked her if she would be willing to change some of Burns' poetry. She angrily replied

'What do you mean by desiring me to correct any thing of Burns? 'Tis asking me 'to paint the lily and add perfume to the violet''.

If only Currie had done what Maria had done and left his own 'corrections' in his own mind, leaving Burns' works to their own devices.

But Maria was intent in getting subscribers for Currie's work, hitting on the highest in London society. Writing to Currie in 1797

'Pray let me know if there will be anything on certain topics, as politics, and so forth, that may render indelicate my requesting persons of any party or persuasion to subscribe. I think if we got the Prince of Wales name, for instance – I mean by way of ornament, for he will never pay the money'. *(He was known for not paying bills.)*

The Riddell's moved to England in 1797, where Maria and her children resided at various addresses. In London in four months they lived at 4 Baker Street, off Portman Square; 13 Bridge Street, Westminster; Duke Street, St James; finally returning to Bridge Street.

In 1797 Walter set out for the 'Leeward Islands'. Maria never saw him again. He died in Antigua on 22nd March (or May) 1802 at Rendevouz Bay.

Though most of 1797 was spent in Dorset, for the next few years Maria spent her time moving between there and London, residing with friends.

In 1798 she was living in Kew Road, Richmond, and there became very ill. As she was to write to Currie

'I was very near giving poor Burns an account 'viva voce' of the progress of his affairs here below'.

Currie received a letter from Maria at Christmas 1799, with an answer to a question he had set as regards Jean Armour. Maria writes

'Burns said little or nothing about his wife to me, but as I believe her conduct, subsequent to their union by marriage, was exemplary towards him, so it is just to add that he always spoke of her with a high tribute of respect and esteem. He did not love her, but he was far from insensible to the indulgence and patience, 'the meekness with which she bore her faculties' on many occasions very trying to the tempers of most individuals of our sex. An illegitimate child of his, born after wedlock, who had lost her mother was, I know, adopted by Mrs Burns, and is, I believe still an inmate of her house and no distinction shown between that and the rest of their children. This trait he told me of with much sensibility'.

In May 1800, Maria was again ill, and 'am recommended the Chalybeate Spring at Tunbridge, to set me rights a little, if possible'. She rented Down Cottage for several months.

In the summer of 1800 she finally received Currie's books. On the whole she was delighted with them, but she was very angry that he had used her 'sketch' from the Dumfries newspaper of August 1796. He had apparently asked to use sections of it, this she had agreed to, but he used it all.

> "Twas horrible, monstrous; you talked of 'availing yourself of it by extracts' and borrowing a few of the thoughts, of which there are some three or four tolerable ones, enwoven in a cobweb of most flimsy fabric, which you have inserted in such a manner that I can neither sweep it away or mend its texture...I should have begged leave to furnish you with a copy I literally have by me at this instant, very much corrected and published since Ann. Dom, 96, when it was printed, mark you – at Syme's request – at 24 hour's notice'.

Even two hundred years later, on reading her letter to Currie you can still feel the rage, frustration and manipulation this woman felt.

In 1802 a second edition of Maria's book on the 'Caribbee Islands', was published in Salem as was 'The Metrical Miscellany', London, which contained eighteen of her poems. This 'Miscellany' became very popular and was quickly followed in 1803 by a second edition.

On the 5th May 1803, Maria was surprised to find that Lord Salisbury, Lord Chamberlain, had signed an authority giving her possession of apartments in Hampton Court Palace. These apartments were situated on the ground floor on the west side of Fountain Court.

1803 was quite a strange year for her. It was suggested to her that she be proposed as suitable to look after the heiress to the throne, Princess Charlotte. The proposer was Thomas Erskine. Maria replied to his letter

> 'If my services in the education of the young Princess can be rendered acceptable through your testimony, to H.R.H., you may rest assured that so flattering an election will excite my ambition to justify the confidence reposed in me, by discharging to the utmost extent of my abilities, so honourable but anxious duty. You are now at liberty, therefore, to propose me to His R.H., and are sufficiently acquainted with my family, my situation in life, my conduct, and those acquirements I have cultivated (chiefly with a view to my own

daughter's education) to be able to afford perhaps every information H.R.H., may require'.

Unfortunately, for both Maria and the young Princess, the responsibility was given to an elderly Dowager, Lady de Clifford, who would not have been in any way in tune with the mind of a seven year old, whose parents, royal or not, hated one another.

Maria became great friends with Jane, the Duchess of Devonshire, and was recommended as guardian to her children when the Duchess was removed abroad, due to her indiscretions. Again the guardianship did not happen, but it does show that Maria was held in great esteem by the highest in the land.

In Spring 1804, the youngest and last remaining Riddell brother, Alexander John, became very ill. According to Maria his 'worthless wife deserted him and broke his heart, and for a time sullied his character most unjustly'. With no family or friend to care for him, though she was ill herself, Maria took on the responsibility for his nursing.

Alexander 'a very affectionate brother-in-law and a most deserving though unfortunate ill-starred young man' died on June 24th 1804.

Maria kept up to date with information regarding Burns' family, through Mrs Scot, the woman who had taken Burns miniature to Maria in 1795. Jean Armour wrote to Maria sometime in 1804 acknowledging her enquiries to her family, which she heard of from the same Mrs Scot

'We still live in the same house that you left us in...James Glencairn is in the Bluecoat School in Newgate Street...It is about sixteen months since James McClure took him to London. He called with James on you at Mr. Banks, but you was in the country. He left his name and where James was to be found, but they had not told you...'

There is a description of Maria, given on 27th May 1804, in the diaries of Sylvester Douglas, Lord Glenbervie, who visited her on that date

'Yesterday I went after church to Hampton Court Palace to pay a visit to Mrs Ridel. She is a lively, handsome little woman, with good teeth and eyes, and a shrill disagreeable voice, which she employs without ceasing on all sorts of subjects...She has a bookcase full of books, the gifts of authors, and showed me a score of them with the circumstances written on the title pages during the course of my visit, and when I came away would have loaded me with half a dozen I happened to say I had not seen. I contrived, however, to escape with two small volumes'.

But Glenbervie was not getting away light handed. The next day, according to his diary, Maria and her daughter visited his house and left another six volumes of the latest Italian compilations with his wife.

On 17th August 1805, Maria wrote to Currie, asking if he would be coming to London.   Currie was very ill.   He read her letter, according to his son, but 'he could not enjoy it'.   Currie died on 31st August 1805.

In 1806 Maria had her portrait painted by Lawrence.   It was exhibited in the Royal Academy that same year.   In Spring 1807 Walter Scott visited her at Hampton Court.   She had not met him before, but via Currie, in November 1804, she had forwarded to Scott a copy of a manuscript 'which I think may please him'.   Scott thanked Maria, via Currie, for her gift.

On 1st May 1807 Maria wrote to Scott, this time enclosing two 'privately printed election ballads' of Burns – 'Buy Braw Troggin' and 'The Election'. She told of how much she misses Scotland.

> 'The years which have elapsed since I have unfortunately ceased to consider Scotland a soil where I was to take root and leave my bones, have not weakened my attachment to it.   I still feel a degree, - a very powerful degree of affinity with all that belongs to, that adorns and honors it...With the Borders Scenery and its traditions, I had, for the happiest and most prosperous days of my life, been familiar...they return upon me like Ossian's Music 'the Memory of past joys, pleasant and mournful to the Soul''.

Maria eventually settled in London where she married circa 30th March 1808, a *Mr Philips Lloyd Fletcher, a Welsh officer of Dragoons.   This surprised everyone as he was ten years younger than she was, but it does appear to be a love-match.   +The actual date of her marriage is unknown, as is where the marriage took place, but it was not at Hampton Court.

*Phillips Lloyd Fletcher was the eldest of a large Welsh family from Gwernhaylod in Flintshire.   The family home was called 'Caean'.   He had three brothers and four sisters. Both his parents were alive at the time of the marriage, but his father was to die in November of the same year.   Fletcher became a Colonel in the 16th Lancers (The Light Dragoons).

+It was one of her earlier biographers, Hugh Gladstone, who gave the date as 30th March, quoting the 'Scots Magazine' of 1808, in which a number of marriages taking part on 30th March are listed.   This list is followed by two undated marriages, one of which is the marriage of Maria and Phillips.

In a letter to Lady Abercorn, dated 26th April 1808, Sir Walter Scott writes

> 'Have you heard, bye the bye, that little Mrs Riddell of Hampton Court (Burns' Mrs Riddell) has married a young officer of Dragoons?   My friend Mathias, will in all probability break his heart upon this melancholy occasion'.

Maria must have had an inkling that she had not long to live, and unlike Burns, put her affairs in order.   Her Last Will and Testament, very minutely detailed, was drawn up ending

> 'P.S. I wish to have my remains interred to Bangor, unless my beloved husband prefers Overton.   I hope that hereafter the same ground will enclose us both'.

Maria died, aged only 36, on 15th December 1808 in Chester, possibly of 'Graves Disease'. She was buried in the family vault at Overton five days later. Her second husband never remarried, and died on 13th April 1863 aged 80. He was buried at Overton, near Maria's grave. There are no other records of him.

In March 1795, Burns mentions Maria Riddell's poem 'To Thee, Loved Nith'. The poem reads as follows

> To thee, loved Nith, thy gladsome plains,
> Where late with careless thought I ranged,
> Though prest with care and sunk with wo,
> To thee I bring a heart unchanged.
> I love thee, Nith, thy banks and braes,
> Though Memory there my bosom tear,
> For there he rov'd that broke my heart,
> Yet to that heart, ah, still how dear!
>
> And now your banks and bonny braes
> But waken sad remembrance' smart;
> The very shades I held most dear
> Now strike fresh anguish to my heart:
> Deserted bower! where are they now –
> Ah! where the garlands that I wove
> With faithful care, each morn to deck
> The altars of ungrateful love?
>
> The flowers of spring, how gay they bloomed
> When last with him I wandered here!
> The flowers of spring are passed away
> For wintry horrors dark and drear.
> Yon osiered stream, by whose lone banks
> My songs have lulled him off to rest,
> Is now in icy fetters locked –
> Cold as my false love's frozen breast!

The first letter Burns wrote to Maria is dated February 1792. Maria had been ill and Burns acknowledges to her

> 'Once more let me congratulate you on your returning health. God grant that you may live at least while I live, for were I to lose you it would leave a Vacuum in my enjoyments that nothing could fill up. Farewell...'
>
> Robt. Burns

Like the true friend she always was, Maria granted his request.

After the death of Robert Riddell, Elizabeth, his widow, refused to let Walter Riddell take over Friar's Carse, and it was put up for sale. This was personal, as she loathed Walter. The professional man they employed to value the lands and buildings was William Stewart, father of 'Lovely Polly Stewart', and close friend of Burns and Robert Riddell.

From 'The Burns Calendar', relating to after the sale of Friar's Carse

'Mrs Riddell continued to live with some kind friends in the neighbourhood for a time, then removed to Edinburgh, and collected into an octavio volume, a collection of original poems, some of which had previously appeared in print, entitled, 'The Metrical Miscellany', London 1802. Seventeen poems were her own composition, and are noted in the table of comments, 'Maria Riddell'. Among other contributers to the volume, it is interesting to notice the Clarinda of Burns (Mrs McLehose, the initial 'M') and her well-known song, 'Talk not of love, it gives me pain'. It is fair to presume they were personally known to each other, and must have been drawn into closer sympathy from a mutual, although a very different, affection for the Poet's wonderful fascination. Mrs Riddell married again in 1808, P.L. Fletcher, Esq., an Irish gentleman connected with the Court, and died in state apartments at Hampton Court Palace'.

After her mother's death, Anna Maria returned to Hampton Court, possibly living with Lady Livingston, a relative. Anna Maria married Captain Charles Montague Walker, R.E., on 6th October 1811, at St George's, Hanover Square. They had nine children. After her husband retired, in 1826, the family settled in Fiesole, Florence, where he husband had a villa. Charles died at Fiesole on 9th July 1833 and Anna Maria died in Florence on 23rd February 1859.

As a footnote, Friar's Carse had it's own history before Burns and the Riddell's, as it was the place where Annie Laurie died on the 5th April 1764 at the grand old age of eighty-one. She was the great grandmother of Robert Riddell, and had married an Alexander Fergusson of Craigdarroch. She was said to have a great addiction to taking snuff and to matchmaking.

Associated Songs:

Song	: Farewell Thou Stream
Tune	: Alace Yat I Cam Ower The Muir
Period	: circa April 1793

Song	: Here Is The Glen
Tune	: Flowers Of Edinburgh (Banks Of Cree-untraced)
Period	: 3rd April 1794

Song	: Here's To Thy Health, My Bonie Lass
Tune	: Laggan Burn
Period	: Undated

31.

MARY (POLLY) STEWART
Born 1775 – Died 1847

Chronology : circa 1788

Mary Stewart was the daughter of *William Stewart of Brownhill, near Closeburn, a village about 12 miles north of Dumfries. William was an acquaintance of Burns and his daughter was reported as being a woman who lived a very erratic lifestyle.

Mary's first marriage was to her cousin Ishmael Stewart of Springfield, with whom she had three sons. Ishmael got himself into a bit of trouble and was forced to flee the country, eventually dying abroad. Nothing more is known of him.

Marriage number two took place in 1801 and was to a George Welsh who farmed Morton Mains and was related to Thomas Carlisle's wife, Jane Welsh, being her grand uncle. There were two daughters to this marriage. The couple did not get on very well due to his serious nature and Mary's entirely opposite of serious nature. Flighty would be the best way to describe her.

George and Mary separated in 1806, and she returned to stay with her father in Maxwelltown, where he now resided.

Mary then fell in love with a Swiss prisoner of war, a soldier of fortune named Fleitz who had been serving in the French army and who had been captured and sent to Dumfries for the duration of the Napoleonic War. When he was repatriated she went abroad with him.

It is reported that the couple went to France first and then on to Switzerland, where he died, date unknown. After Fleitz's death Mary is reported to have resided with her cousin who lived in Florence. Mary eventually settled in Lauffenburg, near Basle where she died at age 72. (tradition says she died in a lunatic asylum, having outlived all her children).

In her later years she seemed to regret leaving her homeland and both sets of children. She wrote to the landlord of the 'King's Arms' in Dumfries, a Mr Pagan, during 1833 asking after her three sons from her first marriage, the sons that she had left behind in Scotland years before.

In these letters her address was given as Laufanburg en Suisse, Canton D'Argavio, styling herself Mary Stewart Fleitz.

The song 'Lovely Polly Stewart' was published in Johnson's Museum in 1796. It is a cheerful composition, despite starting 'The flower it blaws, it fades, it fa's'. Though that first line is a very descriptive prognostication of what Mary's life story became.

*Willam Stewart was born at Closeburn round about 1750, son of an innkeeper. He tried his hand at many jobs even going as far as Lincolnshire in England as a 'travelling Scotchman'.

In 1783 a Mr Menteith purchased the Closeburn estate from a Mr Kirkpatrick, and due to his knowledge of the area, William was appointed factor for the estate. He was also involved in the sale of the Riddell's home, Friar's Carse, after the death of Robert Riddell in 1794. His sister, Catherine was married to a Mr Bacon, landlord of the Brownhill Inn.

William Stewart lived until 1812, and was quite well off when he died, being a shareowner and a landowner. He is buried in Closeburn Churchyard.

Associated Song:

Song   : Lovely Polly Stewart
Tune   : Ye're Welcome Charlie Stewart
Period   : 1794

32.

DEBORAH DUFF DAVIES
Born circa 1772 – Died post May 1793

Chronology : c 1791

Deborah Duff Davies was the youngest daughter of Dr Daniel Davies of Tenby in Pembrokeshire and was connected to Captain Riddell of Glenriddell.

Burns is thought to have met her at Friar's Carse, home of the Riddell's, when she had come to visit them. She was staying at Drungan's Lodge, near Beeswing, home of John McMurdo, father to Jane and Philadelphia when Burns first wrote to her in early October 1791, enclosing a poem dedicated to her. This poem may or may not be 'Lovely Davies'. The letter reads

> 'The inclosed verses I do myself the honor to send you, are a memento exactly of the same kind. – It may be more owing to the fastidiousness of my caprice than the delicacy of my taste, but I am so often tired, disgusted & hurt with the insipidity; affectation & pride of mankind, that when I meet with a person 'after my own heart', I positively feel what an orthodox Protestant would call a species of idolatory, & which acts on my mind like inspiration, and I can no more resist rhyming on the impulse, than an Eolian harp can refuse it's tones to the streaming air'.

Burns says of Deborah

> 'She was positively the least creature I ever saw to be at the same time unexceptionally and indeed uncommonly handsome and beautiful, and besides has the particular felicity to be a favourite of mine'.

Writing on 6th April 1793, enclosing the song 'Bonie Wee Thing' he informs her

> 'Woman is the blood-royal of life; let them be all-sacred. Whether this last statement be right or wrong, I am not accountable; it is an original component of my mind'.

In May of 1793 Burns again wrote to her, enclosing 'Blyth hae I Been On Yon Hill', a song he had dedicated to Lesley Baillie.

> 'Happy is the man, Madam, that has ever had it in his power to contribute to your enjoyments. *Ah quelle enviable sorte!*' - NB if this is

not French, it ought to be so.   *(Burns often made up his own variation of French phrases).*   If the following Song gives you entertainment, it more than repays me for composing it.   It is written on the only toast I have in the world besides yourself – a lovely woman, a Miss Lesley Baillie, of Mayville in Ayrshire...By the bye, I am a great deal luckier than most poets.   When I sing of Miss Davies, or Miss Lesley Baillie, I have only to feign the passion – the charms are real'.

According to 'Honest' Allan Cunningham, from information he supposedly received from her nephew, Deborah had been courted by Captain Delany, and the story is as follows

'He (Captain Delany) made himself acceptable to her by sympathising in her pursuits and writing verses on her, calling her his Stella, an ominous name which might have brought the memory of Swifts's unhappy mistress to her mind.   An offer of marriage was made and accepted, but Delany's circumstances were urged as an obstacle; delays ensued; a coldness on the lover's part followed; his regiment was called abroad – he went with it; she heard from him once and no more, and was left to mourn the change of affection – to droop and die.   He perished in battle, or by a foreign climate, soon after the death of the young lady of whose love he was unworthy.

The following verses on this unfortunate attachment form part of a poem found among her papers at her death: she takes Delany's portrait from her bosom, presses it to her lips saying

> Next to thyself, 'tis all on earth
> Thy Stella dear doth hold;
> The glass is clouded with my breath,
> And as my bosom cold:
> That bosom which so oft has glowed
> With love and friendship's name,
> Where you the seed of love first sowed
> That kindled into flame
>
> You there neglected let it burn,
> It seized the vital part,
> And left my bosom as an urn
> To hold a broken heart:
> I once had thought I should have been
> A tender, happy wife,
> And passed my future days serene
> With thee, my James, through life'.

Allan Cunningham was not considered to be much of a biographer, and even today his stories are considered to be over fanciful, if not downright lies.   But he certainly knew a good tale when he heard one.

It is said by some writers that Deborah went to France because of ill-health and died soon after of consumption.   Apparently Burns received a very chatty letter from her when she was living in Fontainbleau sometime in 1793, but the letter has not been traced.

Associated Songs:

Song   : Lovely Davies
Tune   : Miss Muir
Period : circa October 1791

Song   : Bonie Wee Thing
Tune   : Bonie Wee Thing
Period : 6th April 1793

33.

LESLEY BAILLIE
Born 6th March 1768 – Died 19th July 1843

Chronology : August 1792

Lesley Baillie was the daughter of Robert Baillie and Ann Reid of Mayville House situated just outside Stevenston in Ayrshire.

Burns met Lesley, her sister Grace, (who for some reason was called Maria) and her father in August 1792, when he conveyed her and her family, and a Mr Hamilton of Grange, fifteen miles on their journey through Dumfries to England, 'tho' God knows I could ill spare the time'. According to Burns this good deed was done

> 'out of pure devotion to admire the loveliness of the works of God'.

In a letter dated 22nd August 1792 to Mrs Dunlop, who was friendly with the Baillie family, Burns described how on his way home after performing this good deed, he said he recalled an old ballad called My Bonie Lizie Bailie and 'I parodied it as follows, which is literally the first copy 'unanointed, unannealed,' as Hamlet says

> 'The Bonie Lesley Bailie,
> To see her is to love her'

He declared himself to Mrs Dunlop at the beginning of the same letter

> 'Do you know that I am almost in love with an acquaintance of yours. 'Almost said I – I am in love, souse! Over head & ears, deep as the most unfathomable abyss of the boundless ocean'.

In one of his flights of verbal fancy, he includes in a letter dated 10th September 1792 to Alexander Cunningham

> 'As for the rest of my fancies & reveries – How I lately met with Miss Lesley Bailie, the most beautiful, elegant woman in the world – How I accompanied her and her Father's Family fifteen miles on their journey, out of pure devotion to admire the loveliness of the works of God in such an unequalled display of them – How in galloping home at night, I made a ballad on her of which these two Stanzas make a part (Thou Bonie Lesley, art a queen)…Behold all these things are written in the Chronicles of my imagination, & shall be read by thee, my dear Friend, & by thy beloved Spouse, my other dear Friend, at a more convenient season'.

Reading these two letters, the one to Mrs Dunlop in full, you can see Burns working himself into a complete frenzy over absolutely nothing at all.

Burns had known Lesley Baillie for only a short time and yet he had practically deified her. Sometimes, it seems as if Burns has a very cloying attitude to his 'betters', which makes for uncomfortable reading. For a supposed man of the people he is very sycophantic at times.

At the end of May 1793, Burns sent a copy of 'Blythe Hae I Been On Yon Hill' to Lesley with the opening words

> 'I have just put the last hand to the enclosed song; and I think that I may say of it, as Nature can say of you – 'There is a work of mine, finished in my very finest style'...I have some pretence, Madam, to make you up the theme of my song, as you and I are two downright singularities in human nature. You will probably start at this assertion: but I believe it will be allowed that a woman exquisitely charming, without the least seeming consciousness of it, and a poet who never paid a compliment but where it was justly due, are to of the greatest rarities on earth'.

Lesley married a Mr Robert Cumming in 1799 and died in Edinburgh in July 1843. She is buried in St John's Burying Ground, at the west end of Princes Street. Her tombstone is on the south wall and reads

> 'In memory of Lesley Baillie, widow of Robert Cumming, Esq., of Logie, Morayshire. Born at Mayville, Ayrshire 6th March 1768. Died in Edinburgh 19th July 1843. And of her sister Grace Baillie, born 22nd October 1764. Died 27th August 1841.

Robert Baillie erected a memorial column to his wife in 1784, later the name of his daughter Grace was added. The monument fell derelict at it's first home, near Kerlaw Mains Farm, and various bits of it were taken into safe keeping at Kerlaw House until a more suitable site could be found.

A new location was found, and the monument settled on the east side of Glencairn Street, Stevenston. A dedication took place on 15th June 1929, and on that date Lesley's name was included in the memorial column. It has been known since as the 'Bonie Lesley Memorial'.

Associated Songs:

Song   : Saw Ye Bonie Lesley
Tune   : The Collier's Bonie Lassie
Period : 22nd August 1792

Song   : Blythe Hae I Been On Yon Hill
Tune   : The Quaker's Wife (aka Liggeram Cosh)
Period : May 1793

34.

JEAN LORIMER
(Chloris)
Born 1775 – Died 11ᵗʰ September 1831

Chronology : 1790

Jean Lorimer was born at Craigieburn near Moffat in 1775. She was the eldest daughter of William Lorimer and Agnes Carson of Morton. Her parents were married in 1772.

Jean was a very attractive young woman and had many admirers but unfortunately, in her choice of a marriage partner, she decided on the runt of the litter, a man called Whelpdale who originally came from Cumberland.

Whelpdale had settled in the neighbourhood of Moffat, and was farming at Barnhill in the early 1790's. Sometime after the Lorimers had moved from Craigieburn, Jean met him at a ball given by Colonel William Johnstone at Drumcrieff in 1793. Whelpdale was a year older than Jean.

The couple eloped from her father's house and ran off to Gretna Green to marry in March 1793. Tradition reports that Whelpdale had threatened to kill himself if Jean would not elope with him. She was too young to realise for her future happiness, that it would have been the best thing to happen to him and her.

The marriage lasted only a few weeks when Whelpdale fled the district to Cumberland to avoid paying his debts, leaving his wife to return to her maiden name and to her father's house, with no money to support her.

She did not see Whelpdale again for twenty-three years, until she visited him in Carlisle debtors prison, on hearing from her brother in Sunderland that he had been incarcerated there. He was now partially paralysed. Jean visited him every day for a month, before returning to Edinburgh.

Robert Chambers relates a story of this meeting, which would have taken place around about 1816. The story may or may not be true.

'Having written to ask at the prison for an interview with her husband, she went to the place where he was confined, and was desired to walk in.   His lodging was pointed out to her on the opposite side of a quadrangle, round which, there was a covered walk resembling the ambulatories of the ancient religious houses.   As she walked along one side of this court, she passed a bulky-looking man, slightly paralytic, who shuffled in walking, as from lameness.   As she approached the door, she heard the man pronounce her name.   'Jean'!   he said, and then immediately added 'Mrs Whelpdale'!   It was her husband – the 'gay' young fellow of 1793 transformed into a broken-down, middle-aged man, whom she had passed without even suspecting his identity'.

The tale carries on that when Whelpdale was released from his incarceration, Jean visited him at his lodgings.   But due to the fact that this leopard could not change his spots, though reconciliation was talked about, there was no chance of it being successful.   Their marital life was not resumed.   After that last meeting, Jean never saw her husband again.

Whelpdale eventually returned to Scotland, where he spent his last years in Langholm in Dumfriesshire.   He died in Langholm, in poverty, in 1834.

For her own reasons Jean never divorced him, so till the day she died she remained Mrs Whelpdale, though always referred to as Mrs Lorimer.

Returning to Jean's earlier years.

When her father fell on hard times at Morton, William Lorimer took on the lease of Kemys Hall (Kemmishall) from Robert Riddell in Autumn 1790. Within a short time of moving to the new farm, Lorimer was on the subscription list for Anderson's magazine, 'The Bee', compiled by Burns.

Jean was often a visitor to the home of Burns, which was only two miles away from Kemys.   In fact it is said that the names John Gillespie and Jean Lorimer were scratched on a window in the parlour of Ellisland, at the time they were courting in the first half of 1791.

Gillespie, an Excise Officer and friend of Burns, left the district when he was transferred to Portpatrick in Wigtownshire to work in the division there.   In a letter from Burns to him, Jean is quoted as saying

'I wonder, Mr Burns, what pet Mr Gillespie has taken at this country, that he does not come and see his friends again'?

There must have been a serious disagreement between Jean and John Gillespie, which possibly caused him to request a removal from the district, as Burns says in the same letter

'I drank tea with the young lady at her home yesternight; & on my whispering to her that I was to write you, she begged me to inclose you her Compliments.   – In fact, the lady, to my certain knowledge, is down on her marrowbones of repentance, respecting her usage of a certain gentleman. – I never meet with her, but you are, sooner or later, introduced on the carpet'.

Enclosed in this letter, sometime pre November 1791 from Ellisland, was the first version of the song 'Craigieburn Wood', which Burns was sending to Gillespie in the hope that it would stir him into contacting Jean again. Gillespie didn't, but Jean, being a beauty, was not short of an admirer in a crowd, and according to the letter was already being chased by John Lewars and several other young men of the Excise.

Burns was also attracted to Jean Lorimer, but whether as a lover or poetical inspiration, we will never know. Burns used Jean as the template for many of his poems and songs from 1793-95, conferring on her the Arcadian name of 'Chloris'.

In 1794 Burns would have been thirty-five and Jean nineteen, a girl whom he had known since she was fifteen, and a regular visitor to his home. If a sexual relationship did occur, then it was an insult to Jean Armour given that Jean Lorimer had eaten at her table and shared in her family life.

And yet it's difficult to believe that a sexual liaison didn't happen on reading letters like the one Burns wrote to Alexander Findlater in September 1794.

'I have been among the angelic world this forenoon.

> Ah! Had ye but been whare I had been,
> Ye wad hae been sae canty, O!

But don't be afraid; I did not dare to touch the ark of the Covenant; nor even to cast a prophane eye to the mercy-seat, where it is hid among the feathered cherubim. I am in the clouds elsewhere –

> Ah Chloris, could I now but sit
> As uncommon as when
> Your infant beauty could beget
> Nor happiness nor pain.

Let yesternight – Oh yesternight!

> Kist yestreen - kist yestreen -
> O as she was kist yestreen -
> I'll never forget while the hollin grows green,
> The bonie sweet Lassie I kist yestreen'.

William Lorimer kept Kemys Hall for about five years. He gave up the lease by August 1795, and moved into Dumfries with Jean.

After William died, senile and penniless on 25th October 1808, Jean worked as a governess to various families, some in the North of England.

Eventually she returned to Scotland, this time to Edinburgh, where traditional unsubstantiated gossip states that for many years she lived the life of a vagrant and, may even have turned to prostitution to survive.

According to the poet Thomas Thorburn, sometime contributor to 'Wood's Songs of Scotland', he met Jean in Edinburgh, and relates in a letter to Robert Chambers dated 15th February 1851

'I fell in with Chloris on the mound in Edinburgh in 1816 or 1817, when I was serving an apprenticeship to a WS. She made some amatory proposals, which I declined, but I gave her a shilling, believing her to be an imposter. Our head clerk, however, met her some evenings afterwards, and adjourned to Johnnie Dowie's and discussed a bottle of ale, and by dint of cross-questioning discovered she was the veritable Jean. I regretted afterwards I had not a jaw with her'.

James Hogg the 'Ettrick Shepherd' met with Jean once, round about 1816, the same period as Thorburn stated he met her. Hogg was with three friends who knew of her and of her friendship with Burns.

'She said Burns came to Craigieburn all night every time his business called him to Moffat. I went with some of them one day to see her, and was introduced to her as the successor of Burns, but she held very light of me indeed. Her feelings were of a woman, and, though a ruined one. I loved her for them. She had a lock of his hair keeping in a box. She was then a widow apparently approaching to forty, though she might be younger. She was the ruin of a fine woman, of a fair complexion, and well made, and I heard by her voice that she had once sung well'.

Jean was not then a widow, but it may have suited her to let Hogg think that she was.

It is reported that Jean had been living on the streets for about ten years when, in 1825, an unnamed gentleman discovered who she was and publicised her circumstances in the Edinburgh newspapers, hoping to raise some money for her.

The gentleman's wife sent Jean a copy of the articles in the papers and Jean sent her a reply dated 2nd March 1825

'Burns Chloris is infinitely obliged to Mrs--- for her kind attention in sending the newspapers, and feels pleased and flattered by having so much said and done in her behalf. Ruth was kindly and generously treated by Boaz, perhaps Burns' Chloris may enjoy a similar fate in the fields of men of talent and worth'.

Apparently the lady saw Jean several times and was delighted with her conversation, which 'indicated a gift of humour and native acuteness of understanding'.

Jean obtained employment as a housekeeper to a gentleman in Newington. This was a much-improved situation for her than she had been used to in the previous years. But she contracted what is believed to be Tuberculosis, and had to retire to lodgings in Middleton's Entry, Potterrow, near to where Agnes McLehose stayed when Robert Burns first met her.

Her employer supported her here until she eventually died in September 1831. Jean was one of the first to be buried in the newly opened Preston Street Cemetery/Newington Churchyard.

Whether Burns had an affair with Jean Lorimer or not, cannot be proved. According to Hogg's gossip, Jean admitted that they had. Burns' account to George Thomson said it was a platonic relationship. But Burns wrote twenty-four songs for her, more than anyone else.

After the Autumn of 1795 Chloris is hardly mentioned in either letter or rhyme, but there is an inscription which was copied to Alexander Cunningham in a letter dated 3rd August 1795.

'Written on the blank leaf of a copy of the last edition of my poems, presented to the lady whom, in so many fictitious reveries of passion, but with the most ardent sentiments of real friendship, I have so often sung under the name of 'Chloris''.

Burns' notes in the Scots Musical Museum relate that

'Craigieburn Wood was composed on a passion which a particular friend of mine had for Miss Lorimer, afterwards a Mrs Whelpdale. The young lady was born at Craigieburn Wood. This friend was a John Gillespie, a fellow excise-man'.

In a letter to George Thomson dated 19th October 1794 Burns writes

'The lady on whom it was made is one of the finest women in Scotland, and in fact, (entre nous) is in a manner to me what Sterne's Eliza was to him, - a mistress or friend, or what you will, in the guileless simplicity of Platonic Love...I assure you, that to my lovely friend, you are indebted for many of your best songs of mine'.

Regarding 'Craigieburn Wood', George Thomson replied to Burns on 27th October 1794 saying how much he liked the song

'I wish I knew the adorable she whose bright eyes and witching smiles have so often enraptured the Scottish bard, that I might drink her sweet health when the toast is going round'.

The only problem Thomson had with the song, was the chorus 'Beyond thee dearie etc.' as it could prove to have too strong a sexual connotation, and could not be sung in the company of ladies. He suggested that Burns change the chorus to make it a bit more acceptable and respectable.

In November 1794 Burns replied to Thomson's criticism of 'Craigieburn Wood' saying that he would write a new chorusless 'Craigieburn Wood' altogether, and that the offending chorus, which he would happily write new words to, was not his, but 'part of some old verses to the air'.

From a book, written by Dr James Adams circa 1893, we have a very interesting look at Jean Lorimer a year or so before she died.

Dr Adams apparently met Jean round about 1829, when he was a boy of approximately 14. She lived one stair up in Middleton's Entry, Potterrow, and was a patient of his father's, Dr Alexander Maxwell Adams, who always referred to her as Mrs Lorimer. James had been sent to collect some papers from Jean one Saturday when he had finished school.

In his 'mind's eye' Dr Adams recollects her home thus

> 'On the left side of the room and facing the window was a small chiffonier. On its slab top were a few books. Opposite the entering door was the fire-place, the mantel-shelf of which was decked with several figures or ornaments of common pottery-ware, flanked by two large sea-shells of gorgeous hues and dazzling lustre. At the side of the fire-place, between it and the window, was a stiff, old-fashioned, haircloth arm-chair. Several chairs were ranged along the window side of the room, and in the window recess. Against the wall, facing the fire-place, was a sofa, I think of haircloth. On one side of the sofa was the doorway entering from the little dark lobby. On the other side was a doorway giving admission to an inner room, of which I saw nothing. A small table with a pattern table-cover occupied the centre of the floor, which was carpeted. A few framed small engravings were hung on the walls. The whole betokened snug, cosy comfort; in short, what might be termed in Scottish vernacular a 'snod' little room'.

James was a shy boy, and Jean was aware of this. She asked him about his school and his friends, and drew him out of himself, to the extent of him telling her about a fight he had had with another boy. Of course, 'he had beaten the bigger boy, hadn't he'? enquired Jean. James affirmed this.

He noticed how she accented her apparently favourite word 'really', which she used innumerable times as in 'No really'! 'Are you really'! 'Did you really'! Dr Adams remembers that the word 'really' was not pronounced as 'reely' but *'railly'*.

Realising that he had come from school, school on a Saturday, and that he would be hungry, she offered him a bap and jelly, which she assured him was *'real* good'. He was a bit slow in eating his 'jeely-piece' and Jean encouraged him by saying

'Dinna be blate, laddie, dinna be blate. You teeth are longer than your beard'.

By the time James had finished his bap he had told Jean probably more than he had told anyone else in his life. As he was getting ready to leave he recalled warmly

'She held my hand long in motherly fashion, still plying with questions of my mother, sisters and brothers; and finally and with kindly earnestness said

'Now dinna forget, when you are a big man, that you had the good wish of the 'Lassie Wi' The Lint-White Locks', touching her temples meaningly as she spoke, adding, and with one of her arch, sunny smiles, 'Your father will tell you what I mean'. I never have forgot, but in backward glances have often recalled the incident as a pleasing memory'.

On returning home, his father asked him if he had noticed the colour of her hair, 'Yes, a very pretty colour', he replied. He was told that Mrs Lorimer was at one time called 'The Lassie Wi' The Lint-White Locks', from the colour of her flaxen hair, which had, however, a touch of yellow in it' – that she was proud of her hair and was pleased when its colour was observed.

The package James delivered to his father contained a number of poems and songs in Burns' own hand, which his father, was accepting as payment from Jean for looking after her in her illness. She suffered much from 'winter-cough', today recognised as severe bronchitis.

From Dr James Adams' recollection of her, she was about 54 when they met, he remembered

'She was about five foot seven inches tall. She had a 'fresh' complexion, was comely, straight and tall. Her hair was like pale straw, parted in the centre, on each side in spiral rolls or curls, made with rolling the hair in her fingers, not with using heating tongs. To my boyish apprehension she realised one impression that Burns' description has burnt in upon me.

'Like harmony her motion', are his words, and that I realised as, 'smooth gliding without step' she passed to and from the apartment'.

'Her head was enclosed by a 'mutch'. Her eyes were full with her eyebrows, bushy, and darker than her hair. The expression contained in these eyes was arch and lively'.

'Her voice was pleasing, 'soft and low', while her speech was of the Scottish vernacular, but her accent and pronunciation were different

215

from the society of grown-up persons as I have had access to. If any of my readers have had the opportunity of conversing with an Inverness or a Dublin lady speaking pure English, they will understand what I wish to convey of difference in her dialect from that of the Edinburgh ordinary vernacular'.

Another description he gave was

'Her countenance has been in frequent varied phraseology described as bewitchingly lovely. To me it was only very pleasing. Her hair, abundant, was of what I should at the present time indicate as of pale straw, yellowish lemon colour, of glossy sheen'.

James asked his father Dr Alexander Adams, at a later time, about the life of Jean Lorimer. His father, who liked and respected Jean very much, denied the stories of her vagrant life-style and fall from respectability, putting it all down to lies and mischief making. He replied strongly

'Not at all; nothing of the kind; these are ungenerous aspersions on the good name of an unhappy and much misunderstood lady, originating no doubt in entire ignorance. Contradict them whenever you hear them'.

He went on to inform his son of Jean's history, including the accusations of vagrancy etc.

'After her father's failure in business, when he lost all, a little beyond her twenty-first year (circa 1796), Miss Lorimer had no shelter and was without means. She was unfit for menial country labour, and had to partake herself of plain governessing, needlework, or such shifty, precarious occupations as were then open to women's employment. Necessarily in this straggling, cheerless course of struggle she had to change her residence, and only because of such a struggle for bare subsistence could she be made liable to the improper phrasing of vagrancy or mendicancy. When, at length, in 1822 she sought an abiding place in Edinburgh, her history was communicated to the public through the papers of the day, and among the various notices elicited there were none that in the slightest affected her moral character. On the contrary, there was evoked a disposition to aid, and friends gathered, touched by what was always so obvious of her gentle, amiable disposition and her evil fortunes'.

The old doctor also knew the man who had latterly employed Jean as a housemaid in his residence in 'Blacket Place', and helped look after her until her death, and said that he would never have employed anyone with a dubious background, and that his support for her to the last was a testament to her honest and loyal character.

The employer also settled Jean in her house at 'Middleton's Entry' when she became ill and unable to carry out her housekeeping duties. She lived there in decent comfort, able 'to do her own turns' till near the last.

According to James Adams, Jean Lorimer did not die entirely alone. From her illness to her death she was looked after by a number of ladies who were aware of her history and commiserated with her. Whatever her past entailed, good or bad, it was obvious that these ladies were non-judgemental towards Jean, giving her, in the end, the love and care she deserved.

Burns never spoke or wrote a word concerning Jean Lorimer that could ever lessen her self-esteem, and Jean Armour told John McDiarmid, Editor of the Dumfries Courier when he interviewed her, that she had a warm regard for Jean Lorimer and would not hear anything against her.

Jean Armour also went on to say that William Lorimer had two daughters and three sons and that unfortunately his wife drank, which had a bad effect on the family. *(Or was she the wife of another Lorimer that Burns had been hauled over the coals for by the Excise? I think that Jean Armour's word could definitely be relied upon).

Jean Armour described Jean Lorimer as having very fair hair and of being perfectly virtuous. On the other hand Whelpdale was a reprobate, whose mother had for a time allowed Jean an annuity, due to her son's atrocious behaviour.

How unfortunate Jean's life was in comparison to many women of that time, we don't really know, but she was fortunate in the fact that she gained friends who cared for her right up until the end, and even strangers searched her out to converse with.

Like Agnes McLehose, Jean Lorimer made a wrong choice at a very young age, and was deemed to spend the rest of her life paying for it.

Jean's Lorimer's grave is marked with the only Celtic Cross in Newington Burying Ground, East Preston Street, and is on the south side of the first walk to the left. Carved on the Cross are the words 'Better a wee bush than nae Bield'. There is an inscription carved at the bottom which says

'This stone marks the grave of Jean Lorimer, the 'Chloris' and 'Lassie wi' the lint-white locks' of the poet Burns. Born 1775: Died 1831. Erected under the auspices of the Ninety Burns Club, Edinburgh 1901'.

*It had been said that William Lorimer was involved with smuggling, and that Burns had in some way turned a blind eye to Lorimer's extra-curricular activities. As an Exciseman, this would definitely have been a sacking matter if this had been correct. There is a letter to Alexander Findlater circa June 1791, which reads

'I am both much surprised & vexed at that accident of Lorimer's Stock. The last survey I made prior to Mr Lorimer's going to Edinburgh I was very particular in my inspection &

the quantity was certainly in his possession as I stated it. The surveys I have made during his absence might as well have been marked *'key absent'* as I never found anybody but the lady, who I know is not mistress of keys, &c. to know anything of it, and one of the times it would have rejoiced all Hell to have seen her so drunk. I have not surveyed there since his return. I know the gentleman's ways are, like the grace of God, past all comprehension, but I shall give the house a severe scrutiny tomorrow morning. & send you in the naked facts. I know, Sir, & regret deeply, that this business glances with a malign aspect on my character as an Officer; but as I am really innocent in the affair, & the gentleman is known to be an illicit dealer, & particularly as this is the *single* instance of the least shadow of carelessness or impropriety in my conduct as an Officer, I shall be particularly unfortunate if my character shall fall a sacrifice to the dark manoeuvres of a Smuggler'.

Although it was never stated that Mr Lorimer of Kemys Hall was the smuggler, we do have it on Jean Armour's testament to McDiarmid that 'Jean Lorimer was the daughter of William Lorimer, Farmer, of Kemmis Hall, and in good circumstances, and that his wife was given to drinking, which injured his daughters.

The drunken wife and the smuggler! William Lorimer and his alcoholic wife! Are they one and the same? It certainly is a possibility to be considered.

But if Lorimer was doing a little smuggling on the side, it did not interfere with the friendship that existed between the two families. In a letter to him in August 1795, Burns invited him and Jean to dinner

'I want you to dine with me today. I have two honest Midlothian Farmers (a Mr Wright & Mr Allan) with me, who have travelled threescore miles to renew old friendship with the poet; and I promise you a pleasant party, a plateful of hotch-potch and a bottle of good sound port.

Mrs Burns desired me yesternight to beg the favour of Jeany to come and partake with her, and she was so obliging as to promise that she would. Jeany and you are all the people, besides my Edinburgh friends, whom I wish to see; and if you can come I shall take it very kind. (Dinner at three)'

Above Left : Jean Lorimer's Grave at Preston Street Cemetry in Edinburgh.
Above Right: Jean Lorimer (Chloris) by an unknown artist.

Below: Craigieburn Farm near Moffat where Jean was born.

Associated Songs:

Song   : Craigieburn Wood (Sweet Closes The Evening)
Tune   : Craigieburn Wood
Period : circa 1791(1st version)

Song   : Wilt Thou Be My Dearie
Tune   : The Sutor's Dochter
Period : 4th July 1791, letter to Rev T. Smith

Song   : O Poortith Cauld
Tune   : Cauld Kail In Aberdeen
Period : 27th August 1793

Song   : Come Let Me Take Thee
Tune   : Cauld Kail In Aberdeen
Period : 27th August 1793

Song   : O Whistle And I'll Come To Ye My Lad
Tune   : O Whistle And I'll Come To Ye My Lad
Period : August 1793

Song   : Thine Am I (see Agnes McLehose)

Song   : Sae Flaxen Were Her Ringlets
Tune   : Oonagh's Waterfall
Period : September 1794

Song   : Ah Chloris, Since It May Na Be
Tune   : Major Graham
Period : September 1794

Song   : Sleep'st Thou or Wauk'st Thou
Tune   : De'il Tak The Wars
Period : 19th October 1794

Song   : It Was The Charming Month Of May
Tune   : Dainty Davie
Period : November 1794

Song   : Lassie Wi' The Lint-White Locks
Tune   : Rothiemurche's Rant
Period : November 1794

Song   : Behold My Love, (My Chloris Mark) How Green The Groves
Tune   : My Lodging's On The Cold Ground
Period : November 1794

Song   : Craigieburn Wood (Sweet Fa's The Eve On Craigieburn)
Tune   : Craigieburn Wood
Period : 15th January 1795, letter to Thomson (2nd Version)

Song   : O Wat Ye Wha's In Yon Town (revised for Lucy Oswald in 1795)
Tune   : I'll Gang Nae Mair Tae Yon Toon
Period : Pre 7th February 1795 (originally dated 4th July 1791)

Song   : Can I Cease To Care (On Chloris Being Ill)
Tune   : Ay Waukin O
Period : Mar 1795

Song   : Their Groves O' Sweet Myrtle (see Jean Armour)

Song   : 'Twas Na Her Bonie Blue E'e
Tune   : Laddie Lie Near Me
Period : April 1795

Song   : Mark Yonder Pomp
Tune   : De'il Tak The Wars
Period : May 1795

Song   : Forlorn My Love
Tune   : Will You Lend Me Your Loom, Lass
Period : June 1795

Song   : Why, Why Tell Thy Lover
Tune   : The Caledonian Hunt's Delight
Period : 3rd July 1795

Song   : This Is No My Ain Lassie
Tune   : This Is No My Ain House
Period : circa July/August 1795

Song   : O Bonie Was Yon Rosy Brier
Tune   : I Wish My Love Were In A Mire
Period : circa July/August 1795

Song   : O That's The Lassie O' My Heart (O Wat Ye Wha That Lo'es Me)
Tune   : Morag
Period : August 1795

Song   : I'll Aye Ca' In By Yon Town
Tune   : I'll Gae Nae Mair Tae Yon Toon
Period : Undated, but probably post Autumn 1795

35.

JEAN MCMURDO
Born 1777 – Died 1839

Chronology : circa Summer 1788

Jean McMurdo was the eldest daughter of John McMurdo, Chamberlain to the Duke of Queensberry and Jane Blair, daughter of the Provost of Dundee. She lived at Drumlanrig, near Burns' farm at Ellisland.

Burns became acquainted with John McMurdo in the summer of 1788, and during the period of friendship he loaned him, in December 1793, a copy of 'The Merry Muses' (a collection of bawdy verse, composed or gathered by Burns) with the request

'When you are tired of them, please leave them with Mr. Clint, of the King's Arms. There is not another copy of the collection in the world; and I should be sorry that any unfortunate negligence should deprive me of what has cost me a good deal of pains'.

To Thomson, on 2nd July 1793, Burns wrote

'I have just finished the following ballad, and as I do think it in my best style, send it to you (you had the tune with a verse or two of the song, from me a while ago.) Mr. Clark, who wrote down the air from Mrs. Burns woodnote wild, is very fond of it, and has given it a celebrity by teaching it to some young ladies of the fashion here – The heroine of the foregoing is Miss McMurdo, daughter of McMurdo of Drumlanrig, one of your subscribers. I have not painted her in the rank which she holds in life, but in the dress and character of a cottager, consequently the utmost simplicity of thought and expression was necessary'.

Burns suggested to Thomson that the song be put to the air 'There Was A Lass And She Was Fair'. But Thomson, in his wisdom (which was musically arrogant) decided to put Burns' words to another air 'Willie Was A Wanton Wag'.

Thomson carelessly lost the original music for 'There Was A Lass', even though Burns had specifically requested its return in the letter of the 2nd, if Thomson did not intend to use it.

'If you do not like the air enough to give it place in your collection, please return me the air – the song you may keep, as I remember it'.

The air has remained lost to this day. Burns also mentioned in the letter

'I have some thoughts of inserting in your index, or in my notes, the names of the fair ones, the themes of my songs. I do not mean the name at full; but dashes or asterisks, so as ingenuity may find them out'.

Though this is still more than a little ungenerous on Burns' part to any researcher, I wish he had decided on this before 1793, as it would have made uniting song and recipient so much easier.

Burns wrote, again in July 1793, to John McMurdo, informing him that he had written a song for his daughter Jean, and asked if it was appropriate for him to give the song to her.

'Kings give coronets – alas! I can only bestow a ballad'.

Burns was aware of the immortality he was bestowing on his poetical subjects

'I assure you I am not a little flattered with the idea when I anticipate children pointing out in future publications the tribute of respect I have bestowed on their Mothers. The merits of the Scots airs to which many of my songs are – and more will be – set, gives me this pleasing hope'.

It is not only the children who could point out the tribute, but the grandchildren and the great grandchildren, etc. forever and ever amen.

Sending the song to Jean McMurdo in July 1793, Burns says

'In the enclosed ballad I have, I think, hit off a few outlines of your portrait. The personal charms, the purity of mind, the ingenuous naivety of heart & manners, in my heroine are, I flatter myself, a pretty just likeness of Miss McMurdo in a Cottager'.

He then goes on in the letter to give her what can only be considered a lecture on the behaviour of young women, obviously seeing himself in the position of an 'elder'.

Burns' poem, 'To A Woodlark' was written at the request of Jean's mother, though apparently Burns was not very happy about writing it. He considered it was not one of his best. It was inserted in the Geddes interleaved copy of the first Edinburgh Edition of the Poems.

When researching through many old music books for information on the airs to which Burns put his words, I was surprised and delighted when I discovered what <u>might</u> be the missing music for 'There Was A Lass, And She Was Fair'.

The find is in the Aberdeen Greig-Duncan Folk Song Collection, and may be the tune, or at least a variation of the tune, that Burns, (who had already suggested that the song be married to another Aberdeenshire air, 'Bonnie Jean'), had recommended for Jean McMurdo's song.

There is a provenance in the Collection, in the description of the song, entitled 'There Was A Maid And She Was Fair', regarding the fact that it may be Burns' lost air. The music is very definitely 'ballad' style.

"There was a lass, and she was fair'. Burns song was written for a traditional tune which has been listed as untraced; it seems that this fragment, both words and music, is a version of his source'. (Greig-Duncan, volume 7, note 1335)

Associated Song:

Song   : There Was A Lass And She Was Fair
Tune   : There Was A Maid And She Was Fair
Period : April 1793

36.

PHILADELPHIA (PHILLIS) MCMURDO
Born 1779 – Died 5th September 1825

Chronology : circa Summer 1788

Philadelphia (Phillis) McMurdo was the youngest daughter of John McMurdo, and noted in Drumlanrig for her beauty. She was married to Mr Norman Lockhart of Carnwarth.

Writing to Thomson about 25th August 1793, Burns asks

'Mr Clarke begs you to give Miss Phillis a corner in your Book, as she is a particular Flame of his, & out of compliment to him, I have made the Song- She is a Miss Phillis McMurdo, sister to the 'Bonie Jean' which I sent you some time ago - They are both pupils of his'.

The song was 'Adown Winding Nith'.

Another composition written by Burns was 'Phillis the Fair'. This was at the request of Stephen Clarke, the music master who taught Phillis, and her sister Jean, music and singing. Stephen was secretly in love with Phillis but it is unlikely she reciprocated.

Burns was neither too happy with 'Phillis the Fair', nor the tune, 'Robin Adair', to which it was set.

To Thomson he wrote on 13th August 1793

'I likewise tried my hand on 'Robin Adair', and you will probably think, with little success, but it is such a cursed, cramp, out of the way measure, that I despair of doing any better of it'.

Her marriage to Norman must have been a love match, for when she died, at just forty-six, she was buried in the Lockhart Mausoleum at Carnwarth where, on a white marble stone, her epitaph is carved as follows

This tablet
Is inscribed by Norman Lockhart, Esq.
To record, however inadequately,
his deep sense
of the manifold Christian graces
which adorned the character of
PHILADELPHIA BARBARA MCMURDO
his beloved wife,

who after having been enabled
by divine grace,
to discharge, in an endearing and exemplary manner,
the various duties of a Christian wife and parent
fell asleep in Jesus,
on the 5th day of September 1825,
to awake to the life immortal,
and to be ever with the Lord.

O see how soon the flowers of Life decay!
How soon terrestrial pleasures fade away!
This Star of Comfort for a season given,
First shone on earth, then set to rise in Heaven:
Bur mourn not, as of life bereft, her doom,
Nor, sorrowing, water with thy tears her tomb;
Redeemed by God from Sin, released from pain,
'To her to live was Christ, to die was gain'.

Associated Songs:

Song   : Phillis The Fair
Tune   : Robin Adair
Period : circa 13th August 1793

Song   : Adown Winding Nith
Tune   : The Muckin' O' Geordy's Byre
Period : circa 25th August 1793

37.

JESSY STAIG
Born 1775 – Died 6th March 1801

Chronology : pre-1790

Jessy Staig was the second daughter of Provost David Staig of Dumfries.

When she was about sixteen, she became so ill that she developed a very high fever and was given only a few hours to live by the leading physician in Dumfries, Dr John Gilchrist. Dr William Maxwell who had been helping out Dr Gilchrist as a type of locum, was called in to the girl and gave her some medicine which is reputed to have saved her life.

In September 1794 Burns wrote to Thomson

'Dr. Maxwell was the physician who seemingly saved her from the grave, and to him I address the following

> Maxwell, if merit here you crave,
> That merit I deny;
> You save fair Jessy from the grave?
> An angel could not die'.

This was the same Dr Maxwell, who three years or so later advised Burns to sit in the freezing waters of the Solway, as a cure for his 'flying-gout'.

Not a good suggestion for someone who was emaciated and rheumatic, never mind the added complication of suffering from a bad heart. This prescription certainly helped Burns' life come to a very rapid end.

In enclosing the song 'Young Jessy' in a letter to Miss Staig in the Spring of 1793, Burns writes

'Mr B. would just give the line to Miss S., that should the respectful timidity of any of her lovers deny him his power of speech, that then she will teach him Mr B's song; so that the poor fellow may not lie under the double imputation of being neither able TO SING NOR SAY'.

Jessy was a good and loyal friend. She was very close to a poetess of the time, *Helen Craik (1750-1825) of Arbigland, Kirkbean parish who published five novels between the years 1796-1805. Jessy was one of the few people who stuck by Helen through some amatory troubles which caused her the loss of her good name.

Incidentally, the gardener's son at Arbigland was to become the infamous sea-farer, John Paul Jones, but it is not known if Burns ever met him.

*At the age of 41, the unmarried Helen had a relationship with her father's groom, a man named Dunn, which the family disapproved of. Shortly after the relationship began, Dunn was murdered. The main suspect for the murder was her nephew, Douglas Hamilton Craik, but neither he nor anyone else was brought to justice for the crime.

Because of the relationship, Helen was ostracised by Dumfries society, with the exception of Jessy Staig. Helen Craik died in Flimby Lodge in Cumbria. Burns also knew Helen Craik and wrote to her from Ellisland on 9th August 1790 and 12th January 1792.

Jessy married Major William Miller, son of Patrick Miller of Dalswinton, and they had two sons. She is reportedly long remembered for her charm and gentleness. Jessy is buried in St Michael's Churchyard, Dumfries, beside her father and near Burns' Mausoleum.

After Jessy's death William Miller married Frances Every who is also buried in St Michael's Churchyard.

The song 'Young Jessy' appeared in Thomson's Scottish Airs in 1798.

Associated Song:

Song   : Young Jessie (Truehearted Was He)
Tune   : Bonie Dundee
Period : April 1793

38.

JANET MILLER
Born 25th June 1775 – Died ?

Chronology : 12th December 1786

Janet Miller was the eldest daughter of Patrick Miller of Dalswinton and Jean Lindsay who originally lived at Liberton near Edinburgh.   Her parents, who may not have been married, had five children in all –

William	born 15th February 1772 (married Jessy Staig)
Patrick	born 5th October 1773
Janet	born 25th June 1775
Thomas	born 9th April 1777
Jean	born 5th December 1778

Burns wrote to her on 9th September 1793

'I have taken the liberty to make you the heroine of the song on the foregoing page.   Being little in the secret of young ladies love and lovers – how should I, you know.   I have formed in my fancy a little love story for you.   The air, you know, is excellent, and the verses, I hope and think, are in my best manner'.

The song composed for Janet was 'Where Are The Joys I Have Met In The Morning' which appeared in Thomson's Scottish Airs in 1801.

According to 'Honest' Allan Cunningham, another song, 'Wilt Thou Be My Dearie', was written for Janet during a brief courtship of her by Burns years earlier.   As Burns was married in 1788, it would certainly have had to be a very brief courtship, as Janet would have been at the most thirteen before then. Is this another of 'Honest' Allan's fabrications?

In fact 'Wilt Thou Be My Dearie' was sent to a Rev. Thomas Smith as early as the 4th July 1791 and the charmer of that time was Jean Lorimer. (In a letter from Dumfries dated mid-March 1794 Burns told Captain Patrick Miller that this was a 'new' Scot's song just composed by him)

Janet married Thomas Erskine, later to become the twenty-eighth Earl of Mar and thirteenth Lord Erskine, in 1795.

Associated Song:

Song   : Where Are The Joys
Tune   : Saw Ye My Father (aka The Grey Cock)
Period : 9th September 1793

39.

LUCY OSWALD (LOUISA JOHNSTON)
Born 1760 – Died 14th January 1798

Chronology : post 1793

Lucy Johnston was the daughter of Wynne Johnston of Hylton on Merse, and was a celebrated beauty of her time. On April 23rd 1793, although eleven years older than him, she married, and later had two children to Richard Alexander Oswald of Auchencruive in Ayrshire.

The song, 'O Wat Ye Wha's In Yon Toon', was originally set for Jean Lorimer, but Burns changed the name in it from Jeanie to Lucy and then dedicated it to her in a letter dated May 1795. Burns often changed heads to his songs.

On sending a copy of the song to a Mr John Syme in May 1794, a year before he sent it to Lucy, Burns said

'Do you know that among much that I admire in the characters and manners of those great folks whom I have now the honour to call my acquaintances – the Oswald Family, for instance – there is nothing charms me more than Mr. Oswald's unconcealable attachment to that incomparible woman, his wife? In my song I have endeavoured to do justice to what would be his feelings on seeing, in the scene I have drawn, the habitation of his Lucy. As I am a good deal pleased with my performance, I, in my first fervour, thought of sending it to Mrs. Oswald, but, on second thoughts, what I offer as the honest incense of genuine respect might, from the well-known character of poverty and poetry, be construed into some modification or other of that servility which my soul abhors'.

In a letter to Captain Patrick Miller dated 8th March 1795 Burns writes

'Inclosed, is a Song, I wrote the other day - The lady I mean to complement in it, is, Mrs Oswald; a woman with whom everybody here is quite enchanted. I throw the little drama of my Song – Mr Oswald, seeing the evening sun shine on the habitation of his Lucy'.

Why it took twelve months for Burns to send the song to Lucy is not known, but can be guessed by the tenor of the letter to Syme. He did not want Lucy or her husband to think of him as a 'toady'. Again, why he said to Captain Miller that it was just recently written, is also a little unusual.

Lucy became ill with Pulmonary Tuberculosis and went to Lisbon to recuperate, but died there in the winter of 1798.

The poet Dryden, who had known her before her marriage, wrote of Lucy

'Whate'er she did was done with so much ease,
In her alone 'twas natural to please;
Her motions all accompanied with grace;
And Paradise was open'd in her face'.

Lucy was an accomplished musician and composed the tune 'Captain Cook's Death' to which Burns' poem 'Thou Ling'ring Star' was originally set, though it is now generally sung to another air, 'Mary's Dream'.

Ten Years after Lucy's death her husband married Lady Lilias Montgomerie, widow of Robert Dundas MacQueen of Braxfield.

Associated Song:

Song   : O Wat Ye Wha's In Yon Town (see Jean Lorimer)
Tune   : I'll Gang Nae Mair Tae Yon Toon
Period : May 1794

40.

JESSY LEWARS
Born 1778 – Died 26th May 1855

Chronology : circa 1789/90

When her father died, in 1789, Jessy Lewars was 11 and, even at such a young age, took on some of the duties of the household, especially looking after the family members.

Sometime later she left her home in Ryedale Cottage in Troqueer parish, and moved into Dumfries to her brother John, who was one of Burns fellow Excisemen and who lived across the road from Burns in Millbrae Vennel.

The Burns' house was like a second home to Jessy, and she became a close and trusted friend of Jean Armour. It is reported that she had 'quiet motherly ways' and a very 'pleasing and gentle disposition'. She was also a very gifted singer and competent pianist.

Jessy was the last of the poet's heroines and aided Jean Armour, who was pregnant, nurse Burns through the last six months of his life. As was the wont of Burns, even facing the jaws of death, he imagined himself to be in love with Jessy, writing many lines in her honour.

Although his body was slowly passing from the earth and into the realm of history, in his last months the 'light that led astray', that 'light from heaven' still fired in his soul like a beacon to banish his impending darkness.

In a letter to James Johnson on 16th June 1796 Burns wrote

> 'My wife has a very particular friend of hers, a young lady who sings well, to whom she wishes to present 'The Scots Musical Museum'. If you have a spare copy, will you be so obliging as to send it by the first 'fly' as I am anxious to have it soon'.   RB

Johnson sent three copies to Burns who presented one to Jessy.

Being in the company of Jessy during his last illness, he told her that if she would play for him any of her favourite tunes, for which she desired new verses, he would try to write them. She sat down at the harpsichord and played one several times over, an old song called 'The Wren's Nest'. He was not long in grasping the melody, and very quickly composed his swansong of love 'O Wert Thou In The Cauld Blast'.   Though this song became more popular when sung to another air, 'Lennox Love To Blantyre'.

The verses to 'O Wert Thou In The Cauld Blast', which Jessy had in Burns' own script, were shown by her to Felix Mendelsshon, who was visiting Scotland at the time.   Recognising the depth of emotion in the words he composed an air to the words, and they again supplanted the second air 'Lennox Love To Blantyre'.

According to Jessy, Burns would question and tease her on her male suitors.   One Bob Spalding wouldn't do as

'He has not as much brains as a midge could lean its elbow on'.

Burns told her he could see into the future, 'because being a poet, he was also a prophet – for anciently they were the same thing', and that she would marry the young lawyer James Thomson.   This she did on 3rd June 1799.   They went on to produce two daughters and five sons.

After Burns' death Jessy helped Jean look after the five boys, the eldest, Robert, living with her for about a year.

After her husband's death on 5th May 1849, she spent the rest of her life in Maxwelltown and died on 26th May 1855.

Jessy is buried in St Michael's Churchyard, close to the Burns Mausoleum in Dumfries, as close and good a neighbour to Robert and Jean in death as she was in life.

The notice of Jessy's death taken from the local newspaper and printed in the book 'A New Life and Vindication of Robert Burns', by James Mackenzie, reads as follows

'Mrs Thomson (nee Lewars), Robert Burns' friend, died at her residence in Maxwelltown, Dumfries, on Saturday 26th May 1855, at the advanced age of nearly four score years, up to a recent date Mrs Thomson enjoyed excellent health, but for some months had been gradually sinking.   Persons familiar with the life of the poet will remember that Jessy Lewars was on the most intimate terms with Burns and his family...in the short interval which took place betwixt the poet's return from Brow and his death, Jessy Lewars was unremitting in her attention to Mrs Burns and the children...and conveyed from her brother's house such cordials of all kinds as she supposed would be acceptable to the Bard.   After Burns' death, two of the children, Robert, the eldest, and another, lived with the Lewars family for about fourteen months.   It must not be forgotten that Miss Lewars closed the eyes of the Poet, dimmed with death...Mrs Thomson, in personal appearance, was tall, somewhat stout, with a beautiful blue eye.   She was of a cheerful disposition, a kindness and open-heartedness which endeared her to all; but her warm friendship for, and unremitting attention to, the Poet constitute the claims for which the memory of Jessy Lewars has upon the *grateful remembrance of the admirers of Robert Burns...at the Poet's death Miss Lewars possessed a great many manuscripts and letters of the Poet. These she gave to Dr. Maxwell, of Dumfries, to be forwarded to Dr. Currie, on loan, for the biography, and it was often a cause of great regret to her that none of them were returned...few have lived more respected and beloved than Jessy Lewars, and so long as the human heart beats in unison with anything that is noble in genius and sentiment, so long will the name of Jessy Lewars, the affectionate and constant friend of Robert Burns, be dear to the admirers of Scotland's Poet'.*

Associated Songs:

Song   : O Lay Thy Loof
Tune   : The Cordwainer's March (aka The Shoemaker's March)
Period : Pre May 1795

Song   : Here's A Health To Ane I Lo'e Dear
Tune   : Here's A Health To Them That's Awa
Period : April 1796

Song   : O Wert Thou In The Cauld Blast
Tune   : Lenox Love To Blantyre
Period : Summer 1796

Left : St Michael's Kirk in Dumfries. Burns and Jean Armour are buried in the Mausoleum within the kirkyard only a few yards from their old home in the town.

Below Left: The Mausoleum where buried beside Robert and Jean are the sons Maxwell, Francis, Robert Junior, James and William.

Below Right: Many of Burns' contemporaries are also buried in the Kirkyard. Dumfries Burns Howff Club has recognised them by placing plaques like this on the graves. This one honours one of our lasses, Jessy Staig.

PART THREE

The Songs

PART THREE

Chapter One- The Songs

* **Words and Music**

Listed Chronologically

Note that although Burns occasionally revised and re-issued a song, the sequence listed below is based on what is believed to be the original date of completing the piece.

1.   Handsome Nell
2.   Now Westlin Winds
3.   I Dream'd I Lay
4.   My Nanie O
5.   O Tibbie I Hae Seen The Day
6.   The Lass Of Cessnock Banks
7.   The Rigs O' Barley
8.   Farewell To Eliza
9.   Montgomerie's Peggy
10.   My Girl She's Airy
11.   Mary Morison
12.   The Belles Of Mauchline
13.   O Leave Novels
14.   The Mauchline Lady
15.   The Fornicator
16.   Young Peggy
17.   The Braes O' Ballochmyle
18.   The Rantin Dog, The Daddie O't
19.   The Lament
20.   The Lass O' Ballochmyle
21.   The Highland Lassie O
22.   Tho' Cruel Fate
23.   Again Rejoicing Nature Sees
24.   Blythe, Blythe And Merry Was She
25.   My Peggy's Face
26.   Where Braving Angry Winter's Storms
27.   The Banks Of The Devon
28.   Your Friendship Much Can Make Me Blest (Talk Not Of Love)

29. Go On Sweet Bird
30. Clarinda, Mistress Of My Soul
31 A Rosebud By My Early Walk
32. To The Weavers Gin You Go
33. An' I'll Kiss Thee Yet, Bonie Peggy Alison
34. Of A' The Airts The Wind Can Blaw
35. O Were I On Parnassus Hill
36. The Blue-Ey'd Lassie
37. When First I Saw Fair Jeanie's Face
    (SMM no. 98 for music, but no chorus music)
38. Louis, What Reck I By Thee
39. Afton Water
40. Thou Ling'ring Star
41. Thine Am I, My Faithful Fair
42. Beware O' Bonie Ann
43. On Sensibility
44. Yestreen I Had A Pint O' Wine
45. Out Over The Forth
46. Ye Flowery Banks O' Bonie Doon
47. The Banks O' Doon
48. Wilt Thou Be My Dearie
49. O Wat Ye Wha's In Yon Town
50. Lovely Davies
51. Thou Gloomy December
52. Ae Fond Kiss
53. Behold The Hour, The Boat Arrive
54. Sae Far Awa
55. Craigieburn Wood
56. Saw Ye Bonie Lesley
57. The Bonie Lad That's Far Awa
58. It Isna Jean, Thy Bonie Face
59. Will Ye Go To The Indies, My Mary
60. The Lea-Rig
61. She Is A Winsome Wee Thing
62. Highland Mary
63. I Hae A Wife O' My Ain
64. The Gallant Weaver
65. Wandering Willie
66. Bonie Wee Thing
67. Young Jessie
68. Farewell Thou Stream

69. There Was A Lass, And She Was Fair
(For music - Greig-Duncan volume 7 no. 1335)
70. Blythe Hae I Been On Yon Hill
71. Phillis The Fair
72. O Poortith Cauld
73. O Whistle An' I'll Come To Ye My Lad
74. Adown Winding Nith
75. Come Let Me Take Thee
76. Where Are The Joys
77. Behold, My Love, How Green The Groves
78. Here Is The Glen
(Thomson's Collection 1822 –
Music to which it was set, original 'Banks of Cree' lost)
79. Sae Flaxen Were Her Ringlets
80. Ah Chloris, Since It May Na Be
81. Sleep'st Thou Or Wauk'st Thou
82. It Was The Charming Month Of May
83. Lassie Wi' The Lint-White Locks
84. My Nanie's Awa'
85. O May Thy Morn
86. Lovely Polly Stewart
87. Can I Cease To Care
88. Their Groves O' Sweet Myrtle
89. 'Twas Na Her Bonie Blue E'e
90. O Lay Thy Loof
91. Mark Yonder Pomp
92. Forlorn My Love
93. Why, Why Tell Thy Lover
94. This Is No My Ain Lassie
95. O Bonie Was Yon Rosy Brier
96. O That's The Lassie O My Heart
97. I'll Aye Ca' In By Yon Town
98. Here's A Health To Ane I Lo'e Dear
99. O Wert Thou In The Cauld Blast
100. Altho' My Back Be At The Wa'
101. Here's To Thy Health, My Bonie Lass
102. Fairest Maid On Devon Banks

The Songs
Listed in Alphabetical Order

243

Song 1
Handsome Nell

Slow And Tender　　　　　*Tune : Untitled In The S.M.M.*

O, once I lov'd a bon - nie lass, An'
aye I love her still. An' whilst that vir - tue
warms my breast, I'll love my hand-some Nell

> O, once I lov'd a bonnie lass,
> An aye I love her still.
> And whilst that virtue warms my breast,
> I'll love my handsome Nell.

As bonnie lassies I hae seen,
　And monie full as braw,
But for a modest gracefu' mien
　The like I never saw.

A bonnie lass, I will confess,
　Is pleasant to the e'e;
But without some better qualities
　She's no a lass for me.

But Nelly's looks are blythe and sweet,
　And what is best of a',
Her reputation is complete,
　And fair without a flaw.

She dresses aye sae clean and neat,
　Both decent and genteel;
And then there's something in her gait
　Gars ony dress look weel.

A gaudy dress and gentle air
　May slightly touch the heart;
But it's innocence and modesty
　That polishes the dart.

'Tis this in Nelly pleases me,
　'Tis this enchants my soul;
For absolutely in my breast
　She reigns without control.

Burns first ever song written circa 1774 to the reel air 'I Am A Man Unmarried' (which remains untraced or at least unnamed to this day)

First Commonplace Book, April 1783
Stair Manuscript (September 1786)

Scots Musical Museum (1803) no. 551 printed (without the fal-de-lal chorus in the original copy) - Tune untitled

Read Burns' biographical letter to Dr John Moore August 1787 regarding 'Nell'

Song 2
Now Westlin Winds

Slowly And With Feeling   *Tune : Port Gordon*

Now west-lin winds, and slaught-'ring guns Bring Aut-umn's plea-sant

wea - ther; And the moor-cock springs, on whirr - ing wings, A-

- mang the bloom-ing hea - ther. Now wav - ing grain, wide

o'er the plain, De - lights the wea - ry far - mer; And the

moon shines bright, when I rove at night, To muse up-on my charm - er.

Now westlin winds, and slaught'ring guns
 Bring Autumn's pleasant weather;
And the moorcock springs, on whirring wings,
 Amang the blooming heather.
Now waving grain, wide o'er the plain,
 Delights the weary farmer;
And the moon shines bright, when I rove at night,
 To muse upon my charmer.

The pairtrick lo'es the fruitfu' fells,
 The plover lo'es the mountains;
The woodcock haunts the lonely dells,
 The soaring hern the fountains.
Thro' lofty groves the cushat roves,
 The path o' man to shun it;
The hazel bush o'erhangs the thrush,
 The spreading thorn the linnet.

Thus ev'ry kind their pleasure find,
    The savage and the tender;
Some social join, and leagues combine,
    Some solitary wander;
Avaunt, Away! the cruel sway,
    Tyrannic man's dominion!
The sportsman's joy, the murd'ring cry,
    The flutt'ring gory pinion.

But, Peggy dear, the ev'ning's clear,
    Thick flies the skimming swallow;
The sky is blue, the fields in view,
    All fading-green and yellow;
Come let us stray our gladsome way,
    And view the charms of Nature;
The rustling corn, the fruited thorn,
    And ilka happy creature.

We'll gently walk, and sweetly talk,
    While the silent moon shines clearly!
I'll clasp thy waist, and, fondly prest,
    Swear how I lo'e thee dearly;
Not vernal show'rs to budding flow'rs,
    Not Autumn to the farmer,
So dear can be, as thou to me,
    My fair, my lovely charmer!

Caledonian Pocket Companion (1756) VIII no. 25 – the air
First Commonplace Book August 1785
Kilmarnock Edition (July 1786)
Stair Manuscript (September 1786)
Scots Musical Museum (1792) no. 351
Hastie Manuscript f. 81

Also known as 'Har'st – A Fragment' and 'Song Composed In August'

The words have also been set to the airs – 'When The King Comes O'er The Water', 'Come Kiss With Me', 'I Had a Horse, And I Had Nae Mair', 'Ally Croker'

Song 3
I Dream'd I Lay

Very Slow And Languid   *Tune : I Dream'd I Lay*

I dream'd I lay where flowers were spring-ing Gai-ly in the
sun-ny beam; List' ning to the wild birds sing-ing, By a fall-ing
crys-tal stream; Straight the sky grew black and dar-ing;
Thro' the woods the whirl-winds rave; Trees with ag-ed
arms were war-ring, O'er the swell-ing drum-lie wave.

I dream'd I lay where flowers were springing
  Gaily in the summer beam;
List'ning to the wild birds singing,
  By a falling crystal stream;
Straight the sky grew black and daring,
  Thro' the woods the whirlwinds rave,
Trees with aged arms were warring
  O'er the swelling, drumlie wave.

Such was my life's deceitful morning,
 Such the pleasures I enjoy'd!
But lang or noon, loud tempests, storming,
 A' my flowery bliss destroy'd.
Tho' fickle fortune has deceiv'd me
 She promis'd fair, and perform'd but ill.
Of monie a joy and hope bereav'd me,
 I bear a heart shall support me still.

Scots Musical Museum (1788) no. 146 signed X

Napier's Scots Songs (1792) II no. 88
Hastie Manuscript f. 32
Gray Manuscript

The words have also been set to the air 'The Young Man's Dream' - See Scots Musical Museum (1788) no. 126 by James 'Balloon' Tyler

Song 4
My Nanie O

Slow And Expressive   *Tune : My Nanie O*

Be - hind yon hills where Stin-char flows 'Mang

moors an' moss-es ma-ny, O, The win-try sun the

day has clos'd, An' I'll a-wa to Nan-ie, O. The

west-lin wind blaws loud an' shill; The

night's baith mirk an' rai-ny, O; But I'll get my plaid, an'

out I'll steal, An' owre the hill to Nan-ie, O.

Behind yon hills where Stinchar flows
 'Mang moors an' mosses many, O,
The wintry sun the day has clos'd,
 An' I'll awa to Nanie, O.

The westlin wind blaws loud an' shill,
 The night's baith mirk an' rainy, O;
But I'll get my plaid an' out I'll steal,
 An' owre the hill to Nanie, O.

250

My Nanie's charming, sweet, an' young,
  Nae artfu' wiles to win ye, O;
May ill befa' the flattering tongue
  That wad beguile my Nanie, O.

Her face is fair, her heart is true,
  As spotless as she's bonie,O;
The op'ning gowan, wat wi' dew,
  Nae purer is than Nanie, O.

A country lad is my degree,
  An' few there be that ken me, O;
But what care I how few they be?
  I'm welcome ay to Nanie, O.

My riches a's my penny-fee,
  An' I maun guide it cannie, O;
But warl's gear ne'er troubles me,
  My thoughts are a', my Nanie, O.

Our auld guidman delights to view
  His sheep an' kye thrive bonie, O;
But I'm as blythe that hauds his pleugh,
  An' has nae care but Nanie, O.

Come weel, come woe, I care na by;
  I'll tak what Heav'n will send me, O;
Nae ither care in life have I,
  But live, an' love my Nanie, O.

Orpheus Caledonius (1725) no. 38 - the air
Ramsay's Musick (c1726) – the air
Watt's Miscellany (1730) III no. 126 – the air
British Musical Miscellany (1734) II no. 14 – the air
McGibbon's Scots Tunes (1742) no. 27 – the air
Caledonian Pocket Companion (1753) V no. 3 - the air
Bremner's Scots Songs (1757) no. 17
First Commonplace Book, April 1784 (to tune of 'As I Came In By London O)
Stair Manuscript (September 1786)
See Scots Musical Museum (1787) no. 88 for earlier version of 'My Nanie O'
Poems (1787)
Thomson's Select Collection Of Original Scottish Airs (1793)
Scots Musical Museum (1803) no. 580 (to English air by Thomas Ebdon)

Song 5
O Tibbie, I Hae Seen The Day

Moderate with Attitude　　　　　　　　　　　*Tune : Invercauld's Reel*

O　Tib-bie I　hae seen the day. Ye　wad-na been sae shy; For

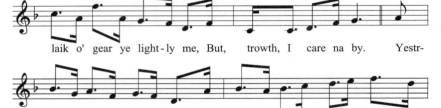

laik o' gear ye light-ly me, But,　trowth, I　care na by.　　Yestr-

- een I　met you on the moor, Ye　spak na but gaed by like stoure: Ye

geck at me be-cause I'm poor, But　fient a　hair care I.

(Chorus)
O Tibbie I hae seen the day, Ye wadna be sae shy;
For laik o' gear ye lightly me, But trowth, I care na by.

Yestreen I met you on the moor,
　Ye spak na, but gaed by like stoure:
Ye geck at me because I'm poor,
　Bur fient a hair care I.

When comin' hame on Sunday last,
　Upon the road as I cam past,
Ye snufft an' gae your head a cast –
　But, trowth, I care na by.

I doubt na lass, but you may think,
　Because ye hae the name o' clink,
That ye can please me at a wink,
　Whene'er ye like to try.

But sorrow tak him that's sae mean,
  Altho' his pouch o' coin were clean,
Wha follows ony saucy quean,
  That looks sae proud an' high!

Altho' a lad were e'er sae smart,
  If that he want the yellow dirt,
Ye'll cast your head anither airt,
  An' answer him fu' dry.

But if he hae the name o' gear,
  Ye'll fasten to him like a brier,
Tho' hardly he for sense or lear,
  Be better than the kye.

But, Tibbie, lass, tak my advice:
  Your daddie's gear maks you sae nice;
The Diel a ane wad spier your price,
  Were ye as poor as I.

There lives a lass beside yon park,
  I'd rather hae her in her sark
Than you wi' a' your thousand mark,
  That gars ye look sae high.

Stewart's Reels (1762) no. 31 - the air
Bremner's Reels (1768) no. 107 – the air
McGlashan's Strathspey Reels (1780) no. 26 - the air
First Commonplace Book, September 1784 (though written before) plus extra verses
Scots Musical Museum (1788) no. 196 signed X
Hastie Manuscript f. 50

Song 6
The Lass Of Cessnock Banks

Moderate/Expressive   *Tune : The Butcher Boy*

On Cess-nock banks a las-sie dwells, Could I des-cribe her shape and mien! Our las-sies a' she far ex-cels, An' she has twa spark-ling, rogue-ish een! She's sweet-er than the morn-ing dawn, When ris-ing Phoe-bus first is seen, When dew-drops twin-kle o'er the lawn, An' she has twa spark-ling, rogue-ish een!

On Cessnock banks a lassie dwells,
   Could I describe her shape and mien!
Our lassies a' she far excels,
   An' she has twa sparkling, rogueish een!

She's sweeter than the morning dawn,
   When rising Phoebus first is seen,
When dew-drops twinkle o'er the lawn,
   An' she has twa sparkling, rogueish een!

She's stately like yon youthful ash,
   That grows the cowslip braes between,
An' drinks the stream with vigour fresh;
   An' she has twa sparkling, rogueish een!

She's spotless like the flow'ring thorn,
   With flow'rs so white an' leaves so green,
When purest in the dewy morn;
   An' she has twa sparkling, rogueish, een!

254

Her looks are like the vernal May,
    When ev'ning Phoebus shines serene,
While birds rejoice on every spray;
    An' she has twa sparkling, rogueish een!

Her hair is like the curling mist,
    That climbs the mountain-sides at e'en,
Then flow'r-reviving rains are past;
    An' she has twa sparkling, rogueish een!

Her forehead's like a show'ry bow,
    When gleaming sunbeams intervene,
An' gild the distant mountain's brow –
    An' she has twa sparkling, rogueish een!

Her cheeks are like yon crimson gem,
    The pride of all the flowery scene,
Just opening on its thorny stem –
    An' she has twa sparkling, rogueish een!

Her bosom's like the nightly snow,
    When pale the morning rises keen,
While hid the murm'ring streamlets flow –
    An' she has twa sparkling, rogueish een!

Her lips are like yon cherries ripe,
    That sunny walls from Boreas screen;
They tempt the taste an' charm the sight –
    An' she has twa sparkling, rogueish een!

Her teeth are like a flock of sheep,
    With fleeces newly washen clean,
That slowly mount the rising steep –
    An' she has twa sparkling, rogueish een!

Her breath is like the fragrant breeze,
    That gently stirs the blossom'd bean,
When Phoebus sinks behind the seas –
    An' she has twa sparkling, rogueish een!

Her voice is like the ev'ning thrush,
    That sings on Cessnock banks unseen,
While his mate sits nestling in the bush –
    An' she has twa sparkling, rogueish een!

But 'tis not her air, her form, her face,
    Tho' matching beauty's fabled Queen!
'Tis the mind that shines in ev'ry grace –
    An' chiefly in her rogueish een!

Scots Musical Museum (1792) no. 304 - the air
Cromek Reliques (1808)

The words have also been set to the airs 'If He Be A Butcher Neat And Trim' and 'The Cardin O't' (aka 'Salt, Fish And Dumplings')

Song 7
The Rigs O' Barley

Lively And Merry　　　　　　　　　　　*Tune : Corn Rigs Are Bonie*

It　　was up-on a　　　Lam-mas night, When　corn　　rigs are

bon-ie,　　Be - neath the moon's un - cloud-ed　light,　I

held a - wa to　An - nie. The　　time flew by, wi'

tent - less heed, Till　'tween the　late and　ear - ly, Wi'

sma' per-sua - sion　she a - greed, To　see me thro' the

bar　-　ley.　　Corn　rigs, an'　bar - ley rigs, An'

corn　rigs are bon　-　ie. I'll　ne'er for-get that

hap-py night, A - mang the rigs wi'　An　-　nie.

(Chorus)
Corn rigs, an' barley rigs,
 An' corn rigs are bonie.
I'll ne'er forget that happy night,
 Amang the rigs wi' Annie

It was upon a Lammas night,
 When corn rigs are bonie,
Beneath the moon's unclouded light,
 I held awa to Annie.
The time flew by, wi' tentless heed;
 Till, 'tween the late an' early,
Wi' sma' persuasion she agreed
 To see me thro' the barley.

The sky was blue, the wind was still,
 The moon was shining clearly;
I set her down, wi' right good will,
 Amang the rigs o' barley!
I ken't her heart was a'my ain;
 I lov'd her most sincerely;
I kiss'd her owre an' owre again,
 Amang the rigs o' barley.

I lock'd her in my fond embrace;
 Her heart was beating rarely;
My blessing on that happy place,
 Amang the rigs o' barley!
But by the moon an' stars so bright,
 That shone that hour so clearly!
She aye shall bless that happy night
 Amang the rigs o' barley.

I hae been blythe wi' comrades dear;
 I hae been merry drinking;
I hae been joyfu' gaith'rin gear;
 I hae been happy thinking;
But a' the pleasures e'er I saw,
 Tho' three times doubl'd fairly –
That happy night was worth them a',
 Amang the rigs o' barley.

Craig's Scots Tunes (1730) no. 42 – the air
Orpheus Caledonius (1733) II nos. 18 & 47 (old version)
McGibbon's Scots Tunes (1742) no. 20 – the air
Caledonian Pocket Companion (1753) V no. 20 (old version)
Bremner's Scots Songs (1757) no. 21 (old version)
Kilmarnock Edition (July 1786)
Scots Musical Museum (1787) no. 93 (old version)
The air was used by John Gay in his opera 'Polly' c1720s

Song 8
Farewell To Eliza

Slow With Thought   *Tune : Gilderoy*

From thee, Eliza, I must go,
  And from my native shore:
The cruel fates between us throw
  A boundless ocean's roar;
But boundless oceans roaring wide
  Between my love and me,
They never, never can divide
  My heart and soul from thee.

Farewell, farewell, Eliza dear,
  The maid that I adore!
A boding voice is in mine ear,
  We part to meet no more!
But the latest throb that leaves my heart,
  While death stands victor by,
That throb, Eliza, is thy part,
  And thine that latest sigh.

(Also suggested to have been written for Elizabeth Miller)

Ramsay's Musick (c1726) - the air
Orpheus Caledonius (1733) II no. 47 - the air
McGibbon's Scots Tunes (1742) no. 26 – the air
Caledonian Pocket Companion (1753) V no. 20 – the air
Bremner's Scots Songs (1757) no. 10 – the air
Kilmarnock Edition (July 1786)
See Biographical letter to Dr. John Moore August 1787

The words have also been set to the air 'Donald'

258

Song 9
Montgomerie's Peggy

Moderate With Caring   *Tune : Galla Water*

Al - tho' my bed were in yon muir, A-
- mang the hea-ther, in my plai-die, Yet hap-py hap-py
would I be, Had I my dear Mont - gom-erie's Peg-gy.

Altho' my bed were in yon muir,
    Amang the heather, in my plaidie,
Yet happy happy would I be,
    Had I my dear Montgomerie's Peggy.

When o'er the hill beat surly storms,
    And winter nights were dark and rainy,
I'd seek some dell, and in my arms
    I'd shelter dear Montgomerie's Peggy.

Were I a Baron proud and high,
    And horse and servants waiting ready,
Then a' 'twad gie o' joy to me –
    The sharin't with Montgomerie's Peggy.

Caledonian Pocket Companion (1756) VIII no. 28 - the air
Stewart's Scots Songs (1772) no. 1 – the air
Neil Stewart's 30 Songs For A Voice And Harpsichord (c1780s) – entitled 'Coming Thro'
The Broom'

Scots Musical Museum (1788) no. 125 - the air
Ritson's Scottish Songs (1794) I no. 84 – the air

First Commonplace Book (1783-85) though written before. Burns wrote that it was "done,
something in imitation of a noble old Scottish Piece called McMillan's Peggy, and sings to
the tune of 'Galla Water'

Song 10
My Girl She's Airy

Fast And Rollicking   *Tune : Black Joke*

My girl she's ai - ry, she's bux - om and gay, Her

breath is as sweet as the bloss-oms in May; A touch of her lips it

ra-vish-es quite; She's al - ways good na-tur'd, good hu-mor'd and free; She

dan - ces, she glan - ces, she smiles with a glee; Her

eyes are the light-enings of joy and de-light; Her slen-der neck, her

hand-some waist, Her hair well buck-l'd, her stays well lac'd, Her

ta - per white leg, with an et, and a c, For her a, b, e, d, and her

c, u, n, t, And Oh, for the joys of a long win-ter night!!!

Bremner's Collection Of Scots Tunes (1759) – adapted air
First Commonplace Book (September 1784)
Merry Muses Of Caledonia

Song 11
Mary Morison

Tenderly Slow   *Tune : Duncan Davidson*

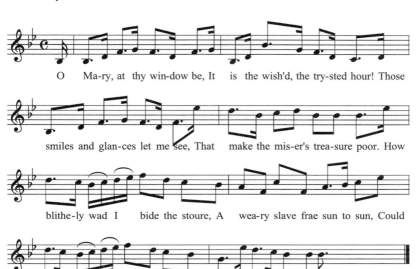

O Mary, at thy window be,
   It is the wish'd the trysted hour!
Those smiles and glances let me see,
   That makes the miser's treasure poor.
How blythely wad I bide the stoure,
   A weary slave frae sun to sun,
Could I the rich reward secure,
   The lovely Mary Morison!

Yestreen, when to the trembling string
   The dance gaed thro' the lighted ha',
To thee my fancy took its wing,
   I sat but neither heard nor saw:
Tho' this was fair, and that was braw,
   And yon the toast of a' the town,
I sighed, and said amang them a' –
   Ye are na Mary Morison!

O, Mary, canst thou wreck his peace
  Wha for thy sake wad gladly die?
Or canst thou break that heart of his
  Whase only faut is loving thee?
If love for love thou wilt na gie,
  At least be pity to me shown:
A thought ungentle canna be
  The thought o' Mary Morison.

(The song is not considered to have been written for the Mary Morison, buried in Mauchline Kirkyard)

Scots Musical Museum (1788) no. 149 - the air
Bremner's Reels (1759) – the air 'Duncan Davidson' entitled 'Ye'll Ay Be Welcome Back Again'

Campbell's Reels (1778) no. 31, entitled 'Duncan Davie'
McGlashan's Strathspey Reels (1780) – the air
Dale's Scots Songs (1794) I no. 58
Currie (1800)
Thomson's Select Collection Of Original Scotish Airs (1818) no. 219
See Burns letter to George Thomson dated 20th March 1792

The words have also been set to the airs 'The Miller, 'The Glasgow Lasses' and ' Bide Ye Yet' (Burns' original choice for the air to the words)

Song 12
The Belles Of Mauchline

Moderate With Teasing   *Tune : Bonie Dundee*

In Mauch-line there dwells six pro-per young Belles, The pride of the

place and its neigh-bour-hood a', Their car-riage and dress a

stran-ger would guess, In Lon'-on or Pa-ris they'd got-ten it a': Miss

Mil-ler is fine, Miss Mark-land's di - vine, Miss Smith she has

wit and Miss Bet-ty is braw; There's beau-ty and for-tune to

get wi' Miss Mor-ton, But AR-MOUR'S the je-wel for me o' them a'.

Skene Manuscript (c1630) - the air entitled 'Adew Dundee'
Playford's Dancing Master (1688) – the air
D'Urfey's Pills To Purge Melancholy (1719) V no. 17 – the air
Craig's Scots Tunes (1730) no. 22 – the air
McGibbon's Scots Tunes (1746) no. 36 – the air
Caledonian Pocket Companion (1751) III no. 4 – the air
Scots Musical Museum (1787) no. 99 - the air
Glenriddell Manuscript (27th April 1791)
Currie (1800)

Song 13
O Leave Novels

Lively With Challenge   *Tune : Ye Mauchline Belles*

O, leave novels, ye Mauchline belles,
  Ye're safer at your spinning wheel;
Such witching books, are baited hooks
  For rakish rooks like Rob Mossgiel.

Your fine Tom Jones and Grandisons,
  They make your youthful fancies reel;
They heat your brains, and fire your veins,
  And then you're prey for Rob Mossgiel.

Beware a tongue that's smoothly hung,
  A heart that warmly seems to feel;
That feeling heart but acts a part,
  'Tis rakish art in Rob Mossgiel.

The frank address, the soft caress,
  Are worse than poisoned darts of steel;
The frank address, and politesse,
  Are all finesse in Rob Mossgiel.

Scots Musical Museum (1803) no. 573 – air untitled
The original title to the air the verses were set to was 'Donald Blue'

Song 14
The Mauchline Lady

Moderate/Pensive   *Tune : I Had A Horse And I Had Nae Mair*

When first I came to Stew-art Kyle My mind it was nae stea-dy: Where - e'er I gaed, where - e'er I rade A Mis-tress still I had ay. But when I came roun' by Mauch-line toun, Not dread - in' an - y bo - dy, My heart was caught, be - fore I thought, And by a Mauch-line La-dy.

Scots Musical Museum (1788) no. 185 – the air.

First Commonplace Book August 1785

There is reportedly a true story regarding the title of the air.   A John Hunter, ancestor of a very respectable farming family, who came from the Galston area, possibly a place called Bar Mill, was a luckless sort of lad and due to some youthful follies, he found it necessary to leave the parish and retreat to the West Highlands, where he fee'd himself to a Highland laird.   On leaving the parish he owned very little, hence the title of the air 'I had a horse, and I had nae mair.'   But on reading the poem, it is clear that though he might only have had one horse to his name, he did have a good eye for the ladies, culminating with a dalliance with the laird's lady that he was fee'd to.

Song 15
The Fornicator

Fast/Lively/Rollicking   *Tune : Clout The Caudron*

Ye jo-vial boys who love the joys, The bliss-ful joys of Lo-vers; Yet

dare a-vow with dauntless brow, When th' bo-ny lass dis-co-vers; I

pray draw near, and lend an ear, And wel-come in a Fra-ter, For I've

late-ly been on qua-ran-tine, A pro-ven For-ni - ca-tor.

Ye jovial boys who love the joys,
  The blissful joys of Lovers;
Yet dare avow with dauntless brow,
  When th' bony lass discovers;
I pray draw near, and lend an ear,
  And welcome in a Frater,
For I've lately been on quarantine,
  A proven Fornicator.

Before the congregation wide
  I pass'd the muster fairly,
My handsome Betsey by my side,
  We gat our ditty rarely;
But my downcast eye by chance did spy
  What made my lips to water
Those limbs so clean where I, between,
  Commenced a Fornicator.

With rueful face and signs of grace
   I paid the buttock-hire,
The night was dark and thro' the park
   I could not but convoy her;
A parting kiss, what could I less,
   My vows began to scatter,
My Betsey fell – lal de lal lal,
   I am a Fornicator.

But for her sake this vow I make,
   And solemnly I swear it,
That while I own a single crown,
   She's welcome for to share it;
And my roguish boy his Mother's joy,
   And the darling of his Pater,
For him I boast my pains and cost,
   Although a Fornicator.

Ye wenching blades whose hireling jades
   Have tipt you off blue-boram,
I tell you plain, I do disdain
   To rank you in the Quorum;
But a bony lass upon the grass
   To teach her esse Mater,
And no reward but for regard,
   O that's a Fornicator.

Your warlike Kings and Heros bold,
   Great Captains and Commanders;
Your mighty Caesar's fam'd of old.
   And Conquering Alexanders;
In fields they fought and laurels bought
   And bulwarks strong did batter,
But still they grac'd our noble list
   And ranked Fornicator!!!

Merry Drollery, London (1661) no. 134 – the air
Tea-Table Miscellany (1724) – the air
Orpheus Caledonius (1733) no. 25 – the air
Scots Musical Museum (1787) no. 23 – the air
Merry Muses of Caledonia

Song 16
Young Peggy

Slow And Tender   *Tune : Loch Eroch Side*

Young   Peg - gy blooms our   bon - iest lass, Her

blush is like the morn -ing, The   ro-sy dawn, the spring -ing grass, With

ear - ly   gems   a - dorn -ing;   Her

eyes out-shine the ra - diant beams That   gild the pass -ing   show-er, And

glit-ter o'er the chrys-tal streams, And   chear each fresh'-ning flow-er.

Young Peggy blooms our boniest lass,
   Her blush is like the morning,
The rosy dawn the springing grass
   With early gems adorning.
Her eyes outshine the radiant beams
   That gild the passing shower,
And glitter o'er the crystal streams,
   And chear each fresh'ning flower.

Her lips, more than the cherries bright –
   A richer dye has graced them –
They charm the admiring gazer's sight,
   And sweetly tempt to taste them.
Her smile is as the evening mild,
   When feather'd pairs are courting,
And little lambkins wanton wild,
   In playful bands disporting.

Were Fortune lovely Peggy's foe,
　　Such sweetness would relent her:
As blooming Spring unbends the brow
　　Of surly, savage Winter.
Detraction's eye no aim can gain
　　Her winning powers to lessen,
And fretful envy grins in vain
　　The poison'd tooth to fasten.

Ye pow'rs of Honor, Love and Truth
　　From ev'ry ill defend her!
Inspire the highly-favour'd youth
　　The destinies intend her!
Still fan the sweet connubial flame
　　Responsive in each bosom,
And bless the dear parental name
　　With many a filial blossom!

The air 'Loch Eroch Side' dates from Pre 1700 and was included in
Agnes Hume's Manuscript (1704) – the air is entitled 'Lady Strathend's'
Aird's Airs (1782) III no. 541 – the air
McGlashan's Reels (1786) no. 46 – the air
Scots Musical Museum (1787) no. 78 – the air
Sime's Edinburgh Musical Miscellany (1793) no. 360
Read Burns' letter to Margaret Kennedy, October 1785
The words have also been set to the airs 'Peggy, I Must Love Thee' and 'The Last Time I
Came O'er The Moor'

'Loch Eroch Side is thought to be the original of the air which is now usually set to the song
'I'm O'er Young To Marry Yet'

Song 17
The Braes O' Ballochmyle

Slow/Pensive   *Tune : The Braes O' Ballochmyle*

The Catrine woods were yellow seen,
  The flowers decay'd on Catrine lea;
Nae lav'rock sang on hillock green,
  But Nature sickened on the e'e;
Thro' faded groves Maria sang,
  Hersel' in beauty's bloom the while;
And aye the wild-wood echoes rang,
  Fareweel the braes o' Ballochmyle.

Low in your wintry beds, ye flowers,
  Again ye'll flourish fresh and fair;
Ye birdies, dumb in with'ring bowers,
  Again ye'll charm the vocal air;
But here, alas! For me nae mair
  Shall birdie charm, or floweret smile;
Fareweel the bonie banks of Ayr!
  Fareweel! fareweel! sweet Ballochmyle!

Burn's words set c1785
Music by Allan Masterton c1787
Scots Musical Museum (1790) no 276 Written for this Work by R. Burns

Song 18
The Rantin Dog, The Daddie O't

Lively With Attitude   *Tune : Whare Wad Bonie Annie Ly*

O, wha my ba-bie - clouts will buy? O,wha will tent me when I cry?

Wha will kiss me where I lie? The ran - tin dog, the dad-die o't!

Wha will own he did the faut? Wha will buy the groan-in maut?

Wha will tell me how to ca't? The ran - tin dog, the dad-die o't!

O, wha my babie-clouts will buy?	When I mount the creepie-chair,
O, wha will tent me when I cry?	Wha will sit beside me there?
Wha will kiss me where I lie? –	Gie me Rob, I'll seek nae mair –
The rantin dog, the daddie o't!	The rantin dog, the daddie o't!
Wha will own he did the faut?	Wha will crack tae me my lane?
Wha will buy the groanin maut?	Wha will mak me fidgin fain?
Wha will tell me how to ca't?	Wha will kiss me o'er again? –
The rantin dog, the daddie o't!	The rantin dog, the daddie o't!

Northumberland Manuscript (1694) – the air is entitled 'Rood House Rant'
Playford's Dancing Master (1695) – the air is entitled 'Red House'

Tea-Table Miscellany (1724) – the air
Watt's Musical Miscellany (1731) V no. 106 – the air is entitled 'Whar'll Our Gudeman Ly'

Scots Musical Museum (1792) no. 324 – the air
Also -Scots Musical Museum (1790) no. 277 signed Z (air – East Nook O' Fife)

'Whare Wad Bonie Annie Lie', is taken from a manuscript seen by James Dick, editor of
'The Songs Of Robert Burns' (1906)

Song 19
The Lament (O Thou Pale Orb)

Slow/Tragic   *Tune : Scots Queen*

O thou pale Orb that silent shines
    While care-untroubled mortals sleep!
Thou seest a wretch who inly pines,
    And wanders here to wail and weep!
With Woe I nightly vigils keep
    Beneath thy wan, unwarming beam;
And mourn, in lamentation deep,
    How life and love are all a dream.

I joyless view thy rays adorn
  The faintly marked, distant hill;
I joyless view thy trembling horn,
  Reflected in the gurgling rill:
My fondly-fluttering heart, be still!
  Thou busy pow'r, Remembrance, cease!
Ah! Must the agonising thrill
  Forever bar returning Peace!

O thou bright Queen, who, o'er th' expanse
  Now highest reign'st, with boundless sway!
Oft has thy silent-marking glance
  Observ'd us, fondly-wand'ring, stray!
The time, unheeded, sped away,
  While love's luxurious pulse beat high,
Beneath thy silver-gleaming ray,
  To mark the mutual-kindling eye.

O! scenes in strong remembrance set!
  Scenes, never, never to return!
Scenes if in stupor I forget,
  Again I feel, again I burn!
From ev'ry joy and pleasure torn,
  Life's weary vale I'll wander thro':
And hopeless, comfortless, I'll mourn
  A faithless woman's broken vow!

Caledonian Pocket Companion (1759) XII no. 1 - the air
Oswald's Companion (c1759) XII no. 1 – the air
Kilmarnock Edition (July 1786)
Scots Musical Museum (1788) no. 190 - the air

The direction to James Johnson was to take the first two verses and the last two verses of
'The Lament' and match them to the air 'Scots (Scotch) Queen'.

Song 20
The Lass O' Ballochmyle

Moderate With Recollection   *Tune : Ettrick Banks*

'Twas even, the dew-y fields were green, On ev-ery blade the
pearls hang; The Ze - phyr wan - ton'd round the bean, And
bore its fra - grant sweets a - lang; In ev' - ry glen the
ma - vis sang, All Na - ture list'-ning seem'd the while, Ex-
- cept where green-wood e - choes rang, A - mang the braes o' Bal-loch-myle.

'Twas even, the dewy fields were green,
 On every blade the pearls hang;
The Zephyr wanton'd round the bean,
 And bore its fragrant sweets alang;
In ev'ry glen the mavis sang,
 All Nature list'ning seem'd the while,
Except where greenwood echoes rang,
 Amang the braes o' Ballochmyle.

With careless step I onward stray'd,
 My heart rejoic'd in Nature's joy,
When, musing in a lonely glade,
 A maiden fair I chanc'd to spy.
Her look was like the morning's eye,
 Her air like Nature's vernal smile,
Perfection whisper'd, passing by: -
 'Behold the lass o' Ballochmyle!'

274

Fair is the morn in flowery May,
　　And sweet is night in autumn mild,
When roving thro' the garden gay,
　　Or wand'ring in the lonely wild;
But woman, Nature's darling child –
　　There all her charms she does compile;
Even there her other works are foil'd
　　By the bonie lass o' Ballochmyle.

O, had but she been a country maid,
　　And I the happy country swain,
Tho' shelter'd in the lowest shed
　　That ever rose on Scotia's plain!
Thro' weary winter's wind and rain
　　With joy, with rapture, I would toil,
And nightly to my bosom strain
　　The bonie lass o' Ballochmyle.

Then Pride might climb the slipp'ry steep,
　　Where fame and honours lofty shine;
And thirst of gold might tempt the deep,
　　Or downward seek the Indian mine!
Give me the cot below the pine,
　　To tend the flocks or till the soil:
And ev'ry day have joys divine
　　With the bonie lass o' Ballochmyle.

Orpheus Caledonius (1733) no. 45 – the air
Tea-Table Miscellany (1740) – the air
Oswald's Curious Collections (1740) – the air
McGibbon's Scots Tunes (1742) – the air
Stair Manuscript (September 1786)
Scots Musical Museum (1787) no. 81 - the air

The Polyhymnia (1799) no. 18 (a collection of poetry original and selected by a society of gentlemen, printed by John Murdoch, Glasgow, song listed as never before published)
Currie (1800)

The words have also been set to the airs 'Johnny's (Jockey's) Grey Breeks' and 'Miss Forbes' Farewell To Banff' (aka 'The Lily Of The Vale Is Sweet')

Song 21
The Highland Lassie O

Slowly With Tenderness   *Tune : McLauchlin's Scots Measure*

Nae gen-tle dames, tho' ne'er sae fair, Shall ev-er be my Mu-se's care: Their ti-tles a' are emp-ty show Gie me my High-land Las-sie, O. *Chorus* With-in the glen sae bush-y, O! A-boon the plain sae ra-shy, O! I set me doon wi' right gude will, To sing my High-land Las-sie, O!

(Chorus)
Within the glen sae bushy, O!
   Aboon the plain sae rashy, O!
I set me doun wi' right guid will,
   To sing my Highland Lassie, O!

Nae gentle dames, tho' ne'er sae fair,
   Shall ever be my Muse's care:
Their titles a' are empty show
   Gie me my Highland Lassie, O!

O, were yon hills and vallies mine,
   Yon palace and yon gardens fine,
The world then the love should know
   I bear my Highland Lassie, O!

276

But fickle fortune frowns on me,
    And I maun cross the raging sea;
But while my crimson currents flow,
    I'll love my Highland Lassie, O!

Altho' thro' foreign climes I range,
    I know her heart will never change;
For her bosom burns with honor's glow,
    My faithful Highland Lassie, O!

For her I'll dare the billows' roar,
    For her I'll trace a distant shore,
That Indian wealth may lustre throw
    Around my Highland Lassie, O!

She has my heart, she has my hand,
    By secret troth and honor's band!
'Till the mortal stroke shall lay me low,
    I'm thine, my Highland Lassie, O!

Farewell the glen sae bushy, O!
    Farewell the plain sae rashy, O!
To other lands I now must go
    To sing my Highland Lassie, O!

Original Scotch Tunes (1700) – the air
Caledonian Pocket Companion (1754) VI no. 28 entitled 'The Inverness Scotch Measure'
Aird's Airs (1782) II no. 95
Scots Musical Museum (1788) no. 117 signed X
Hastie Manuscript f. 25

The words have also been set to the airs 'The White Cockade' and 'The Deuk's Dang O'er
My Daddie' (aka 'Buff Coat' and 'Excuse Me')

Song 22
Tho' Cruel Fate

Moderate/Tender   *Tune : She Rose And Let Me In*

Tho' cru-el fate should bid us part, Far as the pole and line; Her dear i - dea round my heart Should ten-der-ly en- twine. Tho' moun-tains rise, and des - erts howl, And o - ceans roar be - tween; Yet, dear-er than my death - less soul, I still would love my Jean.

Playford's Choice Ayres And Songs (1683) – the air
Margaret Sinkler's Manuscript (1710) – the air
Orpheus Caledonius II (1733) no. 14 - the air
Caledonian Pocket Companion (1743) I no. 21 - the air
Stair Manuscript (September1786)
Scots Musical Museum (1788) no. 118 signed R, Written for this work by R. Burns
Hastie Manuscript f. 26

'She Roasse and Leit Me In' is reported to have been written by Francis Sempill of Belltrees, sometime during the reign of James VI

The words have also been set to the air 'The Northern Lass'

278

Song 23
Again Rejoicing Nature Sees

Briskly With Joy   Tune : *Jockey's Grey Breeks*

(Chorus)
An' maun I still Menie doat,
   An' bear the scorn that's in her e'e?
For it's jet, jet black, an' it's like a hawk,
   An' it winna let a bodie be!

Again rejoicing Nature sees
   Her robe assume it's vernal hues;
Her leafy locks wave in the breeze,
   All freshly steep'd in morning dews.

279

In vain to me the cowslips blaw,
In vain to me the vi'lets spring;
In vain to me, in glen or shaw,
The mavis and the lintwhite sing.

The merry Ploughboy cheers his team,
Wi' joy the tentie Seedsman stalks,
But life to me's a weary dream,
A dream of ane that never wauks.

The wanton coot the water skims,
Amang the reeds the ducklings cry,
The stately swan majestic swims,
An' ev'ry thing is blest but I.

The Sheep-herd steeks his faulding slap,
An' owre the moorlands whistles shill,
Wi' wild, unequal, wand'ring step
I meet him on the dewy hill.

An' when the lark, 'tween light an' dark,
Blythe waukens by the daisy's side,
An' mounts an' sings on flittering wings,
A woe-worn ghaist I hameward glide.

Come Winter, with thine angry howl,
And raging bend the naked tree;
Thy gloom will soothe my cheerless soul,
When nature all is sad like me!

Oswald's Curious Scots Tunes (1741) II no. 6 – the air
Aird's Airs (1782) I no. 59 – the air
Perth Musical Miscellany (1788) no. 256 – the air

(In the Edinburgh edition of Burns Poems, 1787, there is a footnote to the chorus of this song saying 'The chorus is part of a song by a gentleman in Edinburgh, a particular friend of the Author's', but according to William Scott-Douglas, one of the late nineteenth century editors of Burns Work, he believes it to be written by Burns himself about Jean Armour).

Scots Musical Museum (1787) no. 27 – the air.

The words have also been set to the air 'I Wish My Love Were In A Mire'

Song 24
Blythe, Blythe And Merry Was She

Merrily And Lively　　　　　*Tune : Andro And His Cutty Gun*

Blythe, Blythe and mer-ry was she, Blythe was she but and ben; Blythe by the banks of Ern, And blythe in Glen- tu-rit glen. By Ough-ter-tyre grows the aik, On Yar-row banks the bir-ken shaw; But Phe-mie was a bon-ier lass Than braes o' Yar-row ev-er saw.

(Chorus)
Blythe, Blythe and merry was she,
Blythe was she but and ben,
Blythe by the banks of Ern,
And blythe in Glenturit glen.

By Oughtertyre grows the aik,
On Yarrow banks the birken shaw;
But Phemie was a bonier lass
Than braes o' Yarrow ever saw.

Her looks were like a flow'r in May,
Her smile was like a simmer morn;
She tripped by the banks o' Ern,
As light's a bird upon a thorn

Her bony face it was as meek
As ony lamb upon the lee.
The evening sun was ne'er sae sweet
As was the blink o' Phemie's e'e.

The Highland hills I've wander'd wide,
As o'er the Lawlands I hae been.
But Phemie was the blythest lass
That ever trod the dewy green.

Tea-Table Miscellany (1740) – the air
Caledonian Pocket Companion (1754) - the air
Aird's Airs (1782) II no. 37 – the air
Perth Musical Miscellany (1786) no. 133 – the air
Scots Musical Museum (1788) no. 180 signed B, Written by R. Burns
Calliope (1788) no. 410 – the air
Ritson's Scottish Songs (1794) I no. 268

'Andro And His Cutty Gun' is one of the ancient airs in Scottish music and is thought to date from the fifteenth century.

Song 25
My Peggy's Face

Moderate/Caring   *Tune : My Peggy's Face*

My Peg-gy's face, my Peg-gy's form, The frost of her-mit age might warm; My

Peg-gy's worth, my Peg-gy's mind, Might charm the first of hu-man kind. I

love my Peg-gy's an-gel air, Her face so tru-ly heav'n-ly fair, Her

na-tive grace so void of art, But I a-dore my Peg-gy's heart.

My Peggy's face, my Peggy's form,
  The frost of hermit age might warm;
My Peggy's worth, my Peggy's mind
  Might charm the first of humankind.

I love my Peggy's angel air,
  Her face so truly heavenly fair,
Her native grace so void of art,
  But I adore my Peggy's heart.

The lily's hue, the rose's dye,
  The kindling lustre of an eye –
Who but owns their magic sway?
  Who but knows they all decay?

The tender thrill, the pitying tear,
  The generous purpose, nobly dear.
The gentle look that rage disarms –
  These are all Immortal charms.

Scots Musical Museum (1803) no. 501 Written for this Work by R. Burns
Hastie Manuscript f. 40

Burns suggested to Johnson an old Gaelic air called 'Ha A' Chaillich' (included in Glen's
'Early Scottish Melodies (1900)') for the song, subject to musician Stephen Clarke's
agreement.   The air chosen for the song, was probably selected by Clarke.

The words have also been set to the air 'The Ewie Wi' The Crookit Horn', by Skinner.

Song 26
Where Braving Angry Winter's Storms

Moderate/Tender   *Tune : Niel Gow's Lamentation For Abercairney*

Where braving angry winter's storms, The lofty O - chils rise, Far
in their shade, my Peg-gy's charms First blest my wonder-ing eyes; As
one who by some sav-age stream A lone-ly gem sur - veys, A-
ston-ish'd doub-ly marks it beam With art's most pol - ish'd blaze.

Where, braving angry winter's storms,
   The lofty Ochils rise,
Far in their shade, my Peggy's charms
   First blest my wondering eyes;
As one who by some savage stream
   A lonely gem surveys,
Astonish'd doubly marks it beam
   With art's most polished blaze.

Blest be the wild, sequester'd glade,
   And blest the day and hour,
Where Peggy's charms I first survey'd,
   When first I felt their pow'r!
The tyrant Death, with grim control
   May seize my fleeting breath,
But tearing Peggy from my soul
   Must be a stronger death.

Aird's Airs (1782) III no. 542 – the air
Gow's Collection of Strathspey Reels (1784) - the air
Scots Musical Museum (1788) no. 195 signed R, Written for this Work by R. Burns
Hastie Manuscript f. 39

Song 27
The Banks Of The Devon

Tender/Slow   *Tune : Bhannerach Dhon Na Chri*

How pleas-ant the banks of the clear wind-ing De-von, With green spread-ing bush-es and flow'rs bloom-ing fair! But the bo-ni-est flow'r on the banks of the De-von Was once a sweet bud on the braes of the Ayr. Mild be the sun on this sweet blush-ing flow-er, In the gay, ro-sy morn, as it bathes in the dew! And gen-tle the fall of the soft ver-nal show-er, That steals on the even-ing each leaf to re-new.

How pleasant the banks of the clear winding Devon,
 With green spreading bushes and flow'rs blooming fair!
But the boniest flow'r on the banks of the Devon
 Was once a sweet bud on the braes of the Ayr.

Mild be the sun on this sweet blushing flower,
 In the gay rosy morn, as it bathes in the dew!
And gentle the fall of the soft vernal shower,
 That steals on the evening each leaf to renew.

O, spare the dear blossom, ye orient breezes,
  With chill, hoary wing as ye usher the dawn!
And far be thou distant, thou reptile that seizes
  The verdure and pride of the garden or lawn.

Let Bourbon exult in his gay gilded lilies,
  And England triumphant display her proud rose!
A fairer than either adorns the green vallies,
  Where Devon, sweet Devon, meandering flows.

McDonald's Highland Airs (1784) no. 105 (same name but different rudimentary melody to that named above.
Scots Musical Museum (1788) no. 157 signed B, Written for this work by R. Burns.
Hastie Manuscript f. 37

In the Museum the song was originally entitled 'Anglice, The Brown Dairy Maid'. ('Bhannerach dhon na chri' means 'The brown dairy-maid')

From a letter to Peggy Chalmers post October 1787 – 'The air is admiral, true old Highland. It was the tune of a Gaelic song which an Inverness lady sung to me when I was there, and I was so charmed with it that I begged her to write me a set of it from her singing, for it had never been set before'.

The words have also been set to the air 'The Maids Of Arrochar'

Song 28
Your Friendship Much Can Make Me Blest

Very Slow/Tender   *Tune : Banks Of Spey*

Your friend-ship much can make me blest, O' why that bliss de-stroy! Why urge the on-ly, one re-quest You know I will de-ny! Your thought, if love must har-bour there, Con-ceal it in that thought; Nor cause me from my bo-som tear The ve-ry friend I sought.

Your friendship much can make me blest,
  O' why that bliss destroy!
Why urge the only, one request
  You know I will deny!

Your thought, if love must harbour there,
  Conceal it in that thought;
Nor cause me from my bosom tear
  The very friend I sought.

These two verses were added to a poem by Agnes McLehose, which was sent to Burns for his criticism. Agnes' poem appeared in the Scots Musical Museum (1788) no. 186 signed M, By a Lady, with both her verses and Burns' verses included together, and was entitled 'Talk not of love, it gives me pain'.

Burns also changed the first two verses of Agnes' poem to read

> Talk not of love, it gives me pain.
>   For love has been my foe;
> He bound me with an iron chain,
>   And plung'd me deep in woe.
>
> But friendship's pure and lasting joys,
>   My heart was form'd to prove;
> There, welcome win and wear the prize,
>   But never talk of love.

Agnes' poem read -

> 'Talk not of Love – it gives me pain,
>   For Love has been my foe;
> He bound me in an iron chain,
>   And plunged me deep in woe!
>
> But Friendship's pure and lasting joys
>   My heart was formed to prove –
> The worthy object be of those,
>   But never talk of Love!
>
> The Hand of Friendship I accept –
>   May Honour be our guard!
> Virtue our intercourse direct,
>   Her smiles our dear reward'.

McGibbon's Scots Tunes (1755) no. 23 – the air
Caledonian Pocket Companion (c1759) XI no. 20 – the air
McGlashan's Reels (1786) no. 3 – same title to air, but different music

Song 29
Go On Sweet Bird

Slow/Thoughtful

Tune : Scots Queen

Go on, sweet bird, and soothe my care,
   Thy tuneful notes will hush despair;
Thy plaintive warblings void of art,
   Thrill sweetly thro' my aching heart.
Now chuse thy mate, and fondly love,
   And all the charming transport prove;
While I a lovelorn exile live,
   Nor transport or receive or give.

For thee is laughing nature gay;
  For thee she pours the vernal day:
For me in vain is nature drest,
  While joy's a stranger to my breast!
These sweet emotions all enjoy;
  Let love and song thy hours employ!
Go on, sweet bird, and soothe my care;
  Thy tuneful notes will hush despair.

Oswald's Companion (c1759) XII no. 1 – the air
Scots Musical Museum (1788) no. 190 signed M, By a Lady
Hastie Manuscript f. 48

The lady in question was Agnes McLehose, and the above was a revision by Burns of one of her poems. Agnes sent the poem to him on 19th January 1788 asking for his criticism. Her poem read -

Go on, sweet bird, and soothe my care,
Thy cheerful notes will hush despair;
Thy tuneful warblings, void of art
Thrill sweetly through my aching heart.
Now choose thy mate and fondly love,
And all the charming transport prove –
Those sweet emotions all enjoy,
Let Love and Song thy hours employ;
Whilst I, a love-lorn exile, live,
And rapture nor receive nor give.
Go on, sweet bird, and soothe my care,
Thy cheerful notes will hush despair.

Song 30
Clarinda, Mistress Of My Soul

Slow/With Feeling   *Tune : Clarinda*

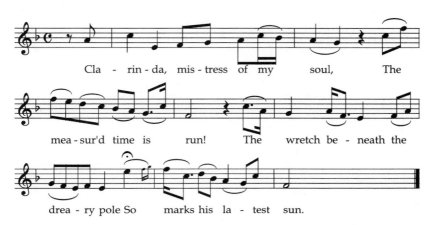

Cla - rin - da, mis - tress of my soul, The
mea - sur'd time is run! The wretch be - neath the
drea - ry pole So marks his la - test sun.

Clarinda, mistress of my soul,
    The measur'd time is run!
The wretch beneath the dreary pole
    So marks his latest sun.

To what dark cave of frozen night
    Shall poor Sylvander hie;
Depriv'd of thee, his life and light,
    The Sun of all his joy?

We part – but by these precious drops,
    That fill thy lovely eyes,
No other light shall guide my steps
    Till thy bright beams arise.

She, the fair Sun of all her sex,
    Has blest my glorious day:
And shall a glimmering Planet fix
    My worship to its ray?

Scots Musical Museum (1788) no. 198 signed B, Written for this Work by R. Burns
The air is by John George Christopher Schetky (1740 -29th November 1824).

Schetky came to Edinburgh in 1772 as principal cellist to the Musical Society. He lived in Ainslie Close and later Foulis's Close, High Street. He is buried in the Canongate Cemetery, and his grave is unmarked. The entry for his burial reads –

1824 - Schetky. Mr John George Christopher Schetky, native of Darmstadt, Upper Rhine; for many years Professor of Music in Edinburgh, died 29th ult., interred in the west side six feet north west of Sharp's ground, and four feet south west of Langley's stone…Old Age.

Song 31
A Rosebud By My Early Walk

Slow And Sweet   *Tune : A Rosebud*

A rose-bud by my early walk
  Adown a corn-inclosed bawk,
Sae gently bent its thorny stalk,
  All on a dewy morning.
Ere twice the shades o' dawn are fled,
  In a' its crimson glory spread,
And drooping rich the dewy head,
  It scents the early morning.

Within the bush her covert nest
  A little linnet fondly prest,
The dew sat chilly on her breast,
  Sae early in the morning.
She soon shall see her tender brood,
  The pride, the pleasure o' the wood,
Amang the fresh green leaves bedew'd,
  Awauk the early morning.

So thou, dear bird, young Jeany fair,
    On trembling string or vocal air,
Shall sweetly pay the tender care
    That tents thy early morning!
So thou, sweet Rose-bud, young and gay,
    Shall beauteous blaze upon the day,
And bless the Parent's evening ray
    That watch'd thy early morning!

Scots Musical Museum (1788) no. 189
Hastie Manuscript f. 47
The air is by David Sillar who was a schoolmaster in Irvine and a good friend of Burns
The words have also been set to the air 'The Shepherd's Wife'

Song 32
To The Weavers Gin Ye Go

Lively Though Pensive   *Tune : To The Weavers Gin Ye Go*

My heart was ance as blythe and free As sim-mer days were lang; But a bon-ie, west-lin wea-ver lad Has gart me change my sang.

To the wea-ver's gin ye go, fair maids, To the wea-ver's gin ye go, I rede you right, gang ne'er at night, To the wea-ver's gin ye go.

(Chorus)
To the weaver's gin ye go, fair maids,
　To the weaver's gin ye go,
I rede you right, gang ne'er at night,
　To the weaver's gin ye go.

My heart was ance as blythe and free
　As simmer days were lang;
But a bonie, westlin weaver lad
　Has gart me change my sang.

My mither sent me to the town,
　To warp a plaiden wab;
But the weary, weary warpin o't
　Has gart me sigh and sab.

A bonie, westlin weaver lad
　Sat working at his loom;
He took my heart, as wi' a net,
　In every knot and thrum.

294

I sat beside my warpin-wheel,
 And ay I ca'd it roun'.
But every shot and every knock,
 My heart it gae a stoun.

The moon was sinking in the west,
 Wi' visage pale and wan,
As my bonie, westlin weaver lad
 Convoy'd me thro' the glen.

But what was said, or what was done,
 Shame fa' me gin I tell;
But Oh! I fear the kintra soon
 Will ken as weel's mysel!

Aird's Airs (1782) II no. 16 - the air
Scots Musical Museum (1788) no. 103 signed X

Song 33
An' I'll Kiss Thee Yet, Bonie Peggy Alison

Moderate With Feeling　　　　　　　*Tune : Braes O' Balquhidder*

An'　I'll kiss thee yet, yet, An'　I'll kiss thee o'er a - gain; An'

I'll kiss thee yet, yet, My　bon - y Peg - gy A - li - son.　Ilk

care and fear, when thou art near, I　ev - er mair de-fy them, O;　Young

kings up-on　their han-sel throne Are　no sae blest as　I am, O!　Ilk

care and fear, when thou art near, I　ev - er mair de - fy them, O; Young

kings up-on their han-sel throne Are　no sae blest as　I am, O!

(Chorus)
An' I'll kiss thee yet, yet,
　An' I'll kiss thee o'er again.
An' I'll kiss thee yet, yet,
　My bonie Peggy Alison.

Ilk care and fear, when thou art near,
　I ever mair defy them, O;
Young kings upon their hansel throne
　Are no sae blest as I am, O!

When in my arms, wi' a' thy charms,
  I clasp my countless treasure, O;
I seek nae mair o' Heav'n to share
  Than sic a moment's pleasure, O!

An' by thy een sae bonie blue
  I swear I'm thine for ever, O;
An' on thy lips I seal my vow,
  An' break it shall I never, O!

Walsh's Caledonian Country Dances (1742) – the air
Bremner's Reels (1758) no. 37 – the air
Aird's Airs (1782) II no. 181 – the air
Scots Musical Museum (1788) no. 193 signed Z

The modern air 'I'm Ower Young To Marry Yet' is a variation on the 'Braes O' Balquhidder'

Song 34
Of A' The Airts The Wind Can Blaw

Moderate and Pensive　　　　*Tune : Miss Admiral Gordon's Strathspey*

Of a' the airts the wind can blaw I dear-ly like the west, For

there the bon-ie las-sie lives, The las-sie I lo'e best. There's

wild woods grow, and riv-ers row, And monie a hill be - tween, But

day and night my fan-cy's flight Is ev - er wi' my Jean.

I see her in the dew-y flowers, I see her sweet and fair; I

hear her in the tune-fu' birds, I hear her charm the air. There's

not a bon-ie flower that springs By foun-tain, shaw, or green, There's

not a bon-ie bird that sings, But minds me o' my Jean.

Of a' the airts the wind can blaw
  I dearly like the west,
For there the bonie lassie lives,
  The lassie I lo'e best.
There's wild woods grow, and rivers row,
  And monie a hill between.
But day and night my fancy's flight
  Is ever wi' my Jean.

I see her in the dewy flowers,
  I see her sweet and fair,
I hear her in the tunefu' birds,
  I hear her charm the air.
There's not a bonie flower that springs
  By fountain, shaw, or green,
There's not a bonie bird that sings,
  But minds me o' my Jean.

Marshall's Collection Of Reels (1781) - the air
McGlashan's Reels (1786) - the air
Scots Musical Museum (1790) no. 235 signed R, Written for this work by R. Burns
Hastie Manuscript f. 55
The air was composed by William Marshall, butler to the Duke of Gordon. The rudiments
of the air can be found in the Skene Manuscript (c1630) under the title 'Alace! I Lie My
Alon I'm Like To Die Auld'

Burns only ever wrote two verses to the above song, others have added verses, extending the
length of the song, on at least two occasions. One set was written by John Hamilton, a
bookseller from Edinburgh, another set was by William Reid of Glasgow, said to have been
a good friend of Burns.

Song 35
O Were I On Parnassus Hill

Slow With Tenderness   *Tune : My Love Is Lost To Me*

O, were I on Parnassus hill!
Or had o' Helicon my fill,
That I might catch poetic skill
  To sing how dear I love thee!
But Nith maun be my Muse's well,
My Muse maun be thy bonie sel',
On Corsincon I'll glow'r and spell,
  And write how dear I love thee.

Then come, sweet Muse, inspire my lay!
For a' the lee-lang simmer's day
I couldna sing, I couldna say,
   How much, how dear I love thee.
I see thee dancing o'er the green,
Thy waist sae jimp, thy limbs sae clean,
Thy tempting lips, thy roguish een –
   By Heav'n and Earth I love thee!

By night, by day, a-field, at hame,
The thoughts o' thee my breast inflame,
And ay I muse and sing thy name –
   I only live to love thee.
Tho' I were doom'd to wander on,
Beyond the sea, beyond the sun,
Till my last weary sand was run;
   Till then – and then – I'd love thee!

Caledonian Pocket Companion (1753) V no. 25 (the air is in two parts and is entitled 'O Jean, I Love Thee)
Calliope (1788) – no. 176
Scots Musical Museum (1790) no. 255 signed R, Written for this Work by R. Burns
301

Song 36
The Blue-Ey'd Lassie

Moderate/Teasing   *Tune : The Blue-Ey'd Lassie*

I gaed a wae-fu' gate yes-treen, A gate I fear I'll dear-ly rue; I gat my death frae twa sweet een, Twa love-ly een o' bon-ie blue! 'Twas not her gold-en ring-lets bright, Her lips like ros-es wat wi' dew, Her heav-ing bo-som li-ly white It was her een sae bon-ie blue.

I gaed a waefu' gate yestreen,
  A gate I fear I'll dearly rue;
I gat my death frae twa sweet een,
  Twa lovely een o' bonie blue!
'Twas not her golden ringlets bright,
  Her lips like roses wat wi' dew,
Her heaving bosom lily-white
  It was her een sae bonie blue.

She talk'd, she smil'd, my heart she wyl'd;
  She charm'd my soul I wist na how;
And ay the stound, the deadly wound,
  Cam frae her een sae bonie blue.
But 'spare to speak, and spare to speed';
  She'll aiblins listen to my vow:
Should she refuse, I'll lay my dead
  To her twa een sae bonie blue.

Scots Musical Museum (1790) no. 294 Written for this Work by R. Burns

The air is by Robert Riddell taken from his New Music (1787) and has a very wide range, covering two octaves plus one note. The song was specifically written for Riddell's air. The words have also been set to the airs 'The Blaitherie O't' and 'My Only Jo And Dearie O'

Song 37
When First I Saw Fair Jeanie's Face

Live And Merry   *Tune : Maggie Lauder*

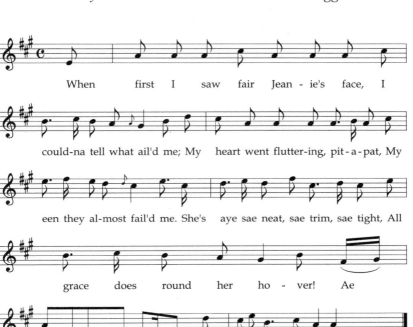

When first I saw fair Jean - ie's face, I

could-na tell what ail'd me; My heart went flutter-ing, pit - a - pat, My

een they al-most fail'd me. She's aye sae neat, sae trim, sae tight, All

grace does round her ho - ver! Ae

look de-prived me o' my heart, And I be-came her lo - ver.

(Chorus)
She's aye, aye sae blythe, sae gay,
    She's aye sae blythe and cheery,
She's aye sae bonie, blythe and gay,
    O, gin I were her dearie!

When first I saw fair Jeanie's face,
    I couldna tell what ail'd me;
My heart went fluttering pit-a-pat,
    My een they almost fail'd me.
She's aye sae neat, sae trim, sae tight,
    All grace does round her hover!
Ae look deprived me o' my heart,
    And I became her lover.

303

Had I Dundas's whole estate,
  Or Hopetoun's wealth to shine in;
Did warlike laurels crown my brow,
  Or humbled bays entwining:
I'd lay them a' at Jeanie's feet,
  Could I but hope to move her,
And, prouder than a belted knight
  I'd be my Jeanie's lover.

But sair I fear some happier swain
  Has gained my Jeanie's favour;
If so, may every bliss be hers,
  Though I maun never have her!
But gang she east, or gang she west,
  'Twixt Forth and Tweed all over,
While men have eyes, or ears, or taste,
  She'll always find a lover.

The air 'Maggie Lauder' is in the Scots Musical Museum (1787) no.98

The song was first published in the New York Mirror of 1846 being taken there by Jean Jaffrey when she emigrated decades before. It has been questioned as to whether the song was one of Burns', but a note, which was given to the song in Alexander Smith's 1868 edition states 'The text has been collated with a copy in the poet's handwriting'.

There is no chorus to the original song 'Maggie Lauder', but the chorus that Burns set to the song can easily be sung as a repeat of the music to the last four lines of each verse.

The air has been used in 'The Quaker's Opera', performed at Lee and Harper's booth in Bartholemew Fair in the year 1728, and also in John Gay's opera 'Achilles' c1733 Bartholemew Fair was banned in 1854, after having been celebrated for centuries, apparently because the people were enjoying it too much.

Maggie Lauder is said to have been written by Francis Semple of Belltrees c1642.

Song 38
Louis, What Reck I By Thee

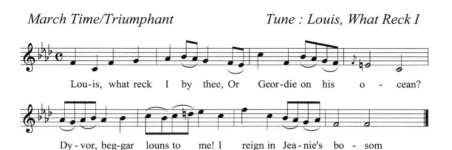

March Time/Triumphant   *Tune : Louis, What Reck I*

Louis, what reck I by thee,
  Or Geordie on his ocean?
Dyvor, beggar louns to me!
  I reign in Jeanie's bosom.

Let her crown my love her law,
  And in her breast enthrone me:
Kings and nations, swith awa!
  Reif randies I disown ye!

Scots Musical Museum (1796) no. 414 signed R, Written for this Work by R. Burns

Burns may have been intending to add extra verses to this short song, as in the Museum the text is followed by asterisks. It is thought that Burns may also have sent the music along with the words to the Museum, as there appears to be no trace of this air before then.

Song 39
Afton Water

Peaceful And Tender   *Tune : Afton Water*

Flow gen-tly, sweet Af - ton, a - mong thy green braes, Flow

gen - tly, I'll sing thee a song in thy praise; My

Ma - ry's a - sleep by thy mur - mur - ing stream, Flow

gen-tly, sweet Af - ton, dis - turb not her dream!

Flow gently, sweet Afton, among thy green braes,
   Flow gently, I'll sing thee a song in thy praise;
My Mary's asleep by thy murmuring stream,
   Flow gently, sweet Afton, disturb not her dream!

Thou stock dove whose echo resounds thro' the glen,
   Ye wild whistling blackbirds in yon thorny den,
Thou green-crested lapwing, thy screaming forbear,
   I charge you, disturb not my slumbering fair.

How lofty, sweet Afton, thy neighbouring hills,
   Far marked with the courses of clear, winding rills;
There daily I wander, as noon rises high,
   My flocks and my Mary's sweet cot in my eye.

How pleasant thy banks and thy vallies below,
   Where wild in the woodlands the primroses blow;
There oft, as mild Ev'ning weeps over the lea,
   The sweet-scented bark shades my Mary and me.

Thy crystal stream, Afton, how lovely it glides,
  And winds by the cot where my Mary resides;
How wanton thy waters her snowy feet lave,
  As, gathering sweet flow'rets, she stems thy clear wave!

Flow gently, sweet Afton, among thy green braes,
  Flow gently, sweet river, the theme of my lays;
My Mary's asleep by thy murmuring stream,
  Flow gently, sweet Afton, disturb not her dream!

(Local tradition suggests the song was written for Mary Murdoch)

Afton Manuscript (1791)
Scots Musical Museum (1792) no. 386 signed B, Written for this Work by R. Burns
Logan Manuscript
It appears that the air 'Afton Water' was sent to the 'Museum' by Burns, along with the words to the air.

The words have also been set to the air 'The Yellow-Haired Laddie'

Song 40
Thou Ling'ring Star

Slow With Remorse   *Tune : Captain Cook's Death*

Thou ling'-ring star, with less-ning ray, That lov'st, to greet the ear - ly morn, A - gain thou ush-er'st in the day My Ma-ry from my soul was torn. O Ma-ry, dear de - part-ed shade! Where is thy place of bliss - ful rest? See'st thou thy lov-er low-ly laid? Hear'st thou the groans that rend his breast?

Thou ling'ring star with less'ning ray,
  That lov'st, to greet the early morn,
Again thou usher'st in the day
  My Mary from my soul was torn.
O Mary, dear departed shade!
  Where is thy place of blissful rest?
See'st thou thy lover lowly laid?
  Hear'st thou the groans that rend his breast?

That sacred hour can I forget?
  Can I forget the hallow'd grove,
Where, by the winding Ayr, we met,
  To live one day of parting love?
Eternity cannot efface
  Those records dear of transports past,
Thy image at our last embrace –
  Ah! Little thought we 'twas our last!

308

Ayr, gurgling, kiss'd his pebbled shore,
  O'erhung with wild-woods, thickening green;
The fragrant birch and hawthorn hoar,
  'Twin'd amorous round the raptur'd scene;
The flowers sprang wanton to be prest,
  The birds sang love on every spray,
Till too, too soon, the glowing west,
  Proclaim'd the speed of winged day.

Still o'er these scenes my mem'ry wakes,
  And fondly broods with miser-care;
Time but th' impression stronger makes,
  As streams their channels deeper wear.
O Mary! Dear departed shade!
  Where is thy place of blissful rest?
See'st thou thy lover lowly laid?
  Hear'st thou the groans that rend his breast?

Scots Musical Museum (1790) no. 279 Written for this Work by R. Burns
The air 'Captain Cook's Death', was written by Lucy Johnson Oswald of Auchincruive

The words have also been set to the airs 'Mary's Dream' and 'Miss Forbes' Farewell To Banff' (aka 'The Lily Of The Vale Is Sweet')

Song 41
Thine Am I, My Faithful Fair

Moderate With Pleasure   *Tune : The Quaker's Wife*

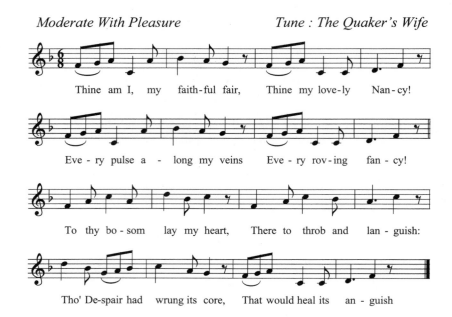

Thine am I, my faith-ful fair, Thine my love-ly Nan-cy!

Eve - ry pulse a - long my veins Eve - ry rov-ing fan - cy!

To thy bo - som lay my heart, There to throb and lan - guish:

Tho' De-spair had wrung its core, That would heal its an - guish

Thine am I, my faithful fair,
  Thine my lovely Nancy!
Every pulse along my veins
  Every roving fancy!

To thy bosom lay my heart,
  There to throb and languish:
Tho' Despair had wrung its core,
  That would heal its anguish.

Take away those rosy lips
  Rich with balmy treasure!
Turn away thine eyes of love
  Lest I die with pleasure.

What is life when wanting Love?
  Night without a morning!
Love the cloudless summer's sun,
  Nature gay adorning.

(This song was subsequently dedicated to Maria Riddell and Jean Lorimer)

Jean Lorimer's version starts –

Thine am I, my Chloris fair,
Well thou may'st discover:
Every pulse along my veins
Tells the ardent Lover

Bremner's Reels (1759) no. 53 – the air entitled 'Merrily Dance the Quaker'
Thomson's Select Collection Of Original Scotish Airs no. 59 (1799)
Neil Gow's Complete Repository (1802) II - 'Merrily Danced The Quaker's Wife'
The air is also known as 'Liggeram Cosh' (Leger M' Chose)

310

Song 42
Beware O' Bonie Ann

Moderate/Teasing

Tune : Bonie Ann

Ye gal - lants bright, I rede you right, Be- ware o' bon-ie Ann! Her come-ly face sae fu' o' grace, Your heart she will tre - pan: Her een sae bright, like stars by night, Her skin is like the swan. Sae jim - ply lac'd her gen - ty waist, That sweet-ly ye might span.

Ye gallants bright, I rede you right,
　Beware o' bonie Ann!
Her comely face sae fu' o' grace,
　Your heart she will trepan:
Her een sae bright, like stars by night,
　Her skin is like the swan.
Sae jimply lac'd her genty waist,
　That sweetly ye might span.

Youth, Grace, and Love attendant move,
　And Pleasure leads the van:
In a' their charms, and conquering arms,
　They wait on bonie Ann.
The captive bands may chain the hands
　But love enslaves the man:
Ye gallants braw I rede you a',
　Beware o' bonie Ann.

Scots Musical Museum (1790) no. 215 signed X

The air is by Allan Masterton, father to 'Bonie Ann' and friend of Burns

Song 43
On Sensibility

Moderate/Sympathetic   *Tune : Cornwallis' Lament For Colonel Moorhouse*

Sensibility how charming,
  Dearest Nancy, thou canst tell;
But distress with horrors arming,
  Thou hast also known too well!

Fairest flower, behold the lily
  Blooming in the sunny ray:
Let the blast sweep o'er the valley,
  See it prostrate on the clay.

Hear the woodlark charm the forest,
　　Telling o'er his little joys;
Hapless bird! a prey the surest
　　To each pirate of the skies!

Dearly bought the hidden treasure
　　Finer feelings can bestow:
Chords that vibrate sweetest pleasure
　　Thrill the deepest notes of woe.

(Original verses were sent to Mrs Dunlop in letters dated 9th July 1790 and 30th July 1790). The verses sent to Agnes McLehose were of a later date.　Agnes replied to the poem in December 1791, her version being entitled 'Sensibility Is Charming', asking 'Let me know what you think of this poor imitation of your style.　The verses are inaccurate, but if it worth while, pray correct them for me'.

Yes, Sensibility is charming
　　Tho' it may wound the tender mind,
Nature's stores, the bosom warning,
　　Yield us pleasures more refined.

See yonder pair of warbling linnets,
　　How their music charms the grove,
What else with rapture fills their minutes,
　　But Sensibility and Love.

E'en should the sportsmen – (cruel rovers)
　　Rob them of their tuneful breath,
How blest the little life-long lovers,
　　Undivided in their death!

A long-loved maid nipt in the blossom,
　　May lie in yonder kirkyard green,
Yet mem'ry soothes her lover's bosom,
　　Recalling many a rapture scene.

Or, musing by the roaring ocean,
　　See him sit with visage wan,
As wave succeeding wave in motion,
　　Mourns the chequer'd life of Man.

Sensibility!　Sweet treasure,
　　Still I'll sing in praise of thee,
All that mortals know of pleasure
　　Flows from Sensibility.

Afton Manuscript (1791)
Scots Musical Museum (1792) no. 329 Written for this Work by R. Burns
Hastie Manuscript f. 68

'Cornwallis's Lament For Colonel Moorhouse', was composed by Malcolm Stewart.

Song 44
Yestreen I Had A Pint O' Wine

Moderate/Tender/Resolute   *Tune : Banks Of Banna*

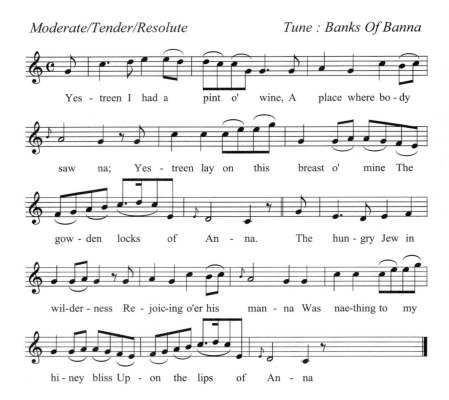

Yes - treen I had a   pint o'   wine, A   place where bo - dy

saw   na;   Yes - treen lay on   this   breast o'   mine The

gow - den   locks   of   An - na.   The   hun - gry Jew in

wil-der - ness Re - joic-ing o'er his   man - na Was   nae-thing to   my

hi - ney bliss Up - on   the   lips   of   An - na

Yestreen I had a pint o' wine,
  A place where body saw na;
Yestreen lay on this breast o' mine
  The gowden locks of Anna.
The hungry Jew in wilderness
  Rejoicing o'er his manna
Was naething to my hiney bliss
  Upon the lips of Anna.

Ye Monarchs take the East and West
  Frae Indus to Savannah:
Gie me within my straining grasp
  The melting form of Anna.
There I'll despise Imperial charms,
  An Empress or Sultana,
While dying raptures in her arms,
  I give and take wi' Anna.

314

Awa, thou flaunting God of Day!
　Awa, thou pale Diana!
Ilk Star, gae hide thy twinkling ray,
　When I'm to meet my Anna!
Come, in thy raven plumage, Night
　(Sun, Moon and Stars, withdrawn a',)
And bring an Angel-pen to write
　My transports with my Anna!

(Added later)
The Kirk an' State may join, an' tell
　To do sic things I maunna:
The Kirk an' State may gae to Hell,
　And I'll gae to my Anna.
She is the sunshine o' my e'e,
　To live but her I canna:
Had I on earth but wishes three,
　The first should be my Anna.

Corri's Scots Songs (1783) no. 14 - the air noted as Irish
Perth Musical Miscellany (1786) no. 75 - the air
Calliope (1788) no. 1 – the air
Glenriddell Manuscript (27ᵗʰ April 1791)

Burns wrote to George Thomson of the song 'I think it is the best love song I ever composed in my life, but in it's original state, is not quite a lady's song'.

'Shepherd's I Have Lost My Love, the original version of the air 'The Banks Of Banna', printed in 'The Charmer' (1782), was written by the Right Honourable George Ogle, who represented Dublin in 1799, and who voted against the Union.

Song 45
Out Over The Forth

Moderate With Yearning   *Tune : Charles Graham's Welcome Hame*

Out o - ver the Forth, I look to the north But

what is the north and its High-lands to me? The south nor the east gie

ease to my breast, The far for-eign land, or the wide roll-ing sea!

But I look to the west, when I gae to rest, That

hap-py my dreams and my slum-bers may be; For far in the west lives

he I lo'e best, The man that is dear to my ba-bie and me.

Gow's Second Collection Of Strathspey Reels (1788) no. 20 - the air
Scots Musical Museum (1796) no. 421
Hastie Manuscript f. 123

Song 46
Ye Flowery Banks O' Bonie Doon

Moderate/Plaintive   *Tune : Cambdelmore*

Ye flowery banks o' bonie Doon,
  How can ye bloom sae fair;
How can ye chant, ye little birds,
  And I sae fu' o' care!

Thou'll break my heart, thou bonie bird
  That sings upon the bough;
Thou minds me o' the happy days
  When my fause luve was true.

Thou'll break my heart, thou bonie bird
  That sings beside thy mate;
For sae I sat, and sae I sang,
  And wist na o' my fate!

Aft hae I rov'd by bonie Doon,
To see the woodbine twine,
And ilka bird sang o' its love,
And sae did I o' mine.

Wi' lightsome heart I pu'd a rose
Frae aff its thorny tree,
And my fause lover staw my rose,
But left the thorn wi' me.

Bremner's Reels (1761) no. 2 – the air
Stewart's Reels (1763) no. 55 – the air
Cumming's Collection Of Strathspeys (1780) no. 7 – entitled 'Ballindalloch's Reel
McGlashan's Strathspey Reels (1780) no. 26 – entitled Gordon Castle
Cromek 'Reliques' (1808)

Read Burns' letter to Alexander Cunningham 11th March 1791

Burns' first version was slightly different.   The first four lines began -

Sweet are the banks, the banks o' Doon,
The spreading flowers are fair,
And everything is blythe and glad
But I am fu' o' care.

It included a last verse thus -

Wi' lightsome heart I pu'd a rose
Upon a morn in June,
And sae I flourished on the morn
And sae was pu'd or noon.

The rest of the poem was the same as before.

The words have also been set to the air 'Katherine Ogie'

Song 47
The Banks O' Doon

Slow And Tender   *Tune : Caledonian Hunt's Delight*

Ye   banks and braes o'   bon - ie Doon, How   can   ye bloom sae

fresh   and fair? How   can ye chant, ye   lit - tle birds, And

I   sae wea - ry   fu'   o' care!   Thou'll   break my heart, thou

warb - ling bird, That   wan - tons thro'   the   flower - ing thorn: Thou

minds me o' de - part - ed joys, De - part - ed nev - er   to   re - turn

Ye banks and braes o' bonie Doon,
  How can ye bloom sae fresh and fair?
How can ye chant, ye little birds,
  And I sae weary fu' o' care!
Thou'll break my heart, thou warbling bird,
  That wantons thro' the flowering thorn:
Thou minds me o' departed joys,
  Departed never to return.

Oft hae I rov'd by bonie Doon
  To see the rose and woodbine twine,
And ilka bird sang o' its luve,
  And fondly sae did I o' mine.
Wi' lightsome heart I pu'd a rose,
  Fu' sweet upon its thorny tree!
And my fause lover staw my rose –
  But ah! He left the thorn wi' me

Gow's Second Collection Of Strathspey Reels (1788) - the air
Scots Musical Museum (1792) no. 374 signed B, Written for this Work by R. Burns
Aird's Airs (1794) IV no. 32 – the air (with the word Irish included)

For a suggested account of the composition of the air, read Burns letter to George Thomson
November 1794. The air may be of Scottish, English or Irish origin. Burns used it first in
1789 for his song 'There Was On A Time' (letter to James Johnson 23rd January 1789)

c1816 two extra verses were added in a book called 'The Pocket Encyclopaedia', by a music
publisher in Glasgow

Song 48
Wilt Thou Be My Dearie

Slow And Tender   *Tune : The Sutor's Dochter*

Wilt thou be my dear-ie? When sor-row wrings thy gen-tle heart, O,

wilt thou let me cheer thee? By the treas-ure of my soul

That's the love I bear thee I swear and vow that on-ly thou Shall

ev-er be my dear-ie! On-ly thou, I swear and vow Shall ev-er be my dear-ie.

Wilt thou be my dearie?
  When sorrow rings thy gentle heart,
  O, wilt thou let me cheer thee?
By the treasure of my soul
  That's the love I bear thee
I swear and vow that only thou
  Shall ever be my dearie!
Only thou, I swear and vow
  Shall ever be my dearie!

Lassie, say thou lo'es me,
  Or, if thou wilt na be my ain,
  Say na thou'lt refuse me!
If it winna, canna be,
  Thou for thine may choose me,
Let me, lassie, quickly die,
  Trusting that thou lo'es me!
Lassie, let me quickly die,
  Trusting that thou lo'es me!

Stewart's Reels (1763) no. 72 - the air entitled 'The Shoemaker's Daughter'
McGlashan's Strathspey Reels (1780) no. 6 – the air entitled 'The Suttor's Daughter'
Cunningham's Strathspeys (1780) no. 10 – the air entitled 'The Duchess Of Buccleugh's Reell'

Scots Musical Museum (1796) no. 470 signed B, Written for this Work by R. Burns Hastie Manuscript f. 145

The song was published in the Morning Chronicle 10th May 1794

Song 49
O Wat Ye Wha's In Yon Town

Lively And Jolly   *Tune : I'll Gang Nae Mair Tae Yon Toon*

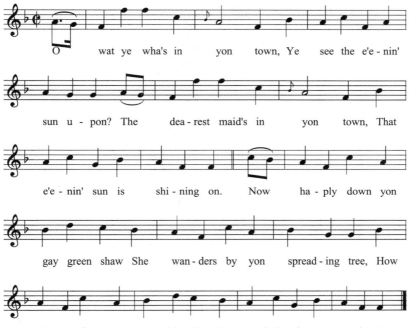

O wat ye wha's in yon town, Ye see the e'e - nin' sun u - pon? The dea - rest maid's in yon town, That e'e - nin' sun is shi - ning on. Now ha - ply down yon gay green shaw She wan - ders by yon spread - ing tree, How blest ye flow'rs that round her blaw! Ye catch the glan-ces o' her e'e.

(Chorus)
O wat ye wha's in yon town,
  Ye see the e'enin sun upon?
The dearest maid's in yon town,
  That e'enin sun is shining on.

Now haply down yon gay green shaw
  She wanders by yon spreading tree,
How blest ye flowers that round her blaw!
  Ye catch the glances o' her e'e.

How blest ye birds that round her sing,
  And welcome in the blooming year!
And doubly welcome be the Spring,
  The season to my Jeanie dear!

321

The sun blinks blythe on yon town,
  Among the broomy braes sae green;
But my delight's in yon town,
  And dearest pleasure is, my Jean.

Without my Love, not a' the charms
  O' Paradise could yield my joy;
But gie me Jeanie in my arms,
  And welcome Lapland's dreary sky.

My cave wad be a lover's bower,
  Tho' raging winter rent the air,
And she a lovely little flower,
  That I wad tent and shelter there.

O, sweet is she in yon town
  The sinking sun's gane down upon!
A fairer than's in yon town
  His setting beam ne'er shone upon.

If angry fate be sworn my foe,
  And suff'ring I am doom'd to bear,
I'd careless quit aught else below,
  But spare me, spare me Jeanie dear!

For, while life's dearest blood is warm,
  Ae thought frae her shall ne'er depart,
And she, as fairest is her form,
  She has the truest, kindest heart.

Bremner's Scots Reels (1757) I no. 6 – the air
Campbell's Reels (1778) no. 17 – the air
Aird's Airs (1782) I no. 35 – the air
Bowie's Reel's (1789) – the air
Scots Musical Museum (1796) no. 458 signed B, Written for this Work by R. Burns

According to Dumfriesshire tradition the song was originally written for Jeanie Scott,
daughter of the postmaster of Ecclefechan, that 'wicked little village', who caught Burns'
eye when he found himself snowed in there round about February 1795. The post office
being situated opposite the Inn where Burns was stormbound.

Song 50
Lovely Davies

Moderate With Pleasure   *Tune : Miss Muir*

O how shall I, un-skil-fu' try The po-et's oc-cu-pa-tion? The tune-fu' powers, in hap-py hours That whis-per in-spi-ra-tion; Even they maun dare an ef-fort mair Than aught they ev-er gave us, Ere they re-hearse in e-qual verse The charms o' love-ly Da-vies. Each eye, it cheers, when she ap-pears, Like Phoe-bus in the morn-ing, When past the shower, and eve-ry flower The gar-den is a-dorn-ing! As the wretch looks o'er Si-be-ria's shore, When win-ter-bound the wave is, Sae droops our heart when we maun part Frae charm-ing, love-ly Da-vies.

O, how shall I, unskilfu' try
   The poet's occupation?
The tunefu' powers, in happy hours
   That whisper inspiration;
Even they maun dare an effort mair
   Than aught they ever gave us,
Ere they rehearse in equal verse
   The charms o' lovely Davies.

Each eye, it cheers, when she appears,
   Like Phoebus in the morning,
When past the shower, and every flower
   The garden is adorning!
As the wretch looks o'er Siberia's shore,
   When winter-bound the wave is,
Sae droops our heart when we maun part
   Frae charming, lovely Davies.

Her smile's a gift frae 'boon the lift,
   That makes us mair than princes,
A sceptered hand, a king's command,
   Is in her darting glances.
The man in arms 'gainst female charms,
   Even he, her willing slave is:
He hugs his chain, and owns the reign
   Of conquering lovely Davies.

My Muse to dream of such a theme
   Her feeble powers surrender,
The eagle's gaze alone surveys
   The sun's meridian splendour.
I wad in vain essay the strain –
   The deed too daring brave is!
I'll drap the lyre, and mute, admire
   The charms o' lovely Davies.

Caledonian Pocket Companion (1756) VIII no 11 - the air entitled 'Port Athol'
Scots Musical Museum (1792) no. 349
Hastie Manuscript f. 79

Song 51
Thou Gloomy December

Slow With Despair   *Tune : Thro' The Lang Muir*

Ance mair I hail thee, thou gloom-y De - cem - ber!

Ance mair I hail thee wi' sor-row and care!

Sad was the part-ing thou makes me re - mem - ber:

Part-ing wi' Nan-cy, O, ne'er to meet mair!

Fond lov-ers' part - ing is sweet, pain-ful pleas - ure,

Hope beam-ing mild on the soft part-ing hour;

But the dire feel-ing, O fare-well for ev - er!

An-guish un - min-gl'd and a - go-ny pure!

Ance mair I hail thee, thou gloomy December!
Ance mair I hail thee wi' sorrow and care!
Sad was the parting thou makes me remember:
Parting wi' Nancy, O, ne'er to meet mair!

Fond lovers' parting is sweet, painful pleasure,
Hope beaming mild on the soft parting hour;
But the dire feeling, O farewell for ever!
Anguish unmingled and agony pure!

Wild as the winter now tearing the forest,
Till the last leaf o' the summer is flown;
Such is the tempest has shaken my bosom,
Till my last hope and last comfort is gone!

Still as I hail thee, thou gloomy December,
Still shall I hail thee wi' sorrow and care;
For sad was the parting, thou makes me remember;
Parting wi' Nancy, O, ne'er to meet mair!

Caledonian Pocket Companion (1755) VII no. 30 - the air
Aird's Airs (1782) I no. 34 – the air
Scots Musical Museum (1796) no. 499 signed R, Written for this work by R. Burns
Hastie Manuscript f. 162

Song 52
Ae Fond Kiss

Tender With Regret   *Tune : Rory Dall's Port*

Ae fond kiss, and then we se-ver! Ae fare-weel, and then for ev-er!

Deep in heart-wrung tears I'll pledge thee, War-ring sighs and

groans I'll wage thee. Who shall say that for-tune grieves him,

While the star of hope she leaves him? Me, nae cheer-fu'

twin-kle lights me, Dark de-spair a-round be-nights me.

Ae fond kiss, and then we sever!
Ae fareweel, and then forever!
Deep in heart-wrung tears I'll pledge thee,
Warring sighs and groans I'll wage thee.
Who shall say that fortune grieves him,
While the star of hope she leaves him?
Me, nae cheerfu' twinkle lights me,
Dark despair around benights me.

I'll ne'er blame my partial fancy,
Naething could resist my Nancy!
But to see her was to love her,
Love but her, and love for ever.
Had we never lov'd sae kindly,
Had we never lov'd sae blindly,
Never met – or never parted,
We had ne'er been broken-hearted.

327

Fare-thee-weel, thou first and fairest!
   Fare-thee-weel, thou best and dearest!
Thine be ilka Joy and Treasure,
   Peace, Enjoyment, Love and Pleasure!
Ae fond kiss, and then we sever!
   Ae fareweel, alas, for ever!
Deep in heart-wrung tears I'll pledge thee,
   Warring sighs and groans I'll wage thee.

Straloch Manuscript (1629) – same title, but different music
Caledonian Pocket Companion (1756) VIII no. 24 - the air
Scots Musical Museum (1792) no. 347 signed X, Written for this Work by R. Burns

Rory Dall was the name of a harper to the MacLeods of Skye, and the word 'Port' is the Gaelic for 'Air'

The words are generally sung today to an old Highland Air, said to be written by Michael Diack

Song 53
Behold The Hour, The Boat Arrive

Slow With Resignation   *Tune : Oran Gaoil*

Be - hold the hour, the boat ar - rive! Thou go-est, the

dar - ling of my heart! Se - vered from thee, can

I sur - vive? But Fate has willed and we must part.

I'll of - ten greet the surg - ing swell, Yon dis - tant

isle will of - ten hail: 'E'en here I took the last fare-

- well; There, la - test mark'd her van - ished sail'.

(First Version)

Behold the hour, the boat, arrive!
  My dearest Nancy, O, fareweel!
Severed frae thee, can I survive,
  Frae thee whom I hae lov'd sae weel?

Endless and deep shall be my grief,
  Nae ray of comfort shall I see,
But his most precious, dear belief,
  That thou wilt still remember me.

329

Along the solitary shore,
  Where flitting sea-fowl round me cry,
Across the rolling, dashing roar,
  I'll westward turn my wistful eye.

'Happy thou Indian grove,' I'll say,
  'Where now my Nancy's path shall be!
While thro' your sweets she holds her way,
  O, tell me, does she muse on me?'

(Second Version)

Behold the hour, the boat arrive!
  Thou goest, the darling of my heart!
Severed from thee, can I survive?
  But Fate has willed and we must part.
I'll often greet the surging swell,
  Yon distant isle will often hail:-
E'en here, I took the last farewell;
  There, latest mark'd her vanished sail.

Along the solitary shore,
  While flitting sea-fowl round me cry,
Across the rolling, dashing roar,
  I'll westward turn my wistful eye:-
'Happy, thou Indian grove,' I'll say,
  'Where now my Nancy's path may be!
While thro' thy sweets she loves to stray,
  O, tell me, does she muse on me?'

Corri's Scots Songs (1783) II no. 29
The original air 'Oran Gaoil' and a translation of a Gaelic song set to it is in the Scots Musical Museum (1790) no. 273

Thomson's Select Collection Of Original Scotish Airs (1805) no. 154

Based on a song published in the 'Edinburgh Magazine' (1774) entitled 'Behold The Fatal Hour Arrive'

Song 54
Sae Far Awa

Moderate With Regret   *Tune : Dalkeith Maiden Bridge*

O sad and hea-vy should I part, But for her sake sae far a - wa; Un - know-ing what my way may thwart, My na - tive land sae far a - wa. Thou that of a' things Ma - ker art, That form'd this Fair sae far a - wa, Gie bo - dy strength, then I'll ne'er start At this my way sae far a - wa.

O, sad and heavy should I part,
  But for her sake sae far awa;
Unknowing what my way may thwart,
  My native land sae far awa.

Thou that of a' things Maker art,
  That formed this Fair sae far awa,
Gie body strength, then I'll ne'er start
  At this my way sae far awa!

How true is love to pure desert!
  So mine in her sae far awa,
And nocht shall heal my bosom's smart,
  While, O, she is sae far awa.

Nane other love, nane other dart
  I feel, but hers sae far awa;
But fairer never touch'd a heart,
  Than hers, the Fair sae far awa.

Aird's Airs (1788) III no 439 - the air
Scots Musical Museum (1796) no. 449 signed B, Written for this Work by R. Burns
Hastie Manuscript f. 136

Song 55
Craigieburn Wood

Moderate With Tenderness　　　　　　*Tune : Craigieburn Wood*

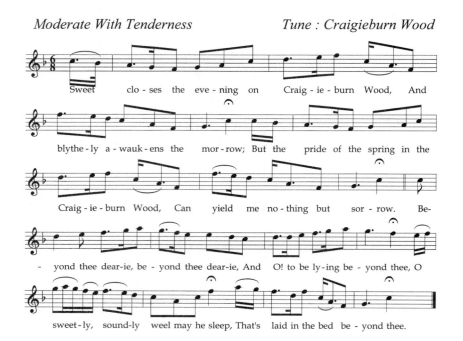

Sweet clo-ses the eve-ning on Craig-ie-burn Wood, And blythe-ly a-wauk-ens the mor-row; But the pride of the spring in the Craig-ie-burn Wood, Can yield me no-thing but sor-row. Be-yond thee dear-ie, be-yond thee dear-ie, And O! to be ly-ing be-yond thee, O sweet-ly, sound-ly weel may he sleep, That's laid in the bed be-yond thee.

(Chorus)
Beyond thee dearie, beyond thee dearie,
　And O! to be lying beyond thee,
O, sweetly, soundly, weel may he sleep,
　That's laid in the bed beyond thee.

Sweet closes the evening on Craigieburn Wood
　And blythely awaukens the morrow,
But the pride of the spring in the Craigieburn Wood
　Can yield me nothing but sorrow.

I see the spreading leaves and flowers,
　I hear the wild birds singing:
But pleasure they hae nane for me,
　While care my heart is wringing.

I can na tell, I maun na tell.
　I daur na for your anger;
But secret love will break my heart
　If I conceal it langer.

332

I see thee gracefu', straight and tall,
    I see thee sweet and bonie;
But O, what will my torments be,
    If thou refuse thy Johnie!

To see thee in another's arms
    In love to lie and languish,
'Twad be my dead, that will be seen –
    My heart wad burst wi' anguish!

But, Jeanie, say thou wilt be mine,
    Say thou lo'es nane before me,
And a' my days o' life to come
    I'll gratefully adore thee.

(Second Version)

Sweet fa's the eve on Craigieburn,
    And blythe awakes the morrow
But a' the pride o' Spring's return
    Can yield me nocht but sorrow.

I see the flowers and spreading trees,
    I hear the wild birds singing:
But what a weary wight can please,
    And Care his bosom is wringing?

Fain, fain would I my griefs impart,
    Yet dare na for your anger;
But secret love will break my heart,
    If I conceal it langer.

If thou refuse to pity me,
    If thou shalt love another,
When yon green leaves fade frae the tree
    Around my grave they'll wither.

Afton Manuscript (1791)
Scots Musical Museum (1792) no. 301 signed B, Written for this Work by R. Burns
Hastie Manuscript f. 58
Read Burns' letters to George Thomson 7th April 1793 & 19th October 1794

333

Song 56
Saw Ye Bonie Lesley

Merry And Live   *Tune : The Collier's Bonie Lassie*

O, saw ye bonie Lesley,
    As she gaed o'er the Border?
She's gane, like Alexander,
    To spread her conquests farther!

To see her is to love her,
    And love but her forever:
For Nature made her what she is,
    And never made anither!

Thou art a queen, fair Lesley –
    Thy subjects, we before thee:
Thou art divine, fair Lesley –
    The hearts o' men adore thee.

The Deil he could na skaith thee,
    Or aught that wad belang thee;
He'd look into thy bonie face,
    And say: - 'I canna wrang thee!'

The Powers aboon will tent thee,
 Misfortune sha'na steer thee:
Thou'rt like themsel sae lovely,
 That ill they'll ne'er let near thee.

Return again, fair Lesley,
 Return to Caledonie!
That we may brag we hae a lass
 There's nane again sae bonie.

Leyden Manuscript (c1690) - the air
Playford's Original Scots Tunes (1700) – the air
Margaret Sinkler's Manuscript (1710) - the air
Orpheus Caledonius (1725) no. 44 - the air
McFarlane Manuscript (1741) – the air
Stewart's Reels (1762) no. 3 – the air entitled 'The Nine Pint Cogie'
Herd's Scottish Songs (1776) II no. 3
Thomson's Select Collection Of Original Scotish Airs (1798) no. 33

Read Burns' letter to George Thomson dated 8th November 1792

The words have also been set to 'The Collier's Dochter'

Song 57
The Bonie Lad That's Far Awa

Slow and Tender   *Tune : The Bonie Lad That's Far Awa*

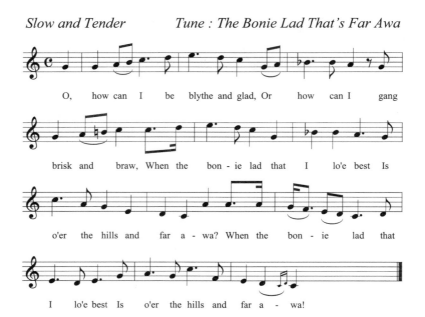

O how can I be blythe and glad,
   Or how can I gang brisk and braw,
   When the bonie lad that I lo'e best
   Is o'er the hills and far awa?

It's no the frosty winter wind,
   It's no the driving drift and snaw;
But ay the tear comes in my e'e,
   To think on him that's far awa.

Ma father pat me frae his door,
   My friends they hae disown'd me a'!
But I hae ane will tak my part –
   The bonie lad that's far awa.

A pair o' glooves he bought to me,
   And silken snoods he gaed me twa,
And I will wear them for his sake,
   The bonie lad that's far awa.

O, weary Winter soon will pass,
   And Spring will cleed the birken shaw,
And my sweet babie will be born,
   And he'll be hame that's far awa!

Scots Musical Museum (1792) no. 317 signed X
Hastie Manuscript f. 67

The air 'The Bonie Lad That's Far Awa' was probably sent to the 'Museum' by Burns, who wrote to George Thomson in October 1794 stating 'O How Can I Be Blythe and Glad is mine'. He may have got the idea of the song from verses in Herd's Scottish Songs (1776) II no. 1, which was an abridgement of a poem c1690 entitled 'The Inconstant Shepherd, Or The Forsaken Lasses Lamentation'

The words have also been set to the air 'Owre the Hills And Far Awa'

Song 58
It Isna Jean, Thy Bonie Face

Slow And Loving

Tune : The Maid's Complaint

It is na, Jean, thy bon-ie face Nor shape that I ad-
- mire, Al - tho' thy beau-ty and thy grace Might
weel a - wauk de - sire. Some - thing in il - ka
part o' thee To praise, to love, I find; But,
dear as is thy form to me, Still dear-er is thy mind.

It is na, Jean, thy bonie face
  Nor shape that I admire,
Altho' thy beauty and thy grace
  Might weel awauk desire.

Something in ilka part o' thee
  To praise, to love, I find;
But, dear as is thy form to me,
  Still dearer is thy mind.

Nae mair ungen'rous wish I hae,
  Nor stronger in my breast,
Than, if I canna make thee sae,
  At least to see thee blest.

Content am I, if Heaven shall give
  But happiness to thee,
And, as wi' thee I wish to live,
  For thee I'd bear to dee.

Oswald's Curious Collections Of Scots Tunes (1740) no. 14 - the air
Caledonian Pocket Companion (1752) IV no. 30 – the air
Scots Musical Museum (1792) no. 333 Written for this Work by R. Burns
Hastie Manuscript f. 72

Song 59
Will Ye Go To The Indies, My Mary

Slow And Tender   *Tune : Ewe-Bughts, Marion*

Will ye go to the In - dies, my Ma-ry, And leave auld Sco-tia's shore? Will ye go to the In - dies, my Ma - ry, A-cross th' At-lan - tic roar? O, sweet grows the lime and the o - range, And the ap - ple on the pine; But a' the charms o' the In - dies Can nev-er e - qual thine.

Will ye go to the Indies, my Mary,
  And leave auld Scotia's shore?
Will ye go to the Indies, my Mary,
  Across th' Atlantic roar?

O, sweet grows the lime and the orange,
  And the apple on the pine;
But a' the charms o' the Indies
  Can never equal thine.

I hae sworn by the Heavens to my Mary,
  I hae sworn by the Heavens to be true,
And sae may the Heavens forget me,
  When I forget my vow!

O, plight me your faith, my Mary,
   And plight me your lily-white hand!
O, plight me your faith, my Mary,
   Before I leave Scotia's strand!

We hae plighted our troth, my Mary,
   In mutual affection to join;
And curst be the cause that shall part us!
   The hour and the moment o' time!

Tea-Table Miscellany (1724) – the air
Orpheus Caledonius (1733) no. 15 – the air
Percy's Reliques (1765) – the air
Stewart's Scots Songs (1781) no. 31
Perth Musical Miscellany (1786) no. 33 – the air
Scots Musical Museum (1787) no. 85 – variation of the air
Aird's Airs (1788) III no. 476 – the air
Ritson's Scottish Songs (1794) II no. 169
Scots Musical Museum (1796) no. 419
Currie (1800)

Song 60
The Lea-Rig

Slow And Pleasurable   *Tune : My Ain Kind Dearie, O*

When o'er the hill the e'en-ing star Tells bught-in time is near, my jo, And

ows-en frae the fur-row'd field Re - turn sae dowf and wea-ry, O, Down

by the burn, where scent-ed birks Wi' dew are hang-ing clear, my jo, I'll

meet thee on the lea - rig, My ain kind dea-rie, O.

When o'er the hill the e'ening star
 Tells bughtin time is near, my jo,
And owsen frae the furrow'd field
 Return sae dowff and weary, O,
Down by the burn, where scented birks
 Wi' dew are hangin clear, my jo,
I'll meet thee on the lea-rig,
 My ain kind dearie, O.

At midnight hour in mirkest glen,
 I'd rove and ne'er be eerie O,
If thro' that glen I gaed to thee,
 My ain kind dearie O:
Altho' the night were ne'er sae wild.
 And I were ne'er sae weary O,
I'd meet thee on the lea-rig,
 My ain kind dearie, O.

The hunter lo'es the morning sun,
   To rouse the mountain deer, my jo,
At noon the fisher takes the glen,
   Adown the burn to steer, my jo;
Gie me the hour o' gloamin grey,
   It maks my heart sae cheery, O,
To meet thee on the lea-rig
   My ain kind dearie, O.

Caledonian Pocket Companion (c1756) VIII no. 20
Bremners Reels (1760) no. 76 – the air
Campbell's Reels (1778) no. 18 – the air
Aird's Airs (1782) I no. 4 – the air
Scots Musical Museum (1787) no. 49 (old version) – the air.
Currie 1800
Thomson's Select Collection Of Original Scotish Airs (1805) no. 195

Song 61
She Is A Winsome Wee Thing

Lively And Cheerily   *Tune : My Wife's A Wanton Wee Thing*

She is a win-some wee thing, She is a hand-some wee thing, She is a lo'e-some wee thing, This sweet wee wife o' mine. I ne-ver saw a fai-rer, I ne-ver lo'ed a dea-rer; And neist my heart I'll wear her, For fear my je-wel tine.

(Chorus)
She is a winsome wee thing,
   She is a handsome wee thing,
She is a lo'esome wee thing,
   This sweet wee wife o' mine.

I never saw a fairer,
   I never lo'ed a dearer,
And neist my heart I'll wear her,
   For fear my jewel tine.

The warld's wrack we share o't;
   The warstle and the care o't,
Wi' her I'll blythely bear it,
   And think my lot divine.

Original Scotch Tunes (1700) – entitled 'Bride Next'
Caledonian Pocket Companion (1754) VI no. 12 - the air
Stewart's Reels (1762) no. 30 – the air
Herd's Scottish Songs (1776) II no. 230
Aird's Airs (1782) I no. 41 – the air
Currie (1800)
Thomson's Select Melodies (1824) VI no. 44 (adapted)
Read Burns letter to Thomson dated 8th November 1792

342

Song 62
Highland Mary

Slow And Tender   *Tune : Lady Catherine Ogie*

Ye banks and braes and streams around
 The castle o' Montgomery,
Green be your woods, and fair your flowers,
 Your waters never drumlie!
There Summer first unfald her robes,
 And there the longest tarry!
For there I took the last fareweel
 O' my sweet Highland Mary.

How sweetly bloom'd the gay, green birk,
 How rich the hawthorn's blossom,
As underneath their fragrant shade,
 I clasp'd her to my bosom!
The golden hours on angel wings
 Flew o'er me and my dearie:
For dear to me as light and life
 Was my sweet Highland Mary.

Wi' monie a vow and lock'd embrace
    Our parting was fu' tender;
And, pledging aft to meet again,
    We tore oursels asunder.
But O! fell Death's untimely frost,
    That nipt my flower sae early!
Now green's the sod, and cauld's the clay,
    That wraps my Highland Mary!

O, pale, pale now, those rosy lips
    I aft hae kiss'd sae fondly;
And clos'd for ay, the sparkling glance
    That dwalt on me sae kindly;
And mouldering now in silent dust
    That heart that lo'ed me dearly!
But still within my bosom's core
    Shall live my Highland Mary.

Apollo's Banquet (1686) – entitled 'A Scotch Tune'
Playford's Dancing Master (1688) – entitled 'Lady Catherine Ogle, A New Dance'
Graham Manuscript (1694) – the air
Bruce Manuscript (1706) – the air

D'Urfey's Pill's To Purge Melancholy (1719) II no. 200 – the air, sometimes entitled
'Bonny Katherine Loggy, A Scotch Song'

Tea-Table Miscellany (1724) – the air
Orpheus Caledonius (1725) no. 22 - the air entitled a seventeenth century English air
Watt's Musical Miscellany (1729) II no. 166
Craig's Scots Tunes (1730) no. 20 – the air
McGibbon's Scots Tunes (1742) no. 20 – the air
Caledonian Pocket Companion (1752) IV no. 2 – the air
Thomson's Select Collection Of Original Scotish Airs. (1799) no. 83

Lady Catherine Ogle was the youngest daughter and one of the co-heirs of the Duke of Newcastle and Baron Ogle. She died in 1691

Song 63
I Hae A Wife O' My Ain

Fast And Proud   *Tune : I Hae A Wife O' My Ain*

I hae a wife o' my ain, I'll par-take wi' nae-bo-dy;

I'll tak cuck-old frae nane, I'll gie cuck-old to nae-bo-dy.

I hae a pen-ny to spend, There thanks to nae-bo-dy!

I hae nae-thing to lend, I'll bor-row frae nae-bo-dy.

I hae a wife o' my ain,	I am naebody's lord,
I'll partake wi' naebody;	I'll be slave to naebody.
I'll take cuckold frae nane,	I'll hae a guid braid sword,
I'll gie cuckold to naebody.	I'll tak dunts frae naebody.
I hae a penny to spend,	I'll be merry and free,
There - thanks to naebody.	I'll be sad for naebody.
I hae naething tae lend,	Naebody cares for me.
I'll borrow frae naebody.	I care for naebody.

Walsh's Caledonian Country Dances – the air
Bremner's Reels (1759) no. 45 - the air
Stewart's Reels (1761) no. 12 - the air
Campbell's Reels (1778) no. 3 – the air
Scots Musical Museum (1792) no 352 signed B, Written for this Work by R. Burns
Hastie Manuscript f. 82

Schumann composed an original lilt on Scottish lines, entitled 'Niemand', as a translation of Burns' song.

Song 64
The Gallant Weaver

Moderate And Tender   *Tune : The Gallant Weaver (The Weaver's March)*

Where Cart rins row-in to the sea By mon-y a flower and spread-ing tree, There lives a lad, the lad for me - He is a gal-lant weav-er. O, I had woo-ers aught or nine, They gied me rings and rib-bons fine, And I was fear'd my heart wad tine, And I gied it to the weav-er.

Where Cart rins rowin to the sea
  By mony a flower and spreading tree,
There lives a lad, the lad for me –
  He is a gallant weaver.
O, I had wooers aught or nine,
  They gied me rings and ribbons fine,
And I was fear'd my heart wad tine.
  And I gied it to the weaver.

My daddie sign'd my tocher-band
  To gie the lad that has the land,
But to my heart I'll add my hand,
  And gie it to the weaver.
While birds rejoice in leafy bowers,
  While bees delight in opening flowers,
While corn grows green in summer showers,
  I love my gallant weaver.

Musical Pocket Book (c1715) – 'The New Swedish Dance' resembles the air
Dancing Master (1728) – the air entitled 'Frisky Jenny' or 'The Tenth Of June'
Aird's Airs (1782) I no 174 – the air, entitled 'Weaver's March', or 'Twenty First Of
August'

Scots Musical Museum (1792) no. 389 signed R, Written for this Work by R. Burns
Thomson's Select Collection Of Original Scotish Airs (1798) no. 39

The words have also been set to the airs 'The Auld Wife Ayont The Fire' and 'Pinkie House'
(aka 'Rothes Lament')

Song 65
Wandering Willie

Moderate/Tender   *Tune : Here Awa, There Awa*

Here a - wa,   there a - wa,   wan - der - ing,   Wil - lie,

Here a - wa,   there a - wa,   haud a - wa   hame;

Come to   my   bo - som, my   ae   on - ly   dear - ie, And

tell me thou   bring'st me my   Wil - lie the   same.

Here awa, there awa, wandering, Willie,
  Here awa, there awa, haud awa hame!
Come to my bosom, my ae only dearie,
  And tell me thou bring'st me my Willie the same.

Loud tho' the Winter blew cauld at our parting,
  'Twas na the blast brought the tear in my e'e,
Welcome now Simmer, and welcome my Willie,
  The Simmer to Nature, my Willie to me.

Rest, ye wild storms, in the cave of your slumber –
  How your wild howling a lover alarms!
Wauken, ye breezes, row gently, ye billows,
  And waft my dear laddie ance mair to my arms.

But O, if he's faithless, and minds na his Nannie,
  Flow still between us, thou wide-roaring main!
May I never see it, may I never trow it,
  But, dying, believe that my Willie's my ain!

347

(Many of the older biographies, c19th century, state that this song was written for Agnes McLehose, some even hint that it was written for Maria Riddell)

Caledonian Pocket Companion (1756) VIII no. 1 – the air entitled 'Here Awa Willie'
Bremner's Second Series Of Scots Songs (1757) no. 22
McGibbon's Scots Tunes (1768) IV no 108
Herd's Scots Songs (1769) no. 291
Herd's Ancient And Modern Scottish Songs (1776) II no. 40 (old version)
Perth Musical Miscellany (1786) no. 17
Scots Musical Museum (1787) no. 57 (old version) – the air.
Calliope (1788) no. 136
Thomson's Select Collection Of Original Scotish Airs (1793) no. 2
Ritson's Scottish Songs (1794) I no. 86.

Song 66
Bonie Wee Thing

Slow And Plaintive   *Tune : Bonie Wee Thing*

Bon - ie wee thing, cann - ie wee thing, Love - ly wee thing,
wert thou mine, I wad wear thee in my bos - om
Lest my jew - el it should tine. Wish - ful - ly I
look and lan - guish In that bon - ie face o' thine,
And my heart it stounds wi' an - guish, Lest my wee thing be na mine.

(Chorus)
Bonie wee thing, cannie wee thing,
 Lovely wee thing, wert thou mine,
I wad wear thee in my bosom
 Lest my jewel it should tine.

Wishfully I look and languish
 In that bonie face o' thine,
And my heart it stounds wi' anguish,
 Lest my wee thing be na mine.

Wit, and Grace, and Love, and Beauty,
 In ae constellation shine!
To adore thee is my duty,
 Goddess o' this soul o' mine.

Straloch's Manuscript Lute-Book (1627) – the air is called 'Wo Betyd Thy Wearie Bodie'
Caledonian Pocket Companion (1758) IX no. 1 - the air.
Bremner's Reels (1758) no. 40 – different air entitled 'The Bonnie Wi' Thing'
Scots Musical Museum (1792) no. 341 signed R, Written for this Work by R. Burns

The words have also been set to the air 'The Lads Of Saltcoats'

Song 67
Young Jessie

Slow And Expressive   *Tune : Bonie Dundee*

True - hear-ted was he, the sad swain o' the Yar-row, And

fair are the maids on the banks o' the Ayr; But

by the sweet side o' the Nith's wind-ing riv-er, Are

lov-ers as faith-ful, and mai-dens as fair: To

e - qual young Jes-sie, seek Sco-tia all o - ver; To

e - qual young Jes-sie, you seek it in vain: Grace,

Beau-ty and El-e-gance fet-ter her lov-er, And

mai-den-ly mo-des-ty fi - xes the chain

True hearted was he, the sad swain o' the Yarrow,
    And fair are the maids on the banks o' the Ayr;
But by the sweet side o' the Nith's winding river,
    Are lovers as faithful, and maidens as fair:
To equal young Jessie seek Scotia all over;
    To equal young Jessie you seek it in vain:
Grace, Beauty and Elegance fetter her lover,
    And maidenly modesty fixes the chain.

Fresh is the rose in the gay, dewy morning,
    And sweet is the lily at evening close;
But in the fair presence o' lovely, young Jessie,
    Unseen is the lily, unheeded the rose.
Love sits in her smile, a wizard ensnaring;
    Enthron'd in her een he delivers his law;
And still to her charms she alone is a stranger,
    Her modest demeanour's the jewel of a'.

Skene Manuscript (c1630) – entitled 'Adew Dundee'
Playford's Dancing Master (1688) – the air
Wit And Mirth, London (1703) – early version of 'Bonie Dundee'
Durfey's Pills (1719) V no. 17 – the air
Collection Of Old Ballads (1723) no. 275 – entitled 'Jockey's Deliverance'
Craig's Scots Tunes (1730) no. 22 – the air
McGibbon's Scots Tunes (1746) no. 36 – the air
Caledonian Pocket Companion (1751) III no. 4 – the air
Herd's Scots Songs (1769) no. 311
'Bonie Dundee' can be found in the Scots Musical Museum (1787) no. 99
Lawrie's Scottish Songs (1791) II no. 91
Thomson's Select Collection Of Original Scotish Airs (1798) no. 46

Song 68
Farewell Thou Stream

Slow and Poignant   *Tune : Alace Yat I Cam Ower The Muir*

Fare - well, thou stream that wind - ing flows A - round Ma - ri - a's

dwel - ling! O mem - 'ry, spare the cru - el throes With - in my bo - som

swel - ling; Con - demn'd to drag a hope - less chain And yet in se - cret

lan - guish, To feel a fire in ev - ery vein, Nor dare dis - close my an - guish.

Farewell thou stream that winding flows
  Around Maria's dwelling!
O mem'ry, spare the cruel throes
  Within my bosom swelling;
Condemn'd to drag a hopeless chain
  And yet in secret languish,
To feel a fire in every vein,
  Nor dare disclose my anguish!

Love's veriest wretch, unseen, unknown,
  I fain my griefs would cover:
The bursting sigh, th' unweeting groan
  Betray the hapless lover.
I know thou doom'st me to despair,
  Nor wilt, nor canst relieve me;
But, O Maria, hear one prayer –
  For pity's sake forgive me!

The music of thy voice I heard,
　Nor wist while it enslav'd me!
I saw thine eyes, yet nothing fear'd,
　Till fears no more had sav'd me!
Th' unwary sailor thus, aghast
　The wheeling torrent viewing,
'Mid circling horrors sinks at last
　In overwhelming ruin.

Skene Manuscript (c1630) – the air
Orpheus Caledonius (1725) no. 6 – the air
Ramsay's Musick (c1726) – the air
Watt's Musical Miscellany (1729) I no. 142 – the air
McGibbon's Scots Tunes (1742) no. 34 – the air
Caledonian Pocket Companion (1745) II no. 24 – the air
Bremner's Scots Songs (1757) no. 9 – the air
Scots Musical Museum (1787) no. 18 – the air
Thomson's Selected Collection Of Original Scotish Airs (1793) no. 21
Ritson's Scottish Songs (1794) I no. 114

Burns choice of air for the above song was 'Nansy's To The Greenwood Gane', Thomson chose 'Alace Yat I Came Ower The Moor'.

Line 2 was originally 'Around Maria's dwelling', but Burns had fallen out with Maria Riddell by now and changed the name from Maria to Eliza, where it appears in many collections.

Song 69
There Was A Lass And She Was Fair

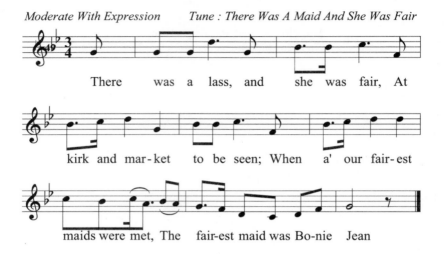

Moderate With Expression　　　*Tune : There Was A Maid And She Was Fair*

There was a lass, and she was fair, At kirk and mar-ket to be seen; When a' our fair-est maids were met, The fair-est maid was Bo-nie Jean

There was a lass, and she was fair,
　　At kirk and market to be seen;
When a' our fairest maids were met,
　　The fairest maid was Bonie Jean.

And aye she wrought her country wark,
　　And ay she sang sae merrilie;
The blythest bird upon the bush
　　Had ne'er a lighter heart than she.

But hawks will rob the tender joys,
　　That bless the little lintwhite's nest,
And frost will blight the fairest flowers,
　　And love will break the soundest rest.

Young Robie was the brawest lad,
　　The flower and pride of a' the glen,
And he has owsen, sheep, and kye,
　　And wanton naigies nine or ten.

He gaed wi' Jeanie to the tryste
　　He danc'd wi' Jeanie on the down,
And, lang ere witless, Jeanie wist,
　　Her heart was tint, her peace was stown!

As in the bosom of the stream,
　　The moonbeam dwells at dewy e'en,
So, trembling pure, was tender love
　　Within the breast of bonie Jean.

And now she works her country's wark,
  And ay she sighs wi' care and pain,
Yet wist na what her all might be,
  Or what wad make her weel again.

But did na Jeanie's heart loup light,
  And didna joy blink in her e'e;
As Robie tauld a tale of love
  Ae e'enin on the lily lea?

While monie a bird sang sweet o' love,
  And monie a flower blooms o'er the dale,
His cheek to hers he aft did lay,
  And whispered thus his tender tale.

'O Jeanie fair, I' lo'e thee dear,
  O canst thou think to fancy me?
Or wilt thou leave thy mammie's cot,
  And learn to tent the farms wi' me?

At barn or byre thou shalt na drudge,
  Or naething else to trouble thee,
But stray amang the heather-bells,
  And tent the waving corn wi' me.'

Now what could artless Jeanie do?
  She had nae will tae say him na!
At length she blushed a sweet consent,
  And love was ay between them twa.

Thomson's Select Collection Of Original Scotish Airs (1805) no. 152

Stephen Clarke took down the original air for this song 'There Was A Lass, And She Was Fair' from the singing of Jean Armour, and Burns sent it to Thomson with a request that if he (Thomson) was not going to use the air, then would he return it, as this was the only copy Burns had. Thomson did not use the air and lost the original. Thomson put the song to 'Willy Was A Wanton Wag', which is also in the Scots Musical Museum (1788) no. 137

To date 'There Was A Lass' has been set to the airs 'Bonie Jean' and 'Willie Was A Wanton Wag'

The air printed to the above song I discovered in the 'Greig-Duncan Collection, with the following quote -

'There Was A Lass and She Was Fair'. Burns song was written for a traditional tune which has been listed as 'untraced'; it seems that this fragment, both words and music, is a version of his source'.

The title of the song in the Greig-Duncan Collection is 'There Was A Maid And She Was Fair' and can be found in Volume 7, no. 1335

Song 70
Blythe Hae I Been On Yon Hill

Moderate And Joyful   *Tune : The Quaker's Wife*

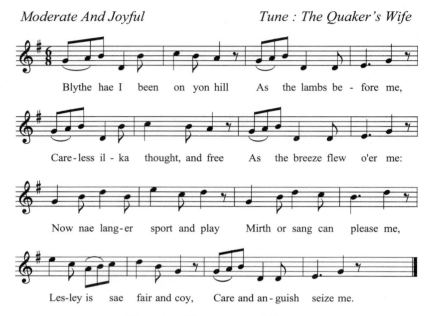

Blythe hae I been on yon hill
  As the lambs before me,
Careless ilka thought, and free
  As the breeze flew o'er me:
Now nae langer sport and play
  Mirth or sang can please me,
Lesley is sae fair and coy,
  Care and anguish seize me.

Heavy, heavy is the task,
  Hopeless love declaring!
Trembling, I do nocht but glow'r,
  Sighing, dumb despairing.
If she winna ease the thraws
  In my bosom swelling,
Underneath the grass-green sod,
  Soon maun be my dwelling.

Bremner's Reels ((1759) no. 53 – the air entitled 'Merrily Dance The Quaker'
Thomson's Select Collection Of Original Scotish Airs (1799) no. 58
Neil Gow's Complete Repository (1802)
The air is also known as 'Liggeram Cosh' (Leger M' Chose)
Read Burns' letter to George Thomson dated May 1793

Song 71
Phillis The Fair

Slow And Light   *Tune : Robin Adair (Eire A Ruin)*

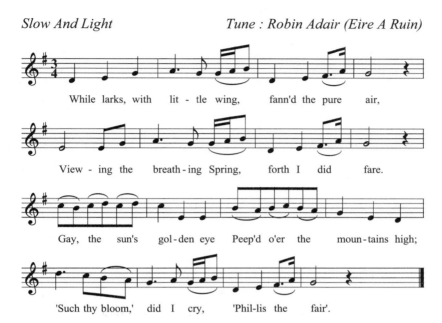

While larks, with lit - tle wing, fann'd the pure air,

View - ing the breath - ing Spring, forth I did fare.

Gay, the sun's gol - den eye Peep'd o'er the moun - tains high;

'Such thy bloom,' did I cry, 'Phil - lis the fair'.

While larks, with little wing, fann'd the pure air,
Viewing the breathing Spring, forth I did fare.
Gay, the suns golden eye
Peep'd o'er the mountains high;
    'Such thy bloom,' did I cry, 'Phillis the fair.'

In each bird's careless song, glad, I did share;
While yon wild flowers among, chance led me there.
Sweet to the opening day,
Rosebuds bent the dewy spray;
    'Such thy bloom,' did I say. 'Phillis the fair!'

Down in the shady walk, doves cooing were;
I mark'd the cruel hawk caught in a snare.
So kind may Fortune be,
Such make his destiny,
    He who would injure thee, Phillis the fair!

Caledonian Pocket Companion (1753) V no. 21- the air entitled Eileen A Roon
McLean's Scots Tunes (1772) no. 28
Currie (1800)
Read Burns' letter to Thomson, August 1793, regarding the origin of the song

Song 72
O, Poortith Cauld

Slow And Pathetic   *Tune : Cauld Kail In Aberdeen*

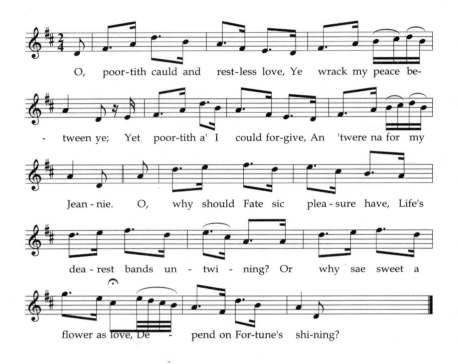

O, poor-tith cauld and rest-less love, Ye wrack my peace be-

- tween ye; Yet poor-tith a' I could for-give, An 'twere na for my

Jean - nie. O, why should Fate sic plea - sure have, Life's

dea - rest bands un - twi - ning? Or why sae sweet a

flower as love, De - pend on For-tune's shi - ning?

(Chorus)
O, why should Fate sic pleasure have,
    Life's dearest bands untwining?
Or why sae sweet a flower as love,
    Depend on Fortune's shining?

O, poortith cauld and restless love,
    Ye wrack my peace between ye;
Yet poortith a' I could forgive,
    An' 'twere na for my Jeanie.

The warld's wealth when I think on,
    Its pride and a' the lave o't –
My curse on silly coward man,
    That he should be the slave o't

358

Her een sae bonie blue betray
How she repays my passion;
But prudence is her o'erword ay;
She talks o' rank and fashion.

O, wha can prudence think upon,
And sic a lassie by him?
O, wha can prudence think upon,
And sae in love as I am?

How blest the wild-wood Indian's fate!
He woos his artless dearie –
The silly bogles, Wealth and State,
Can never make him eerie.

(Suggested to have been written for a Jane Blackstock (later to become a Mrs Whittier of Liverpool) by Gilbert Burns, but remains unsubstantiated)

Herd's Scots Song (1769) no. 314 – old version
Scots Musical Museum (1788) no. 162 – the air.
Dale's Scotch Songs (1794) II no. 61
Thomson's Select Collection Of Original Scotish Airs (1798)
Merry Muses Of Caledonia – 'Gie The Lass Her Fairin, Lad' – the air

The earliest root for the air 'Cauld Kail' can be traced back to an old tune called 'The Sleepy Bodie,' an ancient tune in triple time. Another song called 'The Ploughman' comes from the same source

The words have also been set to the air 'I Had A Horse And I Had Nae Mair'

Song 73
O Whistle An' I'll Come To Ye, My Lad

Lively And Joyous   *Tune : O Whistle An' I'll Come To Ye, My Lad*

O, whis-tle an' I'll come to ye, my lad! O., whis-tle an' I'll come

to ye, my lad! Tho' fa-ther an' mo-ther an' a' should gae mad, O.

whis-tle an' I'll come to ye, my lad! But war-i-ly tent when ye

come to court me, An' come nae un-less the back-yett be a-gee; Syne

up the back-style, an' let nae-bo-dy see, An' come as ye were na

com-in' to me. An' come as ye were na com-in' to me

(Chorus)
O, whistle an' I'll come to ye, my lad!
　O, whistle an' I'll come to ye, my lad!
Tho' father an' mother an' a' should gae mad,
　O, whistle an' I'll come to ye, my lad

But warily tent when ye come to court me,
　An' come nae unless the back-yett be a-jee:
Syne up the back-style, an' let naebody see,
　An' come as ye were na comin' to me.
　An' come as ye were na comin' to me.

360

At kirk, or at market, whene'er ye meet me,
Gang by me as tho' that ye car'd na a flie;
But steal me a blink o' your bonie black e'e,
Yet look as ye were na lookin' to me.
Yet look as ye were na lookin' to me.

Ay vow an' protest that ye care na for me,
An' whyles ye may lightly my beauty a-wee;
But court na anither tho' jokin ye be,
For fear that she wyle your fancy frae me.
For fear that she wyle your fancy frae me.

Herd Manuscript – the old chorus of the song
Scots Musical Museum (1788) no.106 Written for this Work by R. Burns - one verse only

Come down the back stairs when you come to court me;
Come down the back stairs when you come to court me;
Come down the back stairs, and let naebody see;
And come as ye were na' coming to me.
And come as ye were na' coming to me.

Thomson's Select Collection Of Original Scotish Airs (1799) no. 94

In August 1795 Burns asked Thomson to alter the last line of every stanza to 'Thy Jeanie will venture wi' ye, my lad'. Apparently this was at the request of Jean Lorimer herself.

The air was used by John O'Keefe in his opera 'The Poor Soldier' performed at Covent Garden in 1783. The air is also reported to have been composed by a gentleman called John Bruce, an excellent fiddle player from Dumfries circa middle of the 18th century.

Song 74
Adown Winding Nith

Slow And Tender   *Tune : The Muckin' O' Geordy's Byre*

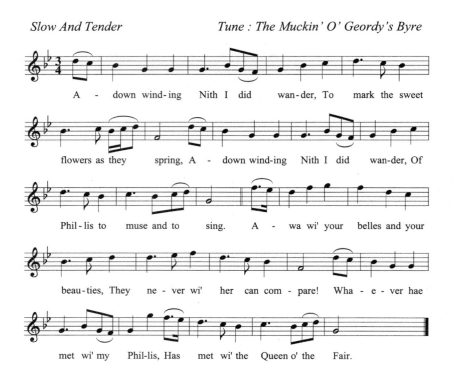

A - down wind-ing Nith I did wan-der, To mark the sweet
flowers as they spring, A - down wind-ing Nith I did wan-der, Of
Phil-lis to muse and to sing. A - wa wi' your belles and your
beau-ties, They ne - ver wi' her can com - pare! Wha - e - ver hae
met wi' my Phil-lis, Has met wi' the Queen o' the Fair.

(Chorus)
Awa wi' your belles and your beauties,
    They never wi' her can compare!
Whaever has met wi' my Phillis,
    Has met wi' the Queen o' the Fair.

Adown winding Nith I did wander,
    To mark the sweet flowers as they spring,
Adown winding Nith I did wander,
    Of Phillis to muse and to sing.

The daisy amus'd my fond fancy,
    So artless, so simple, so wild:
'Thou emblem,' said I, 'O my Phillis' –
    For she is Simplicity's child.

The rosebud's the blush o' my charmer,
  Her sweet balmy lip when 'tis prest.
How fair and how pure is the lily!
  But fairer and purer her breast.

Yon knot of gay flowers in the arbour,
  They ne'er wi' my Phillis can vie:
Her breath is the breath of the woodbine,
  Its dew-drop o' diamond her eye.

Her voice is the song o' the morning,
  That wakes thro' the green spreading grove,
When Phoebus peeps over the mountains
  On music, and pleasure, and love.

But Beauty, how frail and how fleeting!
  The bloom of a fine summer's day!
While Worth in the mind o' my Phillis
  Will flourish without a decay.

Crockatt's Manuscript (1709) – the air
Orpheus Caledonius (1725) no. 33 - the air to the song 'My Daddie's A Delver Of Dykes'
Caledonian Pocket Companion (1745) II no. 37
Herd's Scots Song (1769) no. 311 – a fragment of an earlier version
'Geordie's Byre' can be found in the Scots Musical Museum (1787) no. 96
Thomson's Select Collection Of Original Scotish Airs (1799) no. 66
Read Burns letter to George Thomson, August 1793

The following verse was suppressed by Burns as he thought it was weak

The primrose is o'er for the season,
But mark where the violet is blown;
How modest it peeps from the covert,
So modesty sure is her own.

Song 75
Come Let Me Take Thee

Slow With Expression   *Tune : Cauld Kail In Aberdeen*

Come, let me take thee to my breast, And pledge we ne'er shall sun-der, And I shall spurn as vi-lest dust, The world's wealth and gran-deur: And do I hear my Jea-nie own, That e - qual tran-sports move her? I ask for dea-rest life a-lone, That I may live to love her.

Come, let me take thee to my breast,
   And pledge we ne'er shall sunder,
And I shall spurn as vilest dust,
   The world's wealth and grandeur:
And do I hear my Jeanie own,
   That equal transports move her?
I ask for dearest life alone,
   That I may live to love her.

Thus in my arms, wi' a' her charms,
   I'll clasp my countless treasure,
I'll seek nae mair o' Heav'n to share,
   Than sic a moment's pleasure:
And by thy een sae bonie blue
   I swear I'm thine for ever,
And on thy lips I seal my vow,
   And break it shall I never!

(Also suggested to have been written for Jane Blackstock by Gilbert Burns)
The air 'Cauld Kail' is in the Scots Musical Museum (1788) no. 162
Thomson's Select Collection Of Scotish Airs (1799) no. 93
Read Burns letter to George Thomson dated 28ᵗʰ August 1793
The words have also been set to the air 'Ally Croker'.

Song 76
Where Are The Joys

Slow And Pensive   *Tune : Saw Ye My Father (The Grey Cock)*

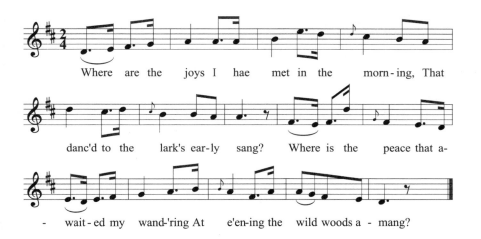

Where are the joys I hae met in the morn-ing, That
danc'd to the lark's ear-ly sang? Where is the peace that a-
-wait-ed my wand-'ring At e'en-ing the wild woods a - mang?

Where are the joys I hae met in the morning,
  That danc'd to the lark's early sang?
Where is the peace that awaited my wand'ring
  At e'ening the wild-woods amang?

Nae mair a-winding the course o' yon river
  And marking sweet flowerets sae fair.
Nae mair I trace the light footsteps o' Pleasure,
  Bur Sorrow and sad-sighing Care.

Is it that Summer's forsaken our vallies,
  And grim, surly Winter is near?
No, no, the bees humming round the gay roses
  Proclaim it the pride o' the year.

Fain wad I hide what I fear to discover,
  Yet lang, lang, too well hae I known:
A' that has caused the wreck in my bosom,
  Is Jenny, fair Jenny alone!

Time cannot aid me, my griefs are immortal,
  Not Hope dare a comfort bestow,
Come then, enamour'd and fond of my anguish,
  Enjoyment I'll seek in my woe!

Herd's Scots Songs (1769) no. 324 – old version of title of air
Herd's Scots Songs (1776) II no 208 – lengthened version of before
Stewart's Scots Songs (1772) no. 14 - the air
Pinkerton's Select Ballads (1783) no. 154
Perth Musical Miscellany (1786) no. 25 - the air
Scots Musical Museum (1787) no. 76 – the air
Thomson's Select Collection Of Original Scotish Airs (1801) no. 102
Read Burns letter to Thomson c 9th September 1793 regarding song

Song 77
Behold My Love, How Green The Groves

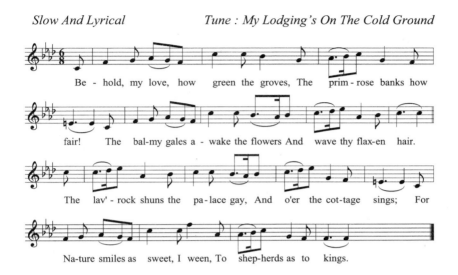

Slow And Lyrical   *Tune : My Lodging's On The Cold Ground*

Behold, my love, how green the groves,
 The primrose bank how fair!
The balmy gales awake the flowers
 And wave thy flaxen hair.

The lav'rock shuns the palace gay,
 And o'er the cottage sings;
For Nature smiles as sweet, I ween,
 To shepherds as to kings.

Let minstrels sweep the skilfu' string,
 In lordly lighted ha';
The shepherd stops his simple reed,
 Blythe in the birken shaw.

The princely revel may survey
 Our rustic dance wi' scorn;
But are their hearts as light as ours,
 Beneath the milk-white thorn?

The shepherd in the flowery glen;
 In shepherd's phrase, will woo:
The courtier tells a finer tale,
 But is his heart as true?

These wild-wood flowers I've pu'd to deck
  That spotless breast o' thine:
The courtier's gems may witness love,
  But, 'tis na love like mine.

Originally entitled 'My Chloris Mark How Green The Groves'

Playford's Dancing Master (1665) – entitled a 17th century English air
Musick's Delight (1666) – the air
Apollo's Banquet (1669) – the air
Vocal Music, London (1775) no. 18 – the air
Thomson's Select Collection Of Original Scotish Airs (1818) no. 201
The above air was composed by Matthew Lock

Nell Gwyn, in a play in 1672 called 'All Mistaken' sang the air to a parody satirizing Moll Davis, her rival, who was short and fat.

  My lodging is on the cold boards
    And wonderful hard is my fare;
  But that which troubles me most is
    The fatness of my dear

The words have also been set to the air 'Down The Burn, Davie'

Song 78
Here Is The Glen

Slow And Gentle   *Tune : The Flowers Of Edinburgh*

Here is the glen, and here the bower, All un-der-neath the bir-chen shade; The vill-age bell has told the hour, O what can stay my love-ly maid. 'Tis not Ma-ri-a's whisp-'ring call; 'Tis but the bal-my breath-ing gale, Mixt with some war-bler's dy-ing fall The dew-y star of eve to hail.

Here is the glen, and here the bower
  All underneath the birchen shade;
The village-bell has told the hour,
  O what can stay my lovely maid?

'Tis not Maria's whispering call;
  'Tis but the balmy breathing gale,
Mixt with some warbler's dying fall
  The dewy star of eve to hail.

Is it Maria's voice I hear –
  So calls the woodlark in the grove
His little faithful mate to cheer:
  At once 'tis music and' tis love!

And art thou come? And art thou true?
  O, welcome, dear, to love and me,
And let us all our vows renew
  Along the flowery banks of Cree!

Scots Musical Museum (1787) no. 13 – the air
Thomson's Select Collection Of Original Scotish Airs (1798) no. 27

Burns at first wished this song to be set to the 'Banks of Cree', an air composed by Lady
Elizabeth Heron, but according to a letter of c May 1794, sent to Thomson, Burns indicates
that he would send the words but not include the music for the 'Banks Of Cree' to Thomson,
as 'the air I feel is not worth your while, else I would send it to you', thus leaving Thomson
free to set Burns' words to any air he chose. Thomson chose 'The Flowers Of Edinburgh'.
The music for the 'Banks of Cree' has not been traced to date.

Song 79
Sae Flaxen Were Her Ringlets

Jaunty And Lyrical   *Tune : Oonagh's Waterfall*

Sae flaxen were her ringlets,
  Her eyebrows of a darker hue,
Bewitchingly o'er-arching
  Twa laughing een o' bonie blue,
Her smiling, sae wyling,
  Wad make a wretch forget his woe!
What pleasure, what treasure,
  Unto those rosy lips to grow!
Such was my Chloris' bonie face,
  When first that bonie face I saw,
And ay my Chloris' dearest charm
  She says she lo'es me best of a'!

370

Like harmony her motion,
   Her pretty ankle is a spy
Betraying fair proportion
   Wad make a saint forget the sky!
Sae warming, sae charming,
   Her fauteless form and gracefu' air,
Ilk feature – auld Nature
   Declar'd that she could dae nae mair!
Hers are the willing chains o' love
   By conquering beauty's sovereign law,
And ay my Chloris' dearest charm
   She says she lo'es me best of a'!

Let others love the city,
   And gaudy show at sunny noon!
Gie me the lonely valley,
   The dewy eve, the rising moon,
Fair beaming, and streaming
   Her silver light the boughs amang,
While falling, recalling,
   The amorous thrush concludes his sang!
Then, dearest Chloris, wilt thou rove
   By wimpling burn and leafy shaw,
And hear my vows o' truth and love,
   And say thou lo'es me best of a'?

Scots Musical Museum (1796) no. 447 signed B, Written for this Work by R. Burns. An Irish Air.

Thomson's Select Collection Of Original Scotish Airs (1805) no. 190
Hastie Manuscript f. 134

Read Burns letter to George Thomson dated September 1794

The air was introduced into Shield's ballad opera 'Marian' (1788)

371

Song 80
Ah Chloris, Since It May Na Be

Slow And Heartfelt   *Tune : Major Graham*

Ah, Chlo-ris, since it may not be, That thou of love wilt hear; If

from the lo-ver thou maun flee, Yet, let the friend be dear. Al-

- tho' I love my Chlo-ris mair Than e-ver tongue could tell; My

pas-sion, I will ne'er de-clare I'll say. I wish thee well. Tho'

all my dai-ly care thou art, And a' my night-ly dream, I'll

hide the strug-gle in my heart, And say it is es-teem.

Gow's Strathspey's (1784) no. 6 – the air
Aird's Airs (1788) III no. 551 - the air
Scots Musical Museum (1796) no. 402 – the air is set to the words of 'A Red Red Rose'
Aldine Edition (1839)

Song 81
Sleep'st Thou Or Wauk'st Thou

Quick And Cheerful   *Tune : De'il Tak The Wars*

Sleep'st thou, or wauk'st thou, fair - est crea-ture? Ro - sy morn now lifts his eye, Num-ber - ing il - ka bud, which Na - ture Wa - ters wi' the tears o' joy. Now to the stream-ing foun-tain Or up the hea - thy moun - tain The hart, hind, and roe, free - ly wild - ly wan - ton stray; In twi - ning ha - zel bow'rs. His lay the lin - net pours; The lave - rock to the sky As - cends wi' sangs o' joy, While the sun and thou a - rise to bless the day

Sleep'st thou, or wauk'st thou, fairest creature?
　Rosy morn now lifts his eye,
Numbering ilka bud, which Nature
　Waters wi' the tears o' joy.
　Now to the streaming fountain
　Or up the heathy mountain
The hart, hind, and roe, freely wildly wanton stray;
　In twining hazel bowers.
　His lay the linnet pours;
　The laverock to the sky
　Ascends wi' sangs o' joy,
While the sun and thou arise to bless the day!

Phoebus, gilding the brow of morning,
　Banishes ilk darksome shade,
Nature gladdening and adorning:
　Such to me my lovely maid!
　When frae my Chloris parted,
　Sad, cheerless, broken-hearted,
The night's gloomy shades, cloudy, dark, o'ercast my sky;
　But when she charms my sight
　In pride of beauty's light,
　When thro' my very heart
　Her beaming glories dart,
'Tis then – 'tis then I wake to life and joy!

Leyden Manuscript (1690) – the air
Atkinson's Manuscript (1694) – the air
D'Urfey's Pills To Purge Melancholy (1719) I no. 297 – entitled 'A Scotch Song'
Oswald's Curious Collection Of Scots Tunes (1740) no. 26 - the air
Caledonian Pocket Companion (1743) I no. 7 – the air
McGibbon's Scots Tunes (1768) IV no. 117 – the air
Perth Musical Miscellany (1786) no. 340 – the air
Scots Musical Museum (1790) no. 262 – the air
Thomson's Select Collection Of Original Scotish Airs (1805) no. 157

Song 82
It Was The Charming Month Of May

Lively And Joyous   *Tune : Dainty Davie*

Lo - vely was she by the dawn, Youth - ful Chlo - e,

char - ming Chlo - e, Trip - ping o'er the pear - ly lawn, The

youth - ful, char - ming Chlo - e. It was the char - ming

month of May, When all the flowers were fresh and gay, One

mor - ning, by the break of day, The youth - ful, char - ming

Chlo - e From peace - ful slum - ber she a - rose, Girt

on her man - tle and her hose, And o'er the flo - wery

mead she goes, The youth-ful, char-ming Chlo - e.

(Chorus)
Lovely was she by the dawn,
    Youthful Chloe, charming Chloe,
Tripping o'er the pearly lawn,
    The youthful, charming Chloe.

It was the charming month of May,
When all the flowers were fresh and gay,
One morning, by the break of day,
    The youthful, charming Chloe,
From peaceful slumber she arose,
Girt on her mantle and her hose,
And o'er the flowery mead she goes –
    The youthful, charming Chloe.

The feather'd people you might see
Perch'd all around on every tree!
In notes of sweetest melody
    They hail the charming Chloe,
Till, painting gay the eastern skies,
The glorious sun began to rise,
Outrival'd by the radiant eyes
    Of youthful, charming Chloe.

Playford's Dancing Master (1680) no 293 – the air
Margaret Sinkler's Manuscript (1710) – the air is untitled
D'Urfey's Pills To Purge Melancholy (1719) I no. 42 – the air
Tea-Table Miscellany (1724) – air put to the song 'Lucky Nancy'
Tea-Table Miscellany (1725) – to be sung to the air 'The Happy Clown'
McGibbon's Scots Tunes (1746) no. 32 – the air
Caledonian Pocket Companion (1753) V no. 22 – the air
Scots Musical Museum (1787) no. 34 – the air
Thomson's Select Collection Of Original Scotish Airs (1799) no. 69

Read Burns letter to Thomson of November 1794 regarding the origin of the song.

Song 83
Lassie Wi' The Lint-White Locks

Slow And Tender   *Tune : Rothiemurche's Rant*

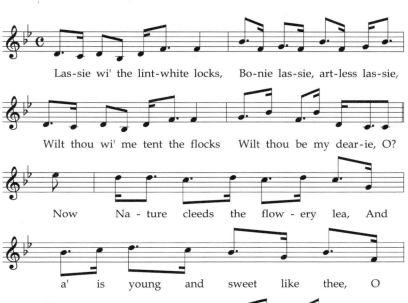

Las-sie wi' the lint-white locks,   Bo-nie las-sie, art-less las-sie,

Wilt thou wi' me tent the flocks   Wilt thou be my dear-ie, O?

Now   Na - ture   cleeds   the   flow - ery   lea,   And

a'   is   young   and   sweet   like   thee,   O

wilt thou share its joys wi' me, And   say thou'll be my dear-ie, O?

(Chorus)
Lassie wi' the lint-white locks,
    Bonie lassie, artless lassie,
Wilt thou wi' me tent the flocks
    Wilt thou be my dearie, O?

Now Nature cleeds the flowery lea,
    And a' is young and sweet like thee,
O wilt thou share its joys wi' me,
    And say thou'll be my dearie, O?

The primrose bank, the wimpling burn,
    The cuckoo on the milk-white thorn,
The wanton lambs at early morn
    Shall welcome thee, my dearie, O.

377

And when the welcome simmer shower
  Has cheer'd ilk drooping little flower,
We'll to the breathing woodbine-bower
  At sultry noon, my dearie, O.

When Cynthia lights wi' silver ray,
  The weary shearer's hameward way,
Thro' yellow waving fields we'll stray,
  And talk o' love, my dearie, O.

And when the howling wintry blast
  Disturbs my lassie's midnight rest,
Enclasped to my faithfu' breast,
  I'll comfort thee, my dearie, O.

Bremner's Scots Reels (1759) no. 42 - the air
McGlashan's Strathspey Reels (1780) no. 17 - the air
Thomson's Select Collection Of Original Scotish Airs (1801) no. 121
Read Burns' letter to Thomson, November 1794, regarding the air 'Rothiemurche's Rant'

Song 84
My Nanie's Awa

Very Slow And Pathetic   *Tune : There Are Few Good Fellows When Jamie's Awa*

Now in her green mantle blythe Nature arrays,
  And listens the lambkins that bleat o'er the braes,
While birds warble welcomes in ilka green shaw,
  But to me it's delightless My Nanie's awa.

The snawdrop and primrose our woodlands adorn,
  And violets bathe in the weet o' the morn;
They pain my sad bosom, sae sweetly they blaw,
  They mind me o' Nanie and Nanie's awa!

Thou lav'rock that springs frae the dews of the lawn
  The shepherd to warn o' the grey-breaking dawn,
And thou mellow mavis, that hails the night-fa',
  Give over for pity My Nanie's awa.

Come Autumn, sae pensive in yellow and grey,
  And soothe me wi' tidings o' Nature's decay!
The dark, dreary Winter, and wild-driving snaw
  Alane can delight me now Nanie's awa.

379

Oswald's Curious Scots Tunes (1740) no 22 – the air is dedicated to Frederick, Prince of Wales

McGibbon's Scots Tunes (1742) no. 30 – the air entitled 'Ther'll Never Be Peace Till Jamie Comes Hame'
Caledonian Pocket Companion (1743) I no. 20 – the air
Thomson's Select Collection Of Original Scotish Airs (1799) no. 99

The words have also been set to the air 'Cooleen'

Song 85
O May Thy Morn

Slow And Poignant   *Tune : The Rashes*

O May, thy morn was ne'er sae sweet As the mirk night o' De - cem - ber! For

spark - ling was the ro - sy wine, And pri - vate was the cham - ber, And

dear was she I dare na name, But I will ay re - mem - ber, And

dear was she I dare na name, But I will ay re - mem - ber

O May, thy morn was ne'er sae sweet
   As the mirk night o' December!
For sparkling was the rosy wine,
   And private was the chamber,
And dear was she I dare na name,
   But I will ay remember:

And here's to them that, like oursel,
   Can push about the jorum!
And here's to them that wish us weel –
   May a' that's guid watch o'er 'em!
And here's to them, we dare na tell,
   The dearest o' the quorum!

Caledonian Pocket Companion XI no. 23 – the air entitled 'When The King Comes O'er The Water'
Oswald's Companion (1753) V no. 26 – the air
Hastie Manuscript f. 141

Set to a different air in the Scots Musical Museum (1796) no. 464 signed B, Written for this Work by R. Burns

The air 'The Rashes' has Jacobite associations, the music, altered from Oswald's Companion, is now known as 'The Wee, Wee German Lairdie'

Song 86
Lovely Polly Stewart

Lively And Merrily   *Tune : Ye're Welcome Charlie Stewart*

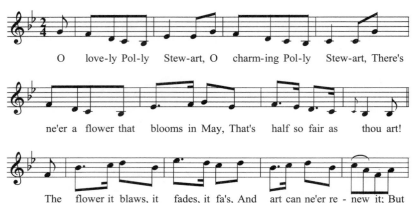

O love-ly Pol-ly Stew-art, O charm-ing Pol-ly Stew-art, There's

ne'er a flower that blooms in May, That's half so fair as thou art!

The flower it blaws, it fades, it fa's, And art can ne'er re - new it; But

worth and truth e - ter-nal youth Will gie to Pol-ly Stew-art.

(Chorus)
O lovely Polly Stewart,
　O charming Polly Stewart,
There's ne'er a flower that blooms in May,
　That's half as fair as thou art!

The flower it blaws, it fades, it fa's,
　And art can ne'er renew it;
But worth and truth eternal youth
　Will gie to Polly Stewart.

May he,whase arms shall fauld thy charms
　Possess a leal and true heart!
To him be given to ken the heaven
　He grasps in Polly Stewart!

Walsh's Caledonian Country Dances (1736) – the air entitled 'The Confederacy'
Bremner's Reels (1758) no. 40 - the air entitled 'Queensberry House'
Aird's Airs (1782) I no 101 – the air
Scots Musical Museum (1796) no. 471 Written for this Work by R. Burns
Hastie Manuscript f. 146

382

Song 87
Can I Cease To Care

Slow And Pathetic   *Tune : Ay Waukin' O*

Long, long the night, Hea-vy comes the mor-row,

While my soul's de-light Is on her bed of sor-row.

Can I cease to care, Can I cease to lan-guish,

While my dar-ling fair Is on the couch of an-guish.

(Chorus)
Long, long the night,
Heavy comes the morrow,
While my soul's delight
Is on her bed of sorrow.

Can I cease to care,
Can I cease to languish,
While my darling fair
Is on the couch of anguish.

Ev'ry hope is fled,
Ev'ry fear is terror;
Slumber ev'n I dread,
Ev'ry dream is horror.

Hear me, Powers Divine:
O, in pity, hear me!
Take aught else of mine,
But my Chloris spare me!

Herd Manuscript – a fragment
Napier's Scots Songs (1790) I no. 61 – from the manuscript of Robert Riddell
See Scots Musical Museum nos. 213 & 382 for origin of the air
Ritson's Scottish Songs (1794) I no. 47
Currie (1800)
Thomson's Select Collection Of Original Scotish Airs (1801) no 111

A sheet song, entitled 'Jess Macfarlan' was issued in 1793 to the music 'Ay Waukin O'.
Jess was reported as being a 'nondescript beauty in Edinburgh about 1740'.

Song 88
Their Groves O' Sweet Myrtle

Moderate And Expressive　　　　　　　*Tune : Humours Of Glen*

Their groves o' sweet myr-tle let for-eign lands reck-on, Where

bright beam - ing sum - mers ex - alt the per - fume! Far

dear - er to me yon lone glen o' green breck - an, Wi' the

burn steal - ing un - der the lang, yel - low broom; Far

dear - er to me are yon hum - ble broom bow - ers, Where the

blue-bell and go-wan lurk low-ly, un-seen; For there, light-ly trip-ping, a-

- mang the wild flow-ers, A - list'-ning the lin-net, aft wan-ders my Jean.

Their groves o' sweet myrtle let foreign lands reckon,
  Where bright beaming summers exalt the perfume!
Far dearer to me yon lone glen o' green breckan,
  Wi' the burn stealing under the lang, yellow broom;
Far dearer to me are yon humble broom bowers,
  Where the blue-bell and gowan lurk lowly, unseen;
For there, lightly tripping amang the wild flowers,
  A-list'ning the linnet, aft wanders my Jean.

Tho' rich is the breeze in their gay, sunny vallies.
  And cauld Caledonia's blast on the wave,
Their sweet-scented woodlands that skirt the proud palace,
  What are they? – The haunt of the tyrant and slave!
The slave's spicy forests and gold-bubbling fountains
  The brave Caledonian views with disdain:
He wanders as free as the winds of his mountains,
  Save Love's willing fetters – the chains o' his Jean.

(Song was written for either Jean Armour or Jean Lorimer)

McLean's Scot's Tunes (1772) no. 31 - the air
Thomson's Select Collection Of Original Scotish Airs (1799) no. 95
Scots Musical Museum (1803) no. 567 – Source of the air.

The air was used in John O'Keefe's opera 'The Poor Soldier'

Traditionally in Ireland, the air was assigned to a family by the name of 'Power' round about the middle of the eighteenth century, who owned an estate near Clonmel.   Glyn or Glen being a small country village midway between Carrick and Clonmel on the river Suir, near Waterford.

Song 89
'Twas Na Her Bonie Blue E'e

Slow And Tender　　　　　　　　　*Tune : Laddie Lie Near Me*

'Twas na her bo - nie blue e'e was my ru - in,

Fair tho' she be, that was ne'er my un - do - ing;

'Twas the dear smile when nae - bo - dy did mind us,

'Twas the be - witch-ing, sweet, stown glance o' kind - ness.

'Twas na her bonie blue e'e was my ruin,
　　Fair tho' she be, that was ne'er my undoing;
'Twas the dear smile when naebody did mind us,
　　'Twas the bewitching, sweet, stown glance o' kindness.

Sair do I fear that to hope is denied me,
　　Sair do I fear that despair maun abide me;
But tho' fell Fortune should fate us to sever,
　　Queen shall she be in my bosom forever.

Chloris, I'm thine wi' a passion sincerest,
　　And thou hast plighted me love o' the dearest,
And thou'rt the angel that never can alter –
　　Sooner the sun in his motion would falter!

Caledonian Pocket Companion (c1760) XII no. 5 – the air
McGibbon's Scots Tunes (1768) IV no. 116 – the air
Original of 'Laddie Lie Near Me' was written by a Dr Blacklock of Edinburgh and is in the
Scots Musical Museum (1790) no. 218 – the air.
Currie (1800)

Song 90
O Lay Thy Loof In Mine Lass

Moderate With Pleasure   *Tune : The Cordwainer's March*

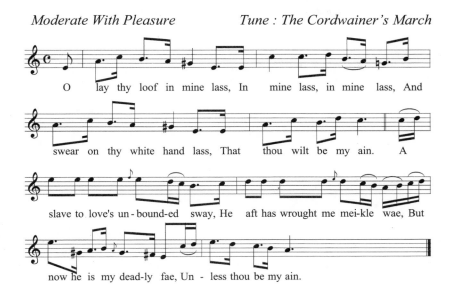

O lay thy loof in mine lass, In mine lass, in mine lass, And
swear on thy white hand lass, That thou wilt be my ain. A
slave to love's un-bound-ed sway, He aft has wrought me mei-kle wae, But
now he is my dead-ly fae, Un-less thou be my ain.

(Chorus)
O lay thy loof in mine lass,
  In mine, lass, in mine lass,
And swear on thy white hand lass,
  That thou wilt be my ain.

A slave to love's unbounded sway,
  He aft has wrought me meikle wae,
But now he is my deadly fae,
  Unless thou be my ain.

There's monie a lass has broke my rest,
  That for a blink I hae lo'ed best;
But thou art queen within my breast,
  For ever to remain.

Aird's Airs (1782) I no 176 - the air is entitled either 'The Cordwainer's March' or 'The Shoemaker's March'

Scots Musical Museum (1803) no. 574 signed B, Written for this Work by R. Burns

Song 91
Mark Yonder Pomp

Cheerfully With Attitude   *Tune : De'il Tak The Wars*

Mark yon - der pomp of cost - ly fa - shion, Round the weal - thy,

ti - tled bride: But when comp - ared with re - al pas - sion,

Poor is all that prince - ly pride. What are their sho-wy treas-ures,

What are their noi - sy pleas - ures, The gay, gau - dy glare of

va - ni - ty and art: The po - lish'd je - wel's blaze May

draw the won - d'ring gaze, And court - ly gran - deur bright The

fan-cy may de-light, But ne-ver, ne-ver can come near the heart

Mark yonder pomp of costly fashion,
  Round the wealthy, titled bride!
But when compared with real passion,
  Poor is all that princely pride.
  What are their showy treasures,
  What are their noisy pleasures,
The gay, gaudy glare of vanity and art:
  The polish'd jewel's blaze
  May draw the wond'ring gaze,
  And courtly grandeur bright
  The fancy may delight,
But never, never can come near the heart.

But did you see my dearest Chloris,
  In simplicity's array;
Lovely as yonder sweet opening flower is,
  Shrinking from the gaze of day.
  O then, the heart alarming,
  And all resistless charming,
In love's delightful fetters, she chains the willing soul!
  Ambition would disown
  The world's imperial crown
  Ev'n Avarice would envy
  His worshipp'd deity,
And feel thro' every being love's raptures roll.

Thomson's Select Collection Of Scotish Airs (1805) no. 157

For musical line of 'De'il Tak the Wars' refer to song no 81

Song 92
Forlorn My Love

Moderate And Gentle　　　　*Tune : Will You Lend Me Your Loom Lass*

O wert thou love, but near me, but near, near, near me, How kind-ly thou wouldst chear me, And min - gle sighs with mine, love! For - lorn, my love, no com - fort near, Far, far from thee I wan - der here; Far, far from thee, the fate se - vere, At which I most re - pine, love.

(Chorus)
O wert thou love, but near me,
　　But near, near, near me,
How kindly thou would chear me,
　　And mingle sighs with mine, love!

Forlorn, my love, no comfort near,
　　Far, far from thee I wander here;
Far, far from thee, the fate severe,
　　At which I most repine, love.

Around me scowls a wintry sky,
　　Blasting each bud of hope and joy,
And shelter, shade, nor home have I,
　　Save in these arms of thine, love.

Cold, alter'd friendship's cruel part,
　To poison fortune's ruthless dart!
Let me not break thy faithful heart,
　And say that fate is mine, love!

But, dreary tho' the moments fleet,
　O, let me think we yet shall meet!
That only ray of solace sweet
　Can on thy Chloris shine, love!

Leyden Manuscript (1685) – the air entitled 'The Goune New Made'
Margaret Sinkler's Manuscript (1710) – the air entitled 'I Would Have My Goune Made'

Caledonian Pocket Companion (1752) IV no. 21 – the air ''Will You Lend Me Your Loom,
Lass

Scots Musical Museum (1792) no. 311 – words set to the air 'Let Me In This Ae Night'
Dale's Scots Songs (1794) II no. 97
Currie (1800)
Thomson's Select Collection Of Original Scotish Airs (1805) no. 156 – the air
Dalhousie Manuscript

Song 93
Why, Why Tell Thy Lover

Slow And Tender   *Tune : Caledonian Hunt's Delight*

Why, why tell thy lo - ver, Bliss he ne - ver must en-joy;

Why, why un - de-ceive him, And give all his hopes the lie?

Oh why, while fan - cy, rap - tured, slum - bers,

Chlo - ris, Chlo - ris all the theme, Why, why

would'st thou cru - el Wake thy lo - ver from his dream?

For history of the air, see song no. 47

Song 94
This Is No My Ain Lassie

Lively And Cheerily   *Tune : This Is No My Ain Hoose*

This is no my ain las - sie, Fair tho' the las - sie be:

Weel ken I my ain las - sie, Kind love is in her e'e. I

see a form, I see a face, Ye weel may wi' the fair-est place, It

wants to me the witch-ing grace, The kind love that's in her e'e.

(Chorus)
This is no my ain lassie,
   Fair tho' the lassie be:
Weel ken I my ain lassie,
   Kind love is in her e'e.

I see a form, I see a face,
Ye weel may wi' the fairest place:
It wants to me the witching grace,
   The kind love that's in her e'e.

She's bonie, blooming, straight, and tall,
And lang has had my heart in thrall;
And aye it charms my very saul,
   The kind love that's in her e'e.

A thief sae pawkie is my Jean,
To steal a blink by a' unseen!
But gleg as light are lover's een,
   When kind love is in the e'e.

It may escape the courtly sparks,
It may escape the learned clerks;
But well the watching lover marks
The kind love that's in her e'e.

Blaikie's Manuscript (1692) – the air entitled 'This Is No My Ain House' or 'Abbeyhill's Rant'

Ramsay's Miscellany (1725) – words and music
Orpheus Caledonius (1733) II no. 32 - the air plus words
Caledonian Pocket Companion (1759) XI no. 8 - the air
Herd's Scots Songs (1769) no. 190
Aird's Airs (1782) II no 176 – the air
Thomson's Select Collection Of Scotish Airs (1799) no. 56

Song 95
O Bonie Was Yon Rosy Brier

Moderate And Tender　　　　　　　*Tune : I Wish My Love Were In A Mire*

O, bon-ie was yon ro - sy brier That blooms sae far frae haunt o' man, and bon-ie she And ah, how dear! It shad-ed frae the e'en-in' sun. Yon rose-buds in the morn - ing dew, How pure a-mang the leaves sae green But pur - er was the lo - ver's vow They wit-ness'd in their shade yestr-een.

O, bonie was yon rosy brier
　That blooms sae far frae haunt o' man,
And bonie she and ah, how dear!
　It shaded frae the e'enin' sun.

Yon rosebuds in the morning dew,
　How pure amang the leaves sae green
But purer was the lover's vow
　They witnessed in their shade yestreen.

All in its rude and prickly bower,
That crimson rose, how sweet and fair!
But love is far a sweeter flower
Amid life's thorny path o' care.

The pathless wild and wimpling burn,
　Wi' Chloris in my arms, be mine,
And I the warld nor wish, nor scorn
　Its joy and griefs alike resign!

Crockatt's Manuscript (1709) – the air
Orpheus Caledonius (1725) no. 5 – the air set to different words by a Mr Phillips
Ramsay's Musick (c1726) – the air
Craig's Scots Tunes (1730) no. 31 – the air

Orpheus Caledonius (1733) no. 5 (The air – Burns choice, Thomson put the words to another tune)

McGibbon's Scots Tunes (1742) no. 15 – the air
Caledonian Pocket Companion (1754) VI no. 9 – the air
Bremner's Scots Songs (2nd Series) 1757 no. 7 – the air
Scots Musical Museum (1787) no. 41
Thomson's Select Collection Of Original Scotish Airs (1801) no. 115

The words have also been set to the air 'The Wee Wee Man'

Song 96
O That's The Lassie O' My Heart

Slow And Wistful   *Tune : Morag*

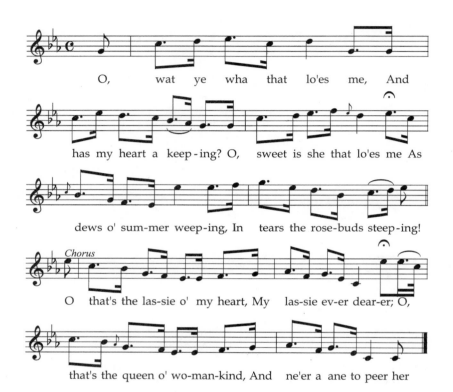

O, wat ye wha that lo'es me, And

has my heart a keep-ing? O, sweet is she that lo'es me As

dews o' sum-mer weep-ing, In tears the rose-buds steep-ing!

Chorus

O that's the las-sie o' my heart, My las-sie ev-er dear-er; O,

that's the queen o' wo-man-kind, And ne'er a ane to peer her

(Chorus)
O, that's the lassie o' my heart,
   My lassie ever dearer!
O, that's the queen o' womankind,
   And ne'er a ane to peer her!

O, wat ye wha that lo'es me,
   And has my heart a keeping?
O, sweet is she that lo'es me
   As dews o' summer weeping,
   In tears the rosebuds steeping.

If thou shall meet a lassie
  In grace and beauty charming,
That e'en thy chosen lassie,
  Erewhile thy breast sae warming,
  Had ne'er sic powers alarming: -

If thou hadst heard her talking
  (And thy attention plighted),
That ilka body talking
  But her by thee is slighted,
  And thou art all-delighted:-

If thou hast met this fair one,
  When frae her thou hast parted,
If every other fair one
  But her thou hast deserted,
  And thou art broken-hearted.

Fraser's Highland Airs no. 119 – reported to be a bad copy of the air
Dow's Scots Music (c1776) no. 46 – the air
Scots Musical Museum (1788) no. 143
Thomson's Select Collection Of Original Scotish Airs (1799) no. 67

Read Burns letter to Mrs Elizabeth Rose of Kilravock, cousin to Henry Mackenzie, dated 17th February 1788. Burns also enclosed a copy of volume II of the Scots Musical Museum with the letter.

The air 'Morag' is an old Highland air Burns learned at Kilravock during his Highland tour of 1787

Song 97
I'll Ay Ca' In By Yon Town

Lively And Merrily   *Tune : I'll Gae Nae Mair Tae Yon Toon*

I'll ay ca' in by yon town And by yon gar-den

green a-gain! I'll ay ca' in by yon town, And

see my bon-ie Jean a-gain. There's nane sall ken, there's

nane sall guess What brings me back the gate a-gain, But

she, my fair-est faith-fu' lass, And stow'n-lins we sall meet a-gain.

(Chorus)
I'll ay ca' in by yon town
   And by yon garden green again!
I'll ay ca' in by yon town,
   And see my bonie Jean again.

There's nane sall ken, there's nane sall guess
   What brings me back the gate again,
But she, my fairest faithfu' lass,
   And stow'nlins we sall meet again.

She'll wander by the aiken tree,
   When trystin time draws near again;
And when her lovely form I see,
   O haith! she's doubly dear again.

Bremner's Scots Reels (1757) I no. 6 - the air
Campbell's Reels (1778) no 17 – the air
Aird's Airs (1782) I no. 35 - the air
Bowie's Reels (1789) – the air
Scots Musical Museum (1796) no. 458
Hastie Manuscript f. 137

Song 98
Here's A Health To Ane I Lo'e Dear

Lively With Tenderness   *Tune : Here's A Health To Them That's Awa*

Here's a health to ane I lo'e dear! Here's a health to ane I lo'e dear! Thou art sweet as the smile when fond lo-vers meet, And soft as their par-ting tear, Jes-sie. Al-tho' thou maun ne-ver be mine, Al-though e-ven hope is de-nied; 'Tis swee-ter for thee de-spai-ring, Than aught in the world be-side, Jes-sie.

(Chorus)
Here's a health to ane I lo'e dear!
   Here's a health to ane I lo'e dear!
Thou art sweet as the smile when fond lovers meet,
   And soft as their parting tear, Jessie.

Altho' thou maun never be mine,
   Altho' even hope is denied;
'Tis sweeter for thee despairing
   Than aught in the world beside, Jessie.

I mourn thro' the gay, gaudy day,
   As hopeless I muse on thy charms;
But welcome the dream o' sweet slumber!
   For then I am lockt in thine arms, Jessie.

I guess by the dear angel smile,
 I guess by the love-rolling e'e;
But what urge the tender confession,
 'Gainst Fortune's fell cruel decree, Jessie.

Scots Musical Museum (1796) no. 412 – the air
Thomson's Select Collection Of Original Scotish Airs (1799) no. 75

A copy of this song, possibly corrected was sent to Alexander Cunningham from Burns on 12th July 1796, with the enclosure "the last I made or probably will make for some time", though the song was originally sent to George Thomson in May 1796.

'The Songs of Robert Burns' by James C. Dick, published 1903, includes the third verse which is given here. Most other publications include only two verses.

The song that is accepted as the last that Burns wrote is 'Fairest Maid On Devon Banks' also dated 12th July 1796, with no earlier copy to date.

Song 99
O Wert Thou In The Cauld Blast

Slow And Heartfelt   *Tune : Lenox Love To Blantyre*

O, wert thou in the cauld blast On yon-der lea, on yon-der lea, My

plaid-ie to the an-gry airt, I'd shel-ter thee, I'd shel-ter thee; Or

did Mis-for-tune's bit-ter storms A - round thee blaw, a-round thee blaw, Thy

bield should be my bo - som, To share it a', to share it a'.

O, wert thou in the cauld blast
  On yonder lea, on yonder lea,
My plaidie to the angry airt,
  I'd shelter thee, I'd shelter thee;
Or did Misfortune's bitter storms
  Around thee blaw, around thee blaw,
Thy bield should be my bosom,
  To share it a', to share it a'.

Or were I in the wildest waste,
  Sae black and bare, sae black and bare,
The desert were a Paradise,
  If thou wert there, if thou wert there;
Or were I monarch o' the globe,
  Wi' thee to reign, wi' thee to reign,
The brightest jewel in my crown
  Wad be my queen, wad be my queen.

Margaret Sinkler's Manuscript (1710) - the air
Bremner's Reels (1757) no. 17 – the air
Stewart's Reels (1761) no. 9 – the air
Campbell's Reels (1778) no 13 – the air
Scots Musical Museum (1796) no. 483 – the air to the old song 'The Wren Shoe'
Currie Second Edition (1801)
Thomson's Select Collection Of Original Scotish Airs (1818) no. 219

The words to the above song are generally sung today to music composed by Felix
Mendelssohn, on 17th October 1742

The story of the name of the air 'Lenox Love To Blantyre' is as follows
Frances Theresa Stewart, daughter of Walter Stewart, (son of the second Lord Blantyre),
born c1647, was the original of the emblem of Britannia on the coinage.   She married
Charles Stuart, forth Duke of Richmond and Lenox.   She died in 1702, leaving a
considerable property to her nephew, Alexander, fifth Lord Blantyre, requesting that an
estate should be purchased in East Lothian, to be named 'Lenox Love to Blantyre'.

Song 100
Altho' My Back Be At The Wa'

Lively With Abandon　　　　　　　　*Tune : The Job Of Journey Work*

Al - tho' my back be at the wa', And tho' he be the fau-tor, Al-
- tho' my back be at the wa', Yet here's his health in wa-ter! O,
wae gae by his wan-ton sides, Sae braw-lie's he could flat-ter, Till
for his sake I'm sligh-ted sair, And dree the kin - tra clat-ter! But,
tho' my back be at the wa', Yet here's his health in wa-ter!

Aird's Airs (1788) III no. 401 — the air
Scots Musical Museum (1796) no. 480, signed Z
Hastie Manuscript f 128

Song 101
Here's To Thy Health My Bonie Lass

Moderate With Attitude   *Tune : The Laggan Burn*

Here's to thy health, my bonie lass; Gude night and joy be wi' thee; I'll come nae mair to thy bower-door To tell thee that I lo'e thee. O, dinna think, my pretty pink, But I can live without thee. I vow and swear, I dinna care How lang ye look about ye!

Here's to thy health, my bonie lass;
  Gude night and joy be wi' thee;
I'll come nae mair tae thy bower-door
  To tell thee that I lo'e thee.
O, dinna think, my pretty pink,
  But I can live without thee.
I vow and swear, I dinna care
  How lang ye look about ye.

Thou'rt ay sae free informing me
  Thou hast nae mind to marry.
I'll be as free informing thee
  Nae time hae I to tarry:
I ken thy freens try ilka means
  Frae wedlock to delay thee;
(Depending on some higher chance),
  But fortune may betray thee.

404

I ken they scorn my low estate
　　But that does never grieve me,
For I'm as free as ony he,
　　Sma' siller will relieve me!
I'll count my health my greatest wealth
　　Sae lang as I'll enjoy it.
I'll fear nae scant, I'll bode nae want
　　As lang's I get employment.

But far off fowls hae feathers fair,
　　And, ay until ye try them,
Tho' they seem fair, still have a care,
　　They may prove as bad as I am.
But at twal at night, when the moon shines bright,
　　My dear I'll come and see thee.
For the man that loves mistress weel,
　　Nae travel makes him weary.

(May not have been meant for Maria Riddell, but has been suggested it was)

Scots Musical Museum (1796) no. 495 signed B, Written for this Work by R. Burns
Hastie Manuscript f 160

Although Johnson states it was written by Burns, this appears to be a revision of an older
song. There is a note in Burns' handwriting at Alloway stating 'as far as I can recollect the
compilation of an illiterate Millwright, about thirty or forty years ago, somewhere in Ayr-
shire'. To date there seems to be no trace of the older version of the song.

Song 102
Fairest Maid On Devon Banks

Slow And Pensive   *Tune : Rothiemurche's Rant*

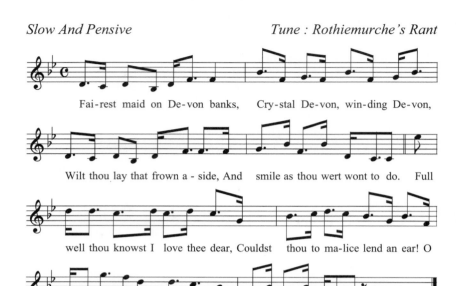

Fai-rest maid on De-von banks,   Cry-stal De-von, win-ding De-von,

Wilt thou lay that frown a - side, And   smile as thou wert wont to do.   Full

well thou knowst I love thee dear, Couldst   thou to ma-lice lend an ear! O

did not love ex-claim. 'For-bear, Nor   use a faith-ful lo-ver so'.

(Chorus)
Fairest maid on Devon banks,
   Crystal Devon, winding Devon,
Wilt thou lay that frown aside,
   And smile as thou were wont to do?

Full well thou know'st I love thee dear –
   Couldst thou to malice lend an ear!
O, did not love exclaim – 'Forbear,
   Nor use a faithful lover so!'

Then come, thou fairest of the fair,
   Those wonted smiles, O, let me share,
And by thy beauteous self I swear
   No love but thine my heart shall know!

(Burns' last song written on 12th July 1796)

Thomson's Select Collection Of Original Scotish Airs (1801) no. 121
Read Burns letter to George Thomson dated 12th July 1796
For information on the air 'Rothiemurche's Rant' see song no. 83

PART THREE
Chapter Two – Notes to the Songs

All the notes quoted are taken from remarks or letters written by Robert Burns, and to his spelling, unless otherwise stated.

Song 1 - Handsome Nell (Tune – Untitled In Scots Musical Museum)
'For my own part I never had the least thought or inclination of turning Poet till I got once heartily in Love, and then Rhyme and Song were, in a manner, the spontaneous language of my heart.   The following composition was the first of my performances, and done in an early period of life, when my heart glowed with honest warm simplicity, unacquainted and uncorrupted with the ways of a wicked world…The subject of it was a young girl who really deserved all the praises I have bestowed on her.   I not only had this opinion of Her then – but actually I think so still, now that the spell is long since broken, and the inchantment at an end'.
(First Commonplace Book, August 1783)

Song 2 - Now Westlin Winds (Tune - Port Gordon)
'Here, though I learned to look unconcernedly on a large tavern-bill, and mix without fear in a drunken squabble, yet I went on with a high hand in my Geometry; till the sun enter Virgo, a month which is always a carnival in my bosom, a charming Fillette who lived next door to the school overset my Trigonometry and set me off on a tangent from the sphere of my studies'.   *(Letter to Dr John Moore, 2nd August 1787)*

Song 3 - I Dream'd I Lay (Tune - I Dream'd I Lay)
'These two stanzas I composed when I was seventeen, and are among the oldest of my printed pieces'.
(Burns' notes in Scots Musical Museum, song 146)

Song 4 - My Nanie O (Tune - My Nanie O)
'I am of opinion that my ballad of 'Nanie O' might perhaps do for one set of verses to the name.   Now don't let it enter into your head that you are under any necessity of taking my verses.   I have long ago made up my mind as to my own reputation in the business of authorship; & have nothing to be pleased, or offended at, in your adoption or rejection of my verses.   In the printed copy of 'My Nanie O', the name of the river is horribly prosaic – I will alter it.   'Girvan' is the river that suits the idea of the stanza best, but 'Lugar' is the most agreeable modulation of syllables'.
(Letter to George Thomson, Friday night, 26th October 1792)

Song 5 - O Tibbie, I Hae Seen The Day (Tune - Invercauld's Reel)
'This song I composed about the age of seventeen'.

Song 6 - The Lass Of Cessnock Banks (Tune – The Butcher Boy)

'I ought in good manners to have acknowledged the receipt of your letter before this time, but my heart was so shocked with the contents of it, that I can scarcely yet collect my thoughts so as to write to you on the subject. I will not attempt to describe what I felt on receiving your letter. I read it over and over again, and though it was in the politest language of refusal, still it was peremptory; 'you were sorry you could not make me a return, but you wish me' what without you I can never obtain, 'you wish me all kinds of happiness'. It would be weak and unmanly to say that without you I never can be happy; but sure I am, that sharing life with you, would have giving it a relish, that, wanting you I can never taste'.
(Letter to Elizabeth Gebbie/Ellison Begbie, June 1781?)

Song 7 – The Rigs O' Barley (Tune – Corn Rigs Are Bonie)

''My Patie is a lover gay', is also unequal. 'His mind is never muddy'. Is a muddy expression indeed. This is surely far unworthy of Ramsay, or your book. My Song, 'Rigs of barley', does not altogether please me, but if I can mend it, & thresh a few loose sentiments out of it, I shall submit it to your consideration'. *(Letter to George Thomson, 7th April 1795)*

Song 8 – Farewell To Eliza/From Thee Eliza (Tune – Gilderoy)

'…excuse my vanity, you should for 'Gilderoy' prefer my own song 'From thee Eliza, I must go'.
(Burns' first letter to George Thomson, 16th September 1792)

Song 9 – Montgomerie's Peggy (Tune – Galla Water)

'The following fragment is done, something in the imitation of the manner of a noble old Scottish piece called 'McMillan's Peggy', and sings to the tune of 'Galla Water'. My Mongomerie's Peggy was my deity for six, or eight months. She had been bred, tho' as the world says, without any just pretence for it, in a style of life rather elegant'.
(First Commonplace Book, September 1785)

Song 10 – My Girl She's Airy (Tune – Black Joke)

'My ailing child is got better – and the mother is certainly in for it again *(Jean Armour)* – and Peggy *(May Cameron?)* will bring a half-Highlander – and I shall get a farm, and keep them all about my hand, and breed them in the fear of the Lord and an oakstick, and I shall be the happiest man upon earth. Take the following random verses to the tune of 'Black Joke' – 'My girl she's airy, she's buxom and gay'. *(Letter to Robert Ainslie 29th July 1787)*

Song 11 – Mary Morison (Tune – Duncan Davidson)

'The song prefixed is one of my juvenile works. I leave it among your hands. I do not think it very remarkable, either for its merits, or demerits. It is impossible, at least I feel it in my stinted powers, to be always original, entertaining & witty'. *(Letter to George Thomson, 20th March 1793)*

Song 12 – The Belles Of Mauchline (Tune – Bonie Dundee)
'Miss Armour is now known by the designation of Mrs Burns'.
(Glenriddell Manuscript)

Song 13 – O Leave Novels (Tune – Ye Mauchline Belles)

Song 14 – The Mauchline Lady
(Tune – I Had A Horse And I Had Nae Mair)
'This story was founded on fact. A John Hunter, ancestor to a very respectable farming family who live in a place in the parish, I think, of Galston called Barr-mill, was the luckless hero that 'had a horse and had nae mair'. For some little youthful follies he found it necessary to make a retreat to the West-Highlands where, 'he fee'd himself to a Highland laird', for that is the expression on all the oral traditions of the song I ever heard. The present Mr Hunter, who told me the anecdote, is great-grandchild to our hero'. *(Burns' notes in the Scots Musical Museum, song 185)*

Song 15 - The Fornicator (Tune - Clout The Caudron)
'A tradition is mentioned in the 'Bee' that the second Bishop Chisholm, of Dunblane, used to say that, if he were going to be hanged, nothing would soothe his mind so much by the way as to hear 'Clout The Caldron' played. I have met with another tradition, that the old song to this tune

> Hae ye onie pots or pans, Or onie broken chanlers?

was composed by one of the Kenmure Family, in the Cavalier times, and alluded to an amour he had, while under hiding, in the disguise of an itinerant tinker. The air is also known by the name of 'The Blacksmith And His Apron', which, from the rhythm, seems to have been a line of some old song to the same tune'.
(Notes, said to be by Burns, taken from Cromek's 'Reliques of Robert Burns')

Song 16 - Young Peggy (Tune - Loch Eroch Side)
'Permit me to present you with the inclosed SONG, as a small, tho' grateful tribute for the honour of your acquaintance. I have, in these verses, attempted some faint sketches of your Portrait, in the unembellished simple manner of descriptive TRUTH. Flattery, I leave to your Lovers; whose exaggerating Fancies may make them imagine you still nearer, if possible, to Perfection than you really are'.
(Letter to Margaret Kennedy, circa early October 1785)

Song 17 - The Braes O' Ballochmyle (Tune - The Braes O' Ballochmyle)
'This air is the composition of my friend Allan Masterton, in Edinburgh. I composed the verses on the amiable and excellent family of Whitefoord's leaving Ballochmyle, when Sir John's misfortune had obliged him to sell the estate'. *(Burns' notes in Scots Musical Museum, song 276)*

Song 18 - The Rantin Dog The Daddie O'T
(Tune - Whare Wad Bonie Annie Ly)

'I composed this song pretty early in life, and sent it to a young girl, a very particular friend of mine, who was at that time under a cloud'.   *(Burns' notes in Scots Musical Museum, song 277, to 'East Nook O' Fife')*

Song 19 - The Lament (Tune - Scots Queen)

'For the tune of the 'Scotch Queen', in Oswald; take the two first, and the two last stanzas of the Poem entitled, 'The Lament' in Burns' Poems'. *(Letter to James Johnson, circa October/November 1787)*

Song 20 - Lass Of Ballochmyle (Tune - Ettrick Banks)

'I think, myself, it has some merit; both as a tolerable description of one of nature's sweetest scenes, a July evening; & one of the finest pieces of Nature's workmanship, the finest indeed we know any thing of, an amiable, beautiful young woman: but I have no common friend to procure me that permission, without which I would not dare to spread the copy'. *(Letter to Catherine Stewart of Stair, September 1786)*

'The inclosed Song was the work of my return home: and perhaps but poorly answers what might have been expected from such a scene.   I am going to print a second Edition of my Poems, but cannot insert these verses without your permission'.   *(Letter to Wilhelmina Alexander, 18th November 1786)*

'My two songs on Miss W. Alexander and Miss P. Kennedy (*Young Peggy*) were likewise tried yesterday by a jury of Literati, and found defamatory libels against the fastidious Powers of Poesy and Taste, and the author forbid to print them under pain of forfeiture of character.   I cannot help almost shedding a tear to the memory of two Songs that cost me some pains, and that I valued a good deal, but I must submit'.   *(Letter to Gavin Hamilton, 8th March 1787)*

Song 21 - The Highland Lassie O (Tune - McLauchlin's Scots Measure)

'This was a composition of mine in very early life, before I was known at all in the world.   My Highland Lassie was a warm-hearted charming young creature as ever blessed a man with generous love.   After a pretty long tract of the most ardent reciprocal attachment, we met by appointment, on the second Sunday of May, in a sequestered spot by the Banks of Ayr, where we spent the day in taking a farewell, before she should embark for the West Highlands, to arrange matters among her friends for our projected change of life.   At the close of autumn following she crossed the sea to greet me at Greenock, where she had scarce landed when she was seized with a malignant fever, which hurried my dear girl to the grave in a few days, before I could even hear of her illness'.
(Notes, said to be by Burns, taken from Cromek's 'Reliques of Robert Burns')

Song 22 – Tho' Cruel Fate (Tune – She Rose And Let Me In)

'The old set of this song (She raisse and loot me in), which is still to be found in printed collections, is much prettier than this; but somebody, I believe it was Ramsay, took it into his head to clear it of some indelicacies, and made it at once more chaste and more dull'. *(Burns notes in Scots Musical Museum, song 83)*

Song 23 - Again Rejoicing Nature Sees (Tune - Jockey's Grey Breeks)

In the Museum the tune 'Johnny's Grey Breeks' is put to the words of 'The Gentle Swain', an Anglicisation of 'Jockie's Gray Breeks'. Burns notes say 'To sing such a beautiful air to such damned verses, is downright sodomy of Common Sense! The Scots verses are indeed tolerable'.

'Though this has certainly every evidence of being a Scottish air, yet there is a well known tune and song in the North of Ireland called 'The Weaver And His Shuttle O', which, though sung much quicker, is every note the very same'. *(Burns' notes in Scots Musical Museum, song 27)*

Song 24 - Blythe, Blythe And Merry Was She
(Tune - Andro And His Cutty Gun)

'The song to which it is set in the Museum, is mine; & was composed on Miss Euphemia Murray of Lintrose, commonly & deservedly called, The Flower of Strathmore'. *(Letter to George Thomson, 19th October 1794)*

'I composed these verses while I stayed at Ochtertyre with Sir William Murray. The lady, who was also at Ochtertyre at the same time, was the well-known toast, Miss Euphemia Murray of Lintrose, who was called, and very justly, The Flower of Strathmore'. *(Burns' notes in Scots Musical Museum, song 180)*

Song 25 - My Peggy's Face (Tune - My Peggy's Face)

'I just now have read yours. The poetic compliments I pay cannot be misunderstood. They are neither of them so particular as to point *you* out to the world at large; and the circle of your acquaintances will allow all I have said. I wish to show to the world the odds between a poet's friends, and those of simple prosement. More for your information *both* the pieces go in. One of them 'Where braving all the Winter's Harms' (earlier title for song no 26), is already set – the tune is 'Neil Gow's lamentation for Abercairney; the other is to be set to an old Highland air in Daniel Dow's 'collection of antient Scots music'; the name is *'Ha a Chaillich air mo Dheith'*. *(Letter to Peggy Chalmers, either 6th November or circa December 1787)*

'I hope against I return, you will be able to tell me from Mr CLARKE if these words will suit the tune. If they don't suit, I must think on some other Air; as I have a very strong private reason for wishing them in the 2nd volume. Don't forget to transcribe me the list of the Antiquarian Music. Farewell'. *(Letter to James Johnson, circa mid-November 1787)*

411

Song 26 - Where Braving Angry Winter's Storms
(Tune - Niel Gow's Lamentation For Abercairney)
'This song I composed on one of the most accomplished of women, Miss Peggy Chalmers that was, now Mrs Lewis Hay, of Forbes & Co's bank, Edinr.'. *(Burns' notes in Scots Musical Museum, song 195)*

Song 27 - The Banks Of The Devon (Tune - Bhannerach Dhon Na Chri)
'I won't say the poetry is first-rate; though I am convinced it is very well: and, what is not always the case with compliments to ladies, it is not only *sincere* but *just*'. *(Letter to Peggy Chalmers, circa 1st December 1787)*

'These verses were composed on a charming girl, a Miss Charlotte Hamilton, who is now married to James McKitrick Adair, Esq. physician. She is sister to my worthy friend Gavin Hamilton of Mauchline; and was born on the Banks of Ayr, but was at the time I wrote these lines residing at Herveyston, in Clackmannanshire, on the romantic banks of the little river Devon. I first heard the air from a lady in Inverness, and got the notes taken down for this work'. *(Burns notes in Scots Musical Museum, song 157)*

Song 28 - Your Friendship Much (Tune - Banks Of Spey)
(Revision to Agnes' Poem 'Talk Not of Love').
'Your last verses to me have so delighted me, that I have got an excellent old Scots air that suits the measure, and you shall see them in print in the 'Scots Musical Museum'...The air is 'The banks of Spey', and is most beautiful'...'I want four stanzas; you gave me but three, and one of them alluded to an expression in my former letter; so I have taken your first two verses with a slight alteration in the second, and have added a third, but you must help me to a fourth'. *(Letter to Agnes McLehose, 4th January 1788)*

'Love never more shall give me pain', has long been appropriated to a popular air of the same title, for which reason, in my opinion, it would be improper to set it to 'My lodging is on the cold ground'. There is a song in the Museum, by a ci-devant Goddess of mine, which I think not unworthy of the air, & suits the rhythm equally with 'Love never more' &c'. It begins 'Talk not of love, it gives me pain'.
(Letter to George Thomson, 19th October 1794)

Song 29 - Go On Sweet Bird (Tune – Scots Queen)
(Revision to Agnes' Poem 'To a Blackbird').
'I am just going to take your Blackbird, the sweetest, I am sure, that ever sang, and prune its wings a little'.
(Letter to Agnes McLehose, 4th February 1788)

Song 30 - Clarinda, Mistress Of My Soul (Tune - Clarinda)
'I am here, absolutely unfit to finish my letter – pretty hearty after a bowl, which has been constantly plied since dinner, till this moment, I have been with Mr Schetki, the musician, and he has set it finely. I have no distinct

ideas of anything, but that I have drunk your health twice tonight, and that you are all my soul holds dear in this world'. *(Letter to Agnes McLehose, Thursday evening, 24th January 1788)*

'Schetki has sent me the song, set to a fine air of his composing. I have called the song 'Clarinda': I have carried it about in my pocket, and thumbed it over all day. I trust you have spent a pleasant day: and that no idea or recollection of me gives you pain'. *(Letter to Agnes McLehose, Sunday night, 27th January 1788)*

'I am sick of writing where my bosom is not strongly interested. Tell me what you think of the following? There, the *bosom* was perhaps a little *interested*. Mr Schetky, the celebrated musician, has done these lines the honour of setting them to music'. *(Letter to Mrs Dunlop, 12th February 1788)*

Song 31 - A Rosebud By My Early Walk (Tune - A Rosebud)
'This song I composed on Miss Jeany Cruikshank, only child to my worthy friend Mr Wm. Cruikshank, of the High School, Edinr. The air is by a David Sillar, quondam merchant, and now Schoolmaster in Irvine. He is the Davie to whom I address my printed poetical epistle in the measure of the 'Cherry and the Slae''. *(Burns' notes in Scots Musical Museum, song 189)*

Song 32 - To The Weavers Gin Ye Go
(Tune – To The Weavers Gin Ye Go)
'The chorus of this song is old the rest of it is mine. Here, once for all, let me apologise for many silly compositions of mine in this work. Many beautiful airs wanted words; in the hurry of some avocations, if I could string a parcel of rhymes together any thing near tolerable, I was fain to let them pass. He must be an excellent poet indeed, whose every performance is excellent'. *(Burns' notes in Scots Musical Museum, song 103)*

Song 33 – An' I'll Kiss Thee Yet (Tune – Braes O' Balquhidder)
'The chorus is the first, or lowest part of the tune. – Each verse must be repeated twice to go through the high, or 2nd part'.
(Burns notes in the Hastie Manuscript, James Kinsley)

Song 34 - Of A' The Airts (Tune - Miss Admiral Gordon's Strathspey)
'This air is by Marshall; the song I composed out of compliment to Mrs Burns. N.B. – It was during the honeymoon'.
(Burns' notes in Scots Musical Museum, song 235)

Song 35 - O Were I On Parnassus Hill (Tune - My Love Is Lost To Me)
'This air is Oswald's; the song I made out of compliment to Mrs Burns'.
(Burns' notes in Scots Musical Museum, song 255)

Song 36 - The Blue-Ey'd Lassie (Tune - The Blue-Ey'd Lassie)
'How do you like the following Song, designed for an Air composed by a friend of mine (Robert Riddell), & which he had christened 'The blue-eyed lassie''. *(Letter to Mrs Dunlop, 29th October 1788)*

Song 37 - When First I Saw Fair Jeanie's Face (Tune - Maggie Lauder)
'Maggie Lauder - is a good tune, but there is, I don't know what, of vulgarism about it; at least to me it has always that effect.   There is an English song to which it is set in the Museum'.
(Letter to George Thomson, circa early September 1793)

Song 38 - Louis What Reck I By Thee (Tune – Louis What Reck I)

Song 39 - Afton Water (Tune - Afton Water)
'There is a small river, Afton, that falls into Nith, near New Cumnock, which has some charming, wild, romantic scenery on it's banks.   I have a particular pleasure in those little pieces of poetry such as our Scots songs, &c. where the names and landskip-features of rivers, lakes, or woodlands, that one knows are introduced.   I attempted a compliment of that kind, to Afton, as follows; I mean it for Johnson's Musical Museum – 'Flow gently, clear Afton, among thy green braes'.
(Letter to Mrs Dunlop, 5ᵗʰ February 1789)

Song 40 - Thou Ling'ring Star (Tune - Captain Cook's Death)
'The song beginning 'Thou ling'ring star' &c. is the last, & in my opinion by much the best of the inclosed compositions.   I beg leave to present it with my most respectful Compliments to Mrs Graham'.
(Letter to Robert Graham of Fintry, 9ᵗʰ December 1789)

Song 41 - Thine Am I, My Faithful Fair (Tune - The Quaker's Wife)
'The following song is one of my latest productions; and I send it you as I would do anything else, because it pleases myself'.
(Letter to Agnes McLehose, circa February 1790)

'I am extremely sorry that the 'Quaker's Wife' is not a wife to your taste.   I am pleased with my song; & very proud of my acquaintance with the lovely Heroine'. *(Letter to George Thomson, circa September 1793)*

'I have just put the hand to the following song: how does it please you'?
(Letter to Maria Riddell, Friday morning, circa October 1793)

'Did I mention to you that I wish to alter the first line of the English song to 'Leiger m' choss', alias, 'The Quaker's wife', from 'Thine am I, my faithful fair' to 'Thine am I, my Chloris fair'.   If you neglect this alteration, I call on all the NINE, conjunctly & severally, to anathematise you'.
(Letter to George Thomson, stamped AU 3 (1795))

Song 42 - Beware O' Bonie Ann (Tune - Bonie Ann)
'Though I give Johnson one edition of my songs, that does not give away the copy-right, so you may take 'Thou ling'ring star with lessening ray,' to the tune of 'Hughie Graham', or other songs of mine; & likewise the song 'Ye gallants bright, I rede you right' &c, for it also is my composition'.
(Letter to George Thomson, 7ᵗʰ April 1793)

'I composed this song out of compliment to Miss Ann Masterton, the daughter of my friend, Allan Masterton, the author of the Air of 'Strathallan's Lament', and two or three others in this work'.
(Burns' notes in Scots Musical Museum, song 215)

Song 43 - On Sensibility
(Tune - Cornwallis' Lament For Colonel Moorhouse)
'I have just, *since I had yours*, composed the inclosed Stanzas.   Let me know your opinion of them.   I have one other Piece in your taste, but I have just a snatch of time'.
(Letter to Agnes McLehose, thought to be circa July 1791, but the verses were first enclosed in a letter to Mrs Dunlop, dated 9th July 1790)

'I have sent in your hair, a part of the parcel you gave me, with a measure, to Mr Bruce the Jeweller in Princes Street, to get a ring done for me.   I have likewise sent in the verses on 'Sensibility', altered to 'Sensibility, how charming, Dearest, Nancy, thou canst tell' &c' in to the Editor of the Scots songs, of which you have three volumes, to set to a most beautiful air, out of the compliment to the first of women, my ever beloved, my ever sacred Clarinda'.   *(Letter to Agnes McLehose, 15th December 1791)*

Song 44 - Yestreen I Had A Pint O' Wine (Tune - Banks Of Banna)
"Shepherd's I have lost my love' *(original words to Banks of Banna)* is to me a Heavenly air. - What would you think of a set of Scots verses to it?   - I have made one, a good while ago, which I think is the best love-song I ever composed in my life; but in it's *original* state, is not quite a lady's song'.
(Letter to George Thomson, 7th April 1793)

'Your Irish airs are pretty, but they are rank Irish.   If they were, like the 'Banks of Banna' for instance, though really Irish, yet in the Scotish taste, you might adopt them'.   *(Letter to George Thomson, circa September 1793)*

Song 45 – Out Over The Forth
(Tune – Charles Graham's Welcome Hame)
'So Goodnight to you!   And sound be your sleep, & delectable your dreams!   Apropros, how do you like this thought in a ballad I have just now on the tapis'?   *(Letter to Alexander Cunningham, 11th March 1791)*

'The enclosed tune is a part of Gow's 'Charles Graham's welcome hame', but I do not think that the close of the second part of the tune happy.   Mr Clarke, on looking over Gow's air, will conceive a better'.
(Written on the copy of the manuscript of the song for the 'Museum', J.C.Dick)

Song 46 - Ye Flowery Banks O' Bonie Doon (Tune – Cambdelmore)
'My song is intended to sing to a Strathspey reel of which I am very fond, called in Cummin's Collection of Strathspeys, 'Ballendalloch's reel'; & in other Collections that I have met with, it is known by the name of 'Camdelmore''.   *(Letter to Alexander Cunningham, 11th March 1791)*

Song 47 - The Banks O' Doon (Tune - Caledonian Hunt's Delight)
'There is another air, 'The Caledonian Hunt's Delight', to which I wrote a
song that you will find in Johnson; this air, I think, might find a place
among your hundred – as Lear says of his Knights – To make room for it,
you may take out (to my taste) either, 'Young Jockey was the blithest lad',
or 'There's nae luck aboot the hoose', or 'The collier's bonie lassie', or 'The
tither morn', or 'The sow's tail' - & put them into your additional list. Not
but that these songs have great merit; but still they have not the pathos of
'The Banks o' Doon''. *(Letter to George Thomson, circa November 1794)*

Song 48 - Wilt Thou Be My Dearie (Tune - The Sutor's Dochter)
'Mr Burns presents his most respectful Compliments to Major Robertson –
begs leave to present him with another copy of the Song- as Mr B. –
understands that in a 'Treaty of Commerce' with a fair Lady, the little song
was among the articles ceded by Major R...As the charms of Major R.'s
voice gave the first celebrity to the Song, Mr B. begs that he will continue
his kindness to his Protegee'.
(Letter to Major William Robertson of Lude, circa February/March 1794)

Song 49 - O Wat Ye Wha's In Yon Town
          (Tune – I'll Gang Nae Mair Tae Yon Toon)
'Do you know the air, I am sure you must know it, 'We'll gang nae mair to
yon toon'? I think, in slowish time, it would make an excellent song. I am
highly delighted with it, & if you should think it worthy of your attention, I
have a fair dame in my eye to whom I would consecrate it'.
(Letter to George Thomson, 7th February 1795)

'I inclose you a Song which I composed since I saw you...As I am a good
deal pleased with my performance, I, in my first fervour, thought of
sending it to Mrs O. *(Lucy Oswald, her name replacing the name of Jeany)*, but
on reflection, perhaps, from the well-known character of Poverty & Poetry,
what I would offer is the honest incense of genuine esteem & grateful
respect, might be construed into some modification of that servility which
my soul abhors'. *(Letter to John Syme, Monday evening, circa May? 1795)*

Song 50 - Lovely Davies (Tune - Miss Muir)
'Though I had lived threescore years a married man, & threescore years
before I was a married man, my imagination would hallow the very idea; &
I am truly sorry that the inclosed stanzas have done such poor justice to
such a subject'. *(Letter to Deborah Duff Davies circa early October 1791)*

Song 51 - Thou Gloomy December (Tune - Thro' The Lang Muir)
'I have written so often to you and have got no answer, that I had resolved
never to lift up a pen to you again, but this eventful day, *the sixth of
December*, recalls to my memory such a scene! Heaven and earth! When I
remember a far distant person'! – But no more of this, until I learn from you
a proper address, and why my letters have lain by you unanswered, as this

is the third I have sent to you'.
(Letter to Mary Peacock, 6th December 1792, regarding Agnes McLehose)

Song 52 - Ae Fond Kiss (Tune - Rory Dall's Port)

'I have yours, my ever dearest Nancy, this moment. I have just ten minutes before the post goes, & these shall employ in sending you some Songs I have just been composing to different tunes for the Collection of Songs, of which you have three volumes - & of which you *shall* have the fourth'.
(Letter to Agnes McLehose, 27th December 1791, also including song no. 51 and first version of song no. 53)

Song 53 - Behold The Hour, The Boat Arrive (Tune – Oran Gaoil)

'They have lately in Ireland, with great pomp, published an Irish air, as they say, called, 'Caun de delish': the fact is, in a publication of Corri's, a great while ago, you find the same air, called a Highland one, with a Gaelic song set to it. I think it is 'Oran Gaoil' - & a fine air it is'.
(Letter to George Thomson, circa mid August 1793)

'The following song I have composed for 'oran-gaoil', the Highland air that you tell me in your last, you have resolved to give a place to in your book. I have this moment finished the song; so you have it glowing from the Mint. If it suits you – Well! If not 'tis also – Well'!
(Letter to George Thomson, circa September 1793)

Song 54 – Sae Far Awa (Tune – Dalkeith Maiden Bridge)

Song 55 - Craigieburn Wood (Tune – Craigieburn Wood)

'The inclosed Song, my dear Sir, is the work of t'other day, based on a bonie Lass, once near & dear to your heart, the charming Miss Lorimer. She was born near Craigieburn-wood, a beautiful place still in her father's possession'. *(Letter to John Gillespie, once suitor to Jean Lorumer, circa 1791?)*

'There is also one sentimental song, of mine, the first in the 4th Vol. of the Museum, which never was known out of the immediate neighbourhood, until I got it taken down from a country girl's singing. It is called 'Craigieburnwood'; & in the opinion of Mr Clarke, is one of the sweetest Scots songs. He is quite an enthusiast about it; & I would take his taste in Scots music against the taste of most connoisseurs'.
(Letter to George Thomson, 7th April 1793)

'Mr Clarke goes to your town by today's Fly...One thing I hope he will do, which would give me high satisfaction, persuade you to adopt my favourite, 'Craigieburnwood', in your Selection, as it is a great favourite of his as of mine. The lady on whom it was made, is one of the finest women in Scotland...' *(Letter to George Thomson, 19th October 1794)*

'I thank you for admitting 'Craigieburnwood'; & I shall take care to furnish you with a new Chorus. In fact, the Chorus was not my work, but a part of some old verses to the air.   If I can catch myself in a more than ordinary propitious moment, I shall write a new 'Craigieburnwood' altogether.   My heart is much in the theme'. *(Letter to George Thomson, circa November 1794)*

'It is remarkable of this air, that it is the confine of that country where the greatest part of our Lowland music (so far as from the title, words, etc, we can localise it), has been composed.   From Craigie-burn, near Moffat, until one reaches the West Highlands, we have scarcely one slow air of antiquity.   The song was composed on a passion which a Mr Gillespie, a particular friend of mine, had for a Miss Lorimer, afterwards a Mrs Whelpdale.   The young lady was born at Craigie-burn-wood.   The chorus is part of an old foolish ballad'.
(Burns' notes in Scots Musical Museum, song 301)

Song 56 - Saw Ye Bonie Lesley (Tune - The Collier's Bonie Lassie)
(After escorting her and her family to the Scottish border)   'Twas about nine, I think, when I left them; & riding home I composed the following ballad, of which you will probably think you have a dear bargain, as it will cost you another groat of postage.   You must know that there is an old ballad beginning with 'My bonie Lizie Bailie', so I parodied it as follows, which is literally the first copy 'unanointed, unannealed', as Hamlet says'.
(Letter to Mrs Dunlop, 22nd August 1792)

'As for the rest of my fancies & reveries.   How I lately met with Miss Lesley Bailie, the most beautiful, elegant woman in the world...How, in galloping home at night. I made a ballad on her...Behold all these things are written in the Chronicles of my imaginations'.
(Letter to Alexander Cunningham, 10th September 1792)

'Now, my dear Sir, with the freedom which characterizes our correspondence, I must not, cannot alter, 'Bonie Lesley'.   You are right, the word 'Alexander', makes the line a little uncouth, but I think the thought is pretty'. *(Letter to George Thomson, 1st December 1792)*

Song 57 – The Bonie Lad That's Far Awa
(Tune – The Bonie Lad That's Far Awa)
'O how can I be blithe and glad' is mine, but as it is already appropriated to an air by itself, both in the Museum & thence into Ritson – (I have got that book) – I think it would be as well to leave it out.   – However, do as you please'. *(Letter to George Thomson, 19th October 1794)*

Song 58 – It Isna, Jean, Thy Bonie Face (Tune - The Maid's Complaint)
'These were originally English verses:- I gave them their Scots dress'.
(Burns' notes in Scots Musical Museum, song 333)

Song 59 - Will Ye Go To The Indies (Tune - Ewe-Bughts, Marion)
'You must know that all my earlier love-songs were the breathings of ardent Passion; & tho' it might have been easy in aftertimes to have given

them a polish, yet that polish to me, whose they were, & who perhaps alone cared for them, would have defaced the legend of my heart which was so faithfully inscribed on them.   Their uncouth simplicity was, as they say of wines, their RACE'.   *(Letter to George Thomson, 26th/27th October 1792)*

Song 60 - The Lea-Rig (Tune - My Ain Kind Dearie, O)
'Let me tell you that you are too fastidious in your ideas of Songs & Ballads...Who shall rise up & say, 'Go to, I will make a better'.   For instance, on reading over 'The lea-rig', I immediately set about trying my hand on it; & after all, I could make nothing more of it than the following, which Heaven knows is poor enough'.
(Letter to George Thomson, Friday night, 26th October 1792)

'Our friend Clarke, than whom, you know, there is not a better judge of the subject, complains that in the air 'Lee-rigg', the accent is to be altered.   But, let our National Music preserve its native features.   They are, I own, frequently wild & unreduceable to the more modern rules; but on that very eccentricity, perhaps, depends a great part of their effect'.
(Letter to George Thomson, stamped 26th April 1793)

Song 61 - She Is A Winsome Wee Thing
(Tune - My Wife's A Wanton Wee Thing)
'In the air, 'My wife's a wanton wee thing', if a few lines, *smoothe & pretty*, can be adapted to it, it is all that you can expect.   The following I made extempore to it; & though, on farther study I might give you something more profound, yet it might not suit the light-horse gallop of the air so well as this *random clink'*.   *(Letter to George Thomson, 8th November 1792)*

Song 62 - Highland Mary (Tune – Lady Catherine Ogie)
'The foregoing Song pleases myself; I think it is in my happiest manner: you will see at first glance that it suits the air.   The subject of the song is one of the most interesting passages of my youthful days; & I own that I would be much flattered to see the verses set to an Air which would insure celebrity.   Perhaps, after all, 'tis the still glowing prejudice of my heart, that throws a borrowed lustre over the merits of the Composition'.
(Letter to George Thomson, 14th November 1792)

'Your remark on the first stanza of my 'Highland Mary' is just, but I cannot alter it without injuring the poetry in proportion as I mended the perspicuity; so, if you please, we will let it stand as it is'.
(Letter to George Thomson, 26th January 1793)

Song 63 – I Hae A Wife O' My Ain (Tune – I Hae A Wife O' My Ain)

Song 64 – The Gallant Weaver (Tune – The Gallant Weaver)

Song 65 – Wandering Willie (Tune – Here Awa, There Awa)

'I leave it to you, my dear Sir, to determine whether the above ('Lang here awa, there awa wandering Willie'), or the old, 'Thro' the lang muir', be the best'. *(Letter to George Thomson, dated MR 27 (1793))*

'My Song, 'Here awa there awa', as amended by Mr Erskine, I entirely approve of, & return to you'. *(Letter to George Thomson April 1793)*

Song 66 - Bonie Wee Thing (Tune - Bonie Wee Thing)

'Nothing less, Madam, than this vile depravity of soul could have made me so long neglect your obliging commands. Indeed I had one apology: the bagatelle was not worth presenting. Besides, so strongly as I am interested in Miss DAVIES'S fate & welfare, in the serious business of life, amid its chances & changes; that to make her the subject of a silly BALLAD is downright mockery of these ardent feelings. ''Tis like an impertinent jest to a dying friend''. *(Letter to Deborah Duff Davies, 6th April 1793)*

Song 67 – Young Jessie (Tune – Bonie Dundee)

'Mr Burns presents his most respectful compliments to Miss Staig & has sent her the Song. Mr B. begs to be forgiven his delaying so long to send it; & allows Miss S. to impute the neglect to any cause under Heaven, except want of respect for her commands'. *(Letter to Jessie Staig, circa Spring 1793)*

Song 68 - Farewell Thou Stream (Tune - Alace Yat I Cam Ower The Muir)

'Mary was the name I intended my Heroine to bear, but I altered it into your ladyship's, as being infinitely more musical. I am afraid that my song will turn out a very cold performance, as I never can do any good with a love theme, except when I am really & devoutly in love'. *(Letter to Maria Riddell, Friday noon, circa April 1793)*

'The following I wrote the other day for a beautiful Scots air, & I think it has some merit, so I send it to you. I have indeed, of late, written a good many things in that way, even though far, far different from the complexion of my mind; but the Editor is a particular friend of mine, & I have pledged myself to assist him'. *(Letter to Mrs Dunlop, 15th December 1793)*

Song 69 - There Was A Lass and She Was Fair
(Tune - There Was A Maid And She Was Fair)

'I send you likewise, to me a beautiful little air, which I had taken down from viva voce. – On the other page, I will give you a stanza or two of the Ballad to it. – I know these songs are not to have the luck to please you, else you might be welcome to them. – Preserve them carefully, & return them to me, as I have no other copy'.
(Letter to George Thomson, April 1793, enclosed also verses to 'Meg o' the Mill')

'In the inclosed ballad I have, I think, hit off a few outlines of your portrait. The personal charms, the purity of mind, the ingenious naivete of heart &

manners, in my heroine are, I flatter myself, a pretty just likeness of Miss McMurdo in a cottager'. *(Letter to Jean McMurdo, circa July 1793)*

'Change the name to 'There was a lass & she was fair' (previously called Bonie Jean) which, by the by, is the old name of the air. Do, make a point of publishing this Song to its own tune, & in your next Number, you will highly oblige me by it'. *(Letter to George Thomson, circa early September 1793)*

Song 70 - Blythe Hae I Been On Yon Hill (Tune – The Quaker's Wife)
'I have some presence, Madam, to make you the theme of my song, as you & I are two downright singularities in human nature. You will probably start at this assertion, but I believe it will be allowed that a woman exquisitely charming without the least seeming consciousness of it; & a poet who never paid a compliment but where it was justly due, are two of the greatest rarities on earth'. *(Letter to Lesley Bailie, circa May 1793)*

'As I propose giving you the designations and names of all my heroines, to appear in some future edition of your work, perhaps half a century hence, you must certainly include *'the boniest lass in a' the warld'* in your Collection'. *(Letter to George Thomson, circa Sept 1793, note 57)*

(The Quaker's Wife aka Liggeram Cosh/Madam Cossy/The Hemp-Dresser)
'Among many of the airs that please me, there is one, well know as a reel by the name of 'The quaker's wife' & which I remember a grand aunt of mine used to sing by the name of 'Liggeram cosh, my bonie wee lass''. *(Letter to George Thomson, stamped JU 30 1793))*

''The Quaker's Wife' – do not give the tune that name, but the old Highland one, Leiger m' chose – the only fragment remaining of the old words, is the chorus, still a favourite lullaby of my old mother from whom I learned it. The current name for the reel to this day, at country weddings is Liggeram Cosh, a Lowland corruption of the original Gaelic'.
(Letter to George Thomson, 19th October 1794)

Song 71 - Phillis The Fair (Tune – Robin Adair)
'I likewise tried my hand on, 'Robin Adair', & you will probably think, with little success; but it is such a d-mned, cramp, out-of-the way measure, that I despair of doing any thing better to it. So much for Namby Pamby. I may after all, try my hand on it in Scots verse. There I always find myself most at home'. *(Letter to George Thomson, stamped AU 13 (1793))*

'That crinkum crankum tune, Robin Adair, has run so in my head, & I succeeded so ill in my last attempt, that I have ventured in this morning's walk, one essay more'. *(Letter to George Thomson, circa mid August 1793)*

Song 72 – O, Poortith Cauld (Tune - Cauld Kail In Aberdeen)
'Many returns of the season to you! my dear Sir. How comes on your publication? Will these two foregoing, be of any service to you?

Disposeth of them as seemeth good in thy sight'.
(Letter to George Thomson, received by him 7th January 1793, other song enclosed, 'Braw Lads o' Galla Water)

'Cauld kail in Aberdeen you must leave with me yet a while. I have vowed to have a song to that air, on the lady whom I attempted to celebrate in the verses 'Poortith cauld & restless love''.
(Letter to George Thomson, stamped MR 27 (1793))

'I have just put the last hand to the song I meant for 'Cauld kail in Aberdeen'. If it suits you, to insert it, I shall be pleased; as the heroine is a favourite of mine: if not, I shall also be pleased, because I wish, & will be glad, to see you act decidedly in the business. 'Tis a tribute as a Man of taste, & as an Editor, which you owe yourself'.
(Letter to George Thomson, stamped AU 13 (1793))

Song 73 - O Whistle An' I'll Come To Ye, My Lad
(Tune - O Whistle An' I'll Come To Ye, My Lad)
'Is 'Whistle & I'll come to you, my lad' one of your airs? I admire it much; & yesterday I set the following verses to it. Urbani, whom I have met with here, begged them of me, as he admires the air much, but as I understand that he looks with rather an evil eye on your WORK, I did not chuse to comply. However, if the song does not suit your taste, I may possibly send it to him'. *(Letter to George Thomson, circa 25th August 1793)*

(In changing the last line of the song to 'Thy Jeany will venture wi' ye, my lad' Burns writes) 'In fact, a fair dame at whose shrine I, the priest of the NINE, offer up the incense of Parnassus; a Dame, whom - the GRACES have attired in witchcraft, & whom the LOVES have armed with lightening – a Fair One, *herself the heroine of the song,* insists on the amendment; & dispute her commands, if you dare'! *(Letter to George Thomson, stamped AU 3 (1795))*

Song 74 - Adown Winding Nith (Tune - The Muckin' O' Geordy's Byre)
'Mr Clarke begs you to give Miss Phillis a corner in your Book, as she is a particular flame of his, & out of compliment to him, I have made the song. She is a Miss Phillis McMurdo, sister to the 'Bonie Jean' which I sent you sometime ago. They are both pupils of his'.
(Letter to George Thomson, circa 25th August 1793)

Song 75 - Come Let Me Take Thee (Tune - Cauld Kail In Aberdeen)
'The last stanza of this song I send you, is the very words that Coila taught me many years ago, & which I set to an old Scots reel in Johnson's Museum. If you think the above will suit your idea of your favourite air, I shall be highly pleased'. *(Letter to George Thomson, 28th August 1793)*

Song 76 - Where Are The Joys (Tune - Saw Ye My Father /The Grey Cock)
'The air, you know, is excellent; & the verses, I hope & think, are in my best manner. It goes into Pleyel's songs: & allow me to tell you a truth (what

your Sex, Youth & Charm, from *my* Sex, may not often hear).   I am Sincerely happy to have an opportunity of shewing, with what respect, I have the honour to be, Madam, your very humble servant'.
(Letter to Janet Miller, 9th September 1793)

'Saw ye my father – is one of my greatest favourites - The evening before last, I wandered out, & began a tender Song, in what I think is its native style.   I must premise, that the old way, & the way to give most effect, is to have no starting note, as the Fiddlers call it, but to burst at once into the pathos…My Song is but just begun; & I should like, before I proceed, to know your opinion of it.   I have sprinkled it with the Scotch dialect, but it may be easily named into correct English'.
(Letter to George Thomson, early September 1793)

Song 77 - Behold My Love (Tune - My Lodging's On The Cold Ground)
'I told you my objections to the song you had selected for 'My lodging is on the cold ground'.   On my visit the other day to my fair Chloris (that is the poetic name of the lovely goddess of my inspiration) she suggested an idea, which I, in my return from the visit, wrought into the following Song. It is exactly in the measure of 'My dearie an thou die', which you say is the precise rhythm of the air.   How do you like the simplicity & tenderness of this Pastoral?   I think it pretty well'.
(Letter to George Thomson, circa November 1794)

Song 78 - Here Is the Glen (Tune - The Flowers Of Edinburgh)
'By my much valued friend, Mr Syme, I sometime ago received a beautiful air which your Ladyship did me the honor to send me, with your obliging commands to suit it with verses.   The inclosed, I am afraid, will not be found in any degree worthy of the charming melody'.
(Letter to Lady Elizabeth Heron, 3rd April 1794)

'I got an air, pretty enough, composed by Lady Elizabeth Heron, which she calls 'The Banks Of Cree'.   Cree is a beautiful romantic stream; & as her ladyship is a particular friend of mine, I have written the following song to it.   The air I fear is not worth your while, else I would send it to you'.
(Letter to George Thomson, circa May 1794)

(Thomson did not like the air 'The Banks of Cree', and appeared to suggest to Burns his words be put to another air.   To which Burns replied,)
''Young Jockey was the blithest lad' (an air) – My English song, 'Here is the glen & here is the bower', cannot go to this air, it was written on purpose for an original air composed by Miss Heron of Heron'.
(Letter to George Thomson, November 1794.   Thomson issued the song, after Burns' death, to the air 'The Flowers of Edinburgh'.   The music to 'The Banks of Cree' remains untraced)

Song 79 - Sae Flaxen Were Her Ringlets (Tune - Oonagh's Waterfall)
'Do you know, my dear Sir, a blackguard Irish song called 'Oonagh's

waterfall', or 'The lock that scattered Oonagh's p-ss'?…The air is charming, & I have often regretted the want of decent verses to it…I intend the following song to the air I mentioned for that work. If it does not suit you as an Editor, but if you know the air, you may be pleased to have verses to it that you may sing it before Ladies'.
(Letter to George Thomson, circa September 1794)

Song 80 – Ah Chloris, Since It May Na Be (Tune – Major Graham)
'This is the second letter of at least my directing which you will receive by this day's post. I have been among the Angelic World this forenoon. Ah!…But don't be afraid I did not dare to touch the ark of the Covenant, nor even cast a prophane eye to the mercy-seat, where it is hid among the feathered Cherubin. I am in the clouds elsewhere'.
(Letter to Alexander Findlater, September 1794)

Song 81 - Sleep'st Thou Or Wauk'st Thou (Tune – De'il Tak The Wars)
'Since the above I've been out in the country taking a dinner with a friend, where I met with the lady whom I mentioned in the second page of this odds & ends of a letter. As usual I got into song; & returning home, I composed the following'. *(Letter to George Thomson, 19th October 1794)*

'I could easily throw this into an English mould, but to my taste, in the simple & tender of the Pastoral song, a sprinkling of the old Scotish, has an imitable effect'. *(Letter to George Thomson, circa November 1794)*

Song 82 - It Was The Charming Month Of May (Tune - Dainty Davie)
'A Song, which, under the same first verse of the first stanza, you will find in Ramsay's Tea-Table Miscellany, & elsewhere, I have cut down for an English dress to your 'Dainty Davie, as follows. Song, altered from an old English one 'It was etc.''. *(Letter to George Thomson, circa November 1794)*

The air Dainty Davie - 'This song, tradition says, and the composition itself confirms it, was composed on the Rev. David Williamson's begetting the daughter of Lady Cherrytrees with child, while a party of dragoons were searching her house to apprehend him for being an adherent to the solemn league and covenant. The pious woman had put a lady's nightcap on him, and had laid him a-bed with her own daughter, and passed him to the soldiery as a lady, her daughter's bed-fellow. A mutilated stanza or two are to be found in Herd's collection, but the original song consists of five or six stanzas, and were their delicacy equal to their wit and humour, they would merit a place in any collection'.
(Notes, said to be by Burns, taken from Cromek's 'Reliques of Robert Burns')

Song 83 - Lassie Wi' The Lint-White Locks (Tune - Rothiemurche's Rant)
'I am now just making verses for Rothiemurche's Rant, an air which puts me in raptures: & in fact, unless I be pleased with the tune I never can make verses to it. Here I have Clarke on my side, who is a judge that I will pit against any of you. Rothiemurche, he says, is an air both original &

beautiful; & on his recommendation I have taken the first part of the tune for a chorus, & the fourth or last part, for the song'.
(Letter to George Thomson, circa September 1794)

'I have finished my song to Rothiemurche's Rant; & you have Clarke to consult, as to the set of the air to singing. The piece has at least the merit of being a regular Pastoral: the vernal morn, the summer noon, the autumnal evening & the winter night, are regularly rounded, if you like it well: if not, I will insert it in the Museum'.
(Letter to George Thomson, circa November 1794)

Song 84 - My Nanie's Awa'
      (Tune – There Are Few Good Fellows When Jamie's Awa)
'It is, I assure you, the pride of my heart to do anything to forward or add to the value of your book, & as I agree with you that the Jacobite song, in the Museum, to 'There'll never be peace till Jamie comes hame', would not so well consort with Peter Pindar's excellent love-song to that air, I have just framed for you the following'. *(Letter to George Thomson, date stamped DE 9 (1794))*

Song 85 – O May Thy Morn (Tune – The Rashes)

Song 86 - Lovely Polly Stewart (Tune – Ye're Welcome Charlie Stewart)

Song 87 - Can I Cease To Care (Tune - Ay Waukin O)
'On Chloris Being Ill'.
(Enclosed with letter to Maria Riddell circa March 1795)
(Enclosed with letter to George Thomson in April 1795)

Song 88 - Their Groves Of Sweet Myrtle (Tune - Humours Of Glen)
'The following I wrote the other day for an Irish air which I highly admire; & for the sake of my verses he *(Pleyel)* has obligingly adopted the air into his Selection'. *(Letter to Maria Riddell, circa March 1795)*

'The Irish air 'The Humours of Glen' is a great favourite of mine, & as, except the silly verses in 'The poor soldier', there are not any decent verses for it, I have written for it, as follows'.
(Letter to George Thomson, circa April 1795)

Song 89 - 'Twas Na Her Bonie Blue E'e (Tune - Laddie Lie Near Me)
'Laddie lie near me – must *lie by me*, for some time.   I do not know the air; & until I am compleat master of a tune, in my own singing, (such as it is) I never can compose for it'.
(Letter to George Thomson, circa early September 1793)

Song 90 - O Lay Thy Loof In Mine Lass (Tune - The Cordwainer's March)
'You say you have the words.   The tune you will find in 'Airds Selection' under the name of The Cordwainer's March'.
(Letter to James Johnson, Weden eve. circa pre 1795)

Song 91 - Mark Yonder Pomp (Tune – De'il Tak The Wars)

'Well! This is not amiss. You see how I answer your orders your tailor could not be more punctual. I am just now in a high fit of Poetizing, provided that the straight-jacket of Criticism don't cure me...I am at this moment, 'holding high converse with the Museum, & have not a word to throw away on such a prosaic dog as you are'.
(Letter to George Thomson, circa 3ʳᵈ May 1795)

Song 92 - Forlorn My Love (Tune – Will You Lend Me Your Loom Lass)

'How do you like the foregoing? I have written it within this hour: so much for the *speed* of my Pegasus; but what say you to his bottom'?
(Letter to George Thomson, circa June 1795)

Song 93 – Why, Why Tell Thy Lover
(Tune – Caledonian Hunt's Delight)

'Such is the damned peculiarity of the rhythm of this air, that I find it impossible to make another stanza to suit it'.
(Letter to George Thomson, 3ʳᵈ July 1795)

Song 94 - This Is No My Ain Lassie (Tune - This Is No My Ain House)

'This is no my ain body' alter into 'This is no my ain lassie''.
(Letter to George Thomson, stamped AU 3 (1795))

'This is no my ain house', is a great favourite air of mine, & if you will send me your set of it, I shall task my Muse to her highest effort'.
(Letter to George Thomson, circa September 1793)

'The tune is an Old Highland Air, called *'Shuan Truish Willighan'*.
(Burns notes in Scots Musical Museum, song 216)

Song 95 - O Bonie Was Yon Rosy Brier
(Tune - I Wish My Love Were In A Mire)

'Do you know that you have aroused the torpidity of Clarke at last? He has requested me to write three or four songs for him, which he is to set to music himself. The enclosed sheet contains two songs for him. I enclose the sheet open that you may copy the song 'O Bonny Was Yon Rosy Briar'. I do not know if I am right, but that song pleases me. If you like the song it may go as Scottish verses to the air 'I wish my love were in a mire', and poor Erskine's English lines may follow'.
(Letter to George Thomson, stamped AU3 (1795))

Song 96 - O That's The Lassie O' My Heart (Tune – Morag)

'I am assisting a friend in a Collection of Scottish songs, set to their proper tunes; every air worth preserving is to be included: among others I have given 'Morag', and some few Highland airs which pleased me most, a dress which will be more generally known, though far, far inferior in real merit'. *(Letter to Mrs Elizabeth Rose of Kilravock, 17ᵗʰ February 1788 – earlier songs composed to 'Morag' were 'Castle Gordon' and 'The Young Highland Rover')*

'The foregoing had been sent to you a long time ago but for reasons which you may have heard. Since I saw you, I have indeed been much the child of disaster. Scarcely began to recover the loss of an only daughter & darling child, I became myself the victim of a rheumatic fever, which brought me to the borders of the grave. After many weeks of a sick bed, I am just beginning to crawl about'. *(Letter to Robert Cleghorn, January 1796)*

Song 97 – I'll Aye Ca' In By Yon Town
(Tune – I'll Gae Nae Mair Tae Yon Toon)
'This tune is evidently the old air *We'll gang nae mair tae yon toon,* and I suspect it is not the best set of the air, but in Bowie's and other collections the old tune is to be found, and you can correct this by these copies'. *(Holographic note on the manuscript of the song in the British Museum, J.C Dick).*

Song 98 - Here's A Health To Ane I Lo'e Dear
(Tune - Here's A Health To Them That's Awa)
'I once mentioned to you an air which I have long admired, 'Here's a health to them that's awa', hiney', but I forgot if you took any notice of it. I have just been trying to suit it with verses, & I beg leave to recommend the air to your attention once more. I have only begun with it'.
(Letter to George Thomson, circa May 1796)

'Did Thomson shew the following song, the last I made or probably will make for some time. The air is my favourite. I shall be impatient to hear from you. As to me, my plan is to address the Board by petition & then if any friend has thrown in a word 'tis a great deal in my favour'.
(Letter to Alexander Cunningham stamped JY 12 (1796). However the July 12th stamp is for the arrival date in Edinburgh. There is also an undated postmark made in Dumfries – confirming that the letter was written sometime before 12th)

Song 99 – O Wert Thou In The Cauld Blast
(Tune – Lenox Love To Blantyre)

Song 100 – Altho' My Back Be At The Wa'
(Tune – The Job Of Journey Work)
'To a Scots critic, the pathos of the line 'Tho' his back be at the wa', must be very striking. It needs not a Jacobite prejudice to be affected with this song'.
(Burns' remarks on a line from 'Lewis Gordon', S.M.M. no.86, quoted in the interleaved copy of the Scots Musical Museum)

Song 101 – Here's Tae Thy Health (Tune – The Laggan Burn)
'As far as I can recollect, the compilation of an illiterate Millwright, about thirty or forty years ago, somewhere in Ayrshire'.
(Burns' annotation written on the manuscript of the song which is held at Alloway)

Song 102 - Fairest Maid On Devon Banks (Tune - Rothiemurche's Rant)
'After all my boasted independence, curst necessity compels me to implore you for five pounds…I do not ask all this gratuitously, for upon returning health, I hereby promise to engage & furnish you with five pounds worth of the neatest song genius you have seen.   I tryed my hand on 'Rothiemurchie' this morning.   The measure is so difficult that it is impossible to infuse much genius into the lines– they are on the other side. Forgive, forgive me'! *(Letter to George Thomson, 12th July 1796)*

BIBLIOGRAPHY

Robert Burns	Autobiographical Letter To Dr Moore		2nd August 1787
'Candidor' (Maria Riddell)	Memoir Concerning Burns	Dumfries Journal	August 1796
Gilbert Burns	Narrative Letter To Mrs Dunlop		1797
Robert Heron	A Memoir Of The Life Of The Late Robert Burns		1796/1797
James Currie	Works Of Robert Burns	Cadell & Davies	1800
R.H. Cromek	Reliques Of Robert Burns	Cadell & Davies	1808
George Thomson Collection	The Songs Of Burns etc.		1822
Allan Cunningham	Songs Of Scotland	John Taylor	1825
J.G. Lockhart	Life Of Robert Burns	Edinburgh	1828
	Illustrated Family Burns	MacKenzie	c1840
Allan Cunningham	The Complete Works Of Robert Burns	George Virtue	c1842
George F. Graham	Songs Of Scotland (3 Volumes)	Wood & Co.	1848
	The Burns Centenary	Nimmo	1859
W.G. Coutts	'The Games' A Nicht Wi' Burns	Coutts	1860
William Gunnyon	Complete Works	Nimmo, Hay, Mitchell	1865
Robert Burns	Poems Chiefly In The Scottish Dialect	James McKie	1869
Robert Chambers (Editor)	The Life & Works Of Burns	Edinburgh	1870
S. Tytler & J. Watson	Songstresses Of Scotland	Strahan	1871
Henry A Bright	Some Account Of The Glenriddell Ms.	Walmsley	1874
William Burnes	A Manual Of Religious Belief	McKie & Drennan	1875
Archibald Anderson	Rambles Through The Land Of Burns	Dunlop & Drennan	1879
William Jack	Burns Second Common-Place Book	Macmillan	1879
Rev Charles Rogers	The Scottish Minstrel	Nimmo, Hay, Mitchell	1885
Charles Annandale	The Works Of Robert Burns	Blackie	1888
Alexander Webster	Burns & The Kirk	McKay	1888
Peter Ross	Songs Of Scotland	Gardner	1893
John D. Ross	Round Burns' Grave	Gardner	1891
Dr J. Adams	Burns 'Chloris'	Glasgow	1893
Wallace Bruce	Here's A Hand	Blackwood & Sons	1893
John Ingram	Anecdotes Of Burns	Morison	1893
John D. Ross	Highland Mary	Gardener	1894
	The Poetical Works Of Burns	Warne & Co.	1894
W. Scott-Douglas	The Works Of Robert Burns	Thin	1896
William A. Craigie	A Primer Of Burns	Methuen	1896
Henley & Henderson	Poetry Of Robert Burns		1896
Archibald Munro	The Story Of Burns & Highland Mary	Gardner	1896
William R. Turnbull	The Heritage Of Burns	Sinclair	1896
W. Wallace (revised)	Chambers Life & Works Of Burns	Waverley	1896
D. McNaught	People's Edition	John Menzies	1897
John D. Ross	Burns' Clarinda	Grant	1897
William Findlay	Burns & The Medical Profession	Gardner	1898
W. E. Henley	Burns, Life, Genius, Achievement	Jack	1898
W. Wallace	Correspondence, Burns & Mrs Dunlop	Hodder	1898
John D. Ross	Early Critical Reviews	Hodge & Co.	1900
Burns' Cottage	Catalogue Of Relics & Engravings	The Trustees	1901
James C. Dick	Songs Of Burns	London	1903
Charles S. Dougall	The Burns Country	Black	1904
John MacIntosh	Life Of Burns	Gardner	1906
Robert Duncan	Story Of The Edinburgh Burns Relics	Elliot	1910
Frank Miller	The Poets Of Dumfriesshire	James MacLehose	1910
	The Kilmarnock Burns	Frowde	1911
D. McNaught	The Truth About Burns	MacLehose	1921
James MacKenzie	A New Life & Vindication	Henderson	1924
John D. Ross	Blue-Eyed Lassie	Paisley	1924
William Stewart	Burns And The Common People	London	1925
Mary D. Stuart	Romance Of The Edinburgh Streets	Methuen	1925

J. Crichton-Browne	Burns From A New Point Of View	Hodder & Stoughton	1926
John D. Ross	Little Book Of Burns Lore	Stirling, Eneas Mackay	1926
John McVie	Burns And Stair	Standard Press	1927
W.D. Fisher	Burns & The Bible	Glasgow	1927
J. F. Gemmill	Natural History In The Poetry Of Burns	Adshead	1928
William Will	Burns As A Volunteer	Smith	1928
James Muir	Burns Till His Seventeenth Year	Standard Press	1929
John D. Ross	Poems Of Clarinda	Mackay	1929
Catherine Carswell	Life Of Robert Burns	Collins	1930
Robert Chambers	Traditions Of Edinburgh	Chambers	1931
J. De Lancey Ferguson	The Letters Of Robert Burns	Clarendon	1931
H.W. Thompson	Henry Mackenzie 'Man Of Feeling'	OUP	1931
A.A. Thomson	The Burns We Love	Jenkins	1931
F.B. Snyder	Life Of Burns	MacMillan	1932
Peter Esslemont	Brithers A' (3 Part Pocket Edition)	The Central Press	1933
Maurice Lindsay	Robert Burns	London	1934
Keith Henderson	Burns – By Himself	Methuen	1938
William S. Douglas	Kilmarnock Edition	Daily Express'	1938
John Lindsey	The Rantin Dog	Chapman & Hall	1938
Peter Esslemont	Brither's A'	Oliphants	1943
Hilton Brown	There Was A Lad	Hamish Hamilton	1949
James Robertson	Robert Burns	James Robertson	1949
John McVie	Robert Burns	Oliver & Boyd	1951
Maurice Lindsay	Robert Burns	MacGibbon & Kee	1954
Christina Keith	The Russet Coat	Hale	1956
James MacKenna	The Homes & Haunts Of Burns	Collins	1959
John C. Hill	Love Songs And Heroines	Dent	1961
William Thomson	Orpheus Caledonius	Folklore	1962
Robert D. Thornton	Currie, The Entire Stranger	Oliver & Boyd	1963
Barke & Smith	The Merry Muses Of Caledonia	Allen	1965
Alan Dent	Burns In His Time	Nelson	1966
Raymond L. Brown	Clarinda	Martin Black	1968
Hugh Douglas	Portrait Of The Burns Country	Hale	1968
James Kinsley	Poems & Songs	Oxford	1968
John McVie	Burns & Edinburgh	Burns Federation	1968
Hyman Shapiro	Scotland In The Days Of Burns	Longman	1968
Raymond L. Brown (Editor)	Common Place Book 1783-85	S.R. Publishers	1969
L. M. Angus-Butterworth	Burns & The 18th Century Revival	AUP	1969
	Glenriddell Manuscripts	E.P. Publishers	1972
Gordon Irving	The Wit Of Burns	Frewin	1972
Donald A. Low	The Critical Heritage	Routledge	1974
Donald A. Low	Critical Essays On Burns	RKP	1975
Angus MacNaghten	Burns' Mrs Riddell	Volturna	1975
Hugh Douglas	Robert Burns – A Life	Hale	1976
Robert D. Thornton	William Maxwell To Robert Burns	Donald	1979
John McVie	Burns Federation Song Book		1980
John Davies	Apostle To Burns	Blackwood	1981
Greig-Duncan	Folk Song Collection (7 volumes)	AUP/Mercat Press	1981
	Bawdy Verse & Folksongs	MacMillan	1982
Robert Burns	The Jolly Beggars	Luath Press	1984
Elizabeth Fraser	Auld Lang Syne	Jarrold	1985
A.M. Boyle	Ayrshire Book Of Burns Lore	Alloway	1986
John Cairney	A Moment White	Glasgow	1986
Raymond Grant	Laughter Of Love	Detselig	1986
Ian Grimble	Robert Burns	London	1986
Donald A. Low	Robert Burns	Scot. Academic Press	1986
John Cairney	The Man Who Played Burns	Mainstream	1987
James Mackay	Complete Letters	Alloway	1987
Michael Turnbull	Edinburgh Portraits	John Donald	1987

430

E. Dunlop & A. Kamen	In The Land O' Burns	Richard Drew	1988
Hugh Douglas	Burns Supper Companion	Alloway	1988
R. H. Fowler	Robert Burns	Routledge	1988
James Mackay	Burns Lore Of Dumfries & Galloway	Alloway	1988
Harold Thomas	Information & Quiz Book	Albyn	1988
Alastair Campsie	The Clarinda Conspiracy	Mainstream	1989
Graham Smith	Burns, The Exciseman	Alloway	1989
Hans Hecht	The Man & His Work	Alloway	1991
Johnson & Burns (Ed. Low)	Scots Musical Museum	Scolar Press	1991
	Robert Burns' Scotland	Jarrold	1992
James Mackay	Burns, A Biography	Mainstream	1992
Alan Bold	Rhymer Rab	Black Swan	1993
Donald A Low	Songs Of Burns	Routledge	1993
Jess Bolton	Love Of Highland Mary	Harper/Collins	1994
Thomas Crawford	Study Of The Poems & Songs	Canongate	1994
David Daiches	Burns, The Poet	Saltire	1994
Norman R. Paton	Thou Ling'ring Star	Sea Green Ribbon	1994
Kenneth Simpson (Ed.)	Burns Now	Canongate	1994
Maurice Lindsay	Burns Encyclopedia	Reprint	1995
Ian McIntyre	Dirt And Deity	Harper/Collins	1995
John Strawhorn	The Scotland Of Robert Burns	Walker & McConnel	1995
Ayrshire Archeological Soc	Mauchline Memories Of Burns	Walker & Connell	1996
Hugh Douglas	The Tinder Heart	Sutton	1996
James Mackay	The Land O' Burns	HMSO	1996
Gavin Sprott	Pride and Passion	HMSO	1996
Edmund Swinglehurst	Robert Burns Country	Lomond	1996
P.J. Westwood	Jean Armour	Creeden	1996
Patrick S. Hogg	The Lost Poems	Clydeside Press	1997
Carol McGuirk	Burns & The Sentimental Era	Tuckwell Press	1997
Kenneth Simpson (Ed.)	Love and Liberty	Tuckwell Press	1997
J. Gray & C. Smith	A Walk On The Southside		1998
David Carroll	Burns Country	Sutton Publishing	1999
Robert Crawford (Ed.)	Burns & Cultural Authority	Polygon	1999
John Cairney	On The Trail of Burns	Luath	2000
Donny O' Rourke	Ae Fond Kiss	Mercat	2000
Norman Watters	Stories Behind Some Burns Songs	Pentland Press	2000
John Cairney	The Luath Burns Companion	Luath Press	2001
The Burns Chronicles			

INDEX